Romans Unplugged

Romans Unplugged

Reading Paul's Letter to the Romans in the Twenty-First Century

LES BRIGHTON

Foreword by
Philip Yancey

WIPF & STOCK · Eugene, Oregon

ROMANS UNPLUGGED
Reading Paul's Letter to the Romans in the Twenty-First Century

Copyright © 2019 Les Brighton. All rights reserved. Except for brief quotations in critical publications or reviews, no part of this book may be reproduced in any manner without prior written permission from the publisher. Write: Permissions, Wipf and Stock Publishers, 199 W. 8th Ave., Suite 3, Eugene, OR 97401.

Wipf & Stock
An Imprint of Wipf and Stock Publishers
199 W. 8th Ave., Suite 3
Eugene, OR 97401

www.wipfandstock.com

PAPERBACK ISBN: 978-1-5326-9069-3
HARDCOVER ISBN: 978-1-5326-9070-9
EBOOK ISBN: 978-1-5326-9071-6

Manufactured in the U.S.A.   08/16/19

For Angela, beloved and faithful companion on the journey.

My task is to make room for God to come.
—Kierkegaard

Contents

Foreword by Philip Yancey | ix
Preface | xiii
Acknowledgements | xv
Introduction | xvii
Endnotes | xxv

1 **Romans 1: 1–7:** Paul's Self-Introduction | 1
2 **Romans 1:8–15:** Why Paul is Writing | 5
3 **Romans 1:16–17:** Paul's Introductory Summary | 8
4 **Romans 1:18—2:5:** The Wrath of God | 18
5 **Romans 2:6–29:** God Has No Favorites | 32
6 **Romans 3:** Much and None | 48
7 **Romans 3:27–31:** The End of Special Status | 71
8 **Endnotes:** Romans 1–3 | 80
9 **Romans 4:1–22:** The Example of Abraham | 107
10 **Romans 4:23—5:11** | 118
11 **Romans 5:12–21** | 144
12 **Romans 6** | 156
13 **Endnotes:** Chapters 4–6 | 171
14 **Romans 7:1–25A** | 189
15 **Romans 7:25b—8:13** | 199
16 **Romans 8:14–30** | 211
17 **Romans 8:31–39** | 226
18 **Endnotes:** Romans 7–8 | 234

APPENDIX 1
The Nature of the Roman Christian Community | 249

APPENDIX 2
Romans 5:1: "We Have or "Let Us Have" Peace with God | 259

APPENDIX 3
Adam and the Creation Story (Romans 5) | 264

Bibliography | 267

Foreword

I met Les Brighton in 2003, on my first visit to New Zealand. Following his recommended route, I hiked in forests and jagged mountain ranges, and drove through rolling green hills dotted with sheep. At the time, that nation of stunning natural beauty had ten times as many sheep as people. Most Kiwis, as they call themselves, have a modest and humble—dare I say shepherd-like?—personality and Les, a warden of a Christian study center, fit the mold.

"Don't let the Kiwis fool you," an Australian later told me. "We Aussies are brash, kind of like you Americans. We think we're athletic and outdoorsy, but the Kiwis are the really tough ones. They started Outward Bound, and were the first to climb Mount Everest. They invented the sports of bungee jumping and black-water rafting—like white-water rafting, only done inside a cave, in the dark. We Aussies face lots of natural dangers: crocodiles, poisonous snakes and spiders, Tasmanian devils, killer jellyfish. New Zealand has none of those. So they have to contrive danger."

As Les recounted his exploits on treks in the Southern Alps, I came to appreciate his toughness. We connected immediately as lovers of nature and theology, for both of us a form of divine revelation. He later took a job with Canterbury University in Christchurch, as marketing director in charge of recruiting international students, and as a result visited my home in Colorado several times. One day we stumbled across a patch of rare Calypso orchids, which grow close to the forest floor. Les reacted as if we had found a solid gold nugget.

Another time, Les's visit coincided with a long season of clinical depression. He described his bouts with the recurring condition as we hiked on the hills behind my mountain home. I led him to a place where each spring a pair of red foxes raises a litter of kits. The parents have grown accustomed to me, and think it not at all strange that I stop in front of the den and whistle a greeting. Sometimes the young ones poke their faces out from a crevice in the rock, sniffing the air and staring at me with alert, shiny eyes. Sometimes I hear them scrabbling around inside. Sometimes I hear nothing.

I warned Les that he may see and hear nothing at all. "They're wild animals, you know," I said. "We're not in charge. It's up to the foxes whether they make an appearance or not."

Foreword

A bold young fox did poke his nose out of the den that day, thrilling my visitor, and a few weeks later I received a letter from Les, back home in New Zealand. As he reflected on it, oddly enough, my comment about foxes helped him understand God. During the season of depression, sometimes God seemed as close as his wife or children. Sometimes he had no sense of God's presence, no faith to lean on. "God is wild, you know," he wrote. "We're not in charge."

A few years later a devastating earthquake hit Christchurch, Les's home city, destroying much of the downtown and tens of thousands of houses. "Everybody knows somebody who died or got injured," Les wrote me. "Angela [his wife] had taught at an English language school in one of the buildings that completely collapsed, so she knew almost all of the staff who died."

In the aftermath of reconstruction, the university eliminated Les's department. In typical fashion, he responded stoically. "Time to move on. The job never was my reason for living. I did get some extra pay, and that has given me the opportunity to do some writing, which has been my dream for a long time. I've started a book on Romans!"

Little did the Brightons know that their greatest challenge lay ahead. In less than a year Les was diagnosed with leukemia. Over the next months, which turned into years, he underwent a series of chemotherapy treatments that caused his health and energy to ebb and flow like a tide. He wrote a poem on that very simile, which begins:

> Spring, like a wave, catches one unawares, spray-shocks.
> Fluorescent-lit offices have no seasons. Townsfolk do not mark the tides.

The end of the poem alludes to his illness:

> The day is over. Log out, lock up, step outside.
> The deck rocks and bucks, the new leaves gather and surge
> The lungs fill as with a driving sou'wester.
> We are riding the tide, over the bar, into the open sea.

Les had already made a good start on his book on Romans when the illness hit. For the next five years, he worked in spurts when his strength allowed it, sometimes from a hospital. "The isolation room he's in is not all that bad," Angela wrote in the midst of one such stay. "Of course he can't get out and about but he has room for books and his computer. So long as he is feeling OK there are times when he can think and read. As well, he has a 'million dollar view' out his window—of the Avon River which runs through Christchurch, and on the other side the Botanic Gardens. Of course the challenge is 'feeling OK.' Fevers come and go."

Both Les and Angela wrote about their spiritual journey throughout the trial. Angela told of her raw faith, so unlike the experiences you hear about from testimonies in church: "You pray, and pray, and there are long stretches of time when nothing happens . . ." Les, buoyed by his book project, expressed a more optimistic tone. As long as he could work, he stayed happy.

Romans is the most systematic treatment of "the big picture" in the entire Bible. The apostle Paul was writing to a sophisticated, erudite city, and the resulting letter has reverberated through the ages, working its effect on such notables as Augustine, Martin Luther, John Wesley, and Karl Barth. Yet Les was convinced that the average reader in modern times may be missing an essential point. "We think the letter is all about us and our salvation," he wrote. "But, surprise, Paul's letter is not all about us, it is first and foremost all about God." Les described the project in its early days:

> The title is *Romans Unplugged*. Our approach to Romans is so massively influenced by the theological amplifiers and mixers of many generations that it is hard to hear Paul himself amidst all the other noise. What I am attempting to do is gently unplug from all that later theology and help us all hear what the man with the guitar is actually singing.
>
> It's such a hugely pretentious thing to try to do. However, the necessary close engagement with the Greek text has proven to be extremely interesting and fruitful. You come to a particular passage already aware of what you will find there—but you're mistaken! The more you look for it the more it isn't there. So, if Paul is not saying that, what is he saying? The answer is tremendous.
>
> My ideal audience is the 20- and 30-year-olds for whom Romans is as yet unknown territory; who, unencumbered by the theological baggage, will read on excited to see what comes next, and into whose heart Paul's message will fall like water and like light.

Les began with the goal of commenting on every chapter of Romans. As the disease progressed, he lowered his sights to completing Romans 1–8. The prayers of friends kept him going. "Like the water and power and other services that run hidden under the streets of the city, maintaining its life, there is this hidden network of prayer and goodwill that, consciously or unconsciously, links person and person and God across communities and across the world. It is the spiritual breath of the planet: awesome to touch the edges of."

In June 2017, prospects looked very grave. All the arduous chemotherapy treatments had proved, in the end, ineffective. Doctors diagnosed Les's condition as terminal, and began speaking in terms of months rather than years of life. "This is a serious email, but I don't want it to be a somber one," Les wrote. "My heart is full of gratitude for so many things, including these friendships, some of them extending over a lifetime. I don't believe death is the end, for any of us. And in the meantime, there is still life to live, friends to meet, things to do."

In August Les wrote in triumph that he had finished the book's chapter on Romans 8. "If I hadn't been well enough to bring things to that point then the whole five years' work would have fallen to the ground. I'm relieved, of course, but also very happy with how it has come together . . . how you start with open hands—and God fills them. It is work but it is also grace."

In that final sentence, Les provides a neat summary of the letter to the Romans. I think of the apostle Paul making notes, outlining, composing, and finally editing the words in this magnificently compressed theological statement, a work that became a gracious gift to us. I think of God's own plan for humanity, an experiment begun in love but that would involve the hardest work of all, the incarnation and crucifixion, a seeming defeat that led to a gift of grace, the salvation of the world. And I think of Les, propped up in a hospital bed, fighting with his febrile brain to squeeze out this timeless message for us modern readers. May it fall like water and like light.

I am recounting the human struggle from which this book emerged because Les would not—he's a Kiwi, after all. You will judge the book by its own merits. As I read it, I hear the boyish voice of Les himself, the guide who pointed out a site not far from his home used for the filming of *The Chronicles of Narnia*, and who exclaimed over yet another Calypso orchid sprouting from dead pine straw in Colorado. I am amazed that my friend sustained such vibrant enthusiasm as he worked on this book of theology while battling a terminal illness.

The whole of creation has been groaning as in the pains of childbirth right up to the present time, Paul wrote in Romans 8. That metaphor may be the most appropriate of all. I recall my first visit to Christchurch, a lovely city of parks and cathedral spires named for Christ Church, Oxford, a gateway to the paradise of New Zealand's South Island—now a city known mainly for its destructive earthquakes and a mass slaughter in a mosque. And I remember my life-giving friendship with Les himself, and the groaning of his own body as he valiantly fought, and finally succumbed to, disease.

Les's last personal email to me closed with a quotation from William Butler Yeats's poem "The Lake Isle of Innisfree":

> And I shall have some peace there, for peace comes dropping slow,
> Dropping from the veils of the morning to where the cricket sings;
> There midnight's all a-glimmer, and noon a purple glow,
> And evening full of the linnet's wings."

Les added his own line: "And look at that band of glory high up and far away in the distance." He died on October 25, 2017, truly believing that, as in childbirth, the pains of all creation would yield new life. This book is his legacy.

Philip Yancey

Preface

I didn't choose Romans, Romans chose me. Thirty years ago as a follow-up to a university dissertation I decided to read through the New Testament letters in order to be sure that I hadn't missed some obvious thing that would invalidate my thesis. But in the event I didn't get past Romans. Using a worn paperback copy of the New English Bible I read the letter through almost at a gulp. And at the end I thought, "Now *that* is interesting!" It was as if I had stepped into an unknown world. I started to read it again, more slowly. And again. Only after six months of reading and rereading did I feel that Romans had released me—for the time.

Over the years that followed the letter continued to haunt me. I preached it and lectured it. There was a thesis, a conference paper, and more reading and thinking. Finally I felt I was beginning to understand what Paul was saying. It blew me away. I began to long to share some of the wonderful things I was discovering. If that was to happen, though, I was sure about one thing. Whatever I wrote had to be written for ordinary people. Of the making of commentaries for specialists there is no end. But where were the books which would enable twenty-first century people to be as challenged and empowered as the little Roman congregation Paul wrote to had been by his letter? I decided to try to write a page-turner on Romans. It was only later that I realised that Paul was doing the very same thing.

As it has happened, I have not been able to complete the full exposition all the way to the end of Paul's letter. Two years into the book's writing I was diagnosed with acute myeloid leukemia. As a consequence I fell off the planet for a year, coming through a bone marrow transplant and the subsequent long convalescence into what appeared at the time to be full recovery.

Getting back to the desk I had a much clearer idea of what the book should be. Especially I realised that there had to be a translation. The text needs to be on the page; besides, my experience with the first three chapters had taught me that you can't write a book where you are continually saying "I know your translation says one thing, but what Paul actually said was quite another." I went back too and re-wrote the main text from the beginning, making it tighter and leaner, and above all ensuring it was true to what Paul actually wrote. It was a voyage of discovery: so much of what the tradition had taught me was in the letter vanished like smoke—and what *was* there was astounding. Engagement with Romans has transformed my understanding of the good news.

After three years of full health my blood counts took a lurch again. It soon became clear that this was no blip: the leukemia had returned. As I write all of the interventions that are possible in this situation have failed. I am living out the final months of my life. In the light of that I am so grateful to have been able to bring the exposition through to the end of chapter 8 of Paul's letter, which in some ways is a natural break point. As I've worked hard to complete the text, his reminder in that chapter that we must suffer with Jesus if we are to share his glory and the discovery—new to me—that the context of the "Abba!" cry is Gethsemane, have not been matters of merely theoretical interest.

In J. R. R. Tolkien's novel *The Lord of the Rings*, an unremarkable character in an unremarkable land finds himself possessed of a ring of power, indeed the one ruling ring that the Dark Lord is bending all of his energies to find. "Keep it safe," the wizard Gandalf tells him. "You have to remember, the ring *wants* to be found." In the service of a very different Lord I have over many months now felt the material in this book trembling under my hand, longing to be set free to do its work in the world. It is a remarkable feeling, nothing to do with any human skill or desire. The good news of Jesus Messiah *wants* to be found.

And so, not without a pang, I commit this book back into the hand of the One who gave me the task so long ago. "My Word shall not return to me empty but shall achieve all that I sent it to do." Yes.

Les Brighton
October 2017

Acknowledgements

THE FOLLOWING PEOPLE WERE part of a reference group that commented, often in extremely helpful detail, on early drafts of chapters 1–3 in particular: Matt Button, Claire Brighton, Dave Festing, Alan Harkness, David Pickering, Paul Trebilco, and Matt Watts.

Others who have sharpened my thinking about particular issues: Ron Hay, Brett Mann, and David Bryant.

I once put Philip Yancey in a position where he felt honor-bound to have a look at an early version of the introduction and chapter 1. He gave me three pieces of advice which became basic principles in the writing and rewriting of the rest of the book.

I'd like especially to thank Ross McKerras for his ready availability to help with Greek language and translation issues.

I also need to acknowledge my home congregation at St. Timothy's church in Burnside, Christchurch, where I have had the privilege of preaching regularly over the years. Books are not written by solitary people in a book-lined room. They spring out of the life of a community, and in particular out of the word of God that comes as a preacher prepares and a congregation expectant reach out their hands and hearts for it. Many of the truths and illustrations that have found their way into the book originally had their source in preaching.

Introduction

Teletype across the bottom of the screen: Jerusalem, AD 56, garrison commander's office, the Fortress of Antonia. The boy is eleven or twelve, with tousled hair and the cheerful boldness of a tomboy: there are dozens like him in the teeming streets and alleys of the city. He is not homeless: the sleeve of his tunic has been torn not long ago, the tribune notices, and mended with careful stitches. A little overawed by being here in the heart of the Antonia, with the armed sentry behind him and the hubbub of a working garrison all around, nonetheless he answers readily enough, and tells what he has overheard. The request that will come from the Jewish Council for a second examination of the defendant. The forty men preparing to ambush the guard party. The vow not to eat or to drink before the prisoner is dead.

The tribune doesn't hesitate. He knows the fundamentalist politics of the place, and the way these things work. The orders are given swiftly. Shortly after dark a massively armed squadron heads out of the city gate and down the main road to the coast. Two hundred foot soldiers, two hundred spearmen, seventy horsemen, all escorting a single prisoner. The bird has flown. Still in chains, Paul of Tarsus has left Jerusalem, and is headed for the safety of Caesarea Philippi.

Teletype chatter once more: Two months previously, the port of Miletus, just south of Ephesus, an hour after sunrise. A steady breeze from the land carries the cry of gulls, the smells of wood smoke, straw and dung, and the aroma of food cooking in hundreds of courtyards. Under the feet of a stream of laden slaves the gangplank creaks and bucks as the cargo is packed into the hold. The captain watches the shadows shortening on the quayside: the high tide is only a couple of hours away, and nowadays both breeze and tide are necessary to negotiate the harbor entrance. He is impatient to be gone.

At the base of the quay the passengers are talking with a group of a dozen or more local people who have come to bid them farewell. Several are older men, but there is a mix of ages. Two are women. It is no casual parting. While they are too far off for him to hear what is being said, the earnestness of what is going on is clear. The leader of the traveling group is the focus: a short man, solidly built, salt and pepper hair, a keen glance under black eyebrows. The captain watches as one by one each of the group grasps his hand and speaks, sometimes with great emotion. Several kiss him on each cheek, as is the custom of those from the western lands. There are tears and cries, and not only from the women. Then suddenly, right there on the stone quayside, the whole group kneels. Out in the open air, far from any temple, clearly they are praying to their god. A final handshake and it is over. The larger group stands back as the traveling party, two of them with the heavy canvas shoulder bags that never leave their sight, head towards the gangplank. They are ready to sail.[1]

Set so closely together in time, these two incidents illustrate the very different responses of the people of his day to the man who wrote the letter to the Romans. The irony of the attempt upon his life (only the latest of a string of such incidents) would not have been lost upon Paul himself. In a former life he too had been that kind of passionate fanatic, convinced that the Christian message was so dangerous to God's revealed truth that those infected with it had to be rooted out and destroyed.[2] As we approach Paul's letter to the Romans, we need to be aware that this is what we are getting: it contains a message that is capable of engendering this kind of reaction. From such a man it would be foolish to expect a soothing sermon of self-congratulation, pious platitudes reinforcing us in what we already know. And indeed it is an incendiary document, designed to challenge the smallness of our vision of God, and to bring us face to face with him in a way that may well be deeply threatening. Are we prepared for this?

The moving farewell by the elders of the church at Ephesus, who had walked the nighttime roads from the city to the port to bid Paul farewell for the last time, shows us the other side of the coin: the deep love and appreciation that people all across the Mediterranean held for the apostle to the nations. They weren't just in love with his ideas, they were warmly attached to the man himself. We catch echoes of this everywhere in the correspondence. In letters to churches like those at Philippi and Corinth, and to individuals like Timothy and Philemon, the warmth of personal appreciation shines out, and this is so even when there are tough issues to deal with. Writing to the Galatian churches Paul reminds them of how when he came to them in a time of need and great bodily weakness they welcomed him "as an angel of God," indeed "as if he were Messiah Jesus himself." They would, he reminds them, have torn out their own eyes and given them to him, if they thought it would have helped.[3] In the Romans letter, too, we see the human qualities of Paul the man: his willingness and honesty in sharing his own personal experience; the earnest pastoral concern that informs everything he says; his pain and grief over the unbelief of his own people, Israel.

CHANGING HISTORY

But it is not for its human dimension alone that the letter to the Romans has been prized by the church down the years since Paul first dictated it. The power of the writing, the depth and the glory of its proclamation of the way God has acted in the world, the earnestness and urgency of its teaching about what it means to live a fully human life, all these have burnt its message into the experience of countless Christians. The letter should have a warning label on it. It has seized upon individuals and upon whole communities over the years, changing them, and in some cases utterly transforming their world. *Martin Luther*, for example, tormented by moral failure and anxiety about his situation before God, found here the secret of peace and freedom—and the theological dynamite of his discovery transformed not only individual lives in his own day, but the political and religious future of a continent. Two hundred years later *John Wesley* heard the Preface to Luther's lectures on Romans read aloud in a small study group. He "felt his heart strangely warmed,"[4] as he later wrote, and it burst upon him that indeed Christ had died for *him*. His life was transformed. Wesley's subsequent preaching ministry, covering 250,000 miles on horseback all over England, introduced many thousands of people to Christ as not just a distant religious figure, but one who could change lives today. The impact of his ministry upon the social life of his time was arguably one of the reasons why England did not suffer a violent revolution in the eighteenth century as had happened in France. Finally, in the early twentieth century the publication of *Karl Barth*'s commentary on this letter was spoken of by one reviewer as "a bombshell dropped on the theologian's playground."[5] Barth himself described it as more like going into a country church in the middle of the night and, stumbling in the dark, grasping hold of the bell rope, bringing all the community running to see what had happened.[6]

These are the stars, of course—very able people whose discovery of Romans has had wide public influence. But, unnoticed by the history books, there are literally millions of people who have found in this letter a deep source of life and hope. I remember reading about a young minister in the nineteenth century who, visiting a miner's house one evening, discovered him reading Romans. Visiting again a month later, he was surprised to find the man still absorbed in the same letter. When he mentioned this, the burly miner looked at him slowly over his spectacles. "Son," he said, "I'm putting a shaft down here."

Yet it has to be acknowledged that Romans is not as easy reading as the Gospels, for example, or the Old Testament history books. We can't just pick it up and grasp all of it all at once, like we might do with the newspaper. Many people will remember reading Shakespeare in school, and having to struggle with the language and unfamiliar concepts in order to break through to the power and excitement of those amazing plays. Shakespeare wrote in English around 400 years ago. But Paul's letter was written in Greek and almost 2,000 years ago. A good modern translation helps a huge amount with the language, of course, but there are still words and ideas in Romans that don't leap off the page. We have to unpack their meaning; we have to take the time to think ourselves into Paul's world a little. As we do that, though, the letter starts to stir under our hand and become a living thing: we hear again the earnest voice of the apostle as with passion and with urgency he uses every technique that he knows to convey the power and the glory of what he has seen in the gospel.

INTRODUCTION

SPOKEN, NOT WRITTEN

One important thing to understand right from the beginning is that Paul did not actually *write* the letter. If we thought about the writing process we might imagine him like some medieval philosopher in an upper room late at night, dipping his quill in the ink, pausing every now and again to think, and then bending once again over the parchment. Not true! In Paul's day only specialists actually wrote anything more than a sentence or two. Paul, like every other educated person, dictated his letters to a scribe. The scribe was the word processor of the time: they were how you wrote things.[7] We know who the scribe was for the letter to the Romans: his name was Tertius, and right at the end of the letter he adds his own personal greeting to the church at Rome (16:22). So, instead of imagining Paul sitting down and writing the letter himself, we have instead to think of him restlessly walking up and down the room, dictating to a scribe. Sometimes the words would come tumbling out, and Tertius would be struggling to keep up. At other times Paul might say "Run that past me again . . . " Tertius would do so, and Paul would then take up his argument at the point he had left off.

The reason it is important to understand this is because it suggests that our aim in working with Romans should be less to *read* the letter than to *hear* it. While he did send letters from time to time, Paul's main calling was as a preacher and teacher. After regular preaching tours across the known world for more than two decades he is superbly skilled at engaging and involving an audience. He is a skilled orator. During all this time he has longed to visit Rome, so far without success (1:9–15). Hence, the letter. As he dictates we have to think of him with the Roman congregation vivid in his imagination as he preaches to them as he has preached to so many audiences over the years. Only in this case, the sermon is written down by a scribe.

Like any good sermon, Paul's letter grabs us by the scruff of the neck and refuses to let us go. There are real surprises: he knows how to play his audience, to lead us along with him all unwittingly until suddenly he turns the argument on its head, and we find ourselves confronted with uncomfortable truths and with the living God. What he says is intensely practical. Paul had no time for a theology that didn't day by day and moment by moment engage with the life-experience of real people. And it is deeply personal. Paul doesn't preach from some elevated place but is completely honest about his own struggles and conflicting emotions. He doesn't talk *at* us, but draws us *with* him on a journey into the truth of God that involves him just as completely as it does us. It is a journey that leads to some astonishing and deeply joyful places.

Which brings us to the final thing we need to say about the letter in this introduction. Provided we give it the respectful attention that is necessary to enter into its world, we will soon enough find that *that world is also in fact our own*, right now in the twenty-first century.[8] One reason for that is because no matter where we find ourselves in history, the pressing issues of human life remain the same. Both joys and challenges, they are fundamental to what it means to be human. But the second reason

INTRODUCTION

is even more significant. Paul's letter is about us only because in the first instance it is about *God*. In that sense, this 2,000-year-old letter is more contemporary than this morning's newspaper. Because through it we find ourselves, right now, directly and personally addressed by the living God. As we read the letter we step into his eternal present. We find ourselves face to face with him.

What lies before us then is not just the task of working out what worthy things there might be to learn from a famous old Christian letter. For this is Scripture. Luther, Wesley, and Barth didn't find Romans so powerful because they were smart or specially gifted people. They are famous because they were those things also, but that was not the source of the power. What each of them testified was that the letter itself gripped them; that it was not what they brought to the letter but God himself speaking through these words into their world that made the difference. The same will be so for us. What we are doing is a bit like working through a pile of papers on a desk, or sorting out and folding away laundry tumbled on a bed. Underneath the pile we find our missing mobile phone. We pick up the phone—and it rings.

WARNING STICKER

The letter itself may not have a warning sticker on it, but perhaps the book you are holding should have at least a small one. If you decide to come on this journey you need to know that you will find yourself, as I have done, in unexpected and surprising places. Before we can get to grips with the meaning of the letter, we will, for example, have to do some careful work in establishing what Paul actually wrote. Even in the very first sections we are going to discover that some of our Bible translations use words that reflect what the translators know Paul *ought* to be saying, rather than what is actually there in the text. Chapter divisions are another problem. In several places (Romans is particularly bad for this) the way the material is broken up into the traditional chapters confuses rather than clarifies Paul's meaning.[9] While we will be reading steadily through the letter, instead of reading each verse in a mechanical sequence like beads on a string we will be trying always to understand the way the argument of each section unfolds as a whole. All along the way things that for some of us have long been familiar will appear in a startling new light.

It is when we do come to understand what Paul is actually saying, however, that the real challenges arise. What has struck me again and again in working through the letter is how shocking, how outrageous, Paul's message must have appeared in his day to all right-thinking religious people. It was not for nothing that zealous and committed men devised the plot to kill Paul that we spoke of in the opening paragraph: it was crucial for the purity and the integrity of the faith that he be silenced. We need to keep this in mind as we read. We don't hear much of this Paul, the uncomfortable Paul, the dangerous Paul, in the current way we read his letters. We have domesticated his Roman letter and have claimed Paul himself as one of our own. His confrontational

INTRODUCTION

message goes right past us; it is directed to someone else, to some other religious person in some other time. But if we are to be honest before God, we cannot fool ourselves like this. Paul's message challenges us right at the heart of our self-understanding as Christians. God looks us in the eye. And it is on this basis alone that we are, perhaps for the first time, able to hear his message of salvation and deliverance.

Are you on for this? The letter to the Romans is not for the faint-hearted. But what we are looking for is not safety and comfort but the word of the Living God; a word which, uncomfortable as it may be at times, is nonetheless a stream of living water in a desert land. Where else can we go? How could we be satisfied with anything less? It is my prayer that through this book, or alongside it—or even perhaps despite it—God himself may speak to us; that Paul's letter to the Romans may fall open to us, and that through it the glory and grace of God that first gripped Paul himself would shine, to the refreshment of our lives, and the transformation of our world.

THE KIND OF BOOK THIS IS

This is not a book for scholars, but for ordinary thoughtful Christians. Paul didn't write for learned people, nor was his letter designed to sit on a library shelf. Like Paul himself I have tried to write a kind of a page-turner; something designed to be read, rather than referred to. You will therefore need to start at the start. Readers flicking through to find out what is said about particular passages will be crucially handicapped by not having the context of what has gone before.

I also (wistfully perhaps) hope that the scholars might also take the time to have a look, even if they have to stoop a little to come in through the doorway of a popular exposition. Again and again what Paul is actually saying in Romans seems to me different from the understanding of the letter that is taken for granted in the literature. In Hillary Mantel's novel of sixteenth-century England, *Wolf Hall* (HarperCollins, 2009), Thomas Cromwell offers his wife a copy of the newly translated (and at that time, contraband) New Testament in English. "Read it," he suggests, and referring to the doctrines of purgatory and priesthood and indulgences and the church structure of that time, "You'll be surprised at what you don't find." That is how it is with Romans. It is surprising what after a close reading of the text you don't find—and completely extraordinary what you do.

My special hope is that this book will filter through to the pastors and the preachers, those whose responsibility is week by week to stand in pulpits and communicate the glory of the good news to their people, yet whose academic training has taught them that Romans is a tough theological book which can only be preached selectively and with caution. It is time that impression was replaced with a different truth. "Unbind him and let him go." It is time that Paul's letter was liberated again to do its work, God's transforming work, in the world.

INTRODUCTION
A NEW TRANSLATION

Although I have at every point consulted the standard English versions, the translation provided here is my own. I should note just a couple of things about that. Translating a text from one language to another, and especially translating something written long ago, can never be a word-for-word business. The *more literal* and word-for-word a translation is the *less accurate* it will be. But there are tight constraints upon the process. Paul was a precise and careful communicator, and dealing with matters of the greatest importance; a cheerful but inexact paraphrase won't do the job. The translation offered here is therefore based on two principles: (1) *Freedom in expression* insofar as that is necessary to communicate what Paul is saying in language that is natural and meaningful to a modern audience without a background of church talk. I haven't hesitated to fill out phrases, to re-order, or to rephrase in order to make clear comprehensible English sentences. The aim throughout is faithfulness not to the individual words, but to the meaning that they express. (2) *Extremely careful concern for accuracy of meaning*, especially in situations where the English translational tradition makes assumptions, or silently interprets the text in the light of what it was later believed to contain. I realize that this will sound alarming to some and presumptuous to others. For those with Greek language skills I can only point to the text itself (please check this end-note.[10]) For all of the rest of us, you will have to trust me. But my hope is that as we go along the text will start to validate itself, and that as we read and think about it we will gain increasing confidence that this really is what Paul was saying. It will hang together and make sense; things that up to now have seemed opaque and merely religious will become understandable in terms of real life outside of Christian culture. I won't get it right every time, of course. For the mistakes and misunderstandings that will undoubtedly crop up I can only seek your pardon, and Paul's.

A NOTE ABOUT NOTES

The notes at the end of the book (indicated by the superscript numbers in the text) provide another layer of engagement with the text for those who want to dig deeper. While the main text is written for the majority of us, those readers who already know Romans well will want more detail about why I take unfamiliar positions about certain key passages; the notes to the translation are there for them. Other notes give more information about first century religious and cultural matters; others extend the theological thinking or the practical outworking of what Paul is saying in a way that would break up the main line of the text if it was included there. Don't be put off by the notes! Treat them like a click-through link on a website. I suggest boldly ignoring them on a first reading. Some people, though, will want to keep a bookmark in the notes section to check them out as they go along, and that is cool too.

Introduction
ROMANS UNPLUGGED

Not every reader will be familiar with the expression "unplugged." Modern musical performances and recordings are heavily technically augmented, by electronic instruments, amplifiers, and speakers, controlled from behind the scenes from a sound mixing desk where the input from the various microphones is balanced and adjusted. To play "unplugged" means that the artist or band puts aside all these artificial aids, and plays directly upon acoustic instruments with no electronic enhancements.

This is a metaphor for what I am trying to do with Paul's letter in this book. Romans has been a key Christian source-document ever since it was written, and rightly so. But that means that it comes to us today so overlaid with all those years of amplification and mixing, theologizing and system-making that it is often impossible to hear what it is saying anymore. What I am trying to do here is to gently unplug for a while from all of that later thinking, and allow Paul alone to stand up there on stage and sing us the song he sang at the beginning. Whether I am successful in that you will have to decide as we go along. There will certainly be surprises. But underneath the ideas and the arguments I hope that we will with increasingly clarity come to hear Paul's living voice: achingly personal, intensely practical, always both challenging and encouraging, pointing us to God. Let us listen to the man.

Endnotes

1. These two stories can be found in Acts 23:16–24 and 20:13–38.
2. The threefold repetition of the story of his own conversion in the public interrogations recorded in Acts reflects his awareness of this—and his desire that others too might experience a similar encounter and transformation.
3. Gal 4:12–15.
4. *John Wesley's Journal* from the entry for May 24, 1738.
5. Quoted by F. F. Bruce, *The Epistle of Paul to the Romans* (Inter-Varsity Press: Leicester, 1983), 60.
6. After completing this introduction I discovered that F. F. Bruce uses the same three illustrations (plus others) in the introduction to his Tyndale commentary on Romans (IVP, revised edition 1985, p. 56.)
7. It was also how you *read* them. Reading one's own letter was much less efficient than giving it to a professional reader/writer to read for you. And reading always involved *speaking out the words*; communication was always a matter of the living voice. In an oral society a letter or a book was treated as we would treat a script or a score: as something to perform. Texts posed a challenge in an only partly literate society, and competent readers were not everywhere to be found. *Silent* reading was still an astonishment and a curiosity well into the Middle Ages. This is, therefore, a fundamental difference between our time and Paul's. For us writing is often the first thing: even sermons and speeches are usually written first, before being spoken. It is initially a silent process. But in the first century *speech* was the primary form. Writing was secondary; it was merely a way of recording speeches for the benefit of those who couldn't attend, or of communicating when you couldn't speak face to face. This is what Paul tells us *Romans* is: a temporary substitute for his personal presence (1:8–15). When it arrived, the letter was not read individually by members of the Roman congregation. Originally there was only one copy; and few people read things as part of their everyday life anyway. The letter was read *to* them, and that was done in the first place by the *letter-carrier*, who was the writer's representative in delivering the letter. There was, of course, no postal service! The letter-carrier was not merely a messenger, but an associate; someone who knew the writer's thinking, and who therefore could read the letter to the recipient or recipients with understanding. In the case of Romans, a number of scholars suggest that the letter-carrier was the Phoebe whom Paul mentions in 16:1. As a respected member of the church in Cenchrae and someone who knew Paul well, she may well have been the kind of person who would have been entrusted with this task. We have no firm evidence. If that was in fact the case, however, it would say a great deal about the openness of the Roman church to such a ministry from a woman in what was still a strongly male-dominated society, and about the power of the Christian gospel to bring that about.
8. Karl Barth describes this process in the work of John Calvin: "How energetically Calvin, having first established what stands in the text, sets himself to re-think the whole material and to wrestle with it, till the walls which separate the sixteenth century from the first become transparent! Paul

Endnotes

speaks, and the man of the sixteenth century hears. The conversation between the original record and the reader moves around the subject-matter, until a distinction between yesterday and today becomes impossible." (Barth, *Epistle to the Romans*, 7.)

9. Although various ways of finding one's way around the text were in use from the fourth century AD, the chapter divisions in our modern Bibles date from the early thirteenth century.

10. Individual translational decisions are defended in the endnote to each text section. On two occasions the differences between the meaning conveyed by the traditional English versions and the meaning of the Greek text are so significant as to damage our understanding of what Paul is saying in the whole of the letter. On these occasions the explanation of the translation I offer is brought into the main text as an optional text box.

1

Romans 1: 1–7
Paul's Self-Introduction

"This letter comes from Paul, slave of Messiah Jesus and a called messenger, set apart for the good news of God. ² Promised beforehand through his prophets in the holy scriptures, ³ that news concerns his Son, who with regard to his physical descent came of David's line, and ⁴ with regard to his holy spirit was declared to be Son of God with power by resurrection from the dead. Through him, Jesus, the Jews' Messiah and the Christians' Lord, ⁵ we have received both the privilege and the commission to bring about the obedience of faith among all the nations, so that his name may be spread far and wide.

⁶ And that includes yourselves, called as you are by Jesus Messiah. ⁷ To all God's beloved in Rome, then, called and holy: grace to you and peace from God our Father and [the] Lord Jesus Messiah."[1]

Christ or Messiah?

What does the word "Christ" mean to you? We use it all the time, but mostly it just functions as a sort of name of honor to refer to Jesus. We don't think of it as having a meaning. But it does . . .

The English word is just a transliteration of *Christos*, the word used by those who first translated the Old Testament into Greek for the Hebrew word "anointed one," i.e., the Messiah, God's promised future king of Israel and the nations. That translation wasn't a particularly useful one, because anointing wasn't part of royal ritual in the Greek and Roman world; besides, the Greek word *christos* meant being smeared with oil or fat: it had more of an unpleasant than a pleasant connotation. Mostly it was taken to be merely a name, passing into Latin for example as "Chrestus." For most of Christian history we too have used "Christ" in much the same way as we would a surname. But *Christos* is not a name. Nor strictly is it a title. It is a *description,* a description of someone sent by God for a particular task, and anointed with oil as a sign both of his authority and his destiny.

The word is central to the message of the New Testament. There was much debate during Jesus' lifetime as to whether he was or was not the promised Messiah. For the religious leaders of the day the death of Jesus proved conclusively that he was not (Mark 15:32, Luke 23:35). But the resurrection changed everything. Peter declared it at Pentecost: "Therefore let the entire house of Israel know with certainty that God has made this Jesus whom you crucified *both Lord and Messiah*" (Acts 2:36). John announced it as the whole purpose of his gospel: "These things are written that you may come to believe that Jesus is *the Messiah, the Son of God*, and that believing you may have life in his name" (John 20:31). The question had changed. No longer was it whether Jesus matched the Old Testament picture of the promised Messiah. Now it was realized that the person of the risen Jesus in his authority and power *defined what the word Messiah had always meant.*

Understanding all this, Paul never uses the word casually. Even when he is speaking in general of "Jesus Christ" (rather than "Jesus the Christ") or of friends in the congregation in Rome as fellow-workers "in Christ," the article "the" is always implicit. Often the meaning of the word is central to his thought: as in this verse, where the description "Messiah" is placed for emphasis before the personal name and foreshadows the identification of Jesus as the Son of God, ruler of the nations (v. 4). And in some sections of the letter (e.g. 3:21–25, 5:6–11 and 8:11) the significance of the word as a descriptive title is completely crucial for understanding what Paul is getting at.

All of this poses a problem for a translator. Because *Messiah* still has meaning in twenty-first-century English, I have chosen to use that original word instead of *Christos*, its Greek translation. We all have some idea about what a Messiah might be, but, unless I am mistaken, little or no idea of what a Christ might be. Even if this feels unfamiliar at first, it will help us understand passages in the letter that will otherwise be puzzling; perhaps too it will help us to rediscover the meaning of the word "Christ" wherever we encounter it in other contexts.

This is Paul's *letterhead*. It explains who the writer is and his authority for writing, it says who the letter is addressed to, and it tells us what it is about. I have a similar letter sitting on my desk as I write. The letterhead says "Tower Insurance," it is addressed to Mr. and Mrs. Brighton, and it tells us that our premiums are going up. Sigh!

Of course no one spends a lot of time gazing at the letterhead of a business letter: we quickly read on to see what the letter itself says. But before we move on from these introductory verses we need to notice three of their extraordinary features.

Firstly, Paul's message is *news*. Christianity is not based on philosophy or theology or general principles such as a scientist might assemble to create a theory. It is nothing human beings could deduce or discover. It is about an *event in history*, an *act of God in the world*, something that breaks in from outside to change things.

Secondly, that act is not a mere happening, it is a *person*: God's Son, the Messiah, prophesied in the Old Testament and now in Paul's lifetime stepping into history. On one level, Paul is saying, Jesus was a man, with a human genealogy like any other person. But the resurrection changes everything we might otherwise have thought about him: it proclaims that he is the Son of God.

When I was younger, verse 4 used to really bother me. Was Paul saying that Jesus was declared to be Son of God only at the resurrection? Doesn't the start of John's Gospel and other passages tell us that he has always been with God and really God from the very beginning? Is there some uncertainty about that?

The key that unlocks the puzzle may sound a little strange at first, and it is this: the title Son of God is in its origin not a *divine* but a *human* title. In the Old Testament it was especially the title of the king: he was God's representative in ruling the nation. He embodied and symbolized God's sovereignty over the people. Psalm 2 expresses the idea especially vividly. God addresses the newly crowned king, and declares

> You are my Son; today I have begotten you.
> Ask me and I will make the nations your inheritance,
> and the ends of the earth your possession.
> You shall break them with an iron rod,
> and smash them to bits like a piece of crockery.[2]

This is the Son of God that Paul is speaking about in verse 4. As to his human pedigree Jesus is the Messiah, the heir of David's promises, the ruler of *the nation* of Israel.[3] But the stunning fact of the resurrection declares something much deeper. Because of who he is, because of the unique spirit he possesses, Jesus has been appointed as the Son of God, the ruler of *the nations*.[4]

And he is that not just in the hopeful and rather militant way that the writer of Psalm 2 envisaged. What Paul is describing is not a merely human "Son of God" but *God's* Son (v. 3): a real human being, yet also, in a way Paul cannot define but is forced to recognize, God himself entering human history and making it his own.[5] To use terminology developed long after his time, the word "Son" for Paul means something like *God incarnate*. Jesus is the reality of which the earlier royal language only hinted. God himself has come.

The blessing at the end of verse 7, therefore, doesn't refer to two persons, but to one. Paul knows that Jesus was a real human being who ate and drank and got tired and laughed and wept as we all do. Nonetheless, he wishes grace and peace to his readers "from God our Father and [the] Lord Jesus Messiah." I have placed the article in square brackets, because it isn't there in the Greek text. One could just as correctly punctuate the sentence "from God, *our Father and Lord Jesus Messiah*."[6]

Finally, notice how Paul honors his listeners. They aren't random individuals trying their best to make a life in the world, they are *loved by God*. Like him, they too have been called by Messiah Jesus; their lives like his have been irrevocably changed by encounter with the holy. Despite the uniqueness of his own commission, he writes to them as his equals: as mature people able to choose and to change, as fellow-participants in a great adventure.

And we too are encountered here. This is not just a letter addressed to other people, far away and long ago. Of course Paul had no idea that his words would be read by people like us two thousand years later. But then, he hadn't met the Roman Christians to whom he was writing, either. Whatever our location in space and time there is no question that we are the people to whom Paul is writing: people loved by God, called into life by the risen Jesus; people who don't understand everything but nonetheless are already being changed by an encounter that we have not initiated. And people eager to go on: eager to learn more about this God, eager to discover in our practical experience what the life is that he calls us into.

2

Romans 1:8–15
Why Paul is Writing

⁸ *"First, to the God who is mine through Jesus Messiah I give thanks for all of you, because your faith is being spoken of everywhere. ⁹God is my witness, the God whom I serve with my whole being in the good news of his Son, how often and how regularly I remember you in my prayers, ¹⁰asking that in his will I may somehow at last succeed in visiting you. ¹¹For I am longing to see you, so that I can share some spiritual gift so that you may be strengthened; ¹²that is, so that we can be mutually encouraged by each other's faith, you by me and me by you. ¹³Brothers and sisters I want to assure you that I have often intended to come to you—but up to now have been prevented from doing so—looking to reap some harvest among you as I have among the rest of the nations. ¹⁴I am a debtor to both Greeks and barbarians, to both wise and foolish: ¹⁵that is why, if I get the chance, I am eager to preach the good news to you who are in Rome as well."*[7]

ONE OF THE APPEALING things about Paul's letters is the personal way in which he engages with those to whom he is writing. We feel his warmth and personality, we sense that he is a real person talking to real people—people among whom, even so many years into his future, we might ourselves be included. From various bits of evidence from Acts and his other letters we can be fairly sure about when Paul wrote this one, and the circumstances that led him to write rather than to visit—as, he tells us, he has for many years longed to do. It seems he is writing from Corinth[8] towards the end of his third missionary journey, that is, in AD 57 or thereabouts. Having been involved for over 20 years in pioneer preaching and church-planting work across most of the Eastern Mediterranean (15:19), he now plans to extend his mission westwards to Spain. That would mean that on the way he would be able to fulfil a long-standing desire to visit Rome. However, there is something he has to do first. For a number of years he has been organizing a relief collection for the church in Jerusalem, and before departing for Spain he must go to see that that is safely delivered.

What Paul was doing single-handedly through his networks was very ambitious: the kind of thing that a whole organisation might be set up to do today.[9] Responding to the practical needs of the impoverished Jerusalem community, the collection is also a gesture of solidarity and fellowship from the non-Jewish churches to the somewhat conservative and very "Jewish" home church in Jerusalem. Paul's hope is that the generous gift to Jerusalem from the non-Jewish churches will show that, despite their freedom from traditional Jewish religious practices, the spirit of Jesus was nonetheless powerfully alive in them. He is hoping that this practical demonstration of care will bring the two parts of the church together.

For these reasons Paul has decided to accompany the group who are escorting the gift to Jerusalem. There are of course no checks or electronic transfers in his world; the money has to be physically transported. And it is not just the money, it is the message. Paul is the only one who can bring the firsthand news of the little congregations away to the west that will make the gift meaningful. And so he turns east, putting aside for a time his mission to Spain and the visit to Rome that he plans to make along the way. In the event, he will visit Rome indeed—as a prisoner in chains, awaiting the results of the personal appeal to the emperor,[10] which he has been forced to make in order to escape the murderous intent of religious extremists in Jerusalem. The decisive action of the tribune in response to the small boy's story in the Antonia will show just how wise he was to have written to his Roman friends from Corinth before his journey to Jerusalem, rather than waiting a month or two until he could make the long-delayed visit after it.

As he explains all these things, Paul's personal qualities shine out. Notice the words that convey emotion: thanksgiving (v. 8), longing (v. 11), eagerness (v. 15). This is a man who feels as well as thinks. He prays for this little church continually (v. 9); he longs to pass on to them some gift from God (v. 11); he looks forward to the encouragement that comes from shared faith (v. 12). He knows that he has been specially equipped and commissioned by God, but that does not mean that he considers himself a cut above others, someone who needs to be always in a teaching role. He knows that when he comes to visit he will be encouraged by the faith of the Roman congregation as much as them by his, and he looks forward keenly to that. While he is sure that he has good things from God to pass on (v. 11), he knows that these gifts don't derive from any wealth of his own. Rather he considers himself *indebted* to those of the nations to whom he is called (v. 14): he has a responsibility to them that he must fulfill.

If those to whom he is writing are already Christians, why does Paul need to preach the good news to them (v. 15)? In the West we tend to think about evangelizing (which is the Greek word used here) as primarily about bringing people to faith for the first time. Paul, though, doesn't see the good news as a one-off thing, a single decision that brings one into the kingdom and nothing more. He has already told us, for example, that he himself serves God "in my spirit, *in* the good news" (v. 9). The good news is not just a set of truths to be believed, it is something that one *lives in*. The truth is not an idea, it is a person (John 14:6), impelling and drawing us on into life. In a letter to another of his churches Paul describes what his own experience of that is like:

> I want to know Messiah and the power of his resurrection and to share in his sufferings; becoming like him in his death in order that by some means[11] I too may arrive at the resurrection from the dead. [12]Not that I have already obtained this or have already reached the goal; but I press on to make it my own, because Messiah Jesus has made me his own. [13]Beloved, I do not consider that I have made it my own; but this single thing I do: forgetting what lies behind and straining forward to what lies ahead, [14]I press on towards the goal for the prize of the heavenly* call of God in Messiah Jesus.[11]

This doesn't mean that Paul is unsure whether he is really a Christian, or whether he will really be raised with Messiah at the last day.[12] Instead it shows the way he understands the good news, not as a single event or a decision, but as the whole course of a life lived day by day in fellowship with the living Jesus. It is "a long obedience in the same direction," to borrow Eugene Peterson's book title. We will hear much more about this in the course of the letter. The good news is like love: not something you can frame on the wall or lodge in the bank, but *a life to be lived* passionately and joyfully day by day. That is why Paul longs to preach the good news to the congregation in Rome.

3

Romans 1:16–17
Paul's Introductory Summary

¹⁶"For I am not ashamed of the good news! To everyone who puts his faith in him, the Jew first, and also the non-Jew, it is God's power for rescue. ¹⁷In it the righteousness of God is revealed, his faithfulness calling forth our faith; as it is written, 'The one who is righteous will live by faith.'"[13]

When I was a schoolboy, hearing verse 16 read always made me a bit uneasy. Paul isn't ashamed of the good news, he says—but why on earth should he be? Was there something I didn't know? Of course, it is an idiom: a colloquial form of speech that, although it sounds strange 2000 years later, would have been completely familiar to Paul's audience.[14] In our extended family there are a couple of people whose way of expressing agreement is to say "You're not wrong!" When someone says this, being wrong is never in view. It is instead an emphatic way of saying "You're right." Paul is not for a moment suggesting that the good news could ever be something to be ashamed of. On the contrary, he means that it is something about which he is deeply proud.[15] We feel this at once, as he goes on to tell us what that good news is. How packed with information these two verses appear! But that is because they are Paul's summary of everything that he will go on to say in the next four chapters.

WRITING AND SPEAKING

Why is such a summary necessary? To find the answer we have to imaginatively think ourselves into Paul's world. It is a world very different to our own in many ways, but perhaps most strikingly in this: it is a world where speaking rather than writing was the primary means of communication. Writing existed, of course—Romans itself is evidence of that. But writing was in every way a secondary medium. It was what you did when you couldn't speak directly. Speaking was primary. Writing was not a thing of its own. It was *speech written down*.

In our world it is writing that is the primary medium. Most of the information we receive comes to us through print, whether on paper or on a screen. But even spoken communication (speeches, sermons, TV news bulletins, weather reports that look spontaneous but are in fact read from auto-prompts off-camera) always start off as written material, which is only then delivered orally. We *receive* it as speech, but it starts off as *writing*.

The complete opposite was true for Paul. In his world even a written letter had its origin in the spoken word. We have already seen that Romans, like all Paul's letters, was dictated, not written. But that is not the only difference. When Paul or any of his contemporaries stood up to speak in public they were not working from a script, not even the most basic of jotted notes. The whole speech was created and held together *in the mind*. For an extended address, this was a significant feat. Most of us in the twenty-first century would be reasonably relaxed about delivering a short speech of welcome or thanks at a club or office gathering—though even then we might have a few notes hidden in a hand to be glanced down at. But how if it was an hour's teaching session, or a scientific or philosophical lecture? What if it was something as complex and as extensive as Romans?

Those who listened faced a similar challenge. There were no PowerPoint slides to look at, no bullet points, no visual headings or sub-headings that an audience could use to gain their bearings. Somehow a speaker had to give their material not only the kind of shape that would enable *them* as a speaker to shape and control it, they also had to build into it the signals, structures, and waypoints that would enable *their audience* to follow and to understand the development of the ideas.

One of the ways in which that was done was to summarize the whole of a thought-sequence at the very beginning. That summary was then unpacked or explained in what followed. Then, at the end, all the strands of the sequence were brought together in a conclusion that echoed the initial summary-statement. And then the next section would begin, the speech developing like this, step by step.[16] It is unfortunate that the chapters in our printed Bibles, designed as they are for readers not hearers, often miss these oral cues.[17] For it is important to realize that the verses we have just read are not just a random statement tacked onto Paul's greeting, but are in fact the summary of all that he wants to tell us in the first section of his letter. That section, Paul's initial line of thought, will conclude with his triumphant testimony to Abraham as a model of all those whose *faith* is "counted to them as *righteousness*" (4:22).

RESCUE

But perhaps your eyes are already beginning to glaze over. Righteousness? Abraham? And of course words like *gospel* and *power* and *salvation*, and something about "Jews and Greeks." I've perhaps used different words and you know that all these things are there in the familiar versions, and that I've just hidden some of them away in order to lull you.

Well, I haven't hidden anything away, I promise you: you will find an explanation of the translation decisions in the notes. What is true for all of us though is that there is a whole collection of words that we use in church that don't ever figure in our ordinary lives or our ordinary conversation. Many of those words are so smoothed and polished with use that they don't register any more—if indeed they ever did. They are religious talismans, giving us a feeling of encouragement and security but little more. Whatever they mean, they are the right words for what we are doing, so we are happy. It is the language of the tribe.

We aren't going to get very far with Romans without taking a second look at some of these words. Not that it is the words themselves that are important; it is the reality they describe. What Paul will do in these four chapters is to make us *experience* some of that reality, so that at the end, the words will shine with meaning in a way we never knew they could. But there are a couple of things that are important to notice at this point so that as the experience unfolds, we will have the language to describe what is going on. First, Paul says, the good news is *God's power for rescue.*

The power of God: we do hear about that quite a lot in church. What does it really mean for us, though? I suspect that mostly it is just something that we sing about, rather than anything that means much in our daily life. Though it isn't something I bring up very often over coffee after church, in the face of the savagery and heartbreak in so many places in our world, a part of me sometimes finds it hard to believe in God's power to change things. But if God *was* now in fact acting in power to change the world, what would that look like? How would we recognize it? We think we know what it would look like, and we don't see what we expect, and so the idea of God's power becomes something we give merely dutiful assent to. It becomes just another religious item.

The reality, though, is very different. Writer Annie Dillard puts it like this:

> On the whole, I do not find Christians, outside of the catacombs, sufficiently sensible of conditions. Does anyone have the foggiest idea what sort of power we so blithely invoke? Or, as I suspect, does no one believe a word of it? The churches are children playing on the floor with their chemistry sets, mixing up a batch of TNT to kill a Sunday morning. It is madness to wear ladies' straw hats and velvet hats to church; we should all be wearing crash helmets. Ushers should issue life preservers and signal flares; they should lash us to our pews.

For the sleeping god may wake someday and take offence, or the waking god may draw us out to where we can never return.[18]

Some of my colleagues in a former job discovered that I preached in church occasionally and were kidding me about it. So the next time my turn came up I sent them all an e-mail saying that, if they were prepared to live dangerously, they were welcome to come along. One woman came up to me afterwards. "If you are prepared to live dangerously?" she asked with a smile. "Well," I said. "I can't guarantee it, but God might turn up as well."

Hmmm. Nice answer. But even that could be just a cute thing to say, couldn't it? Paul however is not talking about something cute or slick, he is talking about something at the heart of reality. The power of God: the power that ignited the Big Bang that brought the material universe in all its finely-tuned complexity into being. The power that calls all living things into existence, and moment by moment holds them in being above the abyss. The power that raised Jesus Messiah from the dead! These are not just ideas or an inspiring story from the past. Paul is describing a God who is in action, creating and shaping his world. The good news is not just something to be believed, he says. It is itself an active power: through it God does things.

And what he does here is *rescue; he saves.* When I was a boy growing up in a wonderful but very conservative Christian community I knew what being saved was. We were told how to get saved at church every Sunday night. It was what happened when you knelt and confessed you were a sinner and asked Jesus into your life. When you had done that you were saved: you were going to heaven, not hell; you were OK. On one occasion I remember one of the older men in the congregation drawing me aside and asking, "Brother, are you saved?" "Yes!" I said. I knew what salvation was; I knew I had fulfilled the requirements.

But the New Testament has a deeper and richer understanding of salvation than this. Of course it knows that God "*has rescued us* (the same word in Greek) from the power of darkness and transferred us into the kingdom of his beloved Son, in whom we are set free" (Col 1:13). But as we read on we find that most of the New Testament references to salvation have a final goal that is *in the future.* So Paul can say about the message of the cross that it is "foolishness to those who are perishing, but to us *who are being saved* it is the power of God" (1 Cor 1:18). He can describe his ministry as "the fragrance of Messiah to God among *those who are being saved* and those who are perishing" (2 Cor 2:15). And at the end of Romans Paul will exhort his readers to watchfulness, because "salvation is getting nearer every day" (Rom 13:11). Clearly salvation is both a fact and a process. We are saved *from* something, absolutely. But we are also saved *for* something, and what that something is we are continually and joyfully discovering.

I dug a series of newspaper pictures out of a file as I was thinking about this. A churning brown torrent is sweeping through the main street of an Australian township. Two young women, chest-high in the water, are clinging desperately to a power pole, while a car floats past, and rescuers struggle to reach them. Which they do. In the final photo the second of the pair is coming back hand over hand along a line, shepherded by the burly firefighter who, with the help of the line, has managed to reach them.

It sometimes seems to me that our idea of God's salvation is too limited. It is only half the story. It is as if we had been rescued from drowning in such a situation but then left in limbo, wet and bedraggled, on the bank. No more choking on water, no more terror of death—but likewise no shower or dry clothes or hot food. No chance to look our rescuer in the eye and grasp his hand and get to know him. No experience of friendship and adventure down the years of the life that has now been given back to us. Rescue is a wonderful thing. But how could we let our imagination be dominated by the nothing, the non-existence we have been delivered from, instead of reaching forward into the something, the future and the life to be lived that that rescue has won for us?

Rescue from what? Paul will tell us very soon. It is worth noting, though, that the word for rescue itself is not common in Romans. After this it doesn't appear again until chapter 10, and then only a handful of other times in the letter. The word that does appear again and again in these early chapters is the word *righteousness*. Notice the "for" at the start of verse 17. Making sinful people into righteous people is *how* God rescues them.[19]

REBOOTING THE CONCEPTS

Righteousness is one of two crucial words that Paul introduces in verse 17: the other one is *faith*. These two ideas dominate this first part of the letter. Before going further, we have to stop and think about them. Trying to read on without understanding what they mean in Paul's thought-world would be a bit like putting on someone else's pair of glasses: everything looking slightly odd in ways hard to define, and a headache coming on. We'll look at *faith* first, and *righteousness* later. But first some background.

We have already talked about the difference between cultures where, as in Paul's world, the primary medium of communication is speech and in another, writing. But there is another difference between the first and the twenty-first century Western worlds that is even more important for our understanding of Romans. Let's start with a big question: what does it mean to be a human being? Western culture's answer to this has been strongly oriented upon the idea of the individual. Descartes's famous aphorism "I think, therefore I am" rang like a bell in the thought-world of his time; it would, however, have been meaningless to Paul. In Paul's world the essence of a person was not what they were in themselves. What defined a person was what they were *in relationship to others*.

This is crucial when we come to think about faith. It is a little-known fact that there is no Greek word for "faith." Instead Greek has a word that can mean either *faith* or *faithfulness*.[20] Hmm. But if that is the case how do we know how to translate the word into English? Which word do we choose? Isn't it confusing? Not at all. Because what is being described is not this or that quality in an individual, but *the nature of a relationship* as seen from one side or the other. One person's faithfulness reaches out towards the faith of another. One person's faith calls forth the faithfulness of the other.[21] Neither faith nor faithfulness is something that anyone can *have*. Faith is not a possession. It is not something that one does. It is not an aspect of character. What is being described is a relationship.

Ever since, in a world rapidly changing from a communal to an individual mentality, Luther rediscovered the power of the word *faith*, translators have learned to come to attention and salute whenever the Greek word "*pistis*" appears in a text. Here is that key word again! Even when a relationship is being described in such a way that the English word *faithfulness* is clearly the most appropriate one, still again and again *faith* is the word that the translators choose. It is a bit like when, in a live performance, the guitarist swings into the opening chords of a famous hit: the audience erupts with applause and cheering and whistles. They already know exactly what is about to come. In the same way we already know what *pistis* means; we don't even have to think about it. It is a problem. Translating the word consistently as *faith* gives the text a serious and religious feel. But it also renders it unintelligible.

The individualistic mindset which sees faith only in terms of what *human beings* do means that in popular teaching faith becomes a quantitative substance, something one can have much or little of. Jesus was at pains to deconstruct that idea. "Think as tiny as you can get—say a mustard seed," he tells us. "If you had only *that tiny* an amount of faith you could move a mountain!"[22] When in other contexts Jesus speaks about great faith he also always means quality, not quantity: he doesn't mean the *amount* of something someone has, but the depth of their understanding of the faithfulness of God.

But what if, thinking back to that live concert, the opening chords of the famous song are played—and from somewhere in the dark of the auditorium a new and different set of chords is struck? A series of notes that in their joy and power somehow *answer* the singer's introduction, calling it on into a further conversation? And so, as the audience holds its breath, stanza by stanza the song encounters an answering song that rises above it and reaches beneath it, completing and complementing: hard as nails, that song, yet as gentle as a breath, making shine for the listeners things that had been there in the words all along, questions understood now only in the light of their answer. And as the music comes to an end the searching spotlight at last finds near the back of the auditorium a guitar on a seat and a young woman standing alone with a microphone in her hand. And the audience realizes that the song *had always been a duet*, even though before that night neither they nor the performer on stage themselves had realized it. Faith and faithfulness: it is a relationship.[23]

This is why Paul can say that in the good news the righteousness of God is revealed, not "through faith for faith" or "by faith from first to last," and especially not (oh dear) "a process begun and continued by our faith," but *his faithfulness* calling forth *our faith*. The expression can mean nothing else.[24]

Paul will unpack the content of that statement in the next three chapters. Sufficient to note here that when God is the subject we are talking about something much more than simply trustworthiness and reliability. God's faithfulness is not an abstract dependability. Of human faithfulness we might say that a good friend will stand by us in a pinch. But God's faithfulness is a living and an active thing; it doesn't wait for the pinch. It steps out to make things happen. As we will see.

THE RIGHTEOUSNESS OF GOD

The problems we encounter by reading a term like *faith* from an individualistic perspective are precisely those which we encounter with the term *righteousness*. It is a key term in Romans: Paul will use it 31 times in the letter, more often than in all his other writings combined. Understanding what he means by it is therefore not an option. But is that so hard? Well, it seems that it is. My *Shorter Oxford* dictionary defines the righteous person as being among other things "virtuous, guiltless, sinless, conforming to the precepts of divine law or accepted standards of morality." Agree? You shouldn't, not for a minute. If we import these ideas into the way the word is used in Romans, we will be lost before we start. Virtually *nothing* in that definition has anything to do with righteousness as Paul understood it. Virtually the only way we use the idea today is when we describe someone as being "self-righteous." But in biblical terms self-righteous is *by definition* something one could never be. "Self-righteous" would for Paul be a meaningless term.

For righteousness is not an individual quality or attribute at all. It is something that can only exist in relation to others. The righteous person is one who can be counted on to be reliable and trustworthy in a friendship, a business encounter, or a marriage. Such a person keeps his or her promises to people, acts justly and unselfishly with regard to them, and values the other person in the relationship as much as themselves. Righteousness is not a static quality. It is active; it only exists in real situations between real persons. What Paul is talking about is not an abstract status or the achievement of virtue according to an impersonal moral or legal standard. To be righteous is to be the kind of person who *lives and acts truly* before God and among others in the actual affairs of human life.[25]

Acting righteously always expects and evokes a corresponding response in the other person. Despite the individualism of Western culture, we still experience relationships like this in practice. We know how friendship offered calls forth friendship in return. We know that receiving the love of someone else calls out the best in us, and calls us to be the person we perhaps aren't yet, but both long and need to be if love is to be real. We know about leadership, which is both something exercised by a person but also calls forth and requires the "followership" of those who affirm and honor that leadership by agreeing to be led.

This is why "self-righteousness" is so impossible as a concept. Righteous for the Bible writers was what *other people* acknowledged you to be, whether with regard to business affairs, the law, family relationships, or how one treated the poor in society. Always the issue was how one behaved as a person with regard to other persons. When you were judged to have acted truthfully, faithfully, and with regard to the other, then you were, in the eyes of your community, a righteous person. But you could never make that judgment of yourself.

This gives us the crucial context for understanding the word "righteousness" in Romans. We are not thinking of some kind of heavenly courtroom and a judge's decision on a case.[26] We shouldn't be visualising halos, either: a virtuous person keeping some kind of moral code. When using this word Paul is talking about what it means to be *a whole person*. He is describing someone who instinctively acts with truth and integrity and faithfulness with regard to God and to other people, and therefore is recognized by them to be that kind of person. Paul is not talking about an ethical quality, but about the completeness of a relationship with God and with others.[27] It is the quality in a person that demonstrates itself in relationships characterized by faith and faithfulness. Righteousness is not then simply a personal matter or a matter of private religion. It has to do with the health and well-being of whole communities; it includes every way in which people relate together.

So much for the general concept of righteousness. But in this verse Paul is speaking about not human righteousness, but the righteousness *of God*.

We need to be cautious when we use the name God. Everyone knows the word, but each of us and at different times in our life understand different things by it. When I was a child my picture of God was heavily influenced by sermons I'd heard on the call of Isaiah, the last judgment in the book of Revelation, and also these early chapters of Romans. My mental picture was of a great high throne, and all the people of the earth standing in front of it for judgment. And none of us were righteous. We all had records as long as our arm. Back then mine included regular stealing from my younger brother's piggy-bank to buy sweets, some pretty serious lies, and a vague feeling of disquiet about various situations where I hadn't really done what I ought to have done. The really discouraging thing was that none of us could get away from these failures. No good deeds we did could ever put them right. It was a nightmare! And the list just kept on growing. Righteousness was theoretically possible, but no one was ever that perfect. That's why we needed Jesus to come and save us. He came to save us from God.

But that childish idea of what righteousness might be was seriously wrong. The real problem with it was not the dread that it instilled in me. If we all aren't a little afraid of God, we should be. It was the inadequacy, the desperate inadequacy of what it said about him. For the great truth burning at the heart of Paul's good news is the righteousness *of God*.[28] That is, God's unshakable commitment to and faithfulness within the relationship with human beings that is implicit in the act of creating us. In the next section of the letter we will be confronted with the anger of God, the judgment of God, and the failure of human beings to be what God intends. But the righteousness of God comes first, and governs how we understand all that follows. Paul's news is first and foremost about something that God is in himself; it is about God's character; it is about God's unfailing commitment to make us, as he always intended, whole people able to stand opposite him in a committed relationship. God is the Righteous One par excellence.[29] This is not a static description. Righteousness, Paul tells us, *does things*. There is no code or law or standard against which God is measured. Our whole understanding of what it means to be righteous derives *from* what we experience God himself to be.

RECLAIMING THE RELATIONSHIP

Paul concludes with a quotation from the Old Testament: "The one who is righteous will live by faith." There is nothing random about the choice: it was a key text of the established religion of his day. (Think of the iconic stature of John 3:16 or Romans 3:23 today.) It comes from the second chapter of Habakkuk, where the prophet set us a contrast between the righteous and the unrighteous that was very important for Jewish people. Habakkuk says that when the tsunami wave of disaster breaks over Israel, the unrighteous person will not survive. The righteous person, on the other hand, *will* live. How? On the basis of a relationship defined by faith/faithfulness (the Hebrew word carries the same duality of concept as the Greek one). All very well, but what does he mean by that? The conservative Judaism of Paul's day knew precisely what he meant. He meant through people's *faithfulness to the requirements of the Law*. Circumcision, the Sabbath, the food laws, strict personal morality: these were the way of salvation. The righteous person was the one who fulfilled all these requirements to the letter. Paul's statement blows all that away. The righteous person lives not by faithfully obeying a law, Paul declares, but by encountering God in a living relationship. The righteous person lives, not by observances, but by *faith in the faithfulness of God*. That, Paul says, is what this famous proof text really means.

Faith, righteousness: with a deeper understanding of these two familiar terms in hand we are now heading off into the main body of the letter. What I hope I've been able to convey is that for the group who first had this letter read to them this was an electric beginning. Paul is writing about *power*, and *deliverance*, and *faith*, and above all, about *the character of God*: some of the most powerful ideas on the planet. As he does that, first of all in his radical reinterpretation of Hab 2:4, and secondly in his declaration that the good news is not just for those within the godly but also for those outside of it, he collides head-on with the most fundamental beliefs of the religion of his day. This is not tame religion. This isn't a man who has a lot of time for pious clichés and tentative suggestions, either. We have been warned. There should be no doubt about the kind of thing to expect as we read on. And indeed, in the following verses Paul begins immediately to draw us in.

4

Romans 1:18—2:5
The Wrath of God

"For God's wrath is made plain from heaven against all the ungodliness and unrighteousness of human beings, who in their unrighteousness suppress the truth. [19] What can be known about God is perfectly clear to them: God has revealed it to them himself. [20] The things about him that can't be seen—his eternal power and divine nature—have been evident ever since the creation of the world in the things that can be seen, the things he has made. So they have no excuse. [21] Although they had that awareness of God they did not honor him as God or thank him: instead their thinking became futile and their foolish hearts dark. [22] Claiming to be wise, they became fools; [23] they exchanged the glory of the immortal God for images of a mortal human being, or birds or animals or reptiles!

[24] As a consequence God gave them up, in the hankering of their hearts after impurity, to dishonoring their bodies among themselves. [25] Their exchange of God's truth for a lie led to their worshipping and serving the created thing rather than the one who created it, God, who is blessed forever. Amen!

[26] For the same reason God gave them up to shameful passions. Their women exchanged natural intercourse for unnatural; [27] likewise the men, giving up natural intercourse with women, were inflamed with desire for one another, men with men acting out the shame and receiving in their own selves the predictable consequence of their wandering.

[28] And, since they did not consider God worth including in their thinking, God gave them up to a distorted mind and therefore to things that should not be done: [29] being filled with every kind of unrighteousness, malice, covetousness and vice; full of envy, murder, quarrelling, craftiness; gossips, [30] slanderers, haters of God, insolent, arrogant, boastful, inventors of evil; disloyal towards parents, [31] foolish, untrustworthy, unloving, ruthless. [32] Knowing God's verdict that those who practice

such things deserve to die, they not only do them themselves but cheer on those who do the same.

2 But all of this means that you too, O judge of everybody else, are without excuse! In passing judgment on others you are condemning yourself: you stand in judgment on others but are doing the very same things. ² Of course we know that God's judgment on people who do such things is justified. ³ But you, so confident in judging others, do you imagine that when you do exactly the same you will escape that judgment? ⁴ Or are the riches of God's kindness and forbearance and patience something you despise? Don't you realize that God's kindness is meant to lead you to repentance? ⁵ But by your hard and impenitent heart you are storing up wrath for yourself on the day of wrath, when God's righteous judgment will be revealed."

THIS IS A DRAMATIC and powerful passage. Can you imagine Paul preaching it? What would it feel like, hearing all of this declaimed by a powerful personality, who used his body and his voice, who spoke directly without notes, making continual eye contact with his audience? Can we feel how the catalogue of iniquity that Paul presents builds from thought to thought and increases in intensity as it goes on? It is one of the most comprehensive and damning descriptions of human evil in any language.

Can I say just one thing before we start to explore it? *Don't get hung up on the statements about same-gender sexuality.* Whether in reading them we shake our head over the depth of human sinfulness or seethe with anger at Paul's ignorance, getting all tied up in that now will only distract us. Only after we have understood and experienced the whole passage will we have the necessary perspective to address that issue—finding ourselves, I am certain, confronted and challenged whatever viewpoint we hold on the matter.

GOD'S ANGER

For any letter, let alone a letter addressed to a group most of whom had not met the writer personally, is this not a pretty scary beginning?[30] This is the *good news* that Paul has just been speaking about? Just for a start, how are we to understand what Paul is saying here about the wrath of God? Everything in the introduction to the letter tells of a personal God who in grace and power calls individuals to himself. How can this God also be—terrifyingly angry? Yes, God is angry, Paul says. God is angry at *the godlessness and wickedness of people who suppress the truth* (v 18). The word translated "wickedness" or "injustice" is the Greek word *unrighteousness*. The contrast with the righteousness spoken of in verse 17 is clear. The way of life of those Paul is talking about is the polar opposite of those who live by faith. For these people the knowledge of God is a joke. The ties of faithfulness and reliability and justice between person and person are for them merely matters of convenience and convention. That is how people like this "*suppress the truth.*" Not just truths but *the* truth, the reality of the universe, the real nature of how things are.[31]

A few years ago there was horror across the world when it was discovered that an Austrian man had imprisoned both his daughter and the children that she had conceived through him in a cramped and windowless cellar beneath the family home for more than 20 years. Pictures of the young woman and the dark and airless chamber that had been her and her children's prison for so long were splashed across every newspaper. The articles trembled with anger and with outrage. And this anger was not wrong. These powerful feelings are completely appropriate reactions to such evil.

Something like this might give us just a small indication of the nature of the anger of God. Perhaps we can see this story as a kind of metaphor for all the chilling ways that human beings continually lock others away in cellars of the mind and body and spirit, in ignorance of the truth. Paul is not simply talking about lies, but about ways in which wicked and unjust *behavior* denies the fundamental truth of the world. Such behavior rouses God to anger. And the anger of God is not a joke.

God wills our joy. *Because that is so* he is angry at those who lock people's thoughts and beliefs up in windowless cellars. *Because that is so* he is angry at injustice between person and person. *Because that is so* he is angry at anything that cripples, distorts, or harms people's lives, or that damages his good creation.

The idea of the judgment of God tends to make us feel uncomfortable. But that is not so in the Bible. Speaking about the coming of the Divine King, for example, Psalm 96 says this:

> Let the heavens be glad, and let the earth rejoice;
> let the sea roar, and all that fills it;
> [12] let the field exult, and everything in it.
> Then shall all the trees of the forest sing for joy
> [13] before the Lord; for he is coming,
> for he is coming to judge the earth.
> He will judge the world with righteousness,
> and the peoples with his truth.

How many hymns are there in our current hymnbooks that are full of such jubilation at the thought of God coming as the righteous Judge? Not too many in my experience! But the psalmist sees God's coming judgment as something in which the whole created world rejoices. Why? Because now, after all the capriciousness and violence of human history *things will be put right*. Injustice and oppression will be ended; righteousness and peace will reign.[32]

If we do not feel anger in the face of injustice or evil there is something wrong. But for human beings anger is a slippery and dangerous power. This is not how it is for God. God is not at the mercy of anger, as human beings so often are. His emotions do not come and go as ours do. God is always and completely himself: love and anger are only the imperfect ways human beings, depending upon where they find themselves within his moral world, describe their encounter with all that he is.[33] Commenting on John the Baptist's warning to the people of his day to flee from the wrath to come (Matt 3:7), Frederick Dale Bruner says this:

> The kingdom of God is much more than the wrath of God, of course, but it is nothing less. The coming of God in Scripture . . . is always at least also the coming of burning justice . . . The wrath of God is not the irritability of God; it is the love of God in friction with injustice. It is the warm, steady, patient but absolutely fair grace of God in collision with manifest selfishness. God's wrath does not contradict God's love; it proves it.[34]

For human beings rage is often an expression of frustration or impotence in a situation. But God is never frustrated or impotent. His anger is an expression of his righteousness towards people. And it is an active power in the world. Recognizing God's wrath against ungodliness and unrighteousness should therefore truly sober us. Yet its existence also brings hope. It makes completely clear that injustice and evil are not just part of the way things are. God's wrath is part of the good news.

UNDERSTOOD THROUGH THE THINGS HE HAS MADE . . .

The climate of thought in the twenty-first-century West is changing. At the very same time as developing scientific knowledge presents us with unexpected and extraordinary support for the existence of a Creator,[35] books of popular atheism tumble off the presses and sell in the hundreds of thousands. One of the techniques of the writers of such books is to set up an opposition between the "objective truths" of science and the merely subjective beliefs, aspirations, and values of religion—and all of the rest of human life. This distinction is itself part of a passionately held belief system, of course, but the rhetoric is very strong[36] and it is easy to be seduced by it. We need to reason carefully and dialogue respectfully with those who hold other beliefs about the nature of reality, including those for whom science is a faith. Paul himself modeled that.[37] But when it comes down to the question of truth Paul is completely unhesitating. "What can be known about God is plain to them," he says, "because God has shown it to them. Ever since the creation of the world his eternal power and divine nature, invisible though they are, have been understood and seen through the things that he has made. So they are without excuse" (v. 19–20).

It is as simple as that. It doesn't need a complicated reasoning process. In fact it doesn't need a reasoning process at all. Truth in this matter isn't something that needs to be deduced, says Paul, for God has actively made it known to us. It may come to us through the mind or the heart or the senses or through creative work or through friendship, but at whatever level of human experience it is equally as plain to the simple as to the wise. So there is no neutral place from which we can make our own judgment as to whether we take God seriously or not. There *is* no neutral knowledge. Everything is a choice: either openness to the truth of God, or a rejection of it.

It is important to note the communal nature of what Paul is saying here. We all know friends who honestly say that they have no concept of God, or who are reluctant to entertain belief in the childish or repellent view of God that has in the past been presented to them. What are we to think about this? Isn't honesty something for which Christians should also strive? Do we ourselves feel compelled to believe a foolish thing simply because it has a coloring of religion about it? Would we ourselves ever believe anything unworthy of God? But Paul isn't speaking about people like this. He is speaking about those who by their wickedness actively suppress the truth (v. 18). And he is also speaking about a whole culture which has come to accept a view of the world based on a lie rather than the truth, in which individual people find themselves caught up. "I'm not a Christian," such a one might say. "I'm more of a scientific sort of person." Here we have the culpability of a culture.

Whether individual or communal, the consequence of rejecting this truth is terrifying. Thinking, which is the essential tool of understanding, becomes *futile*. The heart,[38] instead of being illuminated, becomes *dark*. What images might we find for these things? Futility on an ocean-going yacht is a blown-out mainsail and a rudder that doesn't respond to the wheel. The broken state of the things that should power and steer the vessel mocks their intended purpose. A darkened heart is a demagnetized compass, spinning wildly now north, now south. A small boat's chances of surviving a storm are slim with such equipment. Jesus used a different metaphor: "Your eye is the lamp of your body. If your eye is healthy, your whole body is full of light; if it is not healthy your body is full of darkness. Beware therefore that the light within you is not darkness!"[39] The eye (corresponding to Paul's *heart*), says Jesus, is the source of light for the body. But how if the very source of light comes to be the source of *darkness* instead? That is what happens to the seeing and guiding mechanisms of those who reject the knowledge of God, Paul tells us. What is touted as wisdom turns out to be merely folly; and the truth of the glory of the immortal God is replaced by images representing *mortal* beings: humans, or birds, or other animals (v. 23)!

But wait a second: surely Paul's letter is showing its age here. What has this last bit got to do with us and our twenty-first-century world? Images of *birds or reptiles* today? You've got to be joking! Well, what Paul says might not seem to be a joke for every reader of this book. Some of us do live in lands where carved and decorated images are worshiped as if they were God. If that is your situation you know well the weight and the power of such things.

What though about the culture of the West in the twenty-first century? Surely we have left all that behind? Well, perhaps not. It is hard, though, to see the idolatries in one's own culture. We need to remember that the things which we consider to be folly in the worship of earlier times were not folly to the people back then. On the contrary, they were at the cutting edge of the way people in their day understood the world; they provided the techniques needed to succeed in the practical things of life. So it is with us. Human knowledge grows, but the human heart doesn't change. The secular and scientific West has its own examples that are equally idolatrous.

There are many we could choose, but let's take just one: the theory of "the selfish gene" first popularized by the science writer Richard Dawkins in the late 1970s and now a cliché of popular scientific discussion. Starting from the Darwinian principle of the survival of the fittest, Dawkins ascribes to the units of biochemical code within the DNA molecule called the genes a kind of independent existence, picturing them as being in an endless competition to ensure their own replication and survival down the generations. This is the reason, he tells us—indeed the only reason—that we human beings are here. Here is how he explains it:

> We are survival machines, robot vehicles blindly programmed to preserve the selfish molecules known as genes. . . . [The proto-genes of four thousand million years ago] are past masters of the survival arts. But do not look for them floating loose in the sea; they gave up that cavalier freedom long ago. Now they swarm in huge colonies, safe inside gigantic lumbering robots, sealed off from the outside world, communicating with it by tortuous indirect routes, manipulating it by remote control. They are in you and in me; they created us, body and mind; and their preservation is the ultimate rationale for our existence. They have come a long way, those replicators. Now they go by the name of genes, and we are their survival machines.[40]

Of course it is a picture, and Dawkins was in later years increasingly insistent about that. In the light of what Paul is telling us in this chapter, is it not however extraordinarily revealing? As we hear this idea we need to remember that the "gene" that is being granted this sense of purpose and this far-reaching power is not in itself even an organism. It is not alive. It is simply a segment of wonderfully constructed *chemical code*. I remember a joke that went the rounds when I was a schoolboy. Question: What is an oak tree? Answer: An oak tree is an acorn's way of making another acorn. A comical reversal of logic like this will always delight the cheerful schoolboy mind. But who would have guessed that a highly intelligent writer confident that he represents the best of modern scientific thought would seriously suggest that a human being is a gene's way of making another gene? Our genes "created us, body and mind"—and also, it seems, spirit. Two other very smart thinkers say this about our sense of right and wrong: "Human beings function better *if they are deceived by their genes* into thinking that there is a disinterested objective morality binding upon them, which all should obey."[41] Hmm . . .

All this may seem laughable, but these proposals are not only made seriously but they are *taken* seriously. These writers are expressing the dominant religious understanding of our time. In lectures and in books "selfish gene theory" is solemnly noted as an important contribution to modern thought: a Canadian professor of cognitive science has written a book comprehensively applying it to every aspect of human behavior.[42] But see what has happened: all of human culture in its passion and joy, all our hopes and our strivings, all our creativity and experience of life together has been rendered meaningless. Ultimately all these things are merely by-products of a blind biochemical process: they are as ephemeral as the colors we see when a soap-bubble catches the light. What would Paul write today? "They exchanged the glory of the immortal God for the image of a tiny non-living chain of biochemical code"? How in our shallowness and pride we love to look down on the behavior of people in the past! But comparison with modern idolatries such as this makes the worship of an eagle or a crocodile, a boar or a Buddha seem extraordinarily sensible.[43]

We could go on, for there is no end to the bizarre and foolish ideas that spring from otherwise fine minds when they address the issue of origin and purpose.[44] As G. K. Chesterton said, those who cease believing in God don't believe in nothing, they believe in anything. That is Paul's point exactly. "But they became futile in their thinking," he says. "Claiming to be wise, they became fools." This could have been written yesterday.

GIVEN UP

"Therefore," Paul says, "*God gave them up* . . . for the same reason *God gave them up* . . . since they did not consider God worth including in their thinking *God gave them up*" (v. 24, 26, 28). Three times this somber note sounds, like a bell ringing judgment. And with it, suddenly a chasm opens right at our feet. We humans imagine we can give God up, we can ignore him, we can neglect him. But what if he gave *us* up? "Everything outside God is held constant by God over nothingness" says Karl Barth.[45] That is the seriousness of the issue. We depend upon God for everything, from the reliability of the forces that hold the atoms together to our ability to think and to feel and to live together in relationships and in community. We never consciously think about the oxygen we take in with every breath, but our moment by moment dependence upon God is as crucial to our lives as that. Like the solid wall against which the ivy grows, God's character provides the indispensable structure and foundation for our lives as persons. *What then if he should let us go?* If this thought doesn't absolutely terrify us then we don't understand.

What Paul is making clear is that whatever human beings chose to do or to believe it is always God who is in control. We may think we are acting independently, but we can never step out of the moral world that God set up when he made us. Disbelief doesn't diminish God any more than our faith enhances him. The throne of heaven is not shaken by our small rebellions. Moreover, God is never passive; he is never the object of our attitudes to him. He is always the acting subject. So, in our pride and folly we may think we can take God or leave him. But what if *he* was to leave *us*?

It is then, says Paul, a serious business to be alive. The freedom that has been given us brings with it real responsibility. We need to be careful what we desire, for God may give us what we ask for. We may get what we seek, we may end up where we want to go—and how will it be for us then? What if in response to our pride and our folly God were quietly to withdraw from our lives, leaving us to the terror of the nothingness that our folly has let loose in the world?

Notice how what Paul says here overturns all our ideas about judgment. It is not a matter of punishment or retribution; it is not God somehow paying humanity out for having dared to flout his law and his authority. A sub-Christian understanding of God might lead us to expect that. But Paul has already declared God to be, not the God of punishment, but the God whose purpose and power is directed towards salvation (v. 16). How distorted is the kind of Christian teaching which relishes the idea of God's wrath, misreading the Scripture to find in it a pagan idea of a punitive and vengeful god! Paul knows nothing of such a being. In contrast Paul knows a God whose purpose is to create and not to destroy, a God whose power and glory are unmistakably seen in all that he has made. The anger that Paul describes is not therefore an emotion. It is nothing less than *God's creative power* as it is experienced by those who have turned away from the Creator and who because of that have come to participate in the Nothing which, in the act of creation, God himself has rejected. We all walk the edges of that nothingness, as inadvertently or deliberately we stumble and fall. But how if God should leave us to our failure? What if he should *give us up* to the darkness and the meaninglessness, to the anti-creation that we have chosen? That is free fall in the depths of space: no warmth, no light, no reference point, nothing to push against, just free fall forever. This is why salvation, *rescue*, is so important to God. That is why, as we will see, all his power and his will is bent upon it.

To what does God give up the ungodly and the unrighteous? To the degradation of the body, says Paul (v. 24, 25), to sexual disorder (v. 26–27), and to the failure of the mind to control behavior (v. 28–32). These consequences are not random. They are inherent in our disobedience itself. Each of these disordered situations is a direct result of failure to use our human powers of reason and worship in a God-directed way. A car is a fine way to get from place to place across the city. But take your hands off the steering wheel: the car will act according to its own nature by veering across into another lane, or leaving the road altogether and ploughing into shops or cafes, to the peril of other people. A fire is a wonderful thing in the log burner (I come from a country that is cold in the winter). But let the flames out onto the carpet or into the curtains and they will do what flames do: they will burn the house down. Things act according to their own nature. Ungodliness and unrighteousness bring about idolatry and the breakdown of human relationships *inevitably.*

So it is that *ungodliness* leads to the worship of lesser, created things. But things made by God cannot bear the weight of being treated as if they were God. They become distorted and fracture under the strain. It is impossible for us to believe in nothing, to worship nothing. We are built for worship; as fundamentally as that of any physical constant, the necessity for it is written into the structure of the universe. What changes is *what* we believe and what we worship. If we don't worship God, then we cannot avoid worshiping and obeying a lesser thing—and so, says Paul, we ourselves are also diminished.

In a similar way *unrighteousness* leads to the unpicking of the web of trustworthiness and dependability and fairness that holds relationships and communities together. The personal God makes us persons and therefore beings who are able to enter relationships with others. Forgetting him separates us from the very thing that makes human relationships possible, that enables us to act justly and righteously in our relations with others. That *unrighteousness* follows *ungodliness* is inevitable. If we don't value others we ourselves are devalued. We become less than whole people. Ignoring the central thing that makes us human leads to dehumanizing and inhumanity. What else would we expect?

And so Paul's argument builds to a devastating climax (v. 29–32). The words follow each other in a relentless succession, like hammer-blows driving a nail through timber. "They are filled with evil, covetousness, malice, full of envy, murder, strife, deceit, craftiness; they are gossips, slanderers, God-haters, insolent, haughty, boastful, inventors of evil, disobedient, foolish, faithless, heartless, ruthless . . . " Read it aloud! This is how Paul preached it and how the Roman church first heard it: read aloud by the letter-carrier to the assembled congregation.

It is daunting but it is all very true, isn't it? Written so long ago, isn't this still a completely accurate picture of our world today? As we watch the television or read the newspaper, what leaps out at us from every frame or page? Precisely the ungodly and unrighteous behavior that Paul is describing here; behavior upon which God's righteous anger is poured out.

But of course God is not content with this state of affairs. In response to the desperate wickedness of the world we live in he has acted to put things right. We need immediately to read on into chapter 2 of Paul's letter to see how he has done that.

But all of this means that you too are without excuse, O judge of everybody else!

Wait. This is not what we were expecting!

In passing judgment on others you are condemning yourself: you stand in judgment on others but are doing the very same things.

Hold on a minute, this is not supposed to have anything to do with *us*. It is the wicked ungodly world out there that Paul is describing . . . isn't it?

Of course we know that God's judgment on people who do such things is fully justified. But you, so confident in judging others, do you imagine that when you do exactly the same you will escape that judgment?

But . . .

Or are the riches of God's kindness and forbearance and patience something you despise? Don't you realize that God's kindness is meant to lead you to repentance?

But we are Christians already! We've already repented and been saved! This can't be intended for us!

But by your hard and impenitent heart you are storing up wrath for yourself on the day of wrath, when God's righteous judgment will be revealed.

And the trap is sprung.

CHRISTIANS IN THE CROSSHAIRS

For trap it is. This is the place to which Paul has been working to bring us to all the time, the place where, not the inhabitants of that wicked world *out there*, but we, those who feel confident of our virtue and our standing before God, are suddenly exposed to the searching gaze of the Lord.

Let us not duck the issue by looking over our shoulder and imagining that it is "the Jews" (whoever they are) who are being addressed here. Some Bibles have headings that suggest this. Some commentaries talk about chapter 1 being God's judgment upon the *pagans* and chapter 2 being God's judgment upon the *Jews*.[46] That is such a convenient evasion! God judges the wicked world—but that is not us, is it? And God judges unbelieving Israel—but that is not us either! What Paul says is all very interesting and makes us rather glad, even a little proud, that we don't fit into either of these categories. We only come into the picture in chapters 3 and 4, where Paul speaks once again about living by faith.

Reading the text this way means that nowhere in this whole section of the letter do we find ourselves as Christian people addressed. Does this sound to you like the way the word of God operates? Does this sound like a letter addressed to a Christian church? And in fact, if we look at the actual text we see that this kind of ducking and diving is precisely what Paul is at pains to exclude. "You have no excuse, *whoever you are*," he says, "for in passing judgment on another you condemn yourself" (v. 1). "Do you imagine, *whoever you are*, that when you judge those who do such things and yet do them yourself, you will escape the judgment of God?" (v. 3) The message isn't aimed at any group from which we might distance ourselves. The word "Jew" doesn't in fact appear in the text until verse 9, and then only in a context that means "everybody" ("the Jew first and also the Greek"). After those two "everybody" statements in verses 9 and 10, Paul provides a categorical and unmistakable conclusion: "for God has no favorites" (v. 11). How could he make it plainer?

So we are in God's crosshairs here, right enough, and Paul is extremely anxious that we should recognize that. All of his rhetorical skill is directed towards it. The stakes are high. For if we have the idea that we are somehow "in" with God and others are out, then, says Paul, we run the desperate danger of cutting ourselves off from the mercy and grace that is available only to those who are "out," that is, only to the sinful and lost world for which Jesus died (v. 4, 5).

Now it is true that Paul will later on in the chapter specifically address people of Jewish heritage (e.g., 2:17ff, 3:1ff). But we need to recognize that at the time in which he wrote that included *every Christian in the Roman church*, whether they were ethnically Jewish or not. How is that possible? We tend to forget something that is very obvious in the New Testament, and that is that the gathering of every synagogue right across the Mediterranean world included both ethnic Jews *and non-Jews* who had been attracted to the message of the one true God. Judaism was a missionary religion,[47] and in the religious decline of the empire in the first century the search for something more worthy than paganism was intense.[48] Without being full members of the congregation, these earnest seekers attended every Sabbath service and were as thoroughly educated in the Old Testament and the hope of Israel as any devout Jew.[49] It was to this group in particular that Paul's message came with such impact when, Sabbath after Sabbath, he taught in the synagogues of each city he came to. It was converts from the synagogue, *Jews and non-Jews*, who made up the fledgling Christian churches in each city—including the church in Rome.[50] Paul's address to the philosophers in Athens[51] may have been one of the very few times in his career that he preached the good news to pure pagans.

So the Roman church caught in Paul's sting operation in 2:1 certainly didn't imagine that someone else was being addressed. They knew this message was for them. Let us not then delude ourselves that what Paul says here is addressed to anyone other than we who are reading the text today. Why would we expect it to be otherwise? Scripture is never about other people, it is always God's word to *us*. Go back and read it again.

PROPHETIC CONFRONTATION

When we think about it we can see that what Paul has done is very clever. In addressing those who he knows are already Christians, he starts by launching into a passionate denunciation of the wickedness of the world that is phrased in such a way as to draw us good religious people in. The whole thing is designed to gain our involvement. Of course what Paul says the about the wicked world is *true*—it has to be recognizably truth to draw out the involvement, the mental and moral assent that is the key to what Paul is doing. The attitudes and behaviors that he describes are indeed dreadful things: we are not wrong to agree with him all the way. But Paul's primary purpose is not to define the wickedness of particular behaviors. Instead he is pressing all the right buttons in order to gain our assent, to stir up our outrage, for *the sole purpose* of delivering us to that stunning denunciation of all self-righteousness and sense of special privilege before God that comes in chapter 2:1. Why? Because God isn't interested in teaching us interesting things about the situation of *others*. It is *our* lives he wants to deal with.

The chapter division could not be set in a place more unerringly designed to obscure this. Rom 1:18—2:29 is one integrated rhetorical movement. The Roman Christians are not being educated about the position before God of other people, they are being confronted with their own. The passage is a device, a prophetic device, to bring not the wicked world described in chapter 1 but the pious believers of the little congregations at Rome to the consciousness of their insufficiency in the face of God's glory and their dependence upon him alone for grace and mercy in Jesus. And that means *our* insufficiency and our dependence upon him just as absolutely.

In all of this Paul is emulating the methods of the prophets. This is the same technique as that practiced by Amos in the first chapter of his prophecy. It is worth going back to Amos to have a look. One by one the prophet names Israel's neighbors and enemies, details their terrible crimes, and proclaims God's judgment upon them. It is powerful stuff. But is his book meant for delivery to these faraway nations, these proud kings? No, it is meant as the word of the Lord to the religiously self-confident people of Israel. Hearing these terrible judgments pronounced in solemn order upon the pagans, Amos's hearers surely cheered. God would judge their enemies! But slowly the circle tightens about them as Amos's denunciations work closer and closer to home. Suddenly it is not faraway lands or historic enemies but the southern kingdom of Judah that is in God's line of fire. And then come the dread words "For three transgressions of *Israel*, and for four, I will not revoke the punishment of Israel, because they have rejected the law of the Lord" (Amos 2:6). Having given assent to the righteous judgment of God upon others, Amos's hearers have no way of avoiding that judgment when they find themselves in the path of it. And this is not merely a game. Amos knows that Israel's only hope lies in recognizing their own vulnerability to God's judgment. Only then can they repent and find God's mercy. That is why he does what he does.

Or, to take another example, consider the word of the prophet Nathan to David over the Bathsheba affair in 2 Sam 12. Nathan is given an unenviable task: to go to the absolute ruler of the kingdom, publicly declare that he is an adulterer and a murderer, and call him to account for his crimes before God. Who would want to be a prophet! Well, we know how subtly Nathan goes about it, with his report to the king about a rich man who has stolen his poor neighbor's treasured ewe lamb in order to provide a meal for a guest. David is outraged that such a thing could happen in Israel. "Bring him to me!" he cries in anger. Then "You are the man!" declares Nathan. "You have despised the word of the Lord and done great evil in his sight." And suddenly for David too there is nowhere to hide. He has committed himself to justice in the matter. Now he finds himself inescapably confronted with that very justice.

This then is what Paul is doing in the first chapter of Romans. The denunciation it contains is not intended to be delivered to the wicked world it describes. Nor is it intended to provide interesting information for Christians as to what God thinks about the pagans. No, the passage is intended to engage our wholehearted agreement with

God's righteous judgment upon "all the ungodliness and wickedness of men"—in order that we might at 2:1 in a shock of insight recognize that we too stand in that place, and hence (and only hence) are qualified to share in his gift of righteousness in Jesus.

When I was a boy we learned Rom 3:23 (the way Paul will sum up his argument in these early chapters) as a memory verse. Picked out as an isolated theological statement the emphasis inevitably fell upon the sinfulness of people. "For all have *sinned* and fall short of the glory of God" was how we understood it. However in its actual context in the letter the emphasis is quite different. What these first verses of chapter 2 show us is that what Paul is saying is that "*all* have sinned, and fall short of the glory of God."[52] That is, *everybody*—including the pious, the earnest, the good Christians to whom he was writing the letter, and including we who read the letter today, who recognize and perhaps agonize over the existence of sinful behavior in the world all around and yet in our own self-confidence think we are somehow different—is in danger of missing the truth of the gospel.

Additional Note: Romans 1 and Same-Gender Sexuality

That Paul in Romans 1:26–27 uses same-gender sexual activity[53] as an example of disorder in the human world and of God's abandonment of people to their own devices is something that leaps out at us in the light of modern debates. Recognizing what Paul is doing in these two chapters and who the real target of his teaching is should make us cautious about the way in which we apply what he so forcefully says here. On the one hand *theologically* it is clear that Paul understood same-gender sexual behavior to be a sinful dishonoring of the image of God in human beings, and damaging to the self. This cannot be argued away by special pleading (as for example in the suggestion that Paul is talking about "unnatural" behavior by heterosexual people, rather than what might take place between people who are "naturally" attracted to the same sex). In the few occasions in the biblical materials where it is mentioned, the sexualisation of homosexual desire, like the sexualisation of heterosexual desire outside of marriage, is always described in negative terms, and as something which is not part of God's good will for human beings. On the other hand, *pastorally*, we have to recognize that the force of chapter 1 of Romans is directed not in the first instance at people who behave in this way (or indeed in any of the ways described in the chapter), but at the *self-righteous good Christian people* who give wholehearted assent to Paul's depiction of the wicked world and then find themselves confronted, in those first verses of chapter 2, with their own sinfulness. This is particularly important today in light of the hatred of and prejudice against those sexually and emotionally attracted to the same gender, hatred that regularly claims this among other biblical passages as its justification. The prophetic force of the confrontation in 2:1–5 cannot be evaded by anyone who names God's name. Let us look to ourselves, and come to this passage with seriousness and humility.[54]

If we can face the force of Paul's prophetic challenge in Romans 1 and 2 and not try and deflect it onto some other group, we will quickly realize that picking the statements about same-gender sexual practice out of that rhetorical context and (to put the matter crudely) using them as a club with which to belabor certain other people runs directly counter to the intention of the passage as a whole. Since the primary intention of Romans 1 is not to castigate the wicked world that it describes so vividly, but to bring us self-righteous Christian people to repentance, to take the same-gender verses out of that context is to exhibit precisely what Paul saw as a characteristic and deadly blindness of religious people. No more than Jesus will Paul allow Christianity to be a cover for people to say: "*Them*, those sinful people out there." Instead he insists that we say: "*We*, all of us who stand under the judgment—and therefore the mercy—of God." Those who struggle with the challenge of same-gender desire will of course take their place, with all of the rest of us, in that place of judgment and mercy.

It seems to me that it is material later in the letter, especially the whole section 7:7—8:39, which is *pastorally* more significant for those who daily deal with the burden of same-gender desire—as it is for those who deal with the burden of unfulfilled heterosexual desire, or covetousness, or any other of the kinds of holiness issues that Paul is treating in that section. For the self-righteous and the religious the good new must begin with the recognition of *universal* guilt and need before the holiness and righteousness of God, i.e., with chapters 1–3. For those who know their sinfulness and the desolation of it and who long to be whole and be free, those who cry with Paul "Who will deliver me from this body of death?" the good news begins in chapter 7 and flows on into the work of Jesus Messiah and the gift of the Spirit in chapter 8.

5

Romans 2:6–29
God Has No Favorites

"... but by your hard and impenitent heart you are storing up wrath for yourself on the day of wrath, when God's righteous judgment will be revealed. [6] For he will give to each person the reward of their actions: [7] to those who with untiring good work are seeking glory and honor and immortality, eternal life; [8] to those who are self-seeking, disobedient to the truth and committed to wickedness, anger and fury. [9] There will be bitter trouble and distress for every evildoer: the religious person in the first instance but also the non-religious; [10] but glory and honor and peace to everyone who does good: the religious first and also the non-religious. [11] For God has no favorites.

[12] It is true that those who have sinned outside the Law will perish outside its privilege—and those who have sinned under the Law will be judged by it. [13] Hearing the Law doesn't make a person righteous before God; it is those who do the Law who will be declared to be righteous. [14] When, despite not having the Law, people of other nations act instinctively in accordance with it they are a Law to themselves. [15] They show that the outcome that the Law was designed to bring about is written in their hearts: their own conscience bears witness to it, their reasoning among themselves accusing or even excusing them [16] on that day when, according to the good news I bear, God will judge the secret thoughts of all through Jesus Messiah.

[17] But if you call yourself a believer and rely on the bible; if you boast about your relationship with God [18] and know his will and what is right because of the good teaching you have had; [19] if you are convinced that you are a guide to the blind, a light to those in darkness , [20] a corrector of the foolish and a teacher of children because all knowledge and all truth is, in God's Law, in your possession, [21] you, then, that teach others, will you not teach yourself? While you preach against stealing, do you steal? [22] You that forbid adultery, do you commit adultery? You

that detest the things that take God's place in people's lives, do you rob their temples yourselves? ²³ *You that boast in the Law, do you dishonor God by breaking it?* ²⁴ *For, as the scripture says, 'The name of God is mocked among the nations because of you.'*

²⁵ *Circumcision, the sign of covenant belonging, is indeed of value if you obey the Law. But if you break the Law your sign of belonging has become a sign that you don't belong.* ²⁶ *And if those who don't have the sign nonetheless demonstrate the righteous acts that the Law requires, won't they be considered to be as truly members of the godly community as if the sign was there?* ²⁷ *Then, what an irony: those who don't have the covenant sign will judge those who do have both the letter and the sign, but transgress the Law nonetheless.* ²⁸ *For the person faithful to the covenant is not the one who makes an outward show of it, nor is the real sign of that faithfulness something external and physical.* ²⁹ *Rather, a person is a member of God's people who is one inwardly, and real circumcision is a matter of the heart. It involves the whole person, not just the external form. A person like this receives praise not from others but from God."*⁵⁵

Do you get irritated with Bible readings in church or Bible studies that launch into a passage that begin with "For" or "Therefore"? For or therefore *what*? We can't understand a text like that without knowing where it comes from and its context in the whole argument. So I have to acknowledge that the end of verse 5 was a completely unsatisfactory stopping place for the last section. But for reasons that I hope are now clear we couldn't stop at the end of chapter 1. And because of the confused tradition about who Paul is addressing in the first verses of chapter 2 we couldn't read on beyond verse 5 without clearing that up. So in this section we need to remember that we are following a continuous argument that begins at 1:18 and concludes at the end of chapter 3.

Taking up the text again at 2:6 does, however, draw our attention to something that in traditional readings of Romans often seems to be missed. Listen again to what Paul says:

> God will give to each person the reward of their actions: to those who with untiring good work are seeking glory and honor and immortality, eternal life; to those who are self-seeking, disobedient to the truth and committed to wickedness, anger and fury.

Now, every reader of this book will be coming from a different background. For some this is your first encounter with this amazing letter. Others are here to gain a new perspective on something that has long been familiar. If you are in the first category, can I ask your indulgence for a moment as I talk with those who already know Romans well? For at first sight what Paul says here seems to conflict with what we are sure we know that Romans teaches. Particularly if we happen to be Protestants, "salvation by faith alone" is a truth that we learned at our mother's knee. We can't earn our way to heaven: God's deliverance is an undeserved free gift. So how is it that Paul says here that God *does* in fact give eternal life to those who seek glory by their untiring good work (v. 7)? Judgment on the basis of evil deeds we can understand. But eternal life on the basis of *good* deeds? Isn't Paul going to go on very shortly to say that that is impossible?

The answers to these questions will come as we read on. In the meantime it is important to note what is actually there in *this* text. What we do and how we act, says Paul, is in fact of primary importance to God. God won't judge us on the basis of what we know, or what we believe, but on the basis of *how we actually live*. I wonder how you feel about that. Speaking for myself, I'm appalled. If this is really the case, which of us does not desperately need God's mercy and God's help?

What is the help that we seek? We are not talking about mere forgiveness. It is striking that Paul uses that word only a handful of times in all of his letters. Instead, we are talking about *a transformed life*. The power of God for deliverance that is at the heart of the good news (1:16) is not in the first instance about our future destiny. It is about how we are enabled to act with integrity and faithfulness as a human being now.

The central thrust of Romans is not therefore about how we get to heaven. Of course Paul knows that the life that Messiah gives us is *eternal* life (v. 7): when the living God has dealings with a person their life becomes anchored in eternity. The boundary of bodily death means nothing to that kind of life, any more than it did for Jesus. Paul will have much to say later about the future destiny of God's people, tied up as it is with that of the whole created world (chapter 8). But before then, how do we live? What is the character of the life we live now that will *go on* into eternity? In the day-to-day choices of life we have such a mixed experience. How can we be the fully human beings that God intends us to be? How can we live in the joy and power of right and faithful choices? This is the question that verses 6–11 of chapter 2 pose for us, and what the rest of the letter is written to answer.

It is important then to not sidle past these verses with our eyes averted, because they seem to teach something different to what we expect. Hearing the letter as Scripture means paying close attention to what is really there in the text, and not allowing presuppositions about what it *must* say blind us to what it actually *does* say.[56] Paul hasn't finished what he has to say; his argument will steadily unfold. What these verses do make clear is that the issue for each of us is where we stand before the God who judges on the basis of *the integrity and quality of our lives*.[57] How can we be numbered among the righteous? See how starkly the alternative destinies are painted: *eternal life* versus *anger and fury*; *bitter trouble and distress* versus *glory, honor, and peace*. One of these outcomes will be ours. The stakes could not be higher. All of us will face the same judgment, and, Paul tells us, the religious will face it first (v.9). We will also be those first in the path of God's blessings—blessings which are not, however, restricted to the religious alone. For, Paul says, God has no favorites.

THE LAW WRITTEN ON THE HEART

Each of us has a different heritage and background. Some have had the lifelong privilege of careful instruction about God and his ways. Others come from a completely godless background, where the idea of God is dismissed as childish folly, or is perhaps not even known. Those in Paul's day who had grown up through the Jewish heritage were enormously privileged. They had been instructed in a way of life shaped by the Jewish Law.

What is this Law? In its widest sense the term describes the whole of the first five books of the Old Testament. Some of that material is identity-defining narrative: the stories of creation, of the call of Abraham and his descendants, and of God's extraordinary deliverance of Israel from slavery in Egypt. Other sections are closer to what we today might consider laws: the Ten Commandments, of course, given by God himself in earthquake and in fire on Mount Sinai, but also a whole body of other regulations surrounding the Ten which effectively provided a complete social, religious, and legal system for a people.

None of this was simply regulation. We are not talking about a legal code like that of the Roman Empire, or a moral law like that of the Greeks. What was at issue *was an individual and communal life shaped by relationship with the living God.* The Hebrew name for all of this was Torah. There is no word in either Greek or English that is able to carry its full freight of meaning: when Paul used the Greek word *Law* for the Torah and all that it contained it was shorthand, and both he and his readers knew it. As we read the word "Law" in the Roman letter we also have to keep that broader and deeper Hebrew understanding in mind. In particular, common English usage ("she is studying the law"; "stealing is against the law") will mostly mislead us. What Paul has in view is something much richer and deeper than a mere legal system. Summing up and re-presenting the Torah for a new generation, Moses says, "These are no empty words, *they are your very life.*"[58] This then was the great privilege of the Jewish heritage. Not everybody in the world had that truth, those advantages, and Jewish people were very aware of the joy and responsibility of knowing what they knew.

Does this difference in knowledge mean therefore that people who are ignorant of God and his ways will be let off more lightly? Not so, says Paul. Ignorance of the law is no excuse, whether that is the law of the land or the deeper, richer law of a life lived before God. Those who sin without knowing God's Law will still die (v. 12). And (remembering that this is not an abstract discussion but an actual letter to real Christian people) those who sin *despite knowing the Law* will also inevitably find themselves in the path of the judgment that the Law contains. Knowing the Law isn't enough; it is doing it that counts (v. 13). And this is not just the meeting of an abstract standard, ticking all the right boxes like the rich young ruler whom Jesus met. At issue is the question of *righteousness*, our character as a faithful and trustworthy person in our dealings with others—and with God. It is a question of God's judgment of the quality of our lives; that is, God's declaration about us that we are a righteous person.

What is this *declaration* of righteousness that Paul is speaking of? We will need to come back to this, because the word plays a key part in Paul's discussion in the coming chapters. But first, let us hear the end of Paul's argument:

> [14]*When, despite not having the Law, people of other nations act instinctively in accordance with it they are a law to themselves.* [15]*They show that the effect that the Law was designed to bring about is written in their hearts: their own conscience bears witness to it; their reasoning among themselves accusing or even excusing them* [16]*on that day when God will judge the secret thoughts of all (according to the good news I bear) through Jesus Messiah.*

Can we understand the stunned consternation of Paul's audience, brought up as they were in the knowledge of God through the Law? God not only gives the Law to his people, Paul is saying, he also writes it on the heart of those *outside* the covenant community![59] What then happens to the privilege of being God's specially chosen people, and the sense of security that that provides? Aren't people outside the covenant community by definition just that, *outside*? How can people who do not possess the Law possibly fulfill it? What Paul is saying attacks the whole idea of the faithful religious community.

NO FAVORITES

What is the issue here? Paul is telling us about *what God is like*. It is not possible to own God or to claim him. God is not under special obligation to anybody. God has no favorites (v. 11). What we need to hear is this: the living God deals justly and righteously with every person, whatever their background or their degree of knowledge. And he judges a person not on the basis of what she knows or believes but on the basis of a life lived.

This must have been hard for the good people in the Roman church to hear. Doesn't it make us good Christian people feel a bit uneasy as well?[60] Doesn't it seem to cut across many of the things that we've been taught? We may not have put it into words, but don't we *feel* that at least in some way the church and its members are specially privileged before God? Doesn't faithfulness count for anything? Where is the love of God for the church in all of this?

The answer is that it is right here in what Paul is saying—but perhaps not in quite the way we might expect. I have sometimes startled a congregation by declaring that God doesn't love the church. That grabs the attention, I promise you! But then we turn to John 3:16 and read this: "For God so loved *the world* that he gave his only Son, so that everyone who puts their faith in him may not perish but have eternal life." God does love the church! But he loves us *only* as we are a part of the world into which he came and for which he died.

When Paul speaks about "a Law written on the heart" (v. 15) he is not talking about some vague "moral law of nature." The only Law, the only true standard of human behavior is God's Law, and that Law is not a human legal code or something merely instinctive but a reflection of God's character. But that very Law, Paul says, *people from outside the godly community have written on their hearts*. Who wrote the law there? It can only be God himself. The phrase Paul uses would have been instantly and startlingly recognizable to anyone who knew the Old Testament (which was, of course, the Roman church's only Bible). "There will come a time," God had said through the prophet Jeremiah, "that I will make a new covenant with the house of Israel. I will put my law within them, *and I will write it on their hearts,* and I will be their God, and they shall be my people."[61] This famous promise was precious to every godly person. God would do a new thing. He would make the law *internal*, part of the very essence of a person. Rather than being a response to an external threat or promise, righteous behavior would flow naturally out of a person's innermost being.

The first Christian communities recognized gladly that this prophecy was being fulfilled in their lives.[62] And now what Paul is saying is that many people from among the heathen nations *already experience* the reality of that Old Testament promise. The promise is God's gift to *the whole world*, and in some unacknowledged and partial but nonetheless very real way the whole world is already participating in it. The truth of that, says Paul, will be plain for all to see on the day when God judges the secret thoughts of all.

Judgment! It is a serious word, but Paul makes it clear that it is an essential part of the good news (v. 16). Judgment is a function of God's love, a working out of his good purpose for all of creation. There will come a time in God's good purpose that the secret thoughts of all will be made plain, a time when we will know and others will see who we really are. And judgment, when it comes, will come *through Jesus Messiah*. This is so important. We don't have as a judge someone who hasn't lived in the neighborhood, who doesn't know the territory. In Jesus the living God knows what it is to be human from the inside: the tumult of ideas and desires and emotions, the temptations of power and popularity, the griefs and the struggles, the abuse and the injustice and the temptation to strike back. Tested in every way that we are, yet without sin,[63] he is uniquely qualified to be our judge.[64] Jesus himself, his life, his teaching, his example will be the standard, and he is the one before whom we will stand to give an account of our lives. The way in which this is the most complete good news will occupy Paul now all the way to the end of chapter 8.

GOD'S BUSINESS—AND OUR BUSINESS

It is important not to get distracted by wondering how God will deal with those outside the faith community. Paul is not writing a manual of doctrine. What he says here is not intended to answer idle questions about others but to bring *us* to recognition and repentance. How God will deal with people on the day of judgment is his business, not ours.[65] All of Paul's attention here is directed toward the question of how God will deal with *us*. And so, relentlessly he confronts us again with what is truly our business, the question of where we ourselves stand before the God we say we believe in.

> *But if you call yourself a believer and rely on the Bible; if you boast about your relationship with God and know his will and what is right because of the good teaching you have had; if you are convinced that you are a guide to the blind, a light to those in darkness, a corrector of the foolish and a teacher of children because all knowledge and all truth is, in God's Law, in your possession, you, then, that teach others, will you not teach yourself?* (v. 17–21a)

If you turn up your standard English translation you will see that verse 17 reads: "But if you call yourself a *Jew* and rely on the *Law* and boast of your relationship to God . . ." and that is indeed what the Greek text literally says. But if we read it that way then we miss the force of what Paul is saying—or, more seriously, we avoid it. We end up thinking about a *different race* rather than the *same godly community*; we get hung up on a name for Scripture that is different from the one we use—and so we avoid the issue. But if Paul were writing today he would use the language of our time; there would be no doubt that he is addressing us, the well-meaning Christian community.[66]

Hear how the phrases tumble out as Paul lists all the kinds of things that good religious people might say or think about themselves. Do we brag about our relationship with God and about how important the Bible is to us as a guide to life? Do we feel that we know more than those around us about what is right and how to live? Do we see ourselves as the guardians of public standards of decency and right behavior? How important is it to our self-esteem as Christians to be always teaching or helping others?

None of the things in Paul's list are bad in themselves. But the way he phrases it taps directly into our hidden pride. He is singing a song here that we often sing to ourselves, and forcing us to notice the hesitant notes and the off-key ones. The whole section is heavy with irony. Paul is trying to open our eyes. He knows all too well the way unearned privilege and knowledge freely received can become something that we start to think is to our personal credit. And he will have none of it:

> *While you preach against stealing, do you steal? You that forbid adultery, do you commit adultery? You that detest the things that take God's place in people's lives, do you yourselves rob their temples? You that boast in the Law, do you*

dishonor God by breaking it? For, as the scripture says, "The name of God is mocked among the nations because of you." (v. 21b–24)

Isn't this a bit much, though? Stealing, adultery, temple-robbery? Isn't Paul getting carried away here? It is all too extreme! This isn't us, and honestly it isn't most people in the Christian community—or in the Jewish community, either. There might be the odd person who is guilty in these regards. But not the majority of us. Perhaps we should just move right along.

A couple of things need to be said if we are going to understand what is happening here. Firstly, what Paul is saying is not meant to be analyzed sentence by sentence to see whether we as individuals are guilty or not of any one of these behaviors. To do that misses the point. With the letter written down in front of us we can at leisure take this section and that section, exhaustively analyze every detail of it, and then move on to the next. But we need to remember that all of this for Paul and for his first hearers is *one unified rhetorical movement.* Paul is looking us in the eye, and building and buttressing his argument step by step in order to bring us cumulatively and collectively to the point that "every mouth may be stopped and the whole world may be held accountable to God" (3:19). It is the force and the truth of the whole that is the point. God's message confronts us here in judgment and in hope. This is the good news! If we try to avoid the challenge by chipping away at this or that detail then we avoid the glory and the grace as well.

But the details do hold up. Paul is standing here in a well-known tradition of prophetic denunciation. He was not the first to point out that what we religious people say we believe often fails to match what the surrounding world sees us actually do. Similar lists of hypocritical wrongdoing appear in contemporary writers whom Paul's audience would have been familiar with—not to mention the Old Testament itself: look for example at Psalm 50 and Amos 5:6–24! At issue in such passages is not the behavior of any one individual, but *the honor of God.* How many years of loving and patient work with the poor and needy of the community by thousands of faithful servants of God has been wiped out in public perception by the unfolding stories of sexual abuse of children by a relative handful of clergy in the Roman Catholic church? Nor is it just Catholic Christians: in my own hometown a prominent evangelical spokesman and the former leader of a national Christian political party is serving a jail sentence for similar crimes. A member of our church told me the other day about her son, who was attending a Christian school at the time when the principal suddenly resigned because of an affair between him and a teacher on his staff. "My son just put away his Bible," she told me. "He hasn't been to church since. "Mum, he used to pray with us and teach us about God," he said. "But it didn't mean anything to him. It was just words.'" I remember a friend with a building business who had been cheated by a Christian contractor. "I don't want to offend you, Les," he said, "but I made a vow from then on never to do business with an alcoholic or a Christian."

Unfair, isn't it? These are not things that we ourselves have actually done, perhaps. *But they come out of our community.* Those who did these things knew what we know, they believed what we believe, they went to church and prayed and read their Bibles like we do. But that was not enough. We Christian people are just as radically marked with sin, just as desperately in need of a savior, and we fall just as far short of God's righteousness as any other human being. How could we ever have imagined it was different?

And are we so sure that we are in fact innocent, even of these blatant sexual issues? Can we here, now, confronted with the word of God, bear to be really honest before him about these hidden parts of our life? "We have sinned in ignorance, we have sinned in weakness, we have sinned through our own deliberate fault," says the Confession.[67] And we do confess, and in God's mercy and grace we are forgiven, and we pray daily for any we may have wronged in thought or in act. But what we cannot do is step aside self-righteously as if in what Paul is saying here God was looking at someone other than us.

Think about the websites, the movies, and the television programs of your last week or two. We have given our assent to Paul's robust condemnation of sexual disorder in society in chapter 1, but in all honesty, what do we ourselves tolerate or even, God forbid, welcome in the supposed privacy of our own home in these regards? It is not just a matter of explicitly sinful acts. We would be repulsed at the thought of someone in our neighborhood peeping through windows or keyholes in the dark of the night. But we ourselves are part of a deeply voyeuristic culture, being invited in on every entertainment channel to be a spectator of the most intimate and private acts. The graphic portrayal of violence in entertainment also goes up a notch or two every year. And do we turn it off, do we turn away? Or do we (reluctantly, or perhaps not reluctantly) still give assent to these things?

Sexual sin is one thing, but Paul knows there is more to our sinfulness than this. "Do you steal?" he asks, and "Do you that detest the things that take God's place in people's lives rob their temples yourselves?" Whoa! That sounds pretty far-fetched, doesn't it? How many actual temple robbers were there really in Paul's audience? How many are there among those of us who read this today?

Well, we need to stop pussyfooting around. Here is a practical example. As those of us of a certain age will remember, in late 1988 after a period of extraordinary growth there was an earthquake in stock markets across the world. Suddenly prices were plunging all over the place, and in the first day or two it seemed that for a prudent investor there could be profits to be made by buying cheaply, and selling higher when in a few weeks (don't smile!) the market corrected itself. Angela and I had a small investment portfolio which was the result of ten years of savings towards the deposit on a house of our own. Suddenly it seemed to me that we had an opportunity to make that money grow. I worked out what to do, and gave the instructions to the broker. Time now to wait and see what would happen. I put the phone down and returned to my desk, where the books were spread out as I had left them: I was studying for a coming examination in Old Testament theology. All that day I had been immersed in the prophets, with their godly rage against the idolatry of wealth and possessions in a society that they proclaimed to be under the judgment of God. My call to the broker had at last come through in the middle of all this. And there, when I returned, the books were open before me still.

How often, knowing the encouraging and hopeful things he will surely have to say, we long for God to speak to us. Not this time. The words of Amos and of Malachi flamed off the page that afternoon, and through them I heard the voice of the living God to me, bringing me to tears and driving me to my knees. It was all made worse in that in teaching and preaching I had on several occasions spoken about money and possessions as being one of the idols of our society. That afternoon I realized that in all blindness I was nonetheless involved in heathen worship. In seeking to capitalize upon the movements in the markets I was seeking a financial gain that I had not earned. I had no idea about the business principles of the companies I was investing in; I had no idea of how they treated their employees; I had no idea how or where they sourced their raw materials, and only the vaguest idea of the usefulness of what they produced. None of these things had been considered. I was not doing any work or creating anything. In trying to manipulate the value of our investments, although having often scorned the idol, I was still seeking to rob its temple.

But I shouldn't beat myself up over this, surely? People buy and sell stocks and shares all the time. And I was just trying to do the best for my family, wasn't I?[68] Do these rationalizations really stand up against the force of what God through Paul is saying here? I do not think that they do.

THE STORYBOOK PHARISEE

Do any of us still want to argue Paul's point in all of this? The irony is that his point is even more inescapable for Christians today who have, as neither Paul nor the Roman church did, the full New Testament. For Jesus himself stood in that same tradition of prophetic denunciation. I know we are dealing with Paul and Romans, but trust me in this: before going on, turn up Jesus' sermon in Matthew 23 and read that whole chapter.[69]

What do you think? With my heart in my mouth in attempting this, let us try to transpose what Jesus is saying in that Matthew chapter into language and situations that we are more familiar with today. "Listen to what the religious people teach, he says, but don't follow their example, because they don't practice what they preach" (v. 1–3).

- They preach about how everybody is an utter sinner and falls short of the glory of God, but they don't roll up their sleeves and do anything to actually help pregnant young women, or children at risk, or homeless people, or ex-prisoners trying to get a job, or drug addicts trying to find the way to a new life (v. 4).

- They have their own system of honor and reward and prestige that secretly feeds the soul, and a kind of hierarchy of honor, with famous visiting speakers and church officers and ministers and bishops, and the people who organized the fundraising fair that was so successful back in 1993 (v. 5–12).
- They have a system of doctrine that not only shows that they themselves are far from the Father's heart, but which is also exclusive, teaching that God chooses to call some but not others into the kingdom of heaven (v. 13).
- They expend huge amounts of money and effort upon missionary endeavor but instead of converts to Jesus Messiah make converts to the western theological and cultural mindset that they themselves are trapped in without realizing it (v. 15).

And so it goes on, relentlessly. We could continue: but you have read the chapter.

Does all of this also sound unfair? As a lifelong supporter of missions, just to take that final example, I absolutely feel that it does. And maybe I haven't got all of this totally right. But mustn't this be the *kind* of thing that Jesus is saying? As we read his words are we not, just for a minute, secretly discomforted? Doesn't what he describe feel scarily close to how we sometimes think about things? But then we reassure ourselves: what Jesus says can't be for us, can it? Of course not, it is for the "scribes and Pharisees," those hypocritical and wicked people. Likewise, surely the challenging things Paul is staying can't be intended for the Roman church, for Christian people like us. He is talking about *the Jews*.

WE ARE THE PHARISEES

But who were those scribes and Pharisees that Jesus challenged so forthrightly? Well, we know who they are, of course. They are the regular opponents of Jesus. They are the villains of the story; everything they do or say shows how little they understand and how much they hate Jesus.

But the Gospels are not children's storybooks. Where in the real world, among people and situations we might recognize, would we find a group like the Pharisees? The hugely uncomfortable truth is that we would find them in the churches (and in the synagogues, and in the mosques). The Pharisees in Jesus' day were not some weird group that was constitutionally opposed to all that was right and good. On the contrary. In a society much like ours, with very diverse levels of commitment, they were the church-going, Bible-reading, good-living section of the community. And we know that some of them were also legalists and literalists. But they were these narrower things *as part of the general grouping of good and faithful religious folk.*

People looked up to the Pharisees and gave them respect, just as people do to church-going folk today. They also very often saw through them, realizing in this or in that situation that despite their pious talk and their air of moral superiority these were fallible human beings just as sinful as themselves. And Jesus has no time for the pious air and the superior attitude. As Christians we naturally feel we own Jesus: he is, after all, as we say, *our Lord*. But we have forgotten how impossible he was in his day, how difficult to cope with. The people who were most like us in that society were staggered that Jesus didn't come to their party. He didn't honor them like the good people they were. He went to synagogue, sure, but when he taught there they seemed to be as much in his line of fire as the wicked and careless people he should have been targeting. He broke all their conventions; he ate and drank with prostitutes and dodgy financial dealers. He was threatening, discomforting, and rude to those who should have been his natural allies.

In the response of the Pharisees to Jesus there was as much distress and hurt as outrage. He wasn't being fair; he wasn't seeing how well they were doing. He wasn't acknowledging how faithfully they were seeking to uphold the truth of God in a careless and irreligious world. What brought about Jesus' eventual betrayal to the Romans and his crucifixion? It was not some mysterious group of storybook religious enemies who did this. Let us say it with fear and with trembling and with tears, in that milling crowd in front of Pilate's judgment seat it was as much we good religious people who shouted "Crucify him!" as anyone else. Can we bear to face this?

Paul's confrontation of our religious pride and our sense of privilege in this Romans passage is not then out of step with the rest of the Bible, nor is it alien to the spirit of Jesus. We need to hear it and to bear it and to allow it to cut us to the heart. This is Scripture. This is not the man Paul getting pleasure out of being confrontational. It is the spirit of Jesus himself speaking through Paul for our health and salvation. The good news is first of all for us ("for the religious first"!) before it is what it is finally designed to be, the good news for the world. But how can we hear and grasp it if we think we already have it?

THE SIGNS OF BELONGING

Paul continues to drive his point home:

> *"Circumcision, the sign of covenant belonging, is indeed of value if you obey the Law. But if you break the Law your sign of belonging has become a sign that you don't belong. And if those who don't have the sign nonetheless demonstrate the righteous acts that the Law requires, won't they be considered to be as truly members of the godly community as if the sign was there?"* (v. 25–26)

But hold it! *Circumcision*? You have got to be kidding! Ugh! And that is a Jewish thing, not a Christian one.[70] If Paul was really speaking to the Christian community in Rome, and not to some kind of representative Jew, wouldn't he be talking about baptism instead?' Well, no, I don't think he would. If he was writing to a Christian church *today* of course that is the example that he would have used. "Baptism is all very well," he might have said, "as long as you truly follow the Jesus into whose death you were baptized and in whose life you were raised up. But if you don't live out his life but follow your own self-centered path instead, isn't your baptism just a meaningless bit of ceremony?" In chapter 6 of the letter Paul will, in a different context, make these very points. But at the time he was writing baptism did not fit his argument at this place in his letter simply because it did not have the force and significance *as a mark of exclusive belonging to the covenant community* that circumcision did.[71] During all of this early period Christianity was essentially part of the historic Jewish faith. Example after example throughout the letter show that the division between church and synagogue that is familiar to us was, for Paul and those to whom he was writing, still in the future.[72]

In Paul's day, therefore, the sign of exclusive belonging, *understood as such whether one was inside or outside the notional community that it signified*, was circumcision. It was only later in the history of the church that, in a massive irony, the idea of baptism as an exclusive mark of belonging would grow. And of course those in the Romans community who were Jews by racial descent would have been literally circumcised. For them circumcision and their membership of the Christian community would have been difficult to think of as separate things. They would have understood what Paul was saying instantly. Those in the Roman church who came from different ethnic backgrounds would not normally have been physically circumcised, but they would still have been very aware of the historic significance of circumcision as a mark of belonging. Gentile Christians were in fact in those early days under pressure from some sectors of the community to also undergo the rite in order to "complete" their conversion. We know this from some of Paul's other letters. "What Jesus has done is very wonderful," went the argument, "but you need to be circumcised as well if you want to be a proper Christian."[73] Paul's point would therefore not have been lost on these believers either. They too would have known exactly what Paul was saying.

And so Paul goes on:

> *Then, what an irony: those who don't have the covenant sign will judge those who do have both the letter and the sign, but transgress the Law nonetheless. For the person faithful to the covenant is not the one who makes an outward show of it, nor is the real sign of that faithfulness something external and physical. Rather, a person is a member of God's people who is one inwardly, and real circumcision is a matter of the heart—it involves the whole person, not just the external form. A person like this receives praise not from others but from God.*

What matters, Paul says, is not knowing the truth or having the outward sign of being set apart for God's service. It is doing the truth and living in the way that circumcision was supposed to signify. Baptism is important for Christians today, but not just the external form of it: what is required is to live a baptized life. Notice once again Paul's insistence that what really matters is circumcision of the *heart,* not just of the body. It is a striking image, but the idea was not new. That circumcision was not just a ritual but had to mean something in the heart and the behavior was a familiar theme in the Old Testament.[74] What is shocking in what Paul says here is that it is *those from among the nations*, those outside the knowledge of the Law and the covenant, who are recognized as being circumcised in heart. What is happening is what, long before Paul, Jesus himself had predicted: "The prostitutes and the disreputable financiers go into the kingdom of God before you" (Matt 21:31).

THE CHURCH WITHOUT WALLS

Can you imagine the stunned silence as for the first time Paul's words were read to the Romans community? Might some have wanted to protest? "But Paul can't be saying that, because the Scriptures don't teach that!" Well, in the coming sections Paul will make clear that, yes, they do teach that. In fact, this is not an additional meaning, it is their *fundamental* meaning.

What Paul is telling us is something that we already should know: God is not a fool. Words and profession and right belief are not enough; God looks for something else. There are, says Paul, those who are ignorant of the Scriptures and would never call themselves believers but whose lives put to shame those who say they are Christians but don't act like it. Those who live their lives on the basis of what is right and true will receive God's praise, *whatever they outwardly believe or know.*[75]

The urge to duck and weave in the face of Paul's message in these verses is still strong today. But what else can this passage possibly mean? Various stratagems have over the centuries been devised to explain these verses away. I have already alluded to one of them: that, in order to teach his Christian audience how misguided and lame other people's religious pretensions are, Paul is engaging in a dialogue with *an imaginary Jewish opponent*. There is only one thing I can see going for this idea: it gets us off the hook.[76]

Once again, this is not dogmatic theology. Paul is not trying to lay out some kind of theoretical system which we could use to assess whether a person is righteous before God or not. How could we possibly presume to make such a judgment—even about ourselves?[77] Paul's whole purpose is precisely *not* to engage in such speculation. Working out who is "in" and who is "out" is at the heart of the prideful problem he is challenging. Nor is Paul *addressing* those without knowledge of the Scriptures or outside the distinctives of religious belonging. His presentation of the good news to them would be completely different.[78] Just as the litany of sinfulness in chapter 1 is not designed to satisfy our curiosity about the wicked world but to lure us on into the sting in 2:1, so here Paul's only purpose in talking about those at present outside the covenant community is to confront we who are *within* that community with our total defenselessness against the judgment of God. "The weapons of our warfare," he will say in another of his letters "have divine power to destroy fortresses. We destroy arguments and every proud obstacle raised up against the knowledge of God, and we take every thought captive to obey the Messiah."[79] Who would have thought that those proud obstacles were in fact in our own hearts; that it was *our* thoughts that needed once again to be brought into submission before the Lord Messiah? But, once having heard the force of Paul's relentless argument in this chapter, who can deny that this is the case? What Paul has done is to strip away everything we might have clutched to ourselves as assurance that, as good religious people, we somehow have a privileged standing before God. He has taken away all the illusions. We, like everybody else, stand completely exposed to the judgment of God upon our lives. And *also* exposed to God's grace and mercy, as we shall see. For grace and judgment are not two things, but one.

It is as if we have been having a wonderful worship service in church with a music group and hymns and striking testimonies and—wow, there goes the roof! Suddenly nothing above us but blue sky and a cloud or two. And, goodness, watch out—there goes the back wall! Nothing now between us and the parking lot and the supermarket and the gas station and the liquor store across the street. And then suddenly the side walls are gone. If we look one way we can see the school buildings with the basketball hoops in the playground; if we look the other there is the furniture factory, with machinery humming and a forklift moving about in the yard. And then, quietly and without any fuss, the wall behind the altar fades out and is gone, and the Lord's table stands there in the middle of a suburban street, and there are other streets beyond it, and houses stretching out into the distance.

And there are other people out there! Most of them are just going about their business on a Sunday morning; though one or two are looking at us a little strangely, sitting in rows, all facing the front. Welcome to God's world! Out there are some who have hard and impenitent hearts, and some who patiently do good; there are some who are self-seeking and disobedient to the truth, and some who apparently instinctively live their lives in the light of the law of God. Sometimes those distinctions are completely clear-cut. Mostly, however, they are all somehow mixed up in their lives—as they are in ours.

And the question is, *will we join them*? Are we also a part of the mixed and longing and messed-up and compromised world for which Jesus died? Or will we keep on protesting and arguing that we are somehow different and special—and thereby exclude ourselves from the gospel of grace? Preaching to us here in this church without walls, that is the question Paul forces upon us.[80]

A number of years ago I saw a group of twenty or thirty church people doing some street witnessing in the central square of the town where I live. I hasten to say that I think that is pretty brave: on the few occasions I've ever tried to do such a thing a rabbit in the headlights would have appeared animated in comparison. What this group was doing was very interesting to me nonetheless. They had an earnest prayer time, and then a time of rousing guitar-accompanied singing. But standing in their little joyful group they made a striking sight. Because there in the heart of the city square with people passing all around *they were standing in a circle facing inwards.*

6

Romans 3
Much and None

ALL THAT HAS BEEN said so far is pretty daunting to hear. If what Paul is saying is true, if good religious people are just the same as everybody else before God, what advantage is there in being a Christian at all? That is the way in which we have to ask the question. We have already seen that we can't bat it aside as if Paul was addressing some other group of people and not us. Doesn't that question rise in all of our hearts? If God treats the godless in the same way that he treats the godly, what value is there in being a member of the faithful community? Does religious observance matter? We feel it *ought* to matter, it *ought* to be important: but how can that be so if God treats everybody alike?

Paul poses this question twice in chapter three—and gives a completely different answer each time. "What advantage is there then in being a Jew?"[81] he asks (v. 1). "Huge advantage in every way! For a start, they were entrusted with the Word of God" (v. 2). Later in the chapter, though, he puts the question again: "What then? Do we have a special standing compared to others?" (v. 9) Instantly comes a quite different answer: "Not a bit of it!" The possession of the Scriptures is one of the glories of the people of God—and yet those same Scriptures conclusively demonstrate that all, religious and irreligious alike, are under the judgment of God. There is no privileged place on which to stand.

And then something completely new breaks in. "But now!" Paul will say (v. 21). A great door swings open and the whole discussion turns: the *righteousness of God* is revealed. Someone else steps in on our behalf. God himself acts. This is the good news that Paul has been driving towards all this while, and the unfolding of which will occupy him for the rest of his letter.

ROMANS 3

This then is the structure for chapter 3: a repeated question that reveals first privilege and then poverty, followed by the great news of what God has done to remedy the situation.

And so we start with that first question:

> $^{1"}$ *What advantage is there then in being a Jew? What is the benefit of circumcision, the sign of covenant belonging?* ^{2} *Huge advantage in every way—and especially in that they were trusted with the Word of God.* ^{3} *What if some were unfaithful? Will their faithlessness nullify God's faithfulness?* ^{4} *Impossible! God would still be true even if every human was a liar. As David acknowledged, the result of his sin was 'that you might be recognized as being righteous in what you say, and win the case when you are being judged.'*
>
> ^{5} *But if our unrighteousness brings out God's righteousness more clearly, what then? Is God unrighteous in bringing the Wrath upon us? (This is the way people talk.)* ^{6} *Impossible! For then how could God judge the world?* ^{7} *'Yes, but if my lie means God's truth shines out the more, why am I then judged to be a sinner like everybody else?* ^{8} *And why don't we do evil so that good may come?' This is what some people slander us by saying that we say: they will get what they deserve.*
>
> ^{9} *What then? Do we have a special standing compared to others? No, not a chance! For we have just shown that, whether Jew or Greek, all are under the power of sin.* ^{10} *The scriptures say as much:*
>
> > *No one is righteous, not a single one;*
> > ^{11} *no one has any insight,*
> > *no one is seeking God;*
> > ^{12} *all have turned away, they have become good for nothing;*
> > *there is no one who shows humanity, not even one.*
> > ^{13} *When their mouths open it is like an opening grave:*
> > *their tongues are tools of deceit,*
> > *their lips contain venom like a snake.*
> > ^{14} *Their talk is full of cursing and bitterness;*
> > ^{15} *when murder is afoot they run to meet it.*
> > ^{16} *Ruin and misery are the paths they tread,*
> > ^{17} *and the way of peace they have never known.*
> > ^{18} *From the terror and glory of God they turn away.*
>
> ^{19} *Now we know that whatever the Law says, it says to those who are under the Law, so that every mouth may be shut, and the whole world fall silent before the judgment of God.* ^{20} *This is why no human being will be regarded as righteous by God on the basis of the observances of the Law, for the truth is that what comes through the Law is the knowledge of sin."*[82]

TRUST AND TRUSTWORTHINESS

"Huge advantage in every way!" The expression could scarcely be stronger or more confident. Of those many advantages Paul will however at this point name just one: that historically the Jewish people "were trusted with the words of God."

We need to translate carefully here. Many translations say "*en*trusted." However, this English word sends us off on a wrong tangent. It sounds as if God's words were given to God's people for safekeeping. No! God's words are not given simply to be cherished and preserved. Their purpose is to transform lives and to transform the life of the world. Paul's emphasis is not upon the Scriptures themselves, but upon the character of those who received them.[83] The covenant community *had faith put in them*; they were *trusted*; they were treated as *people who could be trusted*. That is the first thing to notice.

And what they were trusted with was *God's word*: the Law, the prophets, and the writings; our Old Testament. To be put in possession of the word of God is a wonderful thing. Sadly, human behavior so often failed to live up to the truth that is found there. "What if some proved to be unfaithful to that trust?" Paul asks. "Does that bring the faithfulness of God himself into question?" (v. 3)

It is an unusual question. Does it make any sense to you? That a person's failure to be faithful could bring the faithfulness *of someone else* into question isn't the first idea that would spring to our minds. In our Western thought-world there isn't an obvious connection. For us faith and faithfulness are individual qualities and actions, they are aspects of a person's character. What another person does or does not do doesn't alter my character or yours.

But the biblical cultures understood things quite differently. In Paul's world faith and faithfulness are part of *one relationship* where both parties are bound together by both words and actions. We have already noticed how our two English words are expressed by only one word in Greek. We are not talking about individually owned characteristics but about a relationship as it is lived truly or falsely by each of the two parties to it. And those acts of truth or falsehood in the relationship affect the reputation of both.[84]

This idea isn't completely strange to us. We all recognize that when we trust someone we are not only saying something about *them*, we are also saying something about *ourselves*. If the person we trust proves to be a crook, no matter what mitigating factors there might be, our judgment as the one who trusted them still comes into question. In relationships the reputation of both parties are on the line. Think about how we react when a smooth-talking conman persuades a middle-aged couple to "invest" their savings in one of his money-making projects. The conman and the money are never heard of again. He is a villain. But alongside sympathy for the couple don't we also have this feeling that they were foolish to be taken in like that? When the money that a friend pays over the internet to the widow of a Nigerian general who needs help to move a large quantity of gold into their US bank account disappears without trace, don't we immediately think: "you numbskull"?

It is this reciprocal nature of a faith relationship that lies behind the question in verse 3. If some of those whom God trusted with his words proved unworthy of that, doesn't *God's* character come into question? If you don't think this is as much a burning issue in the twenty-first century as it was the first century, you don't get out among non-Christians enough. Are we to think that God was misguided in trusting human beings with his word? If some of his chosen covenant partners fail, does that weaken our confidence in God himself? That is the question here. But Paul will have none of it. "Impossible!" he says. "God would still be true even if *every* human was a liar."

The quotation that follows (v. 4) isn't just a random proof text. Everyone in Paul's audience would have immediately recognized its source in Ps 51, the great penitential psalm of David. In his sinfulness David could not be a more dramatic example of the untrustworthy "some" of verse 3. Yet in this prayer of repentance David declares that his wrongdoing only makes God's righteousness shine. The very Scriptures that God trusted his people with declare the unchallengeable righteousness of God—and therefore expose the folly of these presumptuous questions about his character.

Justification or Being Declared Righteous?

We need to note something else about the Ps 51 quotation. You will see that I've translated the first phrase "that you may be *declared to be righteous* in what you say." If you turn up one of the standard English translations, however, you may well find that it reads "that you may be *justified* in what you say." This introduces a word that, although we will virtually never use it in this book, is so important in the history of theology (think of Luther's famous declaration of "justification by faith alone") that we need to pause for a moment to discuss it.

The word does crop up occasionally in everyday life. "When I challenged him the only *justification* he had to offer was that the wallet had just been lying there." "I don't see how I could possibly *justify* paying that much just to go to a concert." In both cases the speaker is defending the rightness of a course of action. But Paul means nothing like that.

What he does mean is both simple and surprising. Unlikely as it seems from the appearance of the words in English, the Greek word translated "justification" is simply the verbal form of the noun "righteousness." To be "justified" is to be *declared to be righteous.* Isn't this a striking thing? It comes out of left field to find that two such different English words are being used to translate Greek expressions that are this closely related. A new English speaker can take words like *love, lover,* and *beloved* and see immediately from the form of them that they are related. *Create, creation* and *creator* work in the same way. Here, though, there is no similarity at all. There is nothing on the page to alert us to the fact that in our biblical translations the *just* group of words (justify, unjust, justification)[85] and the *right* group of words (righteous, righteousness) are part of the same word family in Greek.[86] In choosing two completely different words to translate such closely linked terms the translators make it virtually impossible to understand what Paul is saying.

This is important, because what Paul is talking about is not some abstract religious concept. It is the central issue of human life. In a marriage, can my wife or husband trust me? In a business relationship, am I scrupulously fair and honest? Do I live generously and compassionately in my family and community, or thoughtlessly and selfishly? Do I keep my promises to God? The question of righteousness is about the *dependability and truthfulness of our relationships with others*, and about the wholeness and integrity in our inner life out of which these qualities flow. It is about being fully human. To narrow this down by introducing words and concepts that direct our thought to judges and judgments and courtrooms is to fail people who come in all good faith trusting that their English translation will be faithful to what Paul intended to say. To avoid this confusion we will therefore not use the words "justify" or "justification" in this book, even when we come to the key section 3:21–25. What Paul is saying is too important to allow even historically hallowed terminology to generate needless uncertainty about what it is.

But that does not mean that we ignore the *concept*. It is crucial. What does it mean to "righteous" somebody, to declare them to be righteous? To find out we need to reach back beyond Paul's day to Old Testament times, when the elders of the community met at the gates of the town to settle disputes.[87] Although individuals were involved, the process was essentially communal. What was at issue was the standing and reputation of individuals *within a community*.

In this context, to "righteous" somebody was to publicly declare that they were the kind of person who would be faithful, honest, and fair in a relationship. In a dispute about property or a contract, for example, after considering the matter the elders would declare that such and such person had acted with integrity and good faith, and were innocent of wrongdoing in the situation. There are two things to notice here. Firstly, such a declaration wasn't something that happened in a shuttered room. It was done in the public square, where anyone could come and watch and listen. It was about the life of the community and the relationships that held it together. Secondly, it was personal. It wasn't about the law as a set of external regulations. Rather, it was about an *internal* thing: being declared righteous was the public recognition of a depth of character in a person's life that had led them to act rightly rather than wrongly in the situation. Furthermore, because it was about the person, not the act, to declare someone to be righteous said as much about the present and the future as about the past. It wasn't a matter of this or that *event*, but of the person's *quality of character* that could be trusted going on into the future.

All of this is quite different from a "not guilty" verdict in a modern law court. A court deals in only the most superficial way with the realities of character. There a verdict of "not guilty" only means that in the opinion of the jury the accused did not break the law *on this occasion*—or that there is sufficient doubt to make a certain judgment impossible. A violent and untrustworthy person may well be judged not guilty of a particular murder: the judgment says nothing about their character, but is a statement only about a single act. In contrast, to *declare as righteous* someone is a statement about the whole person. It is also something that runs both ways. As with faithfulness, when making a declaration to others that an individual can be trusted, the person making the judgment lays their own reputation and integrity on the line.

Now we can understand what is happening in verse 4 of our current passage. David acknowledges that the outcome of his sin has been to demonstrate God's righteousness. He is not saying God is in the right, he is testifying to his unchangeable character. And that, he says, will always be the case: the accusations we throw at God tell us only about ourselves and the place we have chosen to occupy within God's moral world.[88] David declares God to be righteous, not "justifying" him in the modern sense of making excuses for him, but rather declaring that he has experienced the truth of God's character and found it to be completely dependable.

In the verses that follow, Paul will use this word in another, richer context. After David's recognition that God is righteous in all his dealings with us (v. 4) comes God's declaration that *we* are righteous, through the faithfulness of Jesus Messiah (v. 23ff). And the door swings open into another world. For God does not chatter. He speaks and the universe comes into being. His word accomplishes things. So when God himself declares someone to be righteous something *happens*. It is not just a statement, it is an action. Righteousness is formed in the person's life. God pledges his own character and integrity to the ongoing accomplishment of what he declares. Paul will have much more to say about this.[89]

COUNTER-QUESTIONS

This is not the first time Paul has preached all this. As he walks up and down the portico where he and Tertius are respectively dictating and writing the letter, all the debates he has had down the years in the synagogues and the churches come flooding back into his mind. Like a traveling lecturer today, he has heard all the objections and he knows all the questions. And here in verses 5 to 8 they all come tumbling out.

It is important that we hear the tone of voice in these verses. We need to picture Paul the orator still passionately interacting with a vividly imagined audience, as he has been all through the letter so far. We need to hear the tone of irony and scorn. "This is the way people talk!" he says. Paul isn't solemnly working through a series of logical objections. Each question is simply raised in order to show its foolishness. How can we trust a God who trusts the untrustworthy? Where is the righteousness in that? Doesn't the failure of those whom he trusted diminish him? If our failure doesn't damage his honor, how come we find ourselves in the path of his anger? "What nonsense!" says Paul. God is the ruler of the world, not some human being we can turn aside with schoolboy arguments (v. 6). The questions get more and more ridiculous; simply stating them is enough. One can imagine Paul the orator pausing for a moment after each question so the audience can realize its stupidity—and also the implications of the stupidity. Are we really to say: "Let us do evil so that good may come"? Such a logic-chopping, God-dishonoring line of questioning brings us not just to absurdity, but to iniquity.[90]

What Paul is demolishing with these questions is a mindset that considers that, because of his covenant faithfulness, God has somehow become beholden to religious people. We have a special deal. Of course God's wrath will—deservedly—fall upon the wicked world out there. But he would be breaking his covenant promises to inflict wrath upon *us* (v. 5).

What might be the modern equivalent to this? The complacent assurance that God is bound to let us into heaven (as if that was the central concern of the Christian life) because a certain ceremony was performed upon us when we were a babe in arms? The confidence that God will look out for us because we made a "decision for Jesus" at a revival rally when we were a teenager? Of course our eternal destiny *is* secure—and our life and hope here in this life as well. But that is because of God's free and living grace which we experience and live within daily. Salvation is not an entry ticket nor a thing that one could bank. It is not something that one could either gain or lose. It is a relationship. It is grounded in and guaranteed by the character of the living God, the God who calls us to live a life of faith and obedience.

Paul the orator, then—and his argument drives steadily on. It is important to recognize that ongoing movement. Because we are dealing with what is for us an ancient letter, we need to go slowly as we unpack the meaning of terms and trace the line of thought. The danger with that, though, is that we could break the text up into bits, treating each small section as if it stood alone. But Paul was thinking quickly, and his audience was with him all the way. The whole of chapter 3 is one unified line of thought; it is all spoken in one breath, as it were. Any *serious* questions that might arise about God's trustworthiness and righteousness will receive their definitive answer in the section beginning with verse 21. When we get to those verses all this logic-chopping and bargaining with God will be seen to be dead leaves upon the wind.

But in the meantime, Paul has one last nail to drive into the coffin of our religious self-righteousness. The question that was posed at the beginning of the chapter comes again: "What then? Are we any better off?" The answer is again unhesitating, but this time the answer is very different answer: "No, not a chance!" Yes, those of us who stand in the godly tradition of Israel do have huge advantages, not the least of them being the possession of the Scriptures. But in fact the very Scriptures that we cherish clearly demonstrate that everybody in the world (note the globally inclusive "Jew and Greek" terminology appearing again here) is under the power of sin. And that *includes us*.

ROMANS 3

ACCOUNTABLE TO GOD

The long chain of quotations in verses 10 to 18 come from the Psalms and Isaiah.[91] In their original contexts, most of these Scriptures were about "the wicked": people who from the perspective of the godly community were outside the pale of God's favor. But Paul has already demonstrated that such a distinction cannot be made. Notice how confident he is, and how freely he remobilizes the old texts for the new situation in Messiah Jesus. If, as he has shown, God treats all human beings on the same basis, if God has no favorites, then these texts apply to everybody, both the religious and the non-religious. And *especially* they apply to those who possess the Scriptures and who claim to live by them (v. 19). All these objections, all this arguing for special status must end. "Every mouth must be shut, and the whole world fall silent before the judgment of God."

If Paul had had the Gospels in front of him would he have needed to mine the Old Testament for proof texts in the way that he does in these verses? Would he not simply have been able to say something like this: You say you are followers of Jesus? Listen to him then! Hear what he says to the Pharisees, and don't imagine that in addressing them he is talking to anyone other than us good religious people. Listen honestly to the parable of the tax collector and the Pharisee and ask which of those two characters you really are. Listen to the parable of the Good Muslim, or the good Mormon, or whatever the religious-but-theologically-unsound equivalent of the Good Samaritan is for you today. Do you act like the Samaritan—or are you not more like the procession of good religious people who passed by on the other side of the road? Listen to the parable of the sheep and the goats! Can you find any specially privileged group there which stands exempt from God's requirement of righteousness living for all human beings? You say that Jesus is your Master and your Lord; you therefore of all people are the most directly accountable to him. So the arguments and the special pleading must stop. Simply in obedience to him you must take your place with the rest of the world in silence before his judgment.

Let us not, then, read this collection of Old Testament passages and imagine that what Paul is saying here doesn't apply to us. We do have enormous privileges, and especially the responsibility of having been trusted by God with his word to the world. But the very Scriptures we are so proud to possess are those that show our human failure, a failure which both religious and non-religious people share.

But, for both the religious and the non-religious, that is not the end of the story.

ROMANS 3:21–26—"BUT NOW..."

21But now, independently of the Law—but testified to by the Law and the Prophets—God's righteousness has been revealed; 22 ²²God's righteousness through the faithfulness of Jesus Messiah* to all who have faith. There is no distinction. 23 For just as all *have sinned and fall short of God's glory, 24 so now all are by his free grace being made righteous through the liberation that is in Messiah Jesus. 25 God put him forward as a sacrificial means of restoring the relationship, through the ²⁵faithfulness of his own death. This demonstrates his righteousness when in his divine patience he passed over sinful acts in the past. 26 ²⁶It also demonstrates his righteousness now: righteous in himself and righteous as the one who establishes as righteous the person who lives on the basis of the faithfulness of Jesus.*⁹²

The furnishings are sparse: a bed, a washstand, a bucket. Behind the bars on the high window an edge of cloud shows against a pale sky. The man sits on the bed, his knees drawn up to his chest because of the cold. The last appeal has been rejected. Now there are only the years: the ticking of a clock in an empty room. Silence seeps in from the walls; distant dance music from a radio in the guardroom down the corridor only intensifies it. Nothing happens. And nothing happens again and again as the hours drag on towards the dusk and the dark. And then, suddenly, something else. Something unmistakable and electrifying. The sound of a key turning in the lock.

Paul has been merciless. Every barrier of presumption and privilege that separates us from the world for which Jesus died has been torn away. But now he turns our gaze from the embarrassing rags of our religious pride to the glory and the grace of God himself. This is what he has come to tell us about. This is the truth and the wonder that bubbles away in his life and which drives his ministry. This is the story of the mighty act of God to bring about rescue and restoration for everyone who lives by faith in the faithful God. For only now does Paul begin to talk about the good news.

When, in the days before wire fences, the first European settlers of New Zealand brought with them the tough and prickly gorse bush to use as hedges between the fields, they could not have foreseen that in in barely a generation it would be declared a noxious weed. Even today there are large areas in parts of New Zealand where good productive land is choked with gorse.⁹³ When a farmer wishes to reclaim land like this, first the gorse is bulldozed off and heaped into huge piles, and when it is dry it is put to the flames. Only then can the tractors and ploughs do the necessary work of breaking open and tilling the land for the planting of seed.

That is what Paul has been doing up to now. Back in 1:16, 17 he declared his theme: the good news of God's deliverance in Jesus Messiah. But before he could talk about that he had to clear away the gorse of pride and privilege that was thick upon the land, and that process has occupied him for the entire letter up to this point. He has shown how both the religious person and the non-religious person stand defenseless and silent before the holiness and glory of God. Every excuse, all self-justification has been swept away. Now the ploughing and the planting can begin.

ROMANS 3

THE RIGHTEOUSNESS OF GOD

In his summary of his message right at the start of the letter, Paul told us that the good news was about the way "the righteousness of God is revealed, his faithfulness calling forth our faith."[94] Here he tells us that the faithfulness is *the faithfulness of Jesus Messiah* (v. 22). The words *righteousness* and *faithfulness* make clear that we are talking about a relationship. God's side of that relationship will be Paul's theme in this last section of chapter 3. Our side of it, the way we daily reach out to receive the gift of his faithfulness, will be the theme of chapter 4.

These are not just religious words that Paul is shuffling around. The character of God is at stake. Two huge questions have arisen so far in chapter 3. Paul has described the enormous privilege of the covenant people: God has trusted us with his very words. But some have been unfaithful. Doesn't that mean, Paul has asked, *that, as one of the partners in a failed relationship, God's own faithfulness has been compromised?* His certainty about this mirrors our own: "Impossible!" he declares. But how can that certainty be demonstrated? Mightn't it just be wishful thinking? Where is the actual evidence to show that God's faithfulness is not affected by our failure? That is the first issue.

The second is also about the implications of human failure. The Scriptures tell us that all human beings have sinned and fallen short of God's glory, and that raises a huge question. If God, in making a world, has reached out to seek a righteous covenant partner and found "*not one* who is righteous, *not one* who has understanding, *not one* who seeks after God" then what does this mean for God's own righteousness? Righteousness is not an attribute. It only exists as one side of a reciprocal relationship. And if the other side is not there, if it is simply absent, *if there is in all of creation no faithful covenant partner*, then does that not mean that God has failed? Are we to think of him as like a shopkeeper in a tourist town, who stands at the doorway of his shop imploring customers to come in—but everybody walks on by? Is he like a furniture-maker whose every single chair is misshapen and uncomfortable, whose every table is uneven and unstable? How can God truly be the good God if all human beings alike are under the power not of goodness, but of sin? These are the questions that are burning in Paul's mind as he comes to this great "But now!" It is important to remember this as we come to read this section. Historically we have tended to rush on to the question of faith and what God has done for us. But Paul's burning interest is in the character and the trustworthiness of *God*, and how what he has done in Messiah Jesus demonstrates that.

THE FAITHFULNESS OF JESUS MESSIAH

The answer to these questions: a name and a title. Paul declares something that we cannot understand but can only testify to: in Jesus the Messiah God himself has entered our world to live a human life alongside us. Paul never forgets that Jesus is a human being, descended from David, physically raised to life from the death of the body (1:3, 4). But he also recognizes that Jesus' faithfulness is *God's* faithfulness (v. 22); that what he has done demonstrates *God's* righteousness. God has stepped in. In contrast to all the unrighteousness and failure of humanity, Jesus *from within that very humanity* is the faithful covenant partner of God, faithful all the way to death. His death frees human beings from slavery to sin and restores the relationship. In this way God's righteousness is demonstrated beyond doubt or question: his righteousness in the past, his righteousness now, his righteousness in the future. In Messiah Jesus, God himself fulfills the covenant that is *implicit* in creation and *explicit* in the Old Testament Scriptures. God is the utterly faithful God—and also the faithful human partner that both creation and covenant seek.

Faith in Jesus or the Faithfulness of Jesus?

In the translation offered above, Paul declares that God's righteousness has been revealed *through the faithfulness of Jesus Messiah* for all who have faith. In contrast, every major English translation[95] says that the righteousness of God has been revealed *through faith in Jesus Christ*. This is not a minor difference. All of what Paul is saying depends upon getting it right. If we hear correctly what Paul is saying here then what he is saying in the rest of the letter will steadily fall open to us. If we mishear him we will understand something, but it won't be the good news as Paul understood it. It is essential therefore that the reasons for the translation I have made are right out here in the main text. Something so important can't be tucked away in a note at the end of the book.

I am well aware of the startling nature of the claim I am making—and how disturbing it may seem as well. Isn't the doctrine of justification *by faith* the most fundamental thing we know about Paul's teaching in Romans? Isn't Romans about "faith from beginning to end," as some translate 1:17? How can anyone seriously suggest eliminating such an obvious reference to faith, one that is plainly there in the English text before us? And there we have the problem. For the real question is not what the *English* texts say but what is there in the *Greek* text that Paul actually dictated. Hidden behind the standard English translations is the fact that, although all the translations have it, "through faith in Jesus Messiah" is not the natural or obvious way of rendering the Greek sentence. Choosing to translate it as "faith in Jesus" is an attempt to express what it is felt that Paul must be *intending* to say, rather than what he actually does say.

Now of course Romans has much to say about faith, about how in our searing need we reach out empty hands for the gift of righteousness that only God can give. Faith as a life lived in trust in the promises of God will be the theme of all of chapter 4. But here in the last half of chapter 3, Paul is not in the first instance talking about us. He is talking about God. We have had our turn. Brought to a stop by the overwhelming testimony of the Scriptures to the sinfulness of every human being, we like everybody else stand silent before the judgment of God. *But we are not the only actor in this drama.* What has

God himself done about the situation? This is Paul's central interest in these verses. "But now—the righteousness of God has been revealed!" Something awesome has happened. Of course Romans is about faith. But what kind of God do we have faith *in*? That is the question Paul is answering in these verses.

God's righteousness is revealed, Paul says, *through the faithfulness of Jesus Messiah*. This is different from the standard translations in two ways. First of all, it is *faithfulness* rather than *faith*. And secondly, it is the faithfulness *of* Jesus Messiah, not faith *in* Jesus Messiah. Let us take these in turn, beginning with the difference between *faithfulness* and *faith*.

As we have already seen, the Greek word *pistis* describes a relationship between persons. A person has *pistis* (faith) in someone who *also* has *pistis* (faithfulness). Even if there are large differences in power or prestige between the two parties, a faith(fulness) relationship is always reciprocal. God trusts us with the Scriptures, for example. He on his part acts in faithfulness toward us. It is reciprocal. Faith and faithfulness are what the relationship consists of.

English has two words to express this relationship; Greek has only one.[96] The reader of the Greek text depends upon the context to indicate which aspect of the relationship is being described. It is the job of the translator to use that context to decide which of the two English words is most appropriate to translate *pistis* in any particular situation.[97]

In 3:22 that context is clear. God is the subject here. Without any help from the weakness and insufficiency of human religion ("the Law"), God has demonstrated his righteousness. And he has done that not in some general way but specifically (note the repetition of "righteousness") through the faithfulness of Jesus Messiah. Jesus' faithfulness is not just a quality or attribute. It is an act. It is something that God does through Jesus that changes life forever for those who put their faith in that faithfulness (v. 22). Notice how both sides of the relationship are there in the verse: the faithful act of Jesus (v. 22a), and the corresponding faith of those who receive the benefit of what he has done on their behalf (v. 22b).

The second decision for a translator is the choice of English preposition: *in* or *of*. Clearly this is to some extent already determined by our choice of *faithfulness* rather than *faith*. However, the way the Greek phrase works gives us further confidence that this choice is the right one. In English, the relationship between nouns in a sentence is almost always through a preposition. Greek uses prepositions in this way too (*dia*, the word translated *through* is one). But in Greek, a more common way of indicating how one word is related to another is by means of the shape of the word itself: what is called its *case*. In 3:22 the relationship between the word *pistis* and *Jesus Messiah* is indicated in Greek by the genitive case.[98] When we are talking about a person, this particular shape of the word would normally be translated into English as the possessive. We have an example of that in verses 21b and 22a: the word *righteousness* followed by *God* in the genitive case means *the righteousness of God, God's righteousness*.[99] The second half of the sentence explains what that statement means: the righteousness of God (notice the repetition) *through the faithfulness of Jesus*. Even if the phrase stood alone the natural and obvious way of translating it would be as a subjective genitive: "the faithfulness of Jesus."

But the tight link with the similarly constructed phrases in the immediately preceding context makes it even clearer that this is how we must understand it.

And now we have a puzzle. Considerations like these lead virtually every commentator to agree that the most natural way to take the phrase *dia pistis Iesou Christou* in verse 22 is "through the faithfulness *of* Jesus Messiah."[100] But then in the very next breath virtually unanimously they declare that, despite the textual evidence, the phrase must instead be read "through faith *in* Jesus Messiah"![101] This is an extraordinary thing. The reasons, however, are not linguistic but theological. Because of the long history of thought on this passage, we already know what it must say—and that is therefore the way we must translate it despite the contortions we have to go through in order to persuade ourselves that the Greek text is consistent with that translation.

What the commentaries don't usually note when they argue for it is that, while even in general the use of the objective genitive with regard to persons is uncommon,[102] the use of *pistis* plus genitive in the objective sense (faith *in* something or somebody) is extremely rare. There are only a handful of other places *in all of contemporary Greek literature* where reading a *pistis* phrase in this way seems to be demanded by the context.[103] If we were to decide that Paul was using an objective genitive ("faith in") both here and also in Galatians and Philippians[104] (which are the other places in the New Testament where this construction occurs), we would be doubling the total number of the scattered occurrences of this very unusual use of *pistis* with the genitive *in all of the surviving Greek literature from Paul's day*.

Could Paul's use of an objective genitive here be a stylistic eccentricity? We all have them. But the difficulty is that everywhere else in Romans when a quality is linked to a person, Paul uses the genitive with the person as the subject in a perfectly standard way. Genitives indicating possession are everywhere: we have already noted one ("the righteousness *of* God") in the very same sentence in verse 22. And this is what Paul does with *pistis* phrases as well: apart from 3:22–26 there are three other places where he uses *pistis* followed by the genitive, and in every one of these cases the context makes quite clear that he is using the genitive in the way one would expect. In 3:3, for example, it must be the faithfulness *of* God (not "faith in God"),[105] and in 4:12 and 4:16 it must be the faith *of* our father Abraham (not "faith in Abraham"). Understanding the *identical construction* in 3:22, 25, and 26 to mean "faith in" rather than the faith or faithfulness of would therefore be to cut completely across this pattern of normal usage in the surrounding context. How could we justify doing that? Why would Paul say something one way and then just a breath before or a breath after use exactly the same construction in a completely different way? How would he ever expect us to understand him, if he kept chopping and changing the way he used the same words and phrases in the same piece of writing?

Do these considerations seem conclusive to you? Yet, despite it all, translations that read the text as "faith in" still keep appearing, and the major commentaries (but not scholars in general) almost uniformly support that reading. It is a remarkable phenomenon. Quoting a *pistis* sentence in Josephus, one commentator says that "this shows at least that the objective sense of such a genitive is not impossible." Not impossible!

The same commentator tells us, "While [the normal translation of the genitive in this passage] might seem plausible," he says, "*it runs counter to the main thrust of Paul's theology.*"[106] And there we have it. While seldom stated as plainly as this, this is in fact the real issue for translators and commentators alike. The church comes to the text of Romans with two thousand years of theology behind it. Especially we still have ringing in our ears the powerful expositions of this letter by Luther and Calvin (this is the case even, it seems, for the Roman Catholic commentator just quoted), written as they were out of their own personal and cultural context over four hundred years ago. We come to these passages *already knowing* what they say, *already knowing* what Paul's theology is. And so of course we find in the text what we are expecting to find. It is a circular process: we translate the text in the way that we know we must translate it if we are to be true to what we already know that it says. But how can we know what it says if we don't listen to it? How do we know anything about "the main thrust of Paul's theology" unless we allow him to tell us what that theology is?

Finally, apart from the technicalities of language we should notice two further problems with the "faith in Jesus" translation that lie in plain sight on the surface of the English texts themselves. Firstly, this reading produces an awkward verbal duplication in verse 22: "the righteousness of God is revealed *through faith* in Jesus Messiah for *all who have faith*." How does that make sense? The translations tend to blur the difficulty by using two different words: "through faith in Jesus Messiah for all who *believe*" (NRSV). But there is no different word "believe" in Greek. It is the same word *pistis* repeated here twice in the same sentence. The faith/believe stratagem makes us feel that there must be some profound meaning in the repetition. But try working out what that meaning is! And of course, Paul is not saying faith/believe at all, he is opening up his pithy summary of the gospel back in 1:17: God's righteousness is revealed from *pistis to pistis*, from *faithfulness* (God's work, demonstrating who he is) to *faith* (our response to who he is and to what he has done). As we have seen, not only is it impossible to see how this statement makes any sense if it is the Christian who is the subject in both cases, it delivers such a desperately impoverished understanding of what Paul is saying. The standard reading is not only obscure rather than clear; it misses the good news altogether.

And this is the rather more worrying second issue: the deep human-centeredness of the "faith in Jesus" translation. Think for a minute about that standard translation of verse 22 again: "the righteousness of God [has been disclosed] *through faith* in Jesus Messiah." What the translators are saying is that God's righteousness is revealed and demonstrated not by anything that God himself has done, but *by our faith*. Does that seem right to you? Do we really think that God's character is dependent upon how we respond to him? The same issue arises in verse 25. "God put [him] forward as a sacrifice of atonement *through faith* in his blood," says the NIV. The NRSV and NEB are even more explicit: God put Jesus forward as "a sacrifice of atonement by his blood, *effective through faith*." That is, God's work of atonement requires our response for it to be effective; God's plan, if it is going to work properly, requires our assent to it. The sacrifice of Jesus needs to be completed by our participation. Is this not troubling? Are any of us tempted, even for a moment, by any of these ideas? Yet this is what the standard reading of Paul's text drives us to conclude. It is such a sad irony. We have seen how in all of the letter up to this point Paul's whole effort has been directed into demonstrating how nothing that even the most religious human beings can do is enough to bring us back into fellowship with God. God has acted apart from Law, he tells us. Who he is and what he does is independent of all human religiousness. And now, in the standard translations, here we are, exercising our faith so that God's good work may come to completion. Faith has become a work. Paul would weep.

The tragedy is the way in which this understanding of faith has sown confusion and uncertainty in people's lives, instead of joy and confidence. People worry about whether they have enough faith, or whether they really believe the right things, or whether they have the resources to step out into life as the heroes of Hebrews 11 did. If faith is something that you do, how can you be sure that you are doing it the right way? How can you be sure you are doing it enough? But faith is not something that we do. Faith simply means reaching out to the faithfulness of God—God's act of faithfulness which reaches out to us in Messiah Jesus. Where we have been faithless he has been faithful. Where we have failed, he has been steadfast. Where we have been false, he has been true. All that we have longed to be and fallen short of, he is. We can place our lives in his hands and know that those hands will never let us go. This is the liberation that comes through the faithful obedience of Messiah Jesus (v. 24). This is God's own self-giving that restores the relationship (v. 25). This is the good news.

One question before we conclude. If Paul is really speaking here about the faithfulness of Jesus Messiah, what happens to faith in Jesus? Isn't that supposed to be the very heart of the good news? And it is. Those among us who grew up in a Christian community from childhood may well have been given John 3:16 as a memory verse: "God so loved the world that he gave his only Son, that *whoever put their faith in him* will not perish." Later in the same Gospel Jesus himself will say to the disciples: "Don't let your hearts be troubled. Have faith in God; *have faith also in me*. In my father's house are many rooms" (John 14:1). Could anything be clearer than that? To understand these passages we need to read them not as isolated statements, but in their context. Jesus in John is not speaking of faith in himself as anything different from faith in the eternal God. That is the striking thing that the fourth Gospel emphasizes above all: the manifest humanity of the man Jesus, and yet the recognition that in him we see *God himself* stepping into his world to seek and to save. The language of the fourth Gospel is not that of distinction, but of identity: to have faith in Jesus is to have faith in God himself. And this is the case also everywhere else that faith in Jesus is spoken of: faith in Jesus is faith in God; the faithfulness of Jesus is the faithfulness of God. In our daily life faith in Jesus is not so much about what we think but about how we pray. In the struggles and challenges of our human life instinctively we turn to him, just as the disciples placed their confidence and love in him during his life on earth. Prayer to Jesus is the most natural thing in the world. In him God has been a human being too. He knows what it is like.

But faith in Jesus is not in Paul's mind in the letter to the Romans. In Romans faith is always in God (4:3, 5, 17, 20), that is, faith in "him who raised Jesus our Lord from the dead" (4:24). This is not to say that Paul sees Jesus as anything less than God himself, coming among us as a human being to live our life and die our death. Passages like 1:7; 8:9–11; 10:5–17, and especially our current passage 3:21–26 make this crystal clear. But in Romans, Paul presents Jesus as the one who demonstrates God's faithfulness as our representative, rather than being in himself the *object* of our faith. Paul's message is in the first place about God and what he has done, and only secondarily about our response to that. Faith in God as faith in Jesus is something we learn from other parts of the New Testament. But not from this one.

What does the faithfulness of Jesus consist of? In one sense it takes all of the four Gospels to answer that question. But in chapter 5 Paul will sum it up in the one word *obedience*. And, like sunlight through a magnifying glass, where that obedience comes to its most intense and critical focus is his death on the cross. "God put him forward as a sacrificial means of restoring the relationship through the faithfulness of his own death," Paul says in verse 25. "At the right time," he will say a little later, "Messiah died for the ungodly."[107]

Did Paul know the story of Jesus' baptism? Whether he did or not, the line from Jesus' "fulfilling all righteousness" in his baptism by John[108] to his obedient submission to death on the cross is clear and unbroken. He submitted to John's baptism back then, waiting his turn alongside all the rest of us, indistinguishable from any other penitent sinner in the line. Now, three years later, on a day of noise and heat in the crucifying place of Jerusalem, again he stands alongside us, this time staked up alongside two thieves, undergoing the shameful death of an outcast and a criminal. This, says Paul, is God himself, in death as in life standing alongside the ungodly and the despised and the suffering of the world.

Can we get our head around this? Because of who it is who is hanging there, this death has reconciling power. In the cross the broken, guilty, and helpless human world and the righteousness of God are decisively brought together. It is a strange place to look for God. But it is in the cross that Paul sees the light of God's saving glory focused most intensely. Here we see the righteous God taking responsibility for the world he has created.[109] Here he himself steps in to be the obedient, faithful covenant partner that humans have never been able to be. Here we see him walking the way of our sinful life all the way to death itself.

This solitary, majestic act depends in no way at all upon human religion (v. 21). It has nothing to do with buildings and worship services or with Bible studies and robed choirs, nothing to do with the scholars and the commentaries and the earnest religious debates. This is God alone. Who from our human world, even the devout and godly part of it, would ever have dared to imagine such an act on God's part? God entering into human life as a man among men? God on a cross?[110] In the uniqueness and majesty of his action God receives no contribution from the religious effort of human beings. No matter how earnest it is, nothing in our religion can put us right with God. Putting us right is something that God alone can do—and it is something that

God has done, God alone. It is *God's* righteousness, *God's* faithfulness, *God's* liberation, *God's* restoration of the relationship in Jesus Messiah. Human religion only shows us how far short we fall of God's glory (v. 23).[111] But, in Jesus, God has acted.

This is a deeply hopeful truth. Because in sovereign freedom God has acted in this way our salvation is utterly secure. It is founded not on anything from within the human world—and especially not upon human religiosity, however well intended. It is founded upon something that exists within the eternal being of God himself.[112]

"TOO MUCH INFORMATION!"

What Paul is telling us about is the mystery of the world. Not only could God's act in Jesus' act not be imagined or anticipated, it cannot be understood. Not with the tools we have, anyway. How is it possible for the Creator God to assume life within his own creation? How can Jesus be a human being, like every other person utterly dependent upon God for every breath, yet in some way also God himself? We have no idea. All we can do is witness to the truth of these things. There is a danger here for religious people. We can say, for example, that in Messiah Jesus God fulfilled the covenant faithfulness that we could never achieve by ourselves, and that is true. But the danger is that long familiarity could lead us to imagine that just because we can put words to the events, somehow we understand how the events can be. We cannot understand how the events can be. We are looking into mystery and glory. The world should perhaps stop for us here, for a while. It should just rumble to a halt as far as we are concerned, while we simply gaze.

I remember a friend telling me about an encounter he had had with a group of priests from a Hindu temple while he was living in Singapore. He wanted to learn Tamil, they wanted help with their (already fairly fluent) English. As part of the work on the English side it was agreed that they would read the Gospel of John together. No hidden agenda there! But when he met them for the first session they were not ready. The pre-reading had been John 1:1–18, which begins "In the beginning was the Word. And the Word was with God, and the Word was God." The group had only covered a few verses. It wasn't a matter of the challenges of the language. "Too much information!" my friend was told. They had fasted and meditated and had great joy in what they had read. They were keen to go on. But it was going to take time.

If what Paul says is true, what he is describing is the most extraordinary event in the history of the world. Do we understand that anymore? Do we just take these statements in our stride as one more idea among other ideas in the world? But they do not belong among the ideas of the world. While we encounter them as events within the history within which we live, they are in a deeper way alien to human history. They do not rise up from within the human, historical world. Something breaks in from outside. And that something brings with it news of a reality that lies far deeper than human understanding and yet, this Scripture tells us, is powerful for us now in the world in which we live.

REDEEMER AND REPRESENTATIVE

We are not dealing with a theory. The righteousness of God, the faithfulness of Jesus the Messiah, a life lived by faith in that faithfulness: these are not abstract ideas, but describe a living relationship. God in his faithfulness reaches out to needy human beings and human beings respond! And God's righteousness *makes righteous*.[113] "All have sinned and fall short of the glory of God," Paul tells us, "and are now made righteous by his grace as a gift" (v. 24). Making righteous is not about forgiveness, or about wiping away and forgetting the deeds of the past. It is not a matter of a changed status. It is an act of power. It is a new creation, as God through his spirit makes us the righteous human beings we were created to be.

Reaching for words to explain this, Paul uses two pictures, one from everyday life, the other from the world of sacrificial ritual. The first metaphor has become blurred for us because of its common translation as *redemption*, which we mostly know as a religious word used in church talk and Christian songs. We have lost the context that for Paul's audience made it electric. For "redemption" means *liberation:* the delivery of a person from slavery into freedom.

It requires an effort of historical imagination for us today to realize how completely permeated Paul's world was by slavery. It was an everyday reality for everybody and was an essential part of the economic system. Especially in the larger cities like Rome, at any one time between a quarter and a third of the population were slaves. So Paul's audience knew very well what he was talking about. Apart from anything else, almost certainly there were slaves among them; this was a common feature of many of the early Christian congregations. While our word liberation is a general one, in Paul's social situation it meant a very specific and dramatic event. Whether the slave purchased their own freedom, was ransomed by someone else, or was simply freed as a benevolent move on the part of their owner, the change of status was dramatic.[114] One moment, the slave was the chattel, the completely disposable possession of another person. The next they were their own. Perhaps for the first time in their life, they were *free*. So small, so simple a word. Most of us live in societies where it is taken for granted. How do we get our heads around the emotional impact of the word liberation for Paul and for his audience?

It was a prisoner who taught me most about that; coincidentally, his name too was Paul. I met him in a transition facility for prisoners who were right at the end of their sentence and were being prepared for re-entry to ordinary life. He had been in jail for many years. "I did a horrible thing, Les," he said. "I deserved to go to prison. And prison is in your head, you know. Every morning I have to wake up and look at myself in the mirror and realize again that I'm the person who did that." His voice changed then, and a new light was in his eyes. "But today I look out there and I can't see razor wire anywhere. There is not a guard uniform in sight. Yesterday they let me walk down to the store to get an ice cream. And here I am talking to you, a member of the public." Freedom. Not just the absence of walls. But something deep in the heart: sunlight breaking through the clouds, a new world beginning. The liberation that is in Messiah Jesus.

The second metaphor comes from the Old Testament sacrificial system. "God put Jesus forward," Paul says "as a sacrificial means of restoring the relationship, through the faithfulness of his own death." This is less familiar to us: what are we to make of it?

The language of blood and of sacrifice is unfamiliar and even rather repulsive to twenty-first-century readers. But in order to hear what Paul is saying we need to put a rain check on our modern sensibilities. We need to return in imagination to a forgotten time when people lived close to the land and had strong intuitive and practical relationships with the animals upon which their lives and communities depended. The Old Testament sacrificial system was a massive participatory visual aid. The first chapters of Leviticus best describe what was involved. The worshiper would bring an unblemished animal to the priest and lay their hands upon its head. The warm breath, the whole independent life of the beast lay there tremblingly under the hand—just as, the action suggested, our human lives lie under the hand of God. Sins were then confessed, and the animal's life was taken; sacrifice accepted, the person walked on in renewed fellowship with God.[115]

That, Paul says, is a picture of what Jesus' death meant for us. But he is not talking about a merely individual act. The word that I have translated as "a sacrificial means of restoring the relationship"[116] has specific reference to a *communal* event, the great Day of Atonement, upon which the high priest by means of one sacrifice presented the whole repentant community before God. Just as back then the offered lamb symbolically represented the worshiping community, so in his death Jesus represents us. Not a lamb but a real human being now stands in the place of us guilty and helpless human beings.

But not now do we have a lamb passive under the hand of the person offering it. Here we see a choice, an act. God, not a human being, is the one who offers the sacrifice. What he offers is the faithfulness of Messiah Jesus. The human covenant partner stands opposite the divine covenant partner as our representative, and his obedience all the way to death on a cross means that freedom and the grace of God, and the power to live a fully human life become a possibility for every person.[117] And no one is a favorite. The gifts are for everybody. "Just as *all have sinned and fall short of God's glory*, so now *all are by his free grace being made righteous*" (vv. 23–24). What God has done is not some kind of religious thing. It is a change within human nature itself.

ROMANS 3

SIGN AND FULFILLMENT

We are reading a 2,000-year-old letter, and after all that time the idea of being set free resonates more powerfully with us than the idea of a sacrifice. What then does sacrificial symbolism have to do with us, now in the twenty-first century? To be honest, not a lot. The very fact that you are reading this book indicates that you are part of a culture for which the idea of animal sacrifice is far in the past. So we must not get stuck here. The metaphor of the offering of the lamb on the Day of Atonement is an historical image. Whereas for Paul's audience it was something contemporary and powerful, to us today it feels archaic, even unpleasant. We need to understand the idea, because it crops up regularly in the New Testament—and of course because Paul uses it here. Its function is a little like the frame of a photograph. The photograph helps us to recognize the risen Jesus as he in the twenty-first century stretches out his hand to grasp ours. Whether we think the antique frame is beautiful, or ugly, or simply old-fashioned is immaterial when the person themselves stands in front of us. Our job is not to lose ourselves in the religious rituals of a long-gone age. We need to seize the meaning of Paul's image and move on.

And indeed, this is what Paul himself says. The realization has burst upon him like a blaze of light. The sacrificial system didn't give meaning to the death of Jesus, the death of Jesus showed what the sacrificial system meant. What Jesus accomplished was not just an act in history, grounded in a particular cultural context. It was an event in God himself. The sacrifices had always been accepted *only because of the death of Jesus*. This is how God's righteousness in passing over sinful acts in the past is demonstrated (v. 25). Even though for the Old Testament people of God the faithful sacrifice of Jesus was in human terms still to come, in God's being, outside of time, it was already something accomplished.

THE POWER TO BE

And, Paul says, the faithful death of Jesus also demonstrates God's righteousness *in the present*. What happened on the cross involved not only the eternal God, it involved us. The death of Jesus was not only an event for God, it was something that changed human nature forever. From his side God has proved himself to be the completely faithful and dependable God. All the challenges and questions have fallen to the ground. We can trust him absolutely. But on the human side the fully human being, *the* covenant partner, has also been found. In Jesus the Messiah God has himself provided him. God has undertaken not only his own side of the covenant relationship, but, through the incarnation, the human side as well.

This too, Paul tells us, demonstrates God's righteousness. It means that God is completely in the right in trusting *us*. That is what being established as righteous means: God's trust in us, God both declaring us to be and making us righteous. Before all the world, God stands up for us and declares that we are his. He tells us who we truly are. And he calls us to *be* who we are; he gives us the power to be in actual fact the righteous person we were created us to be, as we live by faith (v. 22), as we live on the basis of the faithfulness of Jesus (v. 26).

While many translations of verse 22 say "for all who believe" there is no word in Greek that means this. The word here is the verb *to have faith*, that is, actually stepping out upon what you know to be true about someone. Faith cannot be a possession. It is the *opposite* of possession: it is the reaching of empty hands towards the righteousness and dependability of God. The living by faith that Paul speaks of in verse 22 is not then a matter of belief alone, not even of recognizing our dependence upon God alone. It is a life lived, it is actual daily living done in the light of these things.[118] How would we describe such a lived life? We would describe it as *faithfulness*.

The Christian life is a life lived on the basis and in the power of the faithfulness of Jesus. The mighty work of God in Jesus the Messiah is not just an historical event. It doesn't set up a kind of bank balance upon which we somehow draw. What God has done is to effect a change inside human nature. God's righteous covenant partner has been created, *and we participate in his life now*. The prison door swings open. A possibility for human life has been opened up that was not there before.

Paul is not discussing an idea or a free-floating truth. The significance of the act of God in Jesus is not just that we believe it, but that we daily step out into the new and righteous life that he continues to live out in us through the Spirit. This is the life of faith and of faithfulness. God's making righteous is an on-going process: not merely a status or an abstract benefit, but a stream of power for a life actually lived.[119]

We are not the initiators of this. Although we are called to do something, the new life is not our creation. We are invited to grasp hold of a possibility that God alone has created. This is why the human-centered modern translations that put our faith rather than God's act at the center of these verses are so unfortunate.[120] Paul's topic in this chapter is not human faith but God's righteousness: God's reliability and commitment to us, disclosed and demonstrated through the faithfulness of Jesus Messiah. Our faith is merely a response to that: the flashing reflection of the glory of the rising sun from the window of a house high on the hill.

BUT WHAT IF YOU MAKE A WORLD?

How then to sum up what we mean by the righteousness of God? Some time ago our local newspaper ran a story about the tens of millions of dollars that were outstanding for child support across New Zealand. In our country, when a man fathers a child and then moves on, leaving the mother with the cost and responsibility of raising the child, the government requires the absent parent to pay an annual sum for support. It is a legal obligation. Sadly, many men not only fail to take responsibility for their children by being there as part of an intact family, but also seek in every way they can to avoid making these payments. What can we say about this double abandonment of responsibility? It feels like the essence of faithlessness. We know, and it is in fact written into our laws, that parenthood is no light matter. Life is not a game. You take on a big responsibility when you make a baby.

But what if you make *a world*?

It is no minor debate about Jewish religion that Paul is engaging in in chapter 3. The question is whether God is in the right with regard to his creation. Has he played fair with his world? Doesn't human unfaithfulness damage his credibility as Creator? Isn't God unjust when he shows his anger against human failure and sin? Doesn't God bear some responsibility for making us the way we are? These are the questions.

Now in Jesus Messiah, says Paul, we see the answer. Now we know with piercing insight what up to now we have had to nakedly believe: that God is indeed righteous, that he has not failed to take full personal responsibility for his world. And he has done so in a way undreamed of. Without any contribution from human effort or human religion, God has acted to save. Incomprehensible as that is to us, God has in Jesus Messiah entered our human world, living our life, dying our death. He has taken our part by taking our place. His identification with the human race is complete. He has taken human being into his own being, declaring us to be righteous as he is righteous. And God does not chatter. His declaration is its own accomplishment: he gives us the power—his own power—to live the faithful and complete human life that Jesus made possible for us. This is no small thing! We need to hear the excitement thrilling in every word as Paul recounts it.

Once while visiting Paris on a business trip, a colleague and I set out after dinner one night to find the Eiffel Tower. Exiting from the Champs de Mars Metro station into a small side street we glanced hopefully about, looking for the famous landmark. Then my colleague gave me a nudge. "Look up!" he said. And there it was: the metro station entrance was almost right beneath the tower. It happened to be just the moment when the light-show changes. The little sparkling lights that had been racing up and down the huge silhouette suddenly went out. For a few seconds there was just the blackness of night. And then, bam, all of the main floodlights came on at once.

Now, you can buy little models of the Eiffel Tower on every street corner in Paris. You see stylized drawings of the thing in travel brochures all over the world. But nothing prepares you for this absolutely gigantic structure towering above you into the sky, suddenly flooded with light, and visible from every rooftop all across the city.

Paris was a village and floodlights were science fiction when Paul wrote his letter. But the image captures something of what he means when he talks about God's righteousness being revealed. This is not like turning a page to discover a new and interesting theological fact. It is not like a little child opening their hand to show a precious sixpence. This is the sudden illumination of the character of God towering over his creation, of a defining act that reaches back and forward across time, the revelation of a power that transforms the world; of something that comes as God's completely personal grace to you, now, as you read this book, to me as I write it, and to both of us as we live on in the strength of it all the days of our lives, because of what God in solitary majesty has done in the death and rising of Jesus, freedom and forgiveness, and a power that catches up all our individual lives into God's great purpose of transforming his whole world. This is the good news.

7

Romans 3:27–31
The End of Special Status

27 What basis is there then for boasting? It is ruled out. What kind of Law rules it out? The one that is based on observances? No, a Law that is based on faith. 28 ²⁸For it is clear to us that a person is made righteous by faith, independently of the observances of the Law. 29 ²⁹Or is God the God of Jews only? Is he not the God of the nations also? Yes, of the nations also, 30 ³⁰since there is only one God; and God will make the circumcised person righteous on the basis of faith in his faithfulness and the uncircumcised righteous through the very same faith. 31 ³¹Do we nullify the Law then, through this 'faith'? Not at all! On the contrary, we place the Law upon its true foundation.[121]

DESPITE THE GLORY OF what he has just proclaimed, Paul does not dwell upon the details. That will come later. What he has said is immediately called upon as part of his attack upon religious pride and self-righteousness. A series of questions press his meaning home. If all people everywhere are made righteous by God's grace as a gift (v. 24), what becomes of the idea that we religious people are somehow God's favorites? The answer is not in doubt. Special status just goes. It always was an illusion. In the face of what God has done in Messiah Jesus it cannot be sustained.

Our religion always *pointed towards* what God has done in Messiah Jesus (v. 21). But what he has done doesn't depend upon any human act or attitude. We can't own this thing, because it isn't ours. We rejoice in the fact that we are *his* (v. 26); but that is his sovereign choice. We didn't initiate God's grace nor earn it: how could we boast about it as if it was something unique to us?

RETHINKING WHAT WE HAVE ALWAYS KNOWN

What does that mean for the way we understand the Law (v. 27b)—that is, the Scriptures and the guidance they give us as to the nature of the godly community? Or, as Paul would ask if he was writing today, if there are no favorites, how are we to understand the role of the church in the world? Doesn't religious observance[122] still have something to do with salvation—especially if that religion is Christianity? No, says Paul, it does not. Salvation is about faith in the faithfulness of God. It is not about anything that we do and all about what God has done. A new humanity has been created. Our role as faithful people, our role as the church, is simply to testify to that.

If it wasn't like this, how could God be God of all the world? Do we somehow imagine, Paul asks, that God is the God of good religious people only? Is he not the God of people everywhere?[123] Yes, of course God is God of the nations too. There is only one God! Through the faithfulness of Jesus he will make righteous those who are members of the covenant community (v. 30a). But, through that very same faithfulness, he will *also* declare and empower to be righteous those who are currently outside the traditional religious community (v. 30b). Does this sound strange to us? But haven't we already seen that even the heathen nations have the requirements of the law written on their hearts (2:15)?

How do God's dealings with the nations work in practice? We aren't given any information with which to satisfy our curiosity. As in other places where people outside the normal boundaries of the faithful community are mentioned (e.g., 2:6–16), Paul doesn't elaborate. For elaborating is not his purpose. He is not creating a system, he is testifying to the truth of God. Like his Master Jesus, Paul never gives us time to indulge in speculation about the situation of others.[124] His only interest is in confronting *us*, here, now, with the challenges of the gospel and the call to faith and obedience. How God deals with others is none of our business.

The issue for Paul here as everywhere in the letter is the character of God. God is not beholden to us. We don't own him. He is not bound. He deals faithfully with people both within *and* without what we would recognize as the good religious community. He is not a small God. He is the Ruler of the world.

GOD OF THE NATIONS

Let me tell you a story. During the time that I was writing the first chapters of this book, the city in which I live suffered a devastating earthquake, which destroyed much of the business district, shattered whole suburbs, and caused many deaths. A couple of months after the event, a memorial service was held in one of the city's parks, and thousands of people came to pay their respects. Although the tone of the service was strongly Christian, other faith communities whose members had been among the dead were also invited to participate by offering their prayers as part of the service. It was a most interesting experience. Most of us don't know very much about other faiths, and what we do learn we mostly learn from the outside, through reading about their doctrines and beliefs. But when you listen to people praying, you come right to the heart of what faith means for them.

And so the representatives of the various communities came forward: Muslim and Hindu and half a dozen others. I don't know how it is with the beliefs of Baha'i people in general, but these particular members of the Baha'i faith prayed what seemed to me to be a poem of self-belief in the light of difficult negative circumstances. I don't know how it is with the beliefs of Jewish people in general, but these particular Jewish people told God that they realized life was hard and full of suffering and said that with faith and courage they could accept that. And then the Buddhist representative came forward. His prayer began like this: "O great and compassionate Buddha . . . " In my ignorance I was astounded. I had always understood Buddhism to be a non-theistic philosophy which taught people to free themselves from attachment to the world, because attachment makes one vulnerable to suffering. I had of course seen pictures of the huge statues of Buddha in temples around the world, and seen the incense and offerings placed in front of them. But it was still totally surprising to me that the Buddha, who himself never spoke about God, could be addressed as if he was himself a god.

"O great and compassionate Buddha," the monk continued, "look down on us in pity. There is great destruction and misery and suffering in our city, and some of us have died. We are like travelers looking for a secure home, like people lost in a storm seeking a safe shelter. O great and compassionate Buddha, please accept our prayer. Please grant us your blessing and give us the confidence to live a new life." And as I listened it suddenly struck me to whom this young man was speaking with such earnestness. It was not Buddha, that is certain. Buddha has been dead and in his grave these 2,400 years. But he was talking to *someone*. And there is only One who can be addressed in this way. There is only One who is able to hear and to answer such a prayer. The psalmists prayed to him in exactly the same way (look at Ps 60:1–5 and 102:1–2, for example). The Buddhist monk did not know God's name; he perhaps knew nothing at all about the good news of Jesus. *But he was not talking into the air.* And did the living God, Creator of heaven and earth, not hear him and take his prayer to heart? What would Paul's words in these verses suggest would be the answer?

Let us make no mistake. Not all worship is valid. In 1:18–23 Paul has made it clear that there are kinds of worship that exchange the truth for a lie, and exchange God's glory for lesser and inadequate things. Religion can be toxic. Bad religion exploits our longing and need for God and turns it aside into destructive byways. That is evil and repellent to God, for it makes the very place where one looks for truth into the source of the lie. Nonetheless that same passage from Rom 1 declares that the truth about God is known at some level by all people, because God himself has revealed it to them (1:19–20).[125]

Is Christianity only of minor importance, then, in the history of salvation? Paul has given us the answer to that earlier in the chapter. Not at all! Christians have huge privilege and advantage in every way—and especially in that we have been trusted with the word of God (3:2). Down through all the years of his covenant with Israel the One God has revealed his character to people, and the Old Testament gives us the record of that. Now in an utterly unique way he has revealed himself in Messiah Jesus, and acted to save and to restore all people to himself. We are the witnesses of this! As Peter declared to the guardians of orthodox religion in his day, "There is salvation in no one else. No one anywhere knows of any other name by means of which we can be saved."[126]

Notice how specific Paul's message is. There is no *general religious* way of coming to God. There is no *timeless* way of coming to him. Our world is concrete and specific; it has bright colors and sharp edges. God becomes incarnate in Jesus: he eats fish and bread, he laughs and weeps, he rejoices and suffers, just as we do. And he does these things *in history*, in a specific place and time. History is where human beings live: that is where, if it is to change anything, God's rescue must take place. What Messiah Jesus does is not a religious event that draws a circle of exclusivity around one particular nation or group of followers. It was an event both *within the eternal God* and *within human nature*. Its effectiveness therefore reaches not only back into all of time (3:25), but also across all of the human community. There is only one God. Jesus lived and died and rose again for us all. Which means that God's dealings with people cannot therefore be limited to the relatively small number of us throughout history who through accident of birth or good fortune have come to know of Jesus and learned to speak his name. We *bear witness* to God's truth. Knowing that truth makes us responsible before him. But we do not own him. We do not control the way he chooses to deal with other people, even if they are outside what we might consider to be the exclusive faith community. God is the God of all people. This is what Paul is telling us.[127]

A few years ago I was visiting the island of Guernsey, one of the Channel Islands, and, driving round the island on a cold and rainy Sunday afternoon, came across a path that led to a Neolithic grave site. Buried in a mound, its chamber made of huge standing pillars, its roof massive multi-ton capstones, it was clearly the grave of an important chieftain. As I looked back from inside the chamber there was no sign of civilization. Just gorse-covered rocky outcrops, and rain-swept grasses, and the cries of gulls on the wind from the sea. I tried to imagine the burial party coming around the curve of the hill: what they would have looked like, but also the personalities that would have been there. I wondered what those long-ago mourners would have been thinking and feeling. How *did* people think and feel, how did they understand their world back then, as many thousands of years before Abraham as our modern world is after him? And, especially, what understanding did they have of God? What was God doing in their lives and in their communities so very long ago? Because he *was* at work there. If it is true that in Messiah Jesus God took human nature upon himself in an eternal act, he must have been. Or do we imagine that God's dealings with people started with Abraham? Paul of course had no knowledge of the millennia of human history that lay before the earliest Old Testament stories. But the logic is inescapable.

Even in our own day there is a border between the space where people have had the privilege of knowing that there even was a person called Jesus, and the space where that name is not known. Do we really think that God's dealings with people might stop at that border? How could we begin to think that, Paul will ask in 4:1. Because here is the thing: Abraham, the father of both Israel and Christianity, was *on the far side* of that border when God first spoke to him.[128]

THE TRUE FOUNDATION

I wonder whether some readers might find all of this a bit disturbing. Paul was very aware that that would be the case for his Roman congregation. He anticipates their anxious question. "But doesn't this nullify the Law?" Or, as some of us may be asking, "Doesn't this overthrow our whole understanding of Christianity?" (v. 31) Back comes Paul's characteristic response: Not a chance! On the contrary, this is the *true foundation* of the good news.

We mustn't either minimize the consternation or read Paul's response as some kind of bland reassurance. If we are to take Paul's teaching seriously we need to change the way we think—and that is a threatening thing. Paul himself was more than once at risk of his life because of opposition to his message by the *religious* community. If what Paul is saying is true, though, there is nothing for it: we must give up our exclusive status as those who are "in" with God in a way that others are not. Of course there is a beloved community, but it is not an exclusive community. There is enormous privilege, but no place of special privilege. God's love is rich and potent and joyous, but God has no favorites. All have sinned and come short of the glory of God and are justified by his grace *as a gift*.

Allowing God to change our thinking about these things is a deeply liberating process. As we reorient ourselves to this new reality we are not (as Paul anticipates some might argue) watering down or eroding the fundamentals of the good news. We are being faithful to it. We are talking about what gives the good news its reach and its power. The things it has to say about God and what he has done are broader and deeper, more generous and more radiant with glory than anything we have up to now imagined. "Overthrow the faith? On the contrary," says Paul, "this is the faith's *true foundation*."

THE DRIVER OF MISSION

If God is as fully involved with people outside the formal faith community as he is with those within it, doesn't that take the sting out of mission? Why would we need to go to all peoples and spread the good news, as the risen Jesus commanded us to do? Why not just let people find their own way to God through the means they have?

To use Paul's regular phrase: Impossible! For that is precisely what cannot happen. No wisdom or spiritual insight, no merely human seeking or straining, is sufficient to deduce anything about the ways of God. God must act; God must speak; without that human beings are lost. And the news of God's act and God's word is precisely what Christians have been trusted with. Even if we did not have a direct commission from our Lord, the nature of the knowledge itself drives us into mission. The news isn't ours, it belongs to others. As we tell it we give people what is already their own—their own because Jesus died to win it for them.

Our attitudes within the mission task will be different, though. No superiority to others! No implied sense that we are "in" and others are out. No assumption that the things of God will be wholly unknown to those among whom we minister. No arrogance that leads to unwillingness to hear what others may have to teach us, as well as what we may be privileged to teach them.

For Paul this wasn't just theory. An incident from his own missionary career illustrates these principles perfectly. Harried from town to town in Macedonia by determined troublemakers, Paul is sent off by the local Christians to Athens, far to the south:

> While Paul was in Athens waiting for Silas and Timothy to arrive, he was deeply distressed to see that the city was full of idols. So he argued in the synagogue with the Jews and God-fearing non-Jews, and also in the market-place every day with those who happened to be there. Some Epicurean and Stoic philosophers also debated with him. [*As a result Paul is invited to address the council responsible for public teaching in the city.*] Then Paul stood in front of the Areopagus and said, 'Athenians, I see how extremely religious you are in every way. For as I went through the city and looked carefully at the shrines, I found among them an altar with the inscription, 'To an unknown god.' In your worship you reach out to the unknown—and that is what I am here to talk about. God made the world and everything in it: as the Lord of heaven and earth he does not live in man-made temples. Nor, as though he needed anything, is he dependent upon people serving him; on the contrary it is he himself who gives life and breath and everything else to every creature. Starting with a single ancestor he brought into being all nations to settle across the whole earth; he gave them their histories and their borders. All this was so that they would search for God and perhaps feel after him and find him—though indeed he is not far from each one of us, for 'in Him we live and move and are' and 'we too are descended from Him,' as even some of your own poets have said.
>
> Since we are God's descendants, then, we ought not to think that the divine nature can be represented by gold or silver or stone, an image formed by the art and imagination of human beings. God has overlooked the times of human ignorance. But now he commands all people everywhere to turn their

thinking and their lives around, because he has set a date on which he will judge the world in righteousness by means of a man whom he has appointed—and this he has demonstrated to everybody by raising him from the dead.'

When they heard about the resurrection of the dead, some scoffed; but others said, 'We will hear you again about this.' At that point Paul left them; but some of them joined him and became believers.[129]

Luke makes it clear that Paul is really distressed by the idolatry he sees in the city. But as he stands to address the Areopagus, that is not where he begins. Instead he acknowledges the way in which the religious shrines scattered across the city *reflect the Athenians' seriousness about worship*. He himself shares this seriousness, he tells them. And among all the others he has noticed one shrine to "the unknown God." It is this One God, of whom Athens is already dimly aware, that he has come to proclaim.

God's desire, he tells the council, is that all people "would search for God, and perhaps feel after him, and find him." In this search he recognizes that the Athenians are already genuinely involved. Like him they know that it is a search fundamental to human life, "for in Him we live and move and are."

This sentence and the following one ("for we too are His offspring") are both quotations from the Greek poets.[130] Paul is taking pains to make respectful links to the thought-world of his hearers; the references to the Old Testament that are so appropriate in a letter like Romans would be completely out of place here. What is striking is that *both quotations are from poems in praise of Zeus, the high god of the Greek pantheon.* There is only one God! Paul starts where people are, and shows them the true meaning of things of which they are already half aware. He doesn't attack ignorant paganism, but assumes a real knowledge of God within the pagan forms.

This isn't all, though. Paul cannot leave it at that. Once that common understanding has been established, Paul is then able to go on, as he must, to *critique* the pagan forms on the basis of their limited and earthbound understanding of God. He speaks of how in these last days extraordinary new truth about God has been revealed, and he proclaims the role of the risen Jesus as Judge of the world. And here we come to the heart of it. Always, for Paul and for us, the crucified and risen Jesus is the center of God's revelation, the key to truth and to life. Wherever we start to speak about the good news, this is where we must get to in the end. This is not a point that paganism can reach on its own. It is not deducible from the natural world, or something that can be arrived at by reason. It comes to us as *news*, as a revelation from outside. It is that news—and nothing else—that God has given us the responsibility to carry.

There, in Luke's account of it, the sermon finishes. Some scoff, others want to learn more—and some become believers. For these listeners at least what Paul has said has been not only *appropriate* communication but *effective* communication: genuine encounter between people who share a common humanity before God. That commonality is not subterfuge on Paul's part. He is not attempting to sneak in the gospel under cover of some pretended similarity. What we see in Athens is the theological truth of the last verses of Romans chapter 3 being applied in a living mission encounter.

BEGGARS AND BREAD

Mission there must be. Knowing what we now know about what God has done in Messiah Jesus and the crucial implications of that for every person, can we keep silent?

In his letter Paul supports every point he makes from the Scriptures. Let me do so as well. I want to remind you of an Old Testament story that sums up both the urgency of the good news and also the manner in which it must be proclaimed. The time is somewhere around the year 800 BC, and Samaria, capital city of Israel, is under siege. Encircled by the Aramean army, no one can go in or out. Inside the walls, the situation is desperate. Supplies of food have long ago run out. The most unlikely foodstuffs are sold for enormous prices. Among the poor, some in their utter desperation have turned to cannibalism.

Living in the no-man's-land just outside the city gate, there are four lepers. Outcasts from their own society, they debate about what they can do. If they stay where they are, death is certain. If they go to the Arameans, death is also highly probable. However, there is the remote chance that, instead of killing them, someone might take pity. Perhaps some Aramean soldier, showing off to his mates, might throw them a crust of bread. They decide to stake everything on that remote hope. But as in the early dawn they approach the camp of the besiegers, instead of a bustling community, there is silence. During the hours of darkness a panic has spread through the army, a rumor that a strong mercenary force is approaching to destroy the destroyers. The whole army has fled into the night, leaving the camp untouched.

The four men cannot believe their luck. Going from tent to tent they eat and drink their fill and stash away some treasure, too, as an investment in the future. But then they come to themselves. "What we are doing is wrong," one says to another. "All this is just the most amazing good news. If we are silent and wait until the morning everyone will blame us. We have got to go and tell the king's household." And so they return to the city. After worried discussion a cautious reconnaissance proves their report to be true, and the city is saved. And, in the tragic death of a formerly scornful and skeptical official, the word of Yahweh through his prophet Elisha is vindicated. It is a dramatic story: you need to read it for yourself.[131]

What does all of this have to do with us? Well, we are the four lepers in the story. Are you startled by that? I'm not myself especially thrilled about it. How much we would perhaps like to be the king, or the wealthy merchants in the city, to have some special privilege or standing before God! But the king and the wealthy merchants are dying too. Everybody's situation is desperate. "There is no one that is righteous, not even one," Paul has reminded us. That is the truth of it. The whole world stands silent before the judgment of God. But *that is not the end of the story.* Beyond human failure stands the faithfulness of God. "But now, completely independently of any human religious system . . . the righteousness of God himself has been revealed; the righteousness of God through the faithfulness of Jesus the Messiah." We stumble into the enemy camp and, look, the enemy is gone. Without any input from the inhabitants of the city, God himself has brought about a mighty deliverance.

We who know all this can't just sit around congratulating ourselves on the blessing, can we? We have news to share. We have no special standing before God. What we have, though, is the privilege of being entrusted with astonishing news. That is our dignity. God's deliverance was never intended only for us. His purpose is deliverance for the world. We are the news-carriers: news delivered not in pride or in arrogance or in any sense that we are somehow special. There is no going back to such thinking. Who was it who said that the good news was one beggar telling another beggar where to find bread? That is it precisely.

8

Endnotes
Romans 1–3

1. **Notes to the translation:**
   v. 1: **"slave"**: Translating this word as "servant" is a curiosity restricted to biblical translation. Greek has many words for "servant," *hyperpetes,* and *diakonos,* for example. But Paul doesn't use those words: he speaks of himself as *Paulos doulos*, not someone who chooses to serve but is owned body and soul; a man under orders.

   "called" is an adjective here, not a verb. The usual translation, "called *to be* an apostle" implies a status ("one of the apostles") and therefore an authority deriving from that status. Paul is not talking about an office, but a function. He is a man under orders, with a message to deliver that is not his own.

   v. 3–4: **"physical descent . . . with regard to his holy spirit"**: Literally, "according to flesh . . . according to a spirit of holiness." The latter expression is unique in the New Testament (indeed the word *holiness* is only used on two other occasions). Paul is not speaking of the Holy Spirit in the sense that we would use those capitals to indicate a direct identification with God (although the identification of Jesus with God in v. 7 is crystal clear). Rather, having described Jesus' place in the human world through *physical* descent, he is now describing Jesus' holy *spirit*, his complete commitment and unique relationship with God. This is not a description of Jesus' *makeup*, as if he had on the one hand a physical body and on the other an additional spiritual component. A human being is one thing. All of who Jesus is was descended from David. Rather, the resurrection declares that Jesus is not only David's heir by physical ancestry, but is also the one who filled-full the role of the king as the Son, chosen by God to represent him in leading his people. Now, born into the human line of David, God himself has come.

   "Jesus, the Jew's Messiah and the Christian's Lord": Sanday and Headlam, *Critical and Exigetical Commentary,* 27.

   v. 5: **"nations"**: The Greek word (*ethnos*, equivalent to the Hebrew *goy* and the Latin *gens*) means nation, people-group, and the New Testament virtually always uses it in the plural, whether the reference is to be nations themselves, or the people who comprise them. Though sometimes used of Israel itself (e.g., Luke 7:5), used *by* Israel it mostly means *everybody who is not us*: it is a term reflecting religious exclusivism. Paul's use of it in the context of the good news for everyone is a direct challenge to that attitude. The word *gentile* (commonly used in translations) is somewhat of an historical curiosity, being a transliteration into English of the *Latin* version of the word for nation. As a manufactured religious word without relation to any English idea, and which isn't current in ordinary speech, I think it should be avoided in translation, even if that means that a phrase is needed instead (which might be the case where it refers to *individuals* *from within* a people-group, as it sometimes is). The more common term for individual non-Jews in Paul's world, however, was *Greek* (see the note on the translation of v. 16). Incidentally, not only does using "nation" or "people from among the nations" refresh our understanding of what the word really means, it also makes sudden sense of Paul's argument about the universal scope of the good news in the light of God's promise to Abraham that he would be "the father *of many nations*" (patera pollōn ethnōn, Rom 4:17).

v. 6: "**called as** you **are by Jesus Messiah**": Lit. "you, also called ones of Jesus Messiah." The words "to belong to" in the translations are an interpretation. Paul uses the same word for *called* here as he does in verse 1. His calling is to a specific role, which he describes in verse 5. But then immediately he salutes the Roman church as being just as much (*kai*, in emphatic position) called by the risen Jesus as he is.

v. 7: "**Beloved**": Surely Paul has God's declaration at the baptism of Jesus (e.g., Luke 3:22) in mind—where precisely the same word is used. Note that the terms "beloved," "called," and "set apart" are all historic titles of *Israel*. That Paul has the confidence to address a predominantly non-Jewish congregation in these terms shows the way in which the good news has broken out of its former national boundaries. Cf. Rom 9:1–5.

"**called and holy**": The two words are coordinate. We are not called *to be* holy: Paul is describing what the Roman Christians are *now*. "Holy" is one of those religious words that needs to be rescued from what the tradition has made of it. It conjures up pictures of halos, antique robes, and pale faces unmarked by any real human experience. We have come to see holiness as the *absence* of something: sin, wrongdoing, failure. In fact, it is the *presence* of something: "the shining out of all that God is" as I once heard an old preacher describe it. It can also mean *dedicated, set apart for special use,* and the context suggests that this is probably its central meaning here. What is striking is that the word used here of the Roman Christians is the same word Paul has used just above to describe the spirit of *Jesus*. We will hear more about this later: see 8:28–30.

"**and [the]**": "The use of but one article before a number of nouns indicates that they are conceived as forming a certain unity, if not as identical." Zerwick, *Biblical Greek* §184.

"**Lord**" here is a divine title—as it probably is in v. 4b as well. In the old religion, as the Name of God (YHWH) was considered too holy to be spoken, "Lord" was always substituted for it when the Old Testament was read. Its application to Jesus after the resurrection is therefore an unmistakable recognition of his divine status. At the same time, like "Father" in the preceding phrase, "Lord" reflects *a particular aspect* of God's relationship to us. It is the covenant name: it identifies Jesus as both God himself and also our representative, the one in whom humanity is embodied.

2. Ps 2:7–9. Note that God too can often be addressed as King (especially in the Psalms: see 5:2, 24:7ff, 47:2ff, 74:12, 98:6, etc.). The earthly king represents the heavenly King: that is what "Son of God" means.

3. As the angel declares to Mary at the announcement of Jesus' birth: "He will be great, and will be called the Son of the Most High, and *the Lord God will give to him the throne of his ancestor David*" (Luke 1:31–32). Jesus would inherit David's throne: this is what it meant to be the "Son of God."

4. This is not the only place in the New Testament where this is made plain. Always Jesus' identity as Son is linked to the resurrection. In an evangelistic rather than a declaratory context, Paul's address before the pagan philosophers in Athens in Acts 17:30–31 shows how central this truth is to both the content and the scope of the news he bears. (Look too at Acts 2:36, the words of the risen Jesus in Matt 28:18, and Heb 1:1–4.) The importance of what Paul is saying cannot be overemphasized. *Romans* is not about intriguing religious concepts that might be fascinating and even helpful to those who like such things. The message Paul carries is about *the way God rules the world*. Whatever else it is, his declaration here about Jesus is a political claim. In contrast to the emperor, who styled himself "the son of God" (that is, the son of his divine father the previous emperor), Jesus alone can truly be called the Son of God.

5. While phrases such as this one can readily be translated from one language to another, the

connotations and range of meaning that they carry in each language may be quite different. The biblical languages had a much wider range of meaning for the word "son" than English does, where it is almost exclusively used for the idea of physical descent. Describing their personality, James and John are the "sons of thunder," for example (Matt 3:17); disciples are "sons of light" (John 12:36, 1 Thess 5:5) or "sons of the resurrection" (Luke 20:36); Judas is the "son of perdition" (John 17:12); the name Barnabas (Acts 13) means "son of encouragement." Even within the family non-Western cultures understand the word *son* to mean much more than mere physical descent: the son is the one who resembles the father in character, the one who stands in continuity with the father, the one who bears the father's life on into the next generation. It is in this sense that the letter to the Hebrews speaks of Jesus as "the reflection of the Father's glory and the exact imprint of his very being" (Heb 1:3). Consider also how John 1:1 defines the meaning of "Son" in 1:18 and John 1:49–51, where for Nathaniel, *Son of God* means the same as *the King of Israel*—but then in Jesus' response is given a much richer and deeper meaning (v. 51).

6. That is, both the word *Father* and the phrase *Lord Jesus Messiah* qualify the word *God*. In support of this we should note that everywhere in what precedes and follows through to the end of chapter 8 Jesus is spoken of not as *the* Lord but as *our* Lord. In this verse the possessive pronoun modifies the proper noun "God"—and therefore *both* of the subsequent qualifying descriptions. Understanding the sentence in this way must not blur the fact that in that second term of that united expression Paul is referring to the real, embodied, risen Jesus Messiah. It is not so much that God has descended into human nature, but that in Messiah Jesus humanity has been taken up into the being of God. There is mystery here. "Where is the human being Jesus now?" for example, is a question which is inevitably framed in terms of the physical, space-time world that is the only one that we know. At this point we have neither the concepts with which to frame a better question nor the insight necessary to understand the answer even if it were given to us. It is, I believe, an answer that we will understand not in our mind but in our experience, as we too, crossing the threshold of death, find ourselves caught up into the mighty current of the resurrection life.

7. **Notes to the translation**:

    v. 9 **"with my whole being"**: Lit. "with my spirit." The spirit is not separable part of a person, as classical philosophy and Western theology too often encourages us to believe. Rather it is the essence of a person, the person reaching out in relationship to God and others, the passion and the personality, that which makes a person a person rather than merely an animated body.

    v. 12 **"each other's faith"**: This is the only place in the letter where faith is spoken of as a thing in itself, unrelated to the relationship to God to which it must refer. A strong alternative translation would be to read Paul as speaking about the faith/faithfulness that exists *between himself and the Roman congregation* (cf. "you by me and me by you"). He has promised to come but has not been able to do so; in a sense he has broken faith with them, something which he now means to remedy by means of a visit.

    v. 13 **"Brothers and sisters"** (throughout the translation): In English "brother" and "sister" are quite different words, but Greek has one word, which means "born from the same womb," and which can apply to either male or female siblings; the distinction is indicated by either a masculine or feminine ending (cf. John 11:2, brother, 11:5, sister). The plural (as here) is therefore inclusive: although the ending is masculine (it has to be one or the other) Paul clearly intends to include the women in the congregation, a number of whom are greeted by name in chapter 16, e.g., "our sister (*adelphēn*) Phoebe," 16:1.

    v. 14 **"Civilized and uncivilized"**: Lit. "Greeks and barbarians." This set of four terms is also an idiom: Paul means "everybody, whoever they are"; in English we might say "all, rich and poor, old and young."

    v. 15 **"If I get the chance"**: Free translation; more literally "as for me."

8. Chapter 16 includes greetings to the Roman congregation from Gaius (probably the Gaius of 1 Cor 1:14) and Erastus "the city financial officer." We know from a Corinthian inscription that there was a treasurer of Corinth with this name, and there seems a reasonable possibility that

this is the same person. Phoebe, the deacon mentioned in 16:1, comes from Cenchreae, Corinth's port; if she was the letter-carrier she would have needed to have known Paul well in order to fulfill her commission,

9. The most detailed discussion of the collection that we have is in 2 Cor 8 and 9, but the subject crops up several times in other letters as well.

10. This was the right of every Roman citizen.

11. Phil 3:10–14, from NRSV with my own translation of v. 10.

12. As in the same letter, Phil 1:23 and 3:20–21 make clear.

13. **Notes to the translation:**
v. 16 **"to the Jew first and also the non-Jew"**: Literally *"to the Jew first, and also to the Greek."* The way words have changed their meaning over time can confuse us here. We have noted above (endnote 9) that the word gentile is not (as we often use it today) a singular but a *collective* noun: it means "nation"; the gentiles are the people-groups of the world; where it is used of individuals or groups of individuals that is always the wider context. The term "Greek," on the other hand, *is* the singular noun for a non-Jew; it is the word that applies to individual people (Rom 1:14, 16; 2:9–10; and cf. Mark 7:26, Acts 16:1; 17:12, Gal 2:3. In Gal 3:20 Paul doesn't say "neither Jew nor gentile" but "neither Jew nor *Greek*"). Greeks in this sense don't necessarily come from a land called Greece, though of course they may; rather, they are foreigners in general: the people of every nationality who shared the common Greek culture of the day. That could include Macedonians or Galatians or Romans or Cretans—or indeed, many inhabitants of Palestine and Jerusalem itself (remember the "Hellenist"—Greek—and the "Hebrew" parties in the days of the early church, Acts 6:1). It is a common enough form of speech: the Lummi people of Puget Sound in the American Northwest called all Europeans "Bostons," no matter whether they came from that city, from elsewhere in the United States, or from Europe. As used by Jewish people both *gentiles* (other nations) and *Greek* (non-Jews) had a pejorative overtone (for a pejorative use of the latter see Acts 21:28; in Gal 2:15 Paul uses the former—with ironic intent—as a synonym for "sinner"). Together they meant "the others, everybody else, those who are not the privileged recipients of the covenant as we are." The shocking nature of what Paul is saying here should therefore be immediately apparent: God's salvation is no longer tied to the circumstances of nationality and birthright.

Religious communities have always had expressions like this. We talk about Christians and *non-Christians*—the latter being people whose identity is, apparently, defined by what they are not. Who are they? Well, they aren't us. In my youth we also occasionally, I blush to say, spoke about *outsiders*—and there is the religious meaning of the terms "gentiles" and "Greeks" in a nutshell. The gentiles are the heathen *nations*, the Greeks the individual *outsiders*: "those who don't know God like we do." Later in the letter we will see Paul using the religiously-loaded sense of these terms several times—and doing so completely subversively. From within the exclusive Jewish religious thought-world that he knew so well, and from the Jewish Scriptures themselves, he demonstrates that there is no "inside" and "outside" anymore, and that in fact there never was in the first place. All people without exception are under the judgment—and therefore the mercy—of God. A final comment: it is important not to get distracted by the idea of *Jewish national identity* in these early chapters. Paul will have much to say about the destiny of the Jewish nation in chapters 9–11. Here his point is simply that the good news of God breaks all the traditional boundaries of exclusivism. If he were writing to a Christian church today he would undoubtedly say "to those inside the church—and also those outside of it." There are no lines we can draw that define a zone outside of which the Spirit of God is not at work.

v. 17 **"righteousness"**: this is not a word in common use in twenty-first-century English. Unfortunately we do not have an alternative word that fully expresses the first century concept. Worthy attempts to express the word in twenty-first-century language such as "God's way of righting wrong" (NEB) or "God's saving justice" (JB, following Jerome's similar attempt with the Latin *justicia* in the Vulgate) have the unfortunate weakness of bearing very little relation to the biblical meaning of the word. The only alternative is to retain the word, but to fill it full once again of the meaning it had for Paul and his contemporaries—especially those versed in the Old Testament Scriptures in which it is such a key concept.

14. In a delightful serendipity for twenty-first-century young people the addition of the word "so" restores the idiom exactly: "I am *so* not ashamed!"

15. I have already silently modernized a similar idiom in 1:13, where in the Greek text Paul says "I do not want you to be unaware"—meaning "I want you to clearly know."

16. Storytelling in non-literate cultures works the same way. Agathe Thornton describes her observation of this in New Zealand Maori culture:

    "The oral story-teller's intense eagerness responds to the intensity of listening which surrounds him, and he immediately indicates the whole of the story by telling the beginning and end of it in order to –satisfy at once the desire of his audience to know what they are going to hear about. Then he elaborates 'appositionally' as we shall call it, on the detail of how all this came about . . . this 'appositional expansion' is finally rounded off by a return to its starting point, the 'initial statement' as we shall call it, and from here the story-teller continues with his narration." Thornton, "Two Features," 157.

    We can still see traces of this pattern in the reports of Jesus' oral teaching. One example is Matt 19:30—20:16, where Jesus makes an initial *statement* ("Many who are first will be last, and the last will be first"), *tells a story* to illustrate the point, and then *recapitulates* ("and *that* is how the last will be first and the first will be last!").

17. Although various aids to finding one's way around were used from early times, the system of chapters and verses that we use today was devised early in the thirteenth century.

18. Dillard, *Teaching,* 40–41; punctuation hers.

19. Compare the angel's announcement in Matt 1:21 that the promised child's name would be *Jesus* (God saves) "because *he will save his people from their sins.*" The promised deliverance is not from God's wrath against sin; it is not from judgment or the consequences of sin. It is quite specifically deliverance *from the sins themselves.* People will not have to sin any more. The life and death of Jesus also delivers us from these other things, but that is a downstream effect. They are not the issue in the giving of the name.

20. The Greek word in v. 16, *pisteuō,* is a verb, and is usually translated "to have faith." Which illustrates the problem; the verb "to put one's faith in," or to "trust" is replaced by *another* verb ("have"), with faith as the *noun.* That suggests that faith is something that an individual can *have,* rather than, as it is, *a relationship existing between two persons.* You can't *have* faith. You can only have faith in *someone.* It is a description of one side of a relationship. Hence in the translation I have rendered *pisteuō* as "puts his faith *in him.*" The latter two words must be added in English to make clear something that is implicit in the Greek.

21. A partial comparison can be drawn with the ideas of trust and trustworthiness. No one *has* trust. They put their trust in someone who is trustworthy. Unlike faithfulness, however, trustworthiness *is* a quality that a person can have. Someone can be trustworthy without anyone ever actually putting their trust in them. Faithfulness is never free-floating like that. It is always faithfulness towards someone. It is not an aspect of character, but one side of a relationship.

22. Matt 17:20. Needless to say this is hyperbolic speech: many bizarre conclusions have been drawn from attempts to take it literally. Popular preachers also often miss the irony in the mustard seed saying. "Wow!" their thinking goes. "If that could happen with just such a tiny amount of faith, what could be done with a *spoonful?*" This complete reversal of Jesus' meaning would be hilarious if this kind of teaching had not deluded and discouraged so many good people over the years.

23. "Learn a language, understand a culture." Western culture starts from the individual. The ancient thought-world (and much of the majority world today) starts from community and sees the

individual only in relation to that. Another word in which this is evident is *charis*, which is often translated *grace*. But the same word also means "gratitude." Grace elicits gratitude, gratitude calls forth grace. It is a relationship, as seen from one side or the other.

24. The alternative versions quoted are NRSV, NIV, and Phillips respectively. That the reading in the translation is correct is confirmed in two ways: (1) Paul's omission of both possible pronouns in his citation of Hab 2:4 in the sentence that follows. The Hebrew text of that verse has "the righteous shall live *by faithfulness*." The LXX version, surely also known to Paul, reads "the righteous will live *from my* faithfulness." When Paul cites the quotation he removes the personal pronoun (which is an interpretative addition by the LXX in any case), in order to retain the double sense of *ek pisteōs* in v. 17 that is the point of *ek pisteōs eis pistin* in v. 16 (2). In Rom 3:22, as he proclaims God's answer to our human sin and incapacity, Paul repeats the double statement of this verse: "The righteousness of God has been revealed, that is, the righteousness of God *through the faithfulness* of Jesus the Messiah, towards *all who have faith*."

25. One of the puzzles of biblical theology is the consistent reading of *righteousness* language as *justice* language. Justice is a part of righteousness of course, but only as an aspect of right behavior in interpersonal and communal relationships. If you have a concordance it is worth looking up the word righteousness and running your eye down the entries for the Old Testament to begin with. You will find that every occurrence is personal and relational. "A person is righteous when they meet certain claims which another has on them in virtue of relationship. Even the righteousness of God is primarily his covenantal rule in fellowship with his people" (Schrenk, *Righteousness*). "The way in which it is used shows that *sedeq* [the Hebrew word for righteousness] is out and out a term denoting relationship, and that it does this in the sense of referring to a real relationship between two parties . . . and not to the relationship of an object under consideration to an idea" (H. Cremer, quoted in von Rad, *Old Testament Theology*). This is the concept of righteousness that flows on into New Testament thought.

Despite this biblical evidence we find commentators and theologians everywhere understanding the word *dikaosyne* as an abstract state of guilt or innocence before a law, implicitly God's law. However the discussion begins, the word "forensic" will crop up sooner or later. We know abstractly that when Paul in letters like Romans refers to the Torah, he means the first five books of the Old Testament, including their narrative sections, the whole constituting the factual description of and covenantal basis for a relationship. But when we come to *interpret the text* we do so as if by the term he meant some kind of legal code, the Ten Commandments perhaps. The consequences of this for thought about God and our relationship with him are disastrous. As to understanding the letter, where this understanding doesn't make the text incomprehensible, it twists Paul's meaning into an alien and forbidding shape.

How did this situation come about? The English term "justification" reflects the pervasive influence of the Vulgate, the Latin translation of the Bible that was *the only text available to European scholars for almost 1500 years*. There Jerome translated both the Hebrew *sedaqah* and the Greek *dikaosyne* by the Latin *iustitia*, which means just, equitable, fair, lawful; that is, evaluated by reference to an external standard, especially the law. The Law becomes merely the law. The intensely personal and relational connotations in the biblical texts and in the biblical thought-world are quite lost. Even God himself becomes subject to an external standard to which, though he may have established it himself, he is inexorably bound. The whole concept of righteousness is diminished, depersonalized, and rendered abstract. The translational tradition suggests that the gloomy lenses bequeathed us by all those centuries of dependence upon the Vulgate are hard to throw off. But thrown off they must be if we are to even begin to understand Paul's message of the righteousness of God in Romans.

Those with access to a library and keen to explore the biblical concept of righteousness further might like to consult von Rad, *Old Testament Theology* 1:370ff; Reimer in Van Gemeren, *NIDOTT* 3:744–69; Bultmann, *Theology of the New Testament* 1:270–79; Seebass in Brown, *NIDNTT* 3:352–65; Schrenk in Kittel, *TDNT,* 2:192–210; and Leenhardt, *Epistle to the Romans*, 126–27.

26. Paul does indeed see God as the judge of the world, and righteousness as the standard by which we are judged at the last day. But the measure of that is not a legal code but *the character of God himself*. That is how we could best describe the Old Testament Law: as the character of God written down in terms of human behavior. It is only as that idea was externalized to become an impersonal legal requirement that the problems arose for Israel. The requirements of an abstract legal code and a set of ritual observances are very different from that of a living relationship. Israel hadn't broken the Law, they had *lost God*.

27. English versions translate *dikaiosyne* in different ways, and sometimes that is helpful and sometimes it is confusing. In every case, however, it is the concept of persons that must govern the way we understand the word. Even with regard to the kinds of property or behavior issues that needed to be judicially decided, to act justly was not simply a legal but a *personal* requirement.

28. Readers of editions of the NIV earlier than the 2011 revision may be puzzled that instead of "the righteousness of God" their translation speaks of "a righteousness *that comes from God*." Although not absolutely impossible, this is a very forced reading of the Greek. You don't need to be a Greek scholar to see this. If the text did in fact read "a righteousness that comes from God," then instead of "the power of God" v. 16 should read "a power that *comes from* God"; and instead of "the anger of God," v. 18 should read "an anger that *comes from* God." The Greek construction is identical in all three cases. Why then this reading, which has stood in one of the major English translations for more than 30 years? A particular theological interpretation that goes back to Augustine (*On the Spirit and the Letter*, ch. 9), later picked up by Luther among others, is driving the translation. The arguments that commentators such as Cranfield propose in support of it are theological rather than textual, and are needlessly complicated by the Western misunderstanding of the faith/faithfulness relationship. The early NIV reading does tell us something; it just doesn't tell us anything about what Paul is saying. And this is not a small loss: mistranslation of this phrase together with an understanding of "faith" as a human quality transforms these mighty verses about the character of the God who acts to save into something that is about us. Later in the letter we will indeed learn about a righteousness that God's gift calls into being in us. We will come to that in due time. But here Paul is talking about the revelation of the character of *God*.

29. Our difficulty in recognizing that Paul is speaking about the righteousness of God (rather than a righteousness that *comes from* God) comes from a deficient understanding of righteousness. If righteousness means being impeccable before the law, having a clean slate, if it means the state following forgiveness, then of course none of that applies to God. Biblical people should know better: understood as a description of character, righteousness (alongside faithfulness, uprightness, truthfulness, justice, and other qualities) is freely ascribed to God everywhere in the Old Testament. The Psalms are particularly rich in such references: see 4:1, 7:9, 11:7, 71:24, 116:5, 129:4, 145:17 for examples.

30. Many English versions put in a heading before v. 18, and as a consequence the transition in Paul's thought from what he has said in v. 17 can appear puzzling, even abrupt. For those of his hearers who knew Hab 2:4 in its context, however, Paul's move would have been completely logical. God's call there to Israel to live faithfully is immediately followed by a long denunciation of the wicked, the idolaters (v. 18–19), the drunkards and sexually exploitative (vv. 15–16), the covetous, the haughty, the treacherous, and the ruthless (vv. 5–6, 9–12). For Habakkuk it was the wicked and godless Babylonian invader that was in view (Hab 2:8), but the principles he states clearly apply to wickedness in general. Paul is therefore not just quoting an isolated proof text, but taking the theological thrust of the *whole* of the ancient prophecy and re-preaching it in the personal and individual categories of his day. If this is correct it provides strong support for the case that will be made later for reading Rom 1–3, not with reference to Greek or Roman rhetorical models, Paul's exposure to we can only guess at, but in the light of the rhetorical techniques of the prophets, his mastery of which we can be certain.

31. Notice that God is at the center of Paul's argument. People are not *independently* wicked. Anything that human beings do has meaning and reality only in relation to God. Human beings are

never an "other" over against God. We never create meaning, positively or negatively. Whether we live in faith or turn away, God is always God. This principle will be reaffirmed when Paul turns to the problem of unbelief in chapters 9–11.

32. While it isn't accurate as a translation of the word righteousness, perhaps this is the idea behind the New English Bible's rendering of "the righteousness of God" as "God's way of putting things right."

33. The present tense of the verb indicates the present, living quality of God's anger. It is not a judgment stored up for the future; it is not a thing separable from God himself.

34. Bruner, *Christbook*, 92. Cf. also Barth: "The judgment of God is not in conflict with his mercy. In all its ineluctable sharpness and severity it is a form of the mercy with which he keeps faith with man . . . It is the holy fire of His Creator-love consuming and destroying the sin, rebellion and self-contradiction of man" (*Dogmatics in Outline* 3.2, 32).

35. I am thinking especially of the discovery that the universe had a *beginning* at a time that we can date with remarkable precision; the realization that the fundamental constants of the universe are uniquely set so as to produce a universe that could, in contrast to all other possible universes, produce life; the breaking wave of new discovery that challenges the Darwinian model of evolution as a cycle of random mutation and natural selection which takes millennia and in which organisms themselves are purely passive; and the discovery that particles at the most fundamental level of matter react in the presence of a personal observer.

36. Set alongside recent books like David Bentley Hart's *The Experience of God* (Yale, 2013) which mount a compelling case against atheist simplicities, an older work by Michael Polanyi, *Personal Knowledge* (Routledge, 1962) is particularly helpful in exposing the falsity of the subjective/objective distinction—as well as being hugely illuminating about the nature of knowledge in general.

37. Acts 17:16–33.

38. The Greek word is *kardia*, heart, as in v. 24, where the phrase is translated "the desires of *the heart*." Paul is not repeating himself in the two halves of the verse. Although in biblical thought the heart can sometimes be the source of thought and decision, the concept is wider than merely the *mind* (for which there is a distinct Greek word): it is also the center of the emotions, the will, the whole of the inner life. There are more ways of discerning truth than through reason alone. What Paul is saying is that the instruments of *the whole person* have become clouded and unreliable. There is a refusal to discern, and as a result the equipment that enables discernment has become fundamentally unreliable.

39. Luke 11:34, 35.

40. Dawkins, *Selfish Gene*, 3, 24.

41. Ruse and Wilson, "Moral Philosophy," 179, my italics.

42. See Stanovich, *Robot's Rebellion*.

43. Notice what happens when the knowledge of God is lost, or, as Paul would insist, when it is rejected. It is not that human beings take up God's role, become worshiped as gods themselves—although the last hundred years has produced some striking examples of how that too can be possible. Instead, human beings *diminish*: lost in a vast and indifferent cosmos, we are at the mercy of our animal impulses, constrained by our genetic history, and subject to the remorseless unfolding of a mindless process. It is not as if in rejecting God we gain a brave new freedom and autonomy. Quite the reverse. God gives us up to what we want in our thought as well as in our behavior—and when we get what we choose it turns out to be not quite what we expected. When we cut ourselves off from the source of meaning, we become meaningless. How could we expect anything else?

44. Nothing in these paragraphs should be taken to suggest that we should be other than

passionately interested in the progress of scientific discovery and all that it can tell us about the wonders of our world and our universe. There is nothing to be afraid of in any of this enterprise—although some of the *applications* of scientific research undoubtedly bring with them the possibility of serious physical and moral dangers. The problems occur when scientific discovery is bent to serve the purposes of an atheistic religious ideology. When free of such bias all facts are God's facts, and one of the clearest indications of our nature as being in some way "made in God's image" is our very ability (something explained by no physical theory) to explore, analyze, and discover the world. We are beings able to "think God's thoughts after him," and that very ability should give us pause when we are tempted to accept willfully reductionist theories such as those we have been describing. One of the small delights of each day for me is an email that comes in from a website called Science Daily which contains a summary of the research stories on genetics and evolution that are about to be published in the leading scientific journals—a summary written in language that even an amateur like me can understand. Whether we look out into the universe (where our telescopes can detect galaxies whose light has been traveling towards us almost since the moment of creation 13.7 billion years ago), into the structure of matter (populated by strange particles, some of whose behavior seems strangely purposive), or out across the infinite variety of living things, the wonder and mystery of creation confronts us at every turn. "Glory and honor and power are yours by right, our Lord and God! For you created all things, and by your will they exist now, and were created then." So in John's vision sing the representatives of humanity in response to the worship of the creatures (Rev 4:11). It is a song that we too can share.

45. Barth, *Dogmatics in Outline*, 55.

46. Paul didn't write in chapters. They were added later as a convenient way of finding one's way around. The break here could not be more precisely placed to destroy Paul's argument, and thus throw our understanding of the whole first three chapters into confusion. We will come across similar problems with the placement of the divisions between chapters 4 and 5, plus 7 and 8.

47. In Matt 23:15, for example, Jesus speaks of the Pharisees as those who would "cross sea and land to make a single convert." He assumes that the existence of an organized missionary program is familiar to his audience. In John 7:35, upon hearing Jesus speak about the limited time he has with them, and that soon they would search for him without success, his audience ask, "Does he intend to go to the Dispersion among the Greeks (that is the non-Jews) and teach the Greeks?" The fact that this possibility comes to mind for at least some among Jesus' listeners indicates that the idea of such a mission is not strange to them. It was only after the formal split between Christian congregation and synagogue—which in the case of Rome would occur within less than a decade from the date of Paul's letter—that Judaism turned its back upon foreign mission, retreating inwards once again to its identity as an exclusive "chosen people."

48. Dunn cites a number of Greek and Roman sources bewailing the growing fashionableness of the Jewish religion, and warning of the dangers that it posed for the established religion of the empire (Dunn, *Romans 1–8*, xlvi and l). The phenomenon was not limited to the Mediterranean world, as the story of the (presumably racially African) financial controller for the queen of Ethiopia in Acts 8:26–40 shows.

49. Cf. the report of the Council of Jerusalem in Acts 15:21, where in acknowledging converted gentiles as full members of the Christian community, it is implied they will already be familiar with the Mosaic law, because "in every city for generations past Moses . . . has been read aloud every Sabbath in the synagogues."

50. When, after regular debate in the Corinthian synagogue with "both Jews *and Greeks*," Paul's message is eventually rejected by the Jews (Acts 18:6), he declares his intention to take his message to those traditionally outside the Jewish community. But those to whom he goes are by no means pure pagans: he goes to the house of a non-Jewish God-fearer whose house is right next door to the synagogue (v. 7). From the synagogue itself the presiding official also joins the Christian congregation; and so the mixed-ethnicity, *Old Testament-grounded* church in Corinth is born.

Although Paul himself had not visited Rome that something similar was the case there is clear from chapters 2, 3, 11, 16 of the letter. Cf. also in the story of Pentecost in that detail noted in Acts 2:10 about the pre-Christian situation in Rome.

51. Acts 17:16–34.

52. What does it mean to fall short of God's glory? Coming so soon after the description of willful and deliberate *opposition* to the will of God that appears in some of the Bible verses that Paul has just quoted, it offers a different perspective on the problem. Paul quotes the verses about willful opposition to demonstrate to us good religious people that even our own Scriptures give us no escape route. The metaphor of falling short is something different. Paul elsewhere uses the word that is translated "fall short" to mean *lacking* (1 Cor 1:7), *inferior* (2 Cor 11:5, 12:7), *being in need* (2 Cor 11:9, Phil 4:12). He is describing something that all people are missing, some essential aspect of life that we are deficient in, something we are failing to reach: *the glory of God*. The word "glory" can appear to be just a bit of religious language, but here its meaning is very precise. It means (in Godet's words) "the divine splendor which shines forth from God himself, *and which he communicates to all who live in union with him.*" With regard to human beings, St. Irenaeus summed it up in a famous aphorism: "The glory of God is a person fully alive." To be fully alive! The longing of every human heart . . . and we fail at it. We fall short. Willful and deliberate sin is one thing, but all of us, no matter how we ache to be whole, fail to live a fully human life. What we fail to live up to, though, is not *our* ideals or our aspirations but the glory of *God*. God is the Lord of it—and, Paul tells us, God has acted to secure that glory on our behalf. We fail to be a fully human person, but God through Messiah Jesus both declares and empowers us to be that. "In baptism we have died and been buried with him," Paul will tell us a little later, "so that, just as Messiah was raised by the glory of the Father, *so we too might live a new life*" (6:4). There is no change of subject; verses 23 and 24 are part of the one sentence. The making righteous of v. 24 means nothing other than the act of God that puts right both eternally and in our practical life experience the "falling short" of v. 23.

53. Note that Paul is talking about sexual activity here, i.e., the physical sexualization of same-gender sexual desire. He says nothing about that desire in itself, or about what our culture has taught us to call sexual orientation. It is unlikely that he would have thought in those terms—though Jesus may have: Matt 19:12. At issue for Paul here is simply a matter of behavior.

54. Jesus uses the technique of prophetic confrontation as well. The most obvious example is the story in John 8:1–11 of the woman caught in the act of adultery. "Let those of you without sin hurl the first stone," says Jesus to her accusers, writing in the sand. "And when they heard it," John tells us, "they melted away one by one, until only Jesus and the woman were left. 'Neither do I condemn you,' said Jesus. 'Go your way, and don't sin anymore.'" Both sides of that statement are important. The parable of the Pharisee and the tax collector in Luke 18:9–14 is another example. The Bible-believing Pharisee "prays *with himself,*" so Luke tells us, while the sinful tax collector "goes down to his house justified" (notice the use of this word, so important in Romans). Other examples could be multiplied.

How do we read these stories? As children we learned when listening to a story to identify with the heroes and to despise the villains. Do we as adults still do this with the Gospels? In the Gospel stories it is natural for us to identify with the tax collectors and the scoundrels, because that is what Jesus did. We easily lose sight of how shocking, how subversive of all good behavior, Jesus' behavior seemed to good religious people in their time. Hearing the word Pharisee we instinctively think of the wrong-headed and the hypocritical. In fact the Pharisees were the serious, Bible-believing, moral, God-fearing people of their day. They weren't anything at all like us, were they? Failing to see that they were, we miss the point; the force of Jesus' challenge passes us by completely.

55. **Notes to the translation:**

vv. 9–10 **"religious person . . . non-religious person"**: Lit. "Jew and *Greek.*" In this phrase "Jew" does not have a primarily ethnic reference. "Jew and Greek" is a global expression for "everybody"; "Jew" being shorthand for the good God-fearing person who knows the Law, in contrast to the "Greek" (also not a racial reference) for those outside the religious community who nonetheless show that the knowledge of God is written on their hearts. The issue is not ethnicity in either case. If it was, then there would be no category within which the Roman Christians could find themselves.

v. 12 **"it is true that"** expresses the force of "*gar . . . kai.*"

v. 15 **"The outcome that the Law was designed to bring about"**: Lit. "the work of the Law," not in this case the "*works* of the law," which in Romans is always an expression for something negative or inadequate (3:20, 28, 4:2–6, etc.), but the effect which the law was designed to produce in people's lives.

"Their reasoning among themselves": the words *metaxu allelōn tōn logismōn,* literally "the reasonings between each other" are often taken to mean "conflicting thoughts," i.e., as an explanation of the way conscience works *inside the mind of a person.* On this reading the "others" are thoughts not people. This is, however, a strange way to translate the sentence. (1) It ignores the emphatic place of the phrase "between each other": it is *in parallel with* rather than *descriptive of* the conscience of the individual. (2) It ignores the plural personal pronouns in the surrounding context, which strongly suggest that they and the "between each other" refer to the same subject, i.e., people. Compare a similar usage in 12:16, *eis allelous,* "toward one another." (3) Taking "between each other" to refer to thoughts appears strange: can thoughts really argue and advocate between each other, as individuals might do? I suggest that the translation reflects the influence of what Krister Stendahl called "the introspective conscience of the West," i.e., the overriding importance for us of the struggle within an individual human heart. But Paul is writing about the gentiles, the nations, *as a group*. All of the pronouns are plural; apart from *work* (here translated "the *effect* that the Law was intended to bring about") the word *conscience* alone is singular. *Individually*, Paul says, the conscience bears witness to the truth of God in the heart (v. 15a), and *collectively*, between persons, there is also a witness, a public perception of what just and righteous behavior is. *Together* these two witnesses show that the law of God is written on the heart of the gentiles. What Paul is saying is that *righteousness is not just the property of religious people.* It is also a concern among the nations. In the collective sense of right and justice in the wider world, and the way in which judgments are made on that basis, we have a further witness to the law of God written on the heart of all people. Is it possible that a degree of theological resistance to this conclusion might be a further factor in pushing us towards a different reading? That a particular individual might have some notion of the law of God without the letter of it is one thing; that the nations in general might have it is quite another.

56. This is a particular challenge for those of us who grew up in a strong doctrinal tradition. John White describes how, as a traveling Inter-Varsity Fellowship staff member in Latin America, he was astonished to discover that Roman Catholic students (who in those days had had little or no exposure to Scripture) and communist students were far better at Bible study than students from evangelical churches. In group study, the communists and Catholics were quick to see what the passage *actually said*. Many evangelical students, on the other hand, had a mental block at this point. They seemed only able to see what the Bible was *supposed to say*. It was as though they screened Bible statements through a doctrinal filter, seeing that which they had been trained to expect ("It can't say *that* because the Bible doesn't teach that."). White, *Fight,* 44.

57. Should we still be uneasy about the orthodoxy of this statement we should note that Paul is speaking completely in the spirit of his Master: among the many things that Jesus says on this subject look for example at Matt 7:21–3.

58. Deut 32:47.

59. What Paul is saying here is important lest we misunderstand the force of 1:18–23, where it could appear that God's judgment is poured out particularly on *the pagans,* i.e., those who do not have the Scripture, those outside the covenant community. The pride and sense of special privilege that we can feel when we think that, because of our possession of the truth of God, we are somehow God's favorites is of course precisely the attitude that Paul is playing on in those verses,

in preparation for the dramatic confrontation of 2:1ff. But now that that attitude has been shown up in all its threadbare presumption, Paul leads us deeper into the ways of God with all people, not just those who have had the privilege of his special revelation. The lesson here is the need to pay careful attention to the rhetorical context of any statement of Scripture before we too quickly appropriate it as part of a systematic theology.

60. The passage generates consternation among the theologians as well, as the history of teaching and commentary-writing on this chapter demonstrates. Innumerable pages have been written discussing who the people might be that Paul is referring to here. "It is very foolish to think, as has been thought, that in 2:14–15 Paul was speaking of just any Gentiles who did in fact fulfil the Law because of some moral law of nature written in their hearts" (Barth, *Shorter Commentary*, 6, as one example among many). But putting Barth's Lutheranism and an antipathy to the idea of natural theology aside, it is difficult to conclude that Paul is not saying exactly that—although Barth is correct that he is not talking about some vague "moral law of nature" but very precisely about the Law of the Creator God himself. (Convinced that Paul can't mean what he seems to mean, Barth comes to the conclusion that the only possible candidates are the non-Jewish Christians in the Roman community itself.)

61. Jer 31:31, 33.

62. Heb 10:16,17; 2 Cor 3:3.

63. Heb 4:15.

64. And also and for the same reasons, Paul will go on to say later in the letter, to be our defense counsel. But we anticipate.

65. The conscience of the individual and the way righteous and unrighteous behavior is dealt with within the group will, he says, "accuse *or perhaps* even excuse" the peoples of the nations on the day of judgment. The matter is left indefinite. It is not Paul's concern. It is God's business, not his or ours.

66. As we have already seen (see "Christians in the Crosshairs" above) Paul is writing (1) to a largely non-*racially*-Jewish community, which is however (2) deeply enculturated in the Jewish Scriptures, worship, and religious practice, and for whom therefore (3) the term "Jew" is synonymous with "worshiper of the One True God," i.e., something which they own and strongly identify with. The two circles are distinct *ethnically*, but map onto each other exactly in terms of teaching, and of emotional and religious commitment. They are precisely *one* community.

   A careful reading of Paul's text makes this clear. In 2:14 he describes the situation of gentiles who, while not possessing the Law, nonetheless do what it requires. But this is not of course the group with which the Roman church identifies itself, nor does Paul make that identification. The pronouns alone make that impossible. They, while racially gentile, *do* in fact possess the Law. If this were not so the prophetic confrontation of 2:1ff would be meaningless. So the Roman Christians are not the Greeks, outside the pale of the Law, who nonetheless may possibly do what it requires. Where they must identify themselves in that phrase, and where Paul undoubtedly expects them to identify themselves, is with the term Jew. He knows that the majority of them are not ethnic Jews. Rather, they are what we might call *theological Israel*: outside the racial boundaries, but nonetheless deeply rooted in and committed to Jewish religion. They have been grafted into the rootstock of Israel and are inheritors of the promises (11:17). It is this same theological rather than ethnic shorthand that continues in 2:17. Paul's confrontational gaze does not waver. The pronouns are still "you" all the way. Those he addresses in 2:17 are the same as the "you, whoever you are" in 2:1.

   This is where our literary (rather than oral/aural) culture and our distance from the historical situation become a problem for us. We come to 2:17 and the word "Jew" and say "aha, this is what he is talking about! He is talking about the Jews, who are different from Christians. Therefore he can't really have been talking to us after all! In all of this he is actually talking to those sad failures, the Jews." And so from then on we ignore the pronouns and the whole thrust of the rhetoric. Flicking back and starting again, we construe the passage from 2:1 as if it was descriptive not of us good Christian religious people, but of somebody else.

The problem with this strategy is that it doesn't work. Within an oral culture, such a move was not possible. You couldn't turn back. You couldn't move back and forth within a document. At 2:17 the original audience was still gripped by the relentless flow of Paul's prophetic confrontation. Just as they have recognized that all of chapter 2 up to this point applies directly to them, here too they hear themselves being addressed, this time in the guise of the central owners of the God-fearing religion to which they have been converted. Paul has no other language, no other category with which to address them that would have as much impact or seriousness.

If in any part of this chapter Paul was talking to Jews in distinction from Christians, he would have had to clarify that up front. Otherwise what he was saying would have been incoherent to an audience receiving this not as a written but as a spoken message. But in fact, he never makes that distinction at all: on the contrary, he is at pains to emphasize that the spiritual poverty he speaks of is the situation of every individual, including those in the church to which he is writing. It is always "you, whoever you are." In 2:17ff, then, Paul is not addressing Israelites in contrast to his gentile Christian audience. Rather he is using the term Jew and mentioning circumcision as the key sign of covenant belonging as the epitome of the good religious person set apart for God, *which the Roman Christians know themselves to be*. It is not the language of ethnicity but of allegiance. It is not the language of distinction, it is the language of identification—an identification so close that Paul can without hesitation in 4:1 refer to Abraham as "our forefather, humanly speaking." No less completely than any modern Christian claims the Old Testament, the Roman Christians also understood the Scriptures to be their own: that is, with precisely as little *ethnic* warrant for that, and with as completely real and genuine *spiritual* warrant. When Paul talks about Abraham as "our forefather," the Roman Gentile Christians didn't have to think twice about what he meant. The thought of ethnic literalness didn't cross their mind any more than it does ours. Abraham belongs to us all.

67. *New Zealand Prayer Book*, Liturgy of the Eucharist, available online at: http://anglicanprayerbook.nz/index.html#contents

68. I might note that, as some will remember and all will understand, the whole share market dropped significantly across the board in the next fortnight. My attempt to gain something for nothing was not successful. Painful as the situation was for us and for thousands of others, I remain grateful for God's mercy in this regard.

69. Note that Matthew presents as one tightly organized sermon material that in other Gospels appears in a number of different contexts: e.g., Luke 11:37–54, 20:45–47; Mark 12:37–39, etc.

70. Circumcision is the surgical removal of the foreskin of the penis, an operation in Jewish communities normally performed upon infant boys at 8 days old. The practice is not unique to Jews, being widely practiced even today by such groups as the survivors of the Marsh Arabs of Iraq and by many tribal communities throughout Africa. In virtually every other society it is a manhood initiation rite. For Israel, however, while retaining its sexual and reproductive symbolism, it is a sign of an entry into membership of the covenant community that comes at birth. By its very nature circumcision is performed only on males (the barbaric practice of female circumcision practiced in some parts of Africa was unknown in Israel): the male represents the female in this regard in the solidarity of the overall community.

71. Baptism for purification was already a commonly understood practice *within Judaism*, and was a familiar initiation rite for gentile converts (although, for males, circumcision was generally also required for full acceptance into Israel). While the *significance* of Christian baptism was of course radically different, the external form was quite familiar in Paul's world. The community in which even before Jesus it was a central part of belonging was the sect of the Essenes, with their headquarters in the Judean desert (and whose library, recovered from its hiding place in the last 1940s, is known as the Dead Sea Scrolls). In case it should still be argued that circumcision is an inappropriate value to challenge if this was directed to Christians even if those Christians were deeply rooted in the old Testament and the life of the synagogue, we should note Col 2:11–12,

where the inner meaning of circumcision and that of baptism are equated; and Phil 3:3, where Paul asserts that "we are the true circumcision" (baptism on the other hand is not mentioned in this letter at all).

72. For example, in 1:1 Paul already speaks of Jesus as *Messiah*. In the following verses he speaks of the gospel as having been promised through *the prophets;* he identifies Jesus as *a descendent of David*, Israel's ideal king; and speaks of his proclamation as *Son of God*, the ancient title of the kings of Israel (the latter title now overflowing with new meaning because of the incarnation.) In chapter 4—writing to a mixed congregation, see 9:23–24—he will speak of Abraham as "our ancestor, humanly speaking" (4:1). And in chapter 11 he will speak of Christians from among the nations being *organically grafted into* the olive tree that is Israel (11:17ff). This usage is not restricted to Romans. Compare 1 Cor 10:1–5, where, in writing to what we know was a predominantly gentile congregation, Paul speaks of the Israelites during the exodus as "our ancestors." The letter to the Galatians speaks of those who believe as "descendants of Abraham" (3:7), and automatically assumes the historical continuity of the Christian church with Israel (4:21—5:2); indeed, it asserts its identity with Israel, truly understood (6:16).

    How did the relationship between Christianity and the old faith work during that transition time? Think about the different orders within the Roman Catholic Church. Very different in themselves, the Franciscan or Dominican or Jesuit orders have coexisted for hundreds of years. Each has its own distinguishing marks, and honors its founder and his teaching. Each has its own initiation rites and community rules. But all are still considered to be organically a part of the one church. This is what it was like in the first century too. It was impossible for Christianity and what became Judaism to coexist forever. The new wine could not be contained in the old wineskins: the differences were so radical that eventually a parting of the ways would have to come. But at the time Paul wrote, "Christianity" with its belief in Jesus as Messiah was still strongly rooted within the thought and practice of the historic Old Testament faith.

    It is still rooted there today. Christianity is not a new religion, come to supersede the old. Jesus makes this quite explicit in Matt 5:17–18. It is in full continuity with all that God was doing with his people from the beginning of time, through the Old Testament period, and right up to today. If there is any separation, it is not Christianity that has moved, but what we now call Judaism, which has separated itself from its historic faith as fulfilled in Jesus Messiah. "Branches have been broken off so that you may be grafted in," Paul will tell his listeners from other nations in chapter 11. "For it is we who are the true circumcision," says Paul to the church at Philippi (3:3; "The circumcision" refers not to the physical sign, but to the community that is defined by it as God's people.) And to the Galatian Christians he pronounces the blessing: "Peace be upon the Israel of God" (6:16).

73. This issue, what we might call "Jesus plus something else," was a matter of danger and controversy across a number of Paul's churches, and has continued to be so throughout the history of the church down to the present day. See as a classic example Gal 5:1–12 and 6:11–18, read in the context of that whole letter. It is not impossible that Paul had in mind these pressures upon the gentile section of his audience when he made such a strong point about inward rather than merely external circumcision.

74. E.g., Deut 10:16; Jer 4:4, 9:25–6; Ezek 44:9; and especially Deut 30:6 where *God* is seen as the one who circumcises the heart in the day of salvation.

75. Unthinkingly we tend to use the term "non-Christian." But the whole of Paul's argument will show that the term "non-Christian" is inappropriate: it is judgmental and exclusive in a way that the gospel makes impossible. Paul is here using the *contemporary* term of judgment and exclusivity ("uncircumcised") precisely in order to destroy its power. There are situations where we need a term, however: "not-yet-Christian" is a possibility worth considering; its relative awkwardness is in itself a helpful reminder of the true state of affairs.

    Even as we are startled by the directness of Paul's confrontation, we need to remember that he is not pulling all of this out of the air. Although he never directly quotes Jesus, it is in his power and the authority that he speaks. If you have a Bible handy you might like to consider another Matthew passage: the second half of chapter 25, beginning at v. 31. This passage, too, has been the subject of scandalized interpretation and reinterpretation over the years.

76. I'm aware that this is not a conscious intention; it is the byproduct of a misunderstanding of the rhetorical structure and intent of all that Paul has said up to this point. It is striking that, despite 2:1–5, despite the pronouns and the directness of the address, virtually every commentary interprets the chapter in this way. But as you grapple with the Greek text you find it to be one of those ideas about Romans that the more you look for the more it isn't there.

77. As Paul himself acknowledges in 1 Cor 4:1–5.

78. Acts 17:22–33 is Luke's summary of just such an address by Paul.

79. 2 Cor 10:4–5. The article is present in the Greek text.

80. Again, Paul is following his Master in this: cf. Mark 9:38–41. Jesus' statement in v. 40 is unqualified. The exclusive Christian group is not surrounded by a hostile world. It is set in a world where the love and grace and faithfulness that can come from God alone is constantly demonstrated (v. 41). Hostility there may be; it is possible to actively oppose: but such opposition needs to be actively chosen. According to Jesus you don't have to opt in—though you may choose to opt out.

81. Following on from the discussion of "Jew/Greek" language in endnote 72, it is with perfect consistency that Paul can ask in 3:1, "What advantage then does *the Jew* have?" and then in the very next breath (to a primarily gentile congregation, remember) rephrase the same question: "What then? Do *we* have a special standing compared to others?" (v.9) No more than at 2:17 has Paul suddenly started talking about ethnic Jews. "Not at all!" he answers in response to that second question. "For we have already charged that *both Jews and Greeks* are under the power of sin." Now, some of the Roman congregation may have been literally ethnic Greeks. But not a one of them would have seen themselves in the second of Paul's categories here. For these are not ethnic but religious categories. What Paul is saying is that both *religious* and *non-religious* people, both those inside the faithful community and those outside it, *all* are under the power of sin and therefore under God's judgment—and, astonishingly, also under his mercy and his grace.

82. **Notes to the translation:**

    v. 2 The change from the second person address ("you") in the second half of chapter 2 to the third person ("they") here is Paul's. Just for these few verses the viewpoint becomes more external and historical. The past tense and the third person pronouns simply reflect the fact that those who were first trusted with the Scriptures were our forefathers in the godly community. We are part of a community that has a history. We have inherited the trust that God gave to those who have gone before us. Paul will return to first person address in v. 5, and that is then sustained throughout the chapter. This historical distancing is why I have retained the term "Jew" in the translation of verse 1—which is noteworthy as the last time Paul will use that term of distinction until one further occurrence in chapter 10. From here on, without altering the subject, he continues to address his audience directly and inclusively.

    "the word of God": Lit. "words," the plural in Paul's day carrying exactly the same sense of authority and seriousness as the singular in ours.

    v. 3 **"unfaithful"/"faithlessness"**: Not "not having faith"/"lack of faith" (NIV)!

    v. 4 **"recognized as being righteous"**: Commonly translated "justified." See the "Translation matters" box in the main text.

    "as David confessed to God . . . " These words are added to make clear for a modern reader the location and context of the quotation (Ps 51:4), which Paul assumes his audience will immediately recognize. Paul is quoting from the Greek translation of the Old Testament, which says, not " . . . so that you may prevail in your judging" (NIV, NJB, NRSV, acknowledging the actual text in a footnote!) but " . . . so that you may prevail *when you are judged.*" The English translations reflect perhaps an instinctive avoidance of the idea that God could ever be judged—but in doing so they render the text inexplicable.

    v. 5 **"Righteous/unrighteous"**: Greek *dikaiosyne/adikos,* hence not *justice/unjust* (NRSV). The concept of justice is normally carried by a completely different word group in Greek (*kris-/*

krit-/krin-). This is the word used in the quotation in v. 5 ("that you may win your case when you are *judged*") and in v. 6 ("If that were so, how could God *judge* the world?"). Given that there are specific words in Greek to convey those concepts it is highly confusing when in the same passage justice/injustice language is *also* used for the righteousness group of words. For the NRSV God's *righteousness* in 1:17 and 3:21 in this verse becomes God's *justice*. The NIV correctly translates *dikaiosyne* as *righteousness* in the first half of v. 5 but in the second half joins the NRSV in translating *adikos* as *unjust*. But these words are as closely related as *loving* and *unloving* are in English! Of course, just as is the case in English, the same word can mean different things in Greek depending on the context. But it seems to me that in the current situation what Paul is saying is not being understood. There is an attempt to make sense of individual sentences without any reference to his overall argument. And when *dik-* words are given meanings identical with those of the *krin-* words in the very same context, it is difficult to know how any English reader is supposed to make sense of what Paul is saying.

v. 9 Not "we Jews" (added by NRSV). Paul is back in fully inclusive mode, as he has been since v. 5. It is true that this is the same question repeated, and this time eliciting a different answer from that in v. 1. But that simply indicates that the audience all through these chapters remains the Christian community to whom Paul is writing, and with which he identifies. When Paul speaks of "Jew and Greek" later in the verse, he is not suggesting that there might be some third category, say "Christians," which is different from these. The term just means "everybody without exception," and the point is that the Law's strictures apply *just as much* to the religious (i.e., the Roman church) as to the irreligious.

vv. 10–18 In translating what are quotations in a 2,000-year-old catena of statements that were already ancient in Paul's day, what is necessary is not strict verbal equivalence (this is especially so given that most of the quotations are from poetic texts) but being able to convey in clear twenty-first-century language the force and power of the imagery.

v. 20 **"the observances of the Law"**: Specifically in this context, circumcision (v. 1). Compare 2:25–29, and, a little later in the letter, 4:6 with 4:9.

83. The word translated "entrusted" contains precisely the same idea that is translated as (negatively) *unfaithful* and (positively) as *faithfulness* in the following verse. All are forms of the Greek root *pist-*, and for Greek-speakers their inter-relationship is obvious just from the look of the word. The *pist-* group is of key importance for Romans. From it come the words that are variously translated *faith* or *trust; believe;* and *faithfulness* or *trustworthiness*. These interlinked ideas run through the whole letter. When we come across this range of different words in our English versions we need to keep in mind that it is *one basic idea* that is being expressed. In Greek the form of the words themselves made that obvious.

84. In a relationship of this kind *both* parties exercise faith (in the other) and also faithfulness (in regard to the other). We are used to thinking about our having faith in God, but that in this reciprocal relationship God also *has faith in us* is an awesome thought. Of course God is not as utterly and totally dependent upon us as we are upon him. This is not a relationship between equals, but between Creator and (sinful, struggling, needy) creatures. But that we are the kind of creature in which God *can* put his confidence is a source of massive wonder and hope. For if God trusts us, he has the power to make us trustworthy. If he, the righteous one, calls us into relationship with himself, then he will make us the righteous covenant partner that we need to be and long to be. This is being made righteous; this is the great good news.

85. I haven't included *justice* here because the concept of justice is normally carried by a completely different word group in Greek (*kris-/krit-/krin-*). This is the word used in the quotation in v. 5 ("that you may win your case when you are *judged*") and in v. 6 ("If that were so, how could God *judge* the world?"). Given that there are specific words in Greek to convey those concepts it is highly confusing when some translations in the very same passage also use justice/injustice language for the *righteousness* group of words. For the NRSV, God's *righteousness* in 1:17 and 3:21 becomes God's *justice* in 3:5, and is immediately confused with God's ability to judge (*krinei*) the world in v. 6. The NIV correctly translates *dikaiosyne* as *righteousness* in the first half

of the v. 5 but in the second half joins the NRSV in translating *adikos* as *unjust*. But these words are as closely related as *loving* and *unloving* are in English! Of course in any language the same word can mean different things depending on the context. But it seems to me that in the *present* case, what Paul is saying is not being understood. Some kind of sense is being made of individual sentences without any reference to his overall argument. And when *dik-* words are given meanings identical with those of the *krin-* words in the very same context, it is difficult to know how any English reader is supposed to make sense of what Paul is saying.

86. That the two words look so different on the page is a curious historical accident: the English words for these identical concepts come from two different sources: righteous from the Old English *rhitwis*; justification from the Latin *justitia*, the word which St. Jerome used for righteousness in his translation of the Bible. Because the Vulgate was the only Bible in use in the West for 1,500 years, the word *justification* has survived as a kind of historical relic. It is a powerful relic because of the theology that has gathered round it. But (as was the case for Jerome as well) it is quite unsatisfactory as a translation of the Greek word and, because "justice" has in English become more and more restricted to the law and the court room, it is positively misleading. Based upon the connotations of the word in English, we might subconsciously feel that the "Law" Paul is talking about was something similar to a modern legal system; "justification" could appear to be something similar to the verdict in a trial; and God's role as judge of the world might be limited to something similar to that of a judge in a law court. All of this is very far from Paul's mind.

87. That commentators spend so much time speculating about the degree of Paul's acquaintance with contemporary rhetorical styles and contemporary concepts of law and justice (about which we know almost nothing) and ignore his mastery of the prophetic rhetoric of the Old Testament, and the role of Torah as Law (of which given his rabbinical training we know a great deal) seems misguided.

88. As noted in endnote 82 above, Paul is using the Greek translation of Ps 51, which says in that second clause not "that you may be proved right when you give judgment," but "that you may be proved right *when you are judged*." Understanding the reciprocal commitment involved in the act of judging the character of a person helps us to see that these two translations are not as dissimilar in meaning as they may first appear.

89. Notice the very close link between *faithfulness* in vv. 2 and 3 and *righteousness* in vv. 4 and 5. Paul presents them as complementary. Each illustrates a different aspect of a true relationship between person and person, and between a human being and God. It will be important to keep this in mind when we come later in the letter to the concept of *being made righteous* through *faith*, where the two ideas are brought together in a definitive way.

90. Note that we have here a small hint of the bitter and slanderous opposition that Paul's gospel engendered and that followed him all of his life (Phil 1:16–18). Paul's challenge to religious self-importance and exclusivity in these first chapters of Romans is very bold. Do we understand the opposition that preaching it will arouse among the gatekeepers of the Christian community?

91. Ps 14:1–3; 5:9; 140:3; 10:7; Isa 59:7–8; Ps 36:1. Paul's use of these texts largely follows the LXX (Greek Old Testament) text, but the wording is often very free. He is using the texts as *Scripture*, that is, not as a wooden collection of ancient texts but as a word that God speaks anew each day.

92. **Notes to the translation:**
v. 21 **"independently of the Law"**: The idea is not merely of something on the same level as the Law, but of something that both transcends and encompasses it.

God's righteousness: The repetition of the phrase in this and the following verse is not an accident. Paul's central interest here is the righteousness of God in the light of the questions about that which the human situation raises. Hence the declaration here of the fundamental fact: that God's righteousness has been revealed; and in the following verse how that righteousness is demonstrated.

"the Law and the Prophets": This was the standard expression to refer to the whole of the Old Testament Scripture. Compare Matt 22:40, Luke 16:16.

v. 24 **"being made righteous"**: Most English versions translate as if this was a simple present, describing a state. The Greek word, however, is a present passive participle: Paul is describing something that is ongoing in the present.

"liberation": Often translated *redemption*. But this latter word has a different meaning in modern English to that which Paul intends, which is the freeing of a slave. Also implicit in the English word "redemption" is the idea of something being purchased. But the word *apolutrosis* does not include the mechanism, whatever that mechanism might be; its reference is solely to the change of status of the individual. For a full discussion, see Buchsel in Kittel, *TDNT* 4:351–56; see also endnote 121.

v. 25 **"a sacrificial means of restoring the relationship"**: the word *hilasterion* appears only twice in the New Testament. In its other occurrence (Heb 9:5), it refers to the cover of the ark of the covenant in the holy of holies in the Jerusalem temple, the place where the blood of sacrifice was sprinkled before God on the annual Day of Atonement. Here it refers to the sacrifice itself, a sacrifice which God in his grace had accepted year by year so that the relationship could be put right, and human life could go on. That is however the limit of the similarity. For in this case, the sacrifice is not offered by human beings; it is offered by God himself.

"Through the faithfulness of his own death": The standard English versions are extra creative in finding unusual ways of construing the Greek text. The fixation upon "faith" as the only translation of *pistis* skews everything, producing along the way some extraordinary extra-biblical theology: something God has done is *made effective* by human faith, NEB, NRSV! *Pistis* cannot, however, be translated "faith" here, for God is the only focus and actor in the verse—and indeed, apart from v. 22b—in the whole passage. Although the KJV reading "faith in his blood" is a word for word rendering and sounds impressive, it is difficult to work out what it might mean. Paul never elsewhere speaks of faith in the blood or the death of Jesus. Faith is always in God himself. You can't have faith in a substance, or an event, or even in a truth; it is an interpersonal concept. What Paul is talking about then is *the faithfulness of Jesus* in what he elsewhere describes as "becoming obedient to the point of death—even death on a cross" (Phil 2:8, compare Rom 5:18–21).

"... of his own death": Lit: "in his own blood." There is nothing mystical or mysterious about the word blood. It was in the ancient world understood to be the principle of life, and spilt blood became therefore a sign and image of death (cf. 3:15 and 5:9–10). This was its only significance in the Old Testament sacrificial system. The poured-out blood, therefore, simply represented the death of the animal: not something insignificant, but not something magical either. While Paul undoubtedly uses the word "blood" here because of the sacrificial context, the word order reflects the startling reversal of the old cultic model: the possessive *autou* is in the emphatic position, *his own* death. Note that although it is the death of Jesus that is being referred to, the actor in the sentence is God ("God put him forward"). God's faithfulness and the faithfulness of Jesus Messiah are ultimately not distinguishable.

"Demonstrates": Although like most translations I have used a verb here, we should note that the word *endeixis* is a noun: Paul has in mind a demonstration of the righteousness of God that blows away the foolish questioning of 3:3–8.

"Sinful acts": The word is *hamartama*, sinful acts, not *harmartiai*, sins. Except when quoting the Old Testament (4:7, 11:27), Paul in this letter uses *harmartia* only in the singular, to describe a power that holds people captive.

v. 26 **"righteous in himself . . . "**: The Greek *eis to einai* depends upon *endeixin*; the phrase does not refer to a possibility of *becoming* the one who makes righteous, but to it *becoming known* to all people that he is that one.

" . . . who establishes as righteous": The whole of Paul's argument in these first three chapters comes to a point here. In the main text I have suggested that the opaque English term "justifies" could be better expressed by the expansion "declares to be and makes righteous." The alternative here is a less wordy equivalent: it carries both the idea of a new standing and (Paul uses a participle) an ongoing process.

"the person who lives on the basis of the faithfulness of Jesus": The Greek expression here is *ek pisteōs Iesou*, an identical construction to *ek pisteōs Abraam* in 4:16, which is normally translated "[those who] share the faith of Abraham." In 3:21–26, however, Paul is not exhorting us to share Jesus' own faith in God (which was of course an essential part of his true humanity, as the Gospels and the letter to the Hebrews emphasize). The whole passage so far has been about the way God brings deliverance on the basis of Jesus' faithful life and especially his faithful death. In v. 26 *pisteōs* must therefore be translated not as *faith* but as *faithfulness*—remembering that the distinction between the two English words is only a matter of perspective. What is being described is a relationship. And that relationship between the man Jesus and the eternal God, Paul is saying, is the basis of the new life.

That this is what Paul means is confirmed by the fact that only the human name Jesus is used here, in contrast to the earlier "Jesus Messiah" (v. 22) or "Messiah Jesus" (v. 24). The latter titles focus our attention on the act of God in Jesus and what he accomplished in his life and death. Here in v. 26 the focus is *our human experience*, not just as a matter of belief but as a matter of God's active involvement in our lives, of which Jesus the faithful human being is our example. 8:29, 30 is the best commentary.

This is an important qualification upon historic formulations such as "justification by faith alone." Paul is not talking about an alternative type of human approach to God (faith rather than religious observances). Rather he is declaring, instead of our approach to God, *God's approach to us* as he comes in Messiah Jesus, and to which we respond with faith in his faithfulness. This message is consistent throughout the letter: sin cannot rule over us because another Lord has approached. Into our godlessness God himself steps. The distance is annihilated. God comes.

93. Nuisance as it is, though, how can we not also speak of the beauty of massed gorse in full bloom? Once, coming around a ridge to see a basin in the hills golden with blossom, my 8-year-old daughter exclaimed "Daddy! It looks like God has dropped his paint-pot!" One might also speak of the thick, bee-haunted powdery scent of the gorse as the very spirit of the summer afternoons of my childhood.

94. 1:17; see the explanation of the translation in endnote 28.

95. The *Common English Bible* is an exception, as is *The Message*. Earlier versions that translate the text as the faith (rather than the faithfulness) *of* Jesus Christ are the Vulgate, Wycliffe, the King James Version and the translations of the nineteenth century scholars Young and Darby. How is it that the main translational tradition has become so strong? The problem is, I think, with the word *pistis*, which in the century of both the Reformation and of vernacular Bible translations so obviously could only mean "faith" in a human sense. The prepositions were either ignored or interpreted to conform to that dominant theological message. We have to remember that no one was working with the Greek text at that time: Erasmus's Greek New Testament was only published in 1516. Even then, a working grasp of Greek was as uncommon as it is today—which is why we depend upon our translations being accurate!

96. The advantage of this is precision of meaning; the disadvantage that the emphasis shifts from the *relationship* to what increasingly comes to be seen as *a personal quality*. There will be times when both aspects of the relationship are in view, and then the matter of translation becomes harder. We have to choose one or the other—but in doing so remain aware that it is the whole relationship in its mutuality that is being described, not just what it looks like from the perspective of one or other of the parties. That is the situation especially in 3:31 (as I have tried to signal when I translate those verses later), but the thought runs through every use of *pistis* in the letter.

97. While this is strictly correct we should note that the way the word is used in documents contemporary with Paul is not equally distributed between those two English alternatives. By far the dominant sense for *pistis* in the contemporary Hellenistic Jewish literature (including the Septuagint, the Greek translation of the Old Testament) is *faithfulness, pledge,* or *proof*. In only 16 out of 270 occurrences is the meaning clearly *faith or trust*, with 37 cases ambiguous or exceptional. See the breakdown of these statistics in Howard, "Faith of Christ," 214. It seems that in the literature in general the most usual way in which the *meaning* faith or trust was expressed was through the verb *(pisteueō)*, rather than through the noun. This is, of course, often also a key

way that the concept is expressed in the New Testament, and in Romans (1:16; 3:22; 4:11,18; 6:8; 10:9, 14; 13:11; 14:2; 15:13).

98. I.e., it is not *Iesous Christos* (as it would be written if Jesus was the subject of the sentence), but *pisteōs Iesou Christou*.

99. Readers using a version of the NIV published before 2011 will find in v. 21 not "the righteousness of God" but "a righteousness that comes from God." The 2011 revision eliminates this but paraphrases v. 22 to say the same thing. This therefore needs to be said in words of one syllable: *the NIV version of v. 22 bears no relation to the Greek text of this verse.* It is a pure free-floating interpretation of it in the light of a theology that is being imported into the text. Other problems haunt the NIV translation of this section. In v. 25, Paul's statement that the faithfulness of Jesus reveals God's righteousness in *passing over* sins previously committed becomes God's *leaving unpunished* sins previously committed. God's *mercy* becomes his *restraint from punishment*. The implication is that that punishment remained stored up waiting to be delivered—upon Jesus, in this theology. But the idea of punishment is quite alien to this passage (and indeed to all of Paul's theology): Paul is talking about mercy! And the idea of God as a punishing God is diametrically opposed to all that Paul is saying here about him. This importing into the text of ideas that are alien to it is a matter of deep concern. For this is the Bible version that in good faith millions of faithful and earnest people go to to learn of the ways of God. By, instead of translating what Paul does say, making him say what a particular theological system requires that he says—about God!— the NIV translators take a fearsome responsibility upon themselves. It is all very well-intentioned no doubt. But "God's people were entrusted with his words" (3:2). "What if some were unfaithful?"

100. Or, less likely, "the faith of Jesus," i.e., Jesus' own faith.

101. The major commentaries normally include a bibliography of the discussion for and against the natural sense of the genitive (i.e., "the faith/fullness of Jesus Messiah"), and those interested in researching the full debate should refer to these. (A surprising exception is Cranfield, who, remarkably, fails to mention the issue at all.) Because of the importance of the issue I depart here from my normal practice of avoiding lots of scholarly references by citing the following papers and monographs which to me seem the most useful: **Gabriel Hebert**, "'Faithfulness' and 'Faith,'" *Theology* 57 (1955) 373–79; **Thomas F. Torrance**, "One Aspect of the Biblical Conception of Faith," *Expository Times* 68 (1956/7) 111–14; **George Howard**, "The Faith of Christ," *Expository Times* 85 (April 1974) 212–15; **Douglas A. Campbell**, "Romans 1:17—A *Crux Interpretum* for the ΠΙΣΤΙΣ ΧΡΙΣΤΟΥ Debate," *Journal of Biblical Literature* 113 (1994) 265–85; "The Crisis of Faith in Modern New Testament Scholarship," in *Religious Studies in Dialogue: Essays in Honour of A.C. Moore*, University of Otago Press, 1991, 163–74; "False Presuppositions in the ΠΙΣΤΙΣ ΧΡΙΣΤΟΥ Debate: A Response to Brian Dodd," *Journal of Biblical Literature* 116 (1997) 713–19; **Bruce Longenecker**, "ΠΙΣΤΙΣ in Romans 3:25: Neglected Evidence for the Faithfulness of Christ?" *New Testament Studies* 39 (1993) 478–80; **Richard B. Hays**, *The Faith of Jesus Christ: An Investigation of the Narrative Substructure of Galatians 3:1–4:11*, Eerdmans, 2002. This volume includes as an appendix the following article which can also be accessed independently: "ΠΙΣΤΙΣ and Pauline Christology: What Is at Stake?" in *Society for Biblical Literature Seminar Papers* edited by David J. Lull, Scholars, 1991, 714–29. For those who know these names note also Longenecker's list of articles by **Luke T. Johnson, Bruce Chilton, Leander Keck, Morna Hooker, Stanley Stowers,** and other contemporary scholars. Alone among the major commentators in insisting on the natural reading of the Greek text, **Richard Longenecker** provides an excellent summary of the linguistic and contextual arguments (Longenecker, *Epistle to the Romans*, 408–13.)

102. Where there is no *personal* subject the genitive is often used to indicate, not a characteristic or possession of the original noun, but something which it is *about*, or *to which it is related*. For example, in 1 Cor 1:18 Paul says that "the preaching *of the cross* is foolishness to those that are perishing." In this case the cross is not doing the preaching ("the cross's preaching"), it is the

content of the preaching (it is preaching *about* the cross). The only example that I'm aware of that uses the genitive to express a general link between *persons*, is Luke 6:12, where Jesus offers prayer *tou theou*, that is, prayer to (or with) God ("the rare objective genitive," comments Marshall).

103. Douglas Campbell ("False Presuppositions," 717) notes the following "probable" examples: Mark 11:22 (perhaps, but see William Lane, *The Gospel of Mark,* Eerdmans, 1974); Philo, *De Vita Mosis* 1.90; Josephus, *JW* 1 §485 and *Ant.* 2 §§ 272, 283; 10 §268; and possibly also 17 §327. Fitzmeyer adds 19 §16, but see Howard, "Faith of Christ," on both this and (with regard to all of these citations) the normal sense of *pistis* in the extra-biblical literature in general. Five probable, two possible, and one dubious: that is it.

104. Gal 2:15–16; 3:22. The argument of Gal 2:15—3:29 is very illuminating as a commentary upon Romans. While the pastoral contexts are different, Paul uses virtually the same suite of ideas and examples to explain the gospel and the life of faith in both letters.

Phil 3:9. This passage also repays study because the context is so manifestly a contrast between all that Paul might have to boast about (his faithfulness to his Jewish heritage) and the faithfulness of Jesus upon which he now utterly and joyfully depends. On pages 398–400 of his *Commentary on Philippians* in the NIGNT series (Eerdmans, 1991), Peter T. O'Brien gives an excellent scholarly defense of the *faithfulness of Jesus* reading in that letter.

105. Though we also know that we are to have faith *in* God. Of course! But that is not what Paul is saying here, and not what the words mean. None of the commentaries argue for anything but the normal use of *pistis* plus genitive in these other cases.

106. Fitzmeyer, *Romans,* 345–46, my italics.

107. Rom 5:6.

108. Matt 3:13–17. Gundry notes that the word "fulfill" is normally used in the passive for the fulfillment of prophecy. Here the verb is active. The fulfillment of righteousness is something that Jesus actively does. It is a choice, an act.

109. The biblical term for taking this responsibility is *covenant*. Uniquely among the religions of the world, biblical faith understood that God was not a distant observer of human affairs but that the act of creation implied God's ongoing commitment to and responsibility for that creation. Particularly interesting is the Noah story in Gen 9:8–17, where God commits himself to *human beings* (v. 9), to *the living creatures* (v. 9–10), and to *the earth itself* (v. 13, cf. Rom 8:18–25). Another seminal passage is God's encounter with Abraham in Gen 17:1–8, where we see God committing himself to Abraham as the representative human being ("father of many nations . . . in you all nations will be blessed," vv. 4–6, 18:18, 22:18, 26:4, etc.) Of course, like all these key concepts, that of covenant is reciprocal. Human beings have a response to make and a responsibility to undertake as well. But the biblical testimony is consistent in recognizing that the initiative and the undertaking of responsibility are first of all God's. Two religious misunderstandings are possible: (1) Israel in large part came to see themselves as exclusive recipients of the covenant, as if God's dealings and interest were with them alone, and to feel that the covenant *bound* God to them and to their nation in an exclusive way. The prophets attack that fallacy at its root (e.g., Amos 9:7–8, and Isa 52:13—53:6, in the context of all of II Isaiah). (2) The covenant with Israel can be interpreted as being primary and exclusive to the extent that the Christian good news only exists within it as a kind of subset. This will be dealt with when we come to Rom 9–11. We need to rediscover what it means for God to be Creator, and his commitment to the whole of creation and to all people that is implicit in it—as is made vividly explicit in the Incarnation.

110. The cross has always been offensive to godly people outside of the Christian world. Jews, for example, know, as did the pre-conversion Paul himself, that this kind of death is conclusive evidence that the person concerned was rejected by God. Islam believes Jesus to be a prophet, and on a cross is not the way that prophets die. Rejecting as blasphemous even the idea of incarnation, Muslims hold that on the cross God put someone else in Jesus' place, so enabling him to escape. These are not just differences of opinion, but matters about which people feel

deeply. In a letter to another Christian church Paul speaks about "the offence of the cross," and warns against the danger of downplaying it for fear of persecution (Gal 5:11, 6:12). Is it not then also an offence to us? Is it possible that within the Christian world familiarity and use has tamed and domesticated the scandal and the challenge that it poses for our very existence? Kierkegaard described the situation like this:

"Instead of entering into relation with God we transform it into the history of how God in Christ entered into relation with the apostles or with people. Instead of entering into relation with God, we have turned it into a historical matter which we repeat in diluted form from generation to generation. We imagine that the killing of Christ, that infamous act of the human race, was 2,000 years ago, far in the past, forgotten. Now we are fine people. *But for God it happened today*." (Kierkegaard, *Last Years*, 143, 135, 6; some words omitted for clarity; my italics).

111. What does it mean to fall short of God's glory? It is a striking expression, coming so soon after the description of willful and deliberate *opposition* to the will of God that appears in some of the Bible verses that Paul has just quoted. But those verses are there to demonstrate to us good religious people that even our own Scriptures give us no escape route. This is something different. Paul elsewhere uses the word that is translated "fall short" to mean *lacking* (1 Cor 1:7), *inferior* (2 Cor 11:5, 12:7), and *being in need* (2 Cor 11:9, Phil 4:12). He is describing something that all people are missing, some essential aspect of life that we are deficient in, something we are failing to reach: *the glory of God*. The word "glory" can appear to be just a bit of religious language, but here its meaning is very precise. It means (in Godet's words) "the divine splendour which shines forth from God himself, *and which he communicates to all who live in union with him.*" With regard to human beings, St. Irenaeus summed it up in a famous aphorism: "The glory of God is a person fully alive." To be fully alive! The longing of every human heart . . . and we fail at it. We fall short. Willful and deliberate sin is one thing, but all of us, no matter how we ache to be whole, fail to live a fully human life. What we fail to live up to, though, is not *our* ideals or our aspirations but the glory of *God*. God is the Lord of it—and, Paul tells us, God has acted to secure that glory on our behalf. We fail to be a fully human person, but God in his grace both declares and empowers us to be that, through Messiah Jesus. "In baptism we have died and been buried with him," Paul will tell us a little later, "so that, just as Messiah was raised by the glory of the Father, *so we too might live a new life*" (6:4). There is no change of subject; vv. 23 and 24 are part of the one sentence. The making righteous of v. 24 means nothing other than the act of God that puts right both eternally and in our practical life experience the "falling short" of v. 23.

112. Recognizing this helps us understand what Paul means by the *Law*. Notice the variety of ways in which Paul uses the term in these verses. *The Law* is the Scriptures, and also the teaching that the Scriptures contain (vv. 19, 20; vv. 21b). The *works of the Law* (vv. 20, 27, 28) are the special distinctives of the covenant community: circumcision, the sacrificial system, the food laws, and the Sabbath. Paul can use the word "law" to mean something like an *authoritative principle* (v. 27). And, bracketing our passage here in v. 21 and in v. 31, Law is also a quite general term to describe *true religion*. It is important to grasp this breadth of reference. In our world we think of the law in terms of a legal code, as a set of *laws*. But the biblical view is far wider than this. For example the first five books of the Old Testament, including the stories of creation and covenant in Genesis and God's mighty deliverance of his people from slavery in Exodus, are *all together* described as the Torah, the Law. Although they contain many specific commands and instructions, that is only one aspect of a broad and deep understanding of a life lived in relationship with God in a world that is made by him. Law is much more than laws. It is the total framework of thought and behavior for the faithful people of God.

113. This is what the word "justified" means: declared and empowered to be righteous.

114. Slavery in the first-century Mediterranean world was a diverse and complex institution, much more so than the eighteenth-century slavery in the English colonies and America that we tend to think of when we hear the word. It was for example possible to sell oneself into slavery, in order to raise capital or to secure a particular position. The early Christian writer Clement notes that some Christians had even done this in order to use the money to deliver others from

tyrannical masters. Slaves could own their own property, including other slaves; and it was quite possible for a successful slave to eventually purchase their own freedom. Manumission of slaves by owners for a variety of reasons (including the death of the owner themselves) was a regular occurrence, and it seems that only a tiny proportion of slaves died in that condition without gaining their freedom in one way or another. (For an illuminating discussion see Bartchy, "Slavery.") In the light of this complexity it is clear that the emphasis in Paul's comparison is not on the payment of a purchase price (because purchase of freedom by another was only one of several ways in which freedom could be achieved), but the change of status from slavery to freedom itself. That this is so is confirmed by other occurrences of the word *apolutrōsis* in Pauline and other New Testament material (e.g., Luke 21:28; Rom 8:23; Eph 1:7, 4:30; 1 Cor 1:30; Col 1:14, etc.), where in virtually every case the most appropriate English translation is simply "freedom" or "liberation" (the latter being the word I have used in my own). Where it is a matter of an actual financial payment, the Greek word for buying and selling (*agorazō*) was used. There are a handful of occasions where this word is used metaphorically of Jesus' death (1 Cor 6:20, 7:23; Gal 3:13, 4:5; Rev 5:9, 14:3); that in each case it *is* used metaphorically is indicated by the context, and also by other occurrences of the word such as Eph 5:16. (For a similar usage in the Old Testament, see Isa 52:3, 54:5–8.)

115. In a day when many people choose to be vegetarian and when those who are not have little contact with the living animal and the taking of its life for food (we buy the meat at the supermarket), the idea of animal sacrifice can sound repulsive in a way that most societies for most of history would find curious. Animal sacrifice was ubiquitous across the ancient world. In Israel, the magical, coercive, and propitiatory aspects of its practice was replaced by an understanding based upon God's own gracious act and his commitment to his people through covenant. Instead of a human attempt to manipulate the divine, sacrifice became the means by which guilt was pardoned and relationship restored by God himself. As to the mechanics of the practice, it was *a common and quite normal process* (the taking of an animal life for food) *given special significance*. To eat meat was in Israel always recognized to be a permission rather than a right: it was forbidden, for example, to consume the blood (which was considered to contain the life-principle, and sometimes even to be life itself). With that prior understanding, sacrifice was particularly suitable for expressing the life and death matters of sin and forgiveness. We should note too, that while the burnt offerings were dedicated completely and as a whole to God, in other circumstances (e.g., the "peace" offerings, Lev 7:15–18) the sacrificial animals were afterwards consumed with rejoicing by the worshipers and also the priests (who in this way gained their living). The same was of course true for the Passover, first celebrated as a sign of hope in a promised deliverance; ever after as a glad reminder of and contemporary participation in its meaning.

116. See the notes to the translation.

117. Notice the reversal that has taken place: Jesus' death should have been the conclusive demonstration of the falsity of all his claims, promises, and teaching (as Judaism still believes). Instead of a judgment of rejection upon Jesus, however, Paul says, Jesus' death was a *sacrifice*, put forward by God himself; a demonstration of his righteousness. Jesus was indeed judged, but it was our sinful nature that was judged in him: he carried it to death, accepting the shame. His death was not the end of the story. The *resurrection* is the judgment of God upon Jesus himself, and upon the new humanity in him; the resurrection, not the death of Jesus is the guarantee that the work is complete, that human beings are made righteous (4:24–25).

The identification of Jesus with the Passover lamb is on a handful of occasions in the New Testament made quite explicit: by John the Baptist (John 1:29, 36); once by Paul himself (1 Cor 5:7); in Peter's first letter (1:19); and, most dramatically, in the book of Revelation, where John is told that the Lion of the tribe of Judah has conquered—and looks, and sees, at the heart of the throne of God "a Lamb as if it had been sacrificed." The Lamb is the title of the victorious Messiah in the book from that point on.

118. That faith is not a *possession* does not mean that it is *passive*. In his wonderful account of pioneering missionary work in Africa, *Christianity Rediscovered* (Orbis, 1978), Vincent Donovan

describes a conversation with a Masai elder, who told him that

> the word I had used to convey the idea of faith was not a very satisfactory word in their language. It meant literally 'to agree to.' I myself knew the word had that shortcoming. The elder said 'to believe' like that was similar to a white hunter shooting an animal with his gun from a great distance. Only his eyes and his fingers took part in the act. We should find another word. He said for a man really to believe is like a lion going after its prey. His nose and eyes and ears pick up the prey. His legs give him the speed to catch it. All the power of his body is involved in the terrible death leap and single blow to the neck with the front paw, the blow that actually kills. And as the animal goes down the lion envelops it in his arms (Africans refer to the front legs of an animal as its arms), pulls itself to himself, and makes it part of himself. This is the way a lion kills. This is the way a person believes. This is what faith is.

But that was not all. We are, the elder observed, not the only participant in this drama.

> 'We did not search you out, Padri,' he said to me. 'We did not even want you to come to us. You searched us out. You followed us away from your house into the bush, into the plains, into the steppes where our cattle are, into the hills where we take our cattle for water, into our villages, into our homes. You told us of the High God, how we must search for him, even leave our land and our people to find him. But we have not done this. We have not left our land. We have not searched for him. He has searched for us. He has searched us out and found us. All the time we think we are the lion. But in the end, the lion is God.'

119. The density and the intensity of what Paul is saying here may be a bit overwhelming. After so many years and across a language barrier it takes a lot of words in English to unpack what some of Paul's audience may have understood right off the bat. I'm confident though, that for most people this and other parts of the letter became a continuing resource that they went back to often. That has certainly been the experience of generations of Christians since. We need to note also that this is not all we will hear about these matters. Paul himself will continue to unpack the ideas summarized here, as the letter continues to unfold. We have noted that all the concepts in 3:21–26 are already there in essence in Paul's first pithy statement of theme in 1:16–17. But even now the ideas are still very compressed. The implications of what Paul is saying here will continue to be developed and opened out in the chapters to come.

120. It is a sad irony that among the modern "works of the law" which the Christian community often prizes we would have to add "faith" in the superficial and enfeebled sense of *right believing*. The anthropocentric translations that supplement the work of God with human faith ("a sacrifice of atonement made effective through faith," and similar embarrassments) push us in that direction. They rob God of his glory, and leave us still with a form of human activity or effort—albeit mental or spiritual effort—that is necessary to bring God's work to completion. Ever so subtly faith becomes something that we do, something upon which the success of God's work depends. The result is that we are left with a Romans where, despite 2:1, we Christians are never those who are being confronted, and also with a model of salvation where the work of God has been sidelined, or must be supplemented by a human work. Can we imagine the way in which Paul would treat such a travesty of the good news? But we don't have to imagine. We have it right here in front of us, if we can only learn once again to hear these chapters aright.

121. v. 27 **"What kind of Law?"** Paul is not thinking about different *sorts* of Law, as if there could be several, but about *different models* for understanding the one covenant Law: "*the* Law," v. 31. The article indicates that Paul is referring to a particular way of understanding the Law that is well-known to his readers. In contrast, *nomou* in the following clause has no article, indicating that Paul is suggesting a *new* way of understanding the Law—the one which he has been dealing with in the immediately preceding verses.

ENDNOTES: ROMANS 1–3

"that is based on faith": In this sentence Paul is not contrasting a dependence upon the *humanly performed* signs of special belonging (works of the Law) with a *humanly exercised* faith; he is contrasting something *we* do and perform with something that *God* completely independently has performed, and which we respond to in faith.

v. 28 **"it is clear to us"**: The Greek word (*logizomai*) carries the sense of something logically evaluated. It is not just a belief or a position that Paul is asserting, but something that he logically recognizes must be true in the light of what Jesus has done and the fact that God is one. Strikingly, Paul will use the word later of God reckoning or accounting us to be righteous.

"by faith": The dative of *pistos* following a verb is a unique usage both in Romans and in the New Testament as a whole (see the discussion in Cranfield, among others).

v. 30 **"faith in his faithfulness"**: This is the same phrase (*ek pisteōs*) as in v. 26 (*ek pisteōs Iesuou*). As is the case there we are looking back to the *ek pisteōs eis pistin* of 1:17, and the quotation of Hab 2:4. With that in mind it seems appropriate to make explicit what is always implicit in *pistis* and translate the first of its occurrences as "faith *in God's faithfulness*." Faith is not a free-floating attitude; it is always faith in God.

"on the basis of . . . through": reflecting the different prepositions (*ek* and *dia*) used of the faith of each. The faithfulness of God to which the religious person responds is his faithfulness in Jesus Messiah *to the covenant of which circumcision is the sign*. But because God is God of all, he makes righteous those *without* the sign of the covenant on the basis of the very same (*tes*) faith.

122. This is what the phrase "the works of the Law" means in 3:20, 27, 4:2, etc.: the external signs of religious belonging, like (for Jews and those, like the Roman Christians, still operating within the thought-world of Old Testament religion) circumcision, Sabbath keeping, the food laws. The equivalent for modern Christians might be baptism, the Lord's Supper, church membership, orthodoxy of belief. In the history of Christian interpretation, and especially in reaction to debased teaching in the medieval church in Europe, the phrase has often been taken to mean "good works performed in order to earn God's favor." In Romans, however, *the phrase occurs exclusively in contexts where Christian belonging (not earned merit) is in question*. This is clear from this current passage, where "works of the law" in v. 28 and 29 is immediately defined in terms of the faith community (not virtue). As another example see also 4:1–12, where the discussion in v. 1–6 is directly linked to the "work" of circumcision in v. 9–12.

123. With regard to Paul's use of the term "Jew" here we should note that, although the term "Christian" was known (Acts 11:26) it was almost certainly not in widespread use at the time this letter was written. And where it was in use it described a particular sect *within* Jewish religion, not something over against it.

124. The classic Jesus example is John 21:20–22, where Peter, face to face with the Lord and feeling the heat, looks over his shoulder to John and asks "What about him?" "My dealings with that other disciple [my paraphrase] are none of your business," says Jesus. "Your business is to follow me."

125. Note that what is being talked about is not deduction or speculation or myth-making but *revelation*, that is, God is the one who initiates.

126. Acts 4:12. "Anywhere": literally, anywhere beneath the sky; but this is not an idiom we would normally use today.

127. The most powerful imaginative expression of this truth known to me comes in the seventh of C. S. Lewis's Narnia story, *The Last Battle*. At the end of his fictional world's history Lewis describes a battle of belief between those faithful to the great Lion Aslan (Lewis's symbol for Jesus Messiah) and those who serve Tash, the demon god of the pagans. In the story, corrupt and evil characters, seeking to use religion as a means of gaining power, represent Aslan and Tash as different aspects of one being. A noble young pagan warrior, having served all of his life and seeking to know more of him, passes through death's doorway into a strange and wonderful new world. He describes his meeting with Aslan:

Endnotes: Romans 1–3

The Glorious One bent down his golden head and touched my forehead with his tongue and said, 'Son, thou art welcome.' But I said, 'Alas, Lord, I am no son of thine but the servant of Tash.' He answered, 'Child, all the service thou hast done to Tash, I count as service done to me.' Then by reason of my great desire for wisdom and understanding I overcame my fear and questioned the Glorious One and said, 'Lord, is it then true...that thou and Tash are one?' The Lion growled so that the earth shook (but his wrath was not against me) and said, 'It is false. Not because he and I are one, but because we are opposites, I take to me the services which thou hast done to him. For he and I are of such different kinds that no service which is vile can be done to me, and none which is not vile can be done to him. Therefore if any man swear by Tash and keep it for the oath's sake, it is by me that he has truly sworn, though he know it not, and it is I who reward him. And if any man does a cruelty in my name, then, though he says the name Aslan, it is Tash that he serves, and by Tash his deed is accepted. Dost thou understand, child?' I said, 'Lord thou knowest how much I understand.' But I said also (for the truth constrained me), 'Yet I have been seeking Tash all my days.' 'Beloved,' said the Lion, 'unless thy desire had been for me, thou wouldst not have sought so long and so truly. For all find what they truly seek.'—C.S. Lewis, *The Last Battle* (Penguin, 1964) 148–49.

Lewis suggests, I believe correctly, that as people outside the knowledge of Jesus respond to what God shows to them of his power and his glory through creation (Rom 1:19, 20, 10:18) they will of necessity express that dawning knowledge in the terms of the concepts available to them, for they have no others. This was so for Abraham as well, as we shall see. All of the Genesis stories—and all of the biblical stories, right up to our own day—are about people coming to know and understand the *true character* of the God to whose *bare call* they have at first responded.

128. When I was younger I had the impression that Abraham (who will step onto the stage in the next chapter of Paul's letter) was the first person ever to recognize the call of the one true God; that it was *through Israel exclusively* that God was to be known in the world. But the biblical record makes it clear that this is not the case. Right at the beginning of Abraham's career, for example, returning from battle he is met and blessed by "Melchizedek of Salem, *priest of the Most High God*" (Gen 14:18). The same God speaks personally in a dream to Abimelech (who has unknowingly taken Abraham's wife as his own). Abimelech answers using the name Yahweh: he knows who he is dealing with (18:3). Later on, Laban, who in his day-to-day affairs acknowledges lesser gods, swears when it is a matter of a solemn covenant in the name of Yahweh alone (31:48–49). During the period of the wilderness wanderings after the escape from Egypt, in response to a request from a Moabite chieftain to curse Israel on his behalf, Balaam ben-Beor replies that even if he were to be offered the chieftain's house full of silver and gold he "could not go beyond the command of Yahweh my God, to do less or more" (Num 22:18). The idea that Israel has exclusive knowledge of God, that they somehow own the right to him, is a prideful mistake that arises only later in Israel's history. The prophets challenge it. "'Are you any different from the Ethiopians as far as I'm concerned O people of Israel?' says the Lord. 'Didn't I bring Israel up from the land of Egypt—and the Philistine's from Crete, and the Arameans from Kir?'" (Amos 9:7) The whole purpose of the superbly crafted book of Jonah is to confront any kind of religious exclusivism, even among those who are called to proclaim God's message to the nations (see especially 4:10–11, where the whole story comes to a point.) Above all, we should remember the reaction of the Nazareth congregation when Jesus himself speaks in this way (Luke 4:23–30). What would our reaction have been in that situation? Paul is, then, saying nothing different than his Lord. We don't own God; God owns us. He is sovereign and free and acts to bring about his purpose whether through us or despite us. To borrow the title of a book by Bishop Desmond Tutu, *God is not a Christian*. Well, no, no, of course not! But if, nonetheless, that statement bothers us just a little, then we are beginning to feel the force of what Paul is saying here in Romans 3.

129. Acts 17:16–33.

ENDNOTES: ROMANS 1–3

130. Epiminedes (though similar statements appear in several writers) and Aratus respectively.
131. 2 Kgs 6:24—7:20.

9

Romans 4:1–22
The Example of Abraham

"What did our ancestor Abraham find? ²Because if Abraham was made righteous on the basis of religious observances, he has something to boast about. Not before God, though! ³What does the scripture actually say? 'Abraham put his faith in God, and it was reckoned to him as righteousness.' ⁴A worker's wages aren't considered to be generosity; they are an obligation. ⁵But when someone isn't working for a wage but instead puts his faith in him who makes the ungodly righteous, that faith is reckoned as righteousness. ⁶David says exactly this about the happiness of those to whom God ascribes righteousness irrespective of religious observances:

> ⁷ 'How happy are those whose wrongdoings are forgiven,
> and whose sins are pardoned!
> ⁸ Blessed is the one against whom the Lord will not count sin.'

⁹Is this blessing pronounced only on the circumcised, or also on the uncircumcised? We've just said that faith was reckoned to Abraham for righteousness. ¹⁰But when was it reckoned to him, before or after his circumcision? It wasn't after, but before he was circumcised! ¹¹The sign of circumcision that he received was a confirmation of the righteousness of the faith that he had while he was still uncircumcised. This was so that he could be the ancestor of all who trust without being circumcised and have righteousness ascribed to them, ¹²and likewise the ancestor of the circumcised who are not only circumcised but also follow the example of the faith that our ancestor Abraham had before he was circumcised.

¹³The promise that he would inherit the world didn't come either to Abraham or to his descendants through the Law. It came through the righteousness of faith. ¹⁴If it is the adherents of the Law who are to be the heirs, faith has become empty and the promise meaningless; ¹⁵for the Law brings wrath. But where there is no Law,

neither is there the breaking of it. ¹⁶*The promise comes from faith; it is founded upon grace, therefore it is certain. And this is so for all Abraham's descendants, not only those of the Law but also those who share his faith. For he is the father of all of us:* ¹⁷*as it is written, 'I have made you the father of many nations.'*

Faced with this promise, Abraham put his faith in God, the one who makes the dead live again and calls things that don't exist into existence. ¹⁸ *He trusted, hoping against hope that he would indeed become the father of many nations, for that was the promise: "that is who your descendants shall be!"* ¹⁹*He didn't weaken in faith when he considered that he was no longer capable of fathering a child (for he was about a hundred years old), or when he remembered that Sarah had always been unable to bear one.* ²⁰*With regard to God's promise he never wavered through doubt, but instead was made strong through faith. Acknowledging God to be God* ²¹*and being completely convinced that what God had promised, he is able to do:* ²²*this is what was counted to him for righteousness."*[1]

"Our ancestor Abraham": hearing this, do your eyes glaze over a bit? We aren't into ancestors very much in our culture—which is a pity, because Abraham was a gutsy, practical character, who felt deeply, lived passionately, and had an extraordinary friendship with God; his example has a lot to teach us.[2]

But Paul's aim isn't to give us a character study of Abraham. His interest is quite specific. With regard to the relationship between faith and religious observance, what did our ancestor Abraham find?[3] he asks. What was Abraham's *experience*? And not just his experience in general. This question is simply the next in the series of questions Paul started to ask at the end of chapter 3, and all of them are about God. Paul isn't setting out to tell us anything about Abraham. He is setting out to tell us what Abraham's experience teaches us about *what God is like*.

It is crucial to understand this. A long history of Christian teaching has accustomed us to reading the text—any text—with human beings as the central focus. That means interpreting Paul's question here to mean "What did Abraham find *about how to gain acceptance with God?*" Unconsciously assumed is that we know most of what we need to know about God already. As good Christian people we know that we can't earn approval from the God we assume we know all about by outward shows of religious duty or by doing good deeds. How do we gain his approval then? Well, we gain it *through faith*. It is people of faith who gain God's favor, and that is the sort of person that we need to aim to be. This is how this understanding of the text runs. And all the time the focus is upon us.

But as we have seen from the letter so far, Paul's central interest is *God*, God's character, God's glory, God's solitary and sovereign act of deliverance in the faithfulness of Jesus Messiah. And what that means for us, of course. But God, not us, is the complete center of Paul's attention. Here that God-centered focus never wavers. "Is it a matter of Abraham himself and anything he did?" Paul asks in verse 2. "If so, he has something to boast about. But that is impossible before a God like this!"[4] Abraham had come from a world where the gods were many, each with their own benefits to give, angers to avoid, and rituals to practice in order to gain favor. But the God who had encountered Abraham was not that kind of god. No religious "work" could manipulate or influence him, no sacrifice or good deed earn any claim upon him. Abraham found that the chief characteristic of the kind of God who encountered him was *grace;* he discovered that the only response to such grace was faith. Abraham is our representative, not in what he learned about *how to please* God, but in the journey of discovery God led him on *into who God himself is.*

UNPACKING A KEY TEXT

A second thing to note is that Paul's decision to talk about Abraham here is not random. He is not just introducing an interesting example, he is *expounding the Scriptures.* "What does the scripture say?" he asks. And the Scripture he quotes was an absolutely key one for the way Old Testament religion understood itself: Gen 15:6. "Abraham trusted God, and it was reckoned to him for righteousness."

We have lost the sense of how well-known this verse from Genesis was in the God-fearing world of Paul's day. It was an absolutely key text. We might compare the importance in our Christian world of John 3:16, "For God so loved the world that he gave his only son, that whoever believes in him should not perish but have eternal life." I learned that as a memory verse in Sunday school, and the sense of it ran through all the thinking and the teaching of the little community of which I was then a part. Among the God-fearing people of Paul's day, whether they were full members of the Jewish community or, like most of the members of the fledgling Roman Christian community, converts from among the nations, Gen 15:6 had a similar importance. If Jewish children had memory verses in those days, then this surely was one of them.

The whole of chapter 4 is Paul's careful examination of the meaning of that one key Scripture. He takes each of the three key words in it in turn. First, he asks, what do we mean by righteousness being *reckoned* to Abraham? The answer to that extends from verse 4 to verse 8. Secondly, what significance is there in the fact that it was *Abraham* who put his faith in God? That takes us from verse 9 through verse 12. And, finally, what does it mean that Abraham *had faith*? This is the subject of verses 13 to 22.

It is intriguing to see that Paul's motive in examining this key verse from Genesis is very similar to what we are trying to do with his own letter. The church has always recognized Romans as Scripture, something through which God speaks today. But down the centuries many conflicting voices have gathered around it. Old controversies and theological schemes overlie the text so deeply in some places that Paul's own voice gets lost in the clamor of his commentators. And that was precisely, in Paul's own day, the situation with this Genesis text. Paul is clearing away the misunderstandings and religious presuppositions that over the years had gathered around it. "We've been taught to think about this verse in one particular way," he is saying. "But if we really examine the text, we find that it is saying something very different. It is not in fact about how a person earns God's favor. It is about how a person lives before a God who, without us doing anything, encounters us in grace and in promise."

THE GOD WHO TREATS THE UNGODLY AS RIGHTEOUS

First of all, Paul asks, what do we mean by this word "reckon"? Although their meanings aren't identical, the Hebrew, Greek, and English words for *reckon* or *count* all have this in common: they can be used in two senses.[5] A *secondary* meaning of each has to do with counting: "reckon up, calculate, credit." The primary meaning, however (from which the other is derived), has to do with a personal assessment: "to think, evaluate, consider to be." And immediately we can see what Paul wants to ask about the Genesis passage. Does "reckon" in Gen 15:6 mean *credit* as righteousness (as in a set of accounts)? Or does it mean *treat* as righteousness (as in a personal relationship)? In other words, did Abraham *earn something* by his faith? Or was he *drawn into a relationship* despite anything that he was or anything he had done?

The Jewish rabbis knew the answer to this with certainty. "Abraham became heir of the world *because of the merit of the faith* with which he believed in the Lord," says one ancient commentary. In the same document, as in the Exodus story Israel stands at the brink of the Red Sea, God considers what to do: "The faith with which their father Abraham believed in me *merits* that I should divide the sea for them."[6] And, in the first book of Maccabees, part of the apocryphal Old Testament Scriptures, we read this:

> Remember *the works performed by our ancestors*, each in his generation,
> and you will win great honor and everlasting renown.
> Was not Abraham tested and found faithful,[7]
> was that not considered as *making him righteous*?[8]

Is this how it is, then, asks Paul. Did Abraham *work* for his acceptance with God? For someone who works (v. 4), he points out, wages aren't a matter of the employer's overflowing goodness, they are considered to be fair return, something the worker can claim as a due. Paul isn't talking about the difference between a "gift" (the word doesn't occur here) and "wages." He is thinking about *who has the initiative in the relationship*, and therefore what kind of relationship it is. Is our life lived in joyful dependence upon the free generosity of the gracious God? Or do we have a merely pagan understanding of God as a being whom we can somehow make obliged to us?

What is God like? Well, astonishingly, God is *the God who makes the ungodly righteous* (v. 5), drawing them into relationship with him. This is the reversal of all religious expectation. It comes as a shock. It is not the good-living and the religious, says Paul, but those far away from God whom he calls. But of course *that is every human being*, as he has so conclusively demonstrated in 3:9–20. We Christian people tend to forget. One is reminded of Jesus' retort to the good religious people of his day, "I haven't come to call righteous people, but sinners."[9] It is a comment rich in irony. Implicit is the suggestion that if his hearers don't consider themselves to be in that category, well then, the good news is not for them. But they *are* in fact in that category. Everyone is.

There are no works, then, that we can do to earn God's favor or God's call. How could there be? The initiative is God's completely. So, Paul is telling us, the Genesis 15 passage is not in the first instance about Abraham at all. It is about God. And the God whom it is about is the God of free grace, the God of unearned gifts. "Reckoning" is, then, not crediting. It is the granting of a gift. And what is that gift? It is *righteousness*: God declaring us to be, and transforming us to be, the kind of people who are fit to stand opposite him as partners in a relationship.[10]

MAKING RIGHTEOUS

We need to clear up a misunderstanding. This making righteous is not a legal metaphor. Righteousness has *nothing to do with the law at all*. Although Paul is using every resource at his disposal to make this clear at every step of his discussion, still, somehow, human religion seeps in. We have learned to think that what Paul is saying is that, of course one can't be made righteous *through the Jewish law* (understanding that rather narrowly as a moral code rather than as the whole Torah), but that there is nonetheless *another kind of law*, a heavenly law, under which a penalty for wrongdoing must always be paid. Fortunately Jesus has paid that penalty for us, indeed he has paid the whole huge accumulated punishment incurred by all humanity down all of history, so that we can be made righteous, that is, discharged without conviction.[11] I'm sure we are all familiar with this narrative. What can we say about it? Just this: wherever else in the New Testament that idea might live, Paul knows nothing of it in Romans. His whole point here in these verses is that God does *not* deal with us on these terms. God is not interested in our good or bad deeds, he is interested in *us*; he is not interested in what we do, he is interested in who we *are*. And that is because of who *he* is. He is not the keeping-score god of human religion, he is the living God of sovereign grace and salvation.

Being declared righteous, then, is not a verdict, but God's active word: God declares Abraham to be righteous and therefore he *is* righteous, righteous in an active sense; counted to be so, and enabled to be so. A simple declaration of innocence means nothing. We are not in a courtroom looking back on some isolated deed or deeds in the past. We are here now, standing before God, in the midst of life. What is necessary is *a changed life*—and that is what God gives.[12] We are not talking about wages; we are talking about this *gift*. And it is a gift not only for Abraham. It is a gift for all of us who read and hear and understand, and, like Abraham, raise our empty hands to receive.

NO KEEPING COUNT

Abraham wasn't the only one who had been encountered by a God like this, and the lesson we learn from him is only half the story. Paul now quotes from the first two verses of Ps 32. The psalm is a song of rejoicing in the unearned and undeserved blessings of God. And here, right at the start of the poem, "Blessed are those whose wrongdoings are forgiven!" David cries. This is the further thing Paul wants us to notice. Not only is the free grace of God not dependent upon any *merit* we might have to offer, it is also not diminished or deflected by our *wrongdoings*, the things that burden and shame us, the failures that rise up to haunt us in the night.

Let us not skip too quickly over this. The psalm isn't talking about raiding the cookie jar or getting angry with someone who cuts in front of us on the highway. David had blood on his hands. He was a soldier, and had killed other men in battle: men who had wives and children, and lives to live. He had used his power and charm to steal someone else's wife, and had then ordered the "accidental" death of her husband. Underneath these more spectacular things, the things that got the biblical headlines, lay all the smaller and the hidden things: the angry word that tore someone's heart, the living person that in this or that situation was seen or used merely as a thing, the blunders, the good intentions that never made it into action, the deliberate wrongs. Small or great, our sins and failures weigh upon our lives, and that weight only increases as we get older.

But what David is saying is that, whatever we feel—and the rest of the psalm shows how deeply David himself does feel it—*that is not the way God sees our lives*. As we have seen, our good deeds are not something that God counts up. But, David tells us, *he doesn't count up our failures either*. There is no steadily increasing debt to pay. On the contrary, the wrongdoings which weigh upon our hearts are *forgiven*, our sins are *covered*; the Lord *will not by any means* (the expression is very emphatic) *count them against us* (v. 8).[13] While it goes against all our religious instincts, and is different perhaps from much that we have been taught, the fact is that *sin is not a counting up kind of thing*. Its nature is quite different. Sin is the breaking of a relationship. Only the restoration of that relationship can put it right. And the restoration of that relationship is what making righteous means.[14]

Was Abraham's righteousness something he had earned, then? No, for God is not a bookkeeping God. Our relationship with him is of quite another kind. It is personal, not commercial. There is no credit ledger (v. 4)—and no debit ledger either (vv. 6–8). God is not a god like the gods of paganism who keep score, who must be appeased and placated, who can perhaps be bought or manipulated. He is the Lord, the God of free grace, the God who beyond hope or deserving calls ungodly human beings into relationship with himself. Let us not then, says Paul, continue fooling around with weighing up credit or debt. There is only a relationship or not. And the relationship we have is nothing we have earned. It is *reckoned to us* by God. It is something that he considers us to be—and gives us the power to be. It is his gift. Because that is the kind of God that God is.

THE ANCESTOR OF ALL WHO HAVE FAITH

Having established what "reckoned" means, Paul turns in verse 9 to his second question. Is this blessing only for those within the religious community, or is it also given to those outside it? Well, Paul says, that same Genesis verse gives us the answer. What does it mean that righteousness is reckoned to *Abraham*? Who was Abraham?

Well, we know who he was, of course. If there was a Christian version of the Hollywood Walk of Fame, certain names would have to be on it. Luther, Wilberforce, Florence Nightingale, Desmond Tutu, Mother Theresa, Oscar Romero; each of us could add 20 names to such a list without even trying. And Abraham. On any accounting, Abraham would need to have one of the first and largest stars in any Christian Walk of Fame.

Which is fine, says Paul. Except that *he wasn't a Christian*. And of course he wasn't! We knew that! He was a Jew! But, no, says Paul, *he wasn't a Jew either*. Jews claim descent not from Abraham alone, but more specifically from his grandson, Jacob, whose name, after a memorable encounter, God changed to Israel.[15] And the experience of deliverance and journeying with God that forged a rag-tag rump of Jacob's formerly enslaved descendants into a unified and covenanted people of Israel still lay far in the future. Abraham certainly wasn't a Jew. The idea of being a Jew hadn't been invented yet.

What was Abraham, then? Well, says Paul, he was a *pagan*. He was one of the ungodly (v. 5). He had no theological knowledge, he had no Law, he had no circumcision as a sign of privileged standing, and he had no faithful covenant community. He had only a command from a God previously unknown to him.[16] Taking that command seriously, he found that he had stumbled into a relationship where this God, not the human being, had the initiative. A relationship where ritual and magic and sacrifice and all the ways that people had down the years sought to appease and manipulate the divine were useless. Where there was only the bare encounter between a man and a God who actively sought a relationship with him, a God who called and empowered him to be able to endure that relationship, a God who came to him with grace and with promise beyond hope. "Abraham put his faith in God," says Paul, "and it was reckoned to him for righteousness" (v. 3).

This wasn't a mistake, says Paul (v. 11b). God's purpose in the first place was to make him ancestor of all those who, like him, respond to God's call from outside the religious community, and are welcomed into his friendship. And—notice the reversal here of the order that we in our pride would expect—he is the ancestor *also* of those of us who are not only members of the faithful community, but who also follow the example of the faith in God that Abraham had before there even was such a community.

I speak to those who, like me, have been members of the church for most of their life. Can we bear this word? Can we bear this reversal of all that in our hearts we feel is right and proper, this removal of all that is our due before God? Seriously, our due! We have been faithful members of the Christian community, perhaps for many years. Doesn't that count for something? How can someone outside the church be freely accepted by God, even when they know nothing about him? It reminds us too baldly of that over-the-top saying of Jesus that the dodgy financiers and the prostitutes were going into the kingdom ahead of the faithful. Then there was that other odd thing that Jesus said about *religious people* needing to be born all over again; about the freedom of God's spirit to blow where it pleases. Just between the two of us, don't you sometimes, even as a Christian, find Jesus hard to cope with? Isn't it fundamentally wrong, for example, that story about the latecomers to the vineyard earning as much as those who had worked all through the day? And wasn't it just outrageous for him on the cross to say to a man who had been a thief and perhaps a murderer "today you will be with me in Paradise"?[17]

Oh dear. Perhaps we should pause for a moment to let what Paul is saying here sink in. For underneath all the layers, this is the truth that the example of Abraham confronts us with. This is what it means that *Abraham* was reckoned to be righteous by God. This is also, incidentally, the teaching of Paul's which so inflamed the religious authorities in Jerusalem that they gave silent assent to the plot to ambush and murder him. Do we begin to understand that, now? At the most fundamental level this is also the teaching for which Jesus of Nazareth was crucified. We are faced with a decision. Can we hear this word? For this is what Abraham found. There is only one God. And this is what that God is like.

THE HOPE AND THE PROMISE

As challenging to our pride as Paul's teaching may be, it is also a message of hope. It sets our feet on the right path again. It helps us understand who we are. Like Abraham we too are wanderers on the earth, looking for a home. And like him we also find ourselves addressed, called, drawn in fear and awe into a relationship with the living God. The God we encounter is the same God that Abraham knew. A God who doesn't count up either our good deeds or our bad ones, but simply places us in the position of those who are fit to stand opposite him in a covenant relationship. A God who commits himself to enabling us to be that righteous human being—the person whom we are not yet, but whom in his grace and his good time we will become. A God who will plant that in us and draw that out of us. A God of grace. Isn't David's shout of joy precisely right? How truly and utterly blessed are those who find themselves called by God, forgiven, redeemed and restored! And these words were not written for Abraham's sake alone, says Paul. They were written also for us.

God's dealings with Abraham did not stop with giving him a standing as his counterpart in a relationship. He also gave him a promise; that is, a goal and a purpose. His life was to be a life that had meaning. And that promise, says Paul, came through *the righteousness of faith* (v. 13). But what does it mean to have faith in God?[18] And so Paul comes to the third thing he wants to unpack from the story told in Genesis 15: the meaning of faith itself.

He is not setting out to define a word. We already know about the word faith: that it describes a relationship; a relationship seen now from one side, now the other. Faith is on the one hand the trust and confidence two friends or business partners or lovers *place in* one another, and on the other hand the reliability and faithfulness that they *offer* each other. Faithfulness generates trust, and trust evokes an answering trustworthiness. Friends look after each other, partners rely upon one another, lovers love each other. We are not dealing with an abstract quality. Faith always has to do with *this relationship*, here, now.[19]

The question Paul is asking, then, is not about the meaning of the word in general (for everyone knew that), but *what meaning it must bear in the Gen 15:6 context*. Why ask that question? Well, as we have seen, the Jewish rabbis knew the meaning it must have there. Abraham was *faithful to God's commands*, they believed, and that faithfulness earned him God's favor. Abraham had fulfilled his side of the bargain, and because of that God was bound to fulfill his side.

Nonsense, says Paul. The Genesis text makes clear that God's promise is totally unqualified. God was not bound to do anything at all. Nor did he require Abraham to do anything. Abraham found himself encountered by a God who *promised* rather than demanded. He found that God was *a promising God*. None of this has anything to do with a Law (v. 13). God didn't give Abraham rules to obey or actions to perform. Instead, Abraham trusted what God said about himself. He believed that when God said something, he would do it. That was all. Abraham staked his life on God's promise. And so he became, as with great boldness a later Old Testament writer would say, *God's friend*.[20] Friendship! That is what the righteousness of faith means.

Think about it. The God who encounters Abraham asks nothing of him. He seeks no merit. The momentum of his gracious approach to Abraham pushes all wrongs and failures behind him. Instead of laying these kinds of requirements upon Abraham, God astonishingly pledges *himself*. He commits his own character and credibility in offering to Abraham not only his blessing and friendship now in the present, but also the promise of his settled purpose to bless him and his descendants down all the future generations. Is this not remarkable? But, Paul says, this is the kind of God that

God is. What did God promise? He promised that Abraham would "inherit the world" (v. 9). Childless in his old age, nonetheless God declared him to be "the father of many nations" (v. 17–18).

What was the significance of such a promise for Abraham? It was twofold: it *gave him a standing in the world now,* and it *guaranteed him a future.* In the first case it meant that he was no isolated individual, with some individual personal religion. God was telling him that his life and what he had learned about God was bound up with the whole life of the world: with the settled inhabitants of the land in which he wandered, with the traders and explorers who moved through it, and ultimately with that of the great empires over the horizon. His life was to influence the world's destiny. That would be so for him *and for his descendants.* It is not a matter of merely physical descent. The source is not Abraham, but the God in whom he trusted. "He is the father of us all," Paul declares. "As it is written, "I have made you the father of many nations.""[21]

The fulfillment of these promises was the basis of Abraham's hope (v. 18). But as a careful reader of the Scriptures, Paul makes another observation. He notes the remarkable fact that God's promise is not couched in the future tense, as Abraham's hope has to be. It is in the past tense: "I *have made* you the father of many nations" (v. 17). The promises of God are not anticipations. They are facts. God says it, and it is done. All Abraham is asked to do is to watch it come about.

Once again, Paul has driven us back to the character of God. What did Abraham learn about God? He learned that he was a *promising* God. The problem with those who "adhere to the Law" (v. 14) rather than to the God who gave the Law is, Paul says, that they have a cramped and diminished understanding of God. One who replaces allegiance to God by allegiance to the Law comes to see God as primarily wrathful, a God needing to be placated by unceasing vigilance about rules of behavior and observance. But where there is no Law standing between us and God, then keeping or breaking the rules is not the issue (v. 15). It never was the issue.

That is where faith comes in (v. 16). Faith isn't another kind of activity that we need to learn how to do. It is a description of an *actual relationship.* Faith grounds the promise not on anything that we could do, but in God's character. "It is founded upon grace, therefore it is certain," says Paul. And certain for all: not only for those who by grace and by accident of birth have grown up within the community of the faithful, but also to all who reach out in faith to God, just as Abraham did.

THE PROMISE AND THE PROMISER

What was all of that like in Abraham's actual experience? Now Paul moves from the theology of the thing, the way faith is grounded not in anything that we do but in the character of God, to ask *what that faith felt like in the actual experience of Abraham.* And it was a mixed experience! As when once he looked up at the night sky and heard

God's promise about the number of his descendants, sometimes it was great. But other times, when the years went by and he and his wife weren't getting any younger, it was tough. Abraham was no plaster saint, as both Paul and his readers knew. Living this way stretched his resources. Often his situation was that of "hoping against hope" (v. 18), an expression that from this letter has passed into the language. Because what God had asked him to trust in wasn't easy. Abraham knew the facts of biology as well as we do. There comes an age when a man's sexual ability falls away. And Sarah was barren: they had been trying for a child ever since they had married, with no success.[22] The fulfillment of God's promise wasn't just hard to believe, it was *impossible* to believe.

Now, the word "impossible" is an idea. But what did the knowledge of the impossible mean in Abraham's daily experience? It meant a shadow that colored every joy. It meant a shut door where the future should be. It meant a heaviness in going about everyday tasks and wondering whether they meant anything. But despite all that, "with regard to God's promise he never wavered through doubt," Paul tells us (v. 20). Or, as one translation brilliantly puts it, "He didn't allow his doubts to shake his faith." Does that sound like a contradiction? Not at all. Abraham was no starry-eyed dreamer but a practical and intelligent man. He knew the score. *He didn't believe this could happen.* He would have been stupid to believe it. So, he didn't believe the promise. Instead *he put his faith in the one who promised.*

Which brings us to the heart of Paul's teaching about the nature of faith. Faith is precisely *not* something that we bring, something that we have, something that we do. Faith is God's hand extended to us in blessing beyond hope or imagination, his promise that comes to us in spite of our disbelief, our failure, our lack of anything to offer or to bring. Faith is God's grace through and through as we lift up our empty hands to receive it.

"So this is what that old Scripture really means," Paul tells us. "This is what was counted to Abraham for righteousness." But we are not talking about Abraham alone. We don't have an interesting story about someone long ago, from which we can learn general truths. Like the sun through a magnifying glass Paul now gathers together all that he has said so far and focuses it with burning intensity upon our own lives. Gen 15:6 was not written just about Abraham, he tells us (v. 23), it was written for us. For we too stand in the path of the promise of the living God.

10

Romans 4:23—5:11

"Now these words, 'it was reckoned to him', were written not only about him ²⁴but also about us. It will be reckoned to us also, to those who put their faith in the one who raised Jesus our Lord from the dead. ²⁵He was given up because of our wrongdoings and was raised because of our being made righteous.

^{5:1} Having then been made righteous on the basis of faith, let us have peace with God through our Lord Jesus the Messiah, ²the one through whom by faith we have come to stand in this place of grace and privilege. Let us boast in our hope of the glory of God. ³And not only that, let us also boast in our sufferings, recognizing that suffering produces endurance, ⁴and endurance produces character, and character produces hope,⁵and hope does not let us down, because God's love has been poured into our hearts through the holy Spirit that has been given to us. ⁶Indeed, while we were still weak, at the right time the Messiah died for the godless. ⁷Almost no-one would die for another person, no matter how righteous they were—though perhaps, for a truly good person, someone might actually dare to do it. ⁸But God demonstrates his love for us in that while we still were still sinners the Messiah died for us.

⁹Much more certainly then, having now been made righteous in his sacrificial death, will we be rescued from the Wrath through him. ¹⁰For if while we were enemies, we were restored to fellowship with God through the death of his Son, much more certainly, given that renewal of relationship, will we be rescued in his life. ¹¹But that isn't all: we boast in God through our Lord Jesus the Messiah, because through him we have been given that restored relationship now."[23]

DESPITE THE WAY THINGS are laid out in our printed Bibles, the final verses of chapter 4 are not the conclusion of something. Instead, they are the start of something: they are the *statement of topic* for the next section of Paul's letter. They are that familiar compressed initial summary which we now recognize to be characteristic of Paul's style and characteristic of oral teaching in his time: this is the bud from which his argument in the following four chapters will open out, blossoming at last in the triumphant conclusion of chapter 8.

And the change of tone is obvious. From *confrontation* (of our religious self-righteousness) and *declaration* (of God's mighty act to save his world) Paul now moves into a section in which the dominant note is *exhortation*. What has been learned must now be lived. Just as Abraham followed so long ago, so we too must follow.

Abraham came to know God, and what he learned was something fundamental: the same faithfulness and commitment to his world that he found we see dramatically demonstrated in the life, death, and resurrection of Jesus. But knowing God is not just a matter of believing certain truths. We only truly come to know him by living a life. Abraham didn't come to know God by hearing about him. In fact he didn't know that the Living God even existed until he heard his call and stepped away from the little gods of paganism to follow that call. He learned who God was, not through a vision or by thinking deep thoughts, but by experiencing his faithfulness in practice, in the thick of the challenges of life. The righteousness God reckoned to him was not an abstract status. It was a relationship that was worked out in daily living. And so it will be for us. We enter into the righteousness Messiah has won for us not by believing things but by actively following God's call. Just as Abraham did.

The next four chapters, then, are a sustained and passionate exhortation to live a new life in the power of the resurrection. "Those words "it was reckoned to him" are not just about Abraham," Paul tells us. "They are also about us." Notice the future tense in what follows: "Righteousness will be reckoned to us also, to those who put their faith in the one who raised Jesus our Lord from the dead." It *will be* reckoned. God's gift is not a pronouncement, but the power to live a life. It is the power of the resurrection of Jesus. It is the power of the spirit of God at work in us as it was in him. And it will be reckoned *to us*: we in the twenty-first century hear God's promise to us just as directly as Abraham did so long ago.

GIVEN UP

Hmm. We have heard this kind of thing before, haven't we? Righteousness, new life, the Spirit's power: these are phrases we have heard preachers use in a million sermons. They sound full of promise. We feel we should value them and believe them. But sometimes the language seems hard to relate to anything much in our weekday lives. Am I alone in feeling this? The phrases are grand, but when we leave the building on Sunday morning we tend to leave all that behind us too. It feels like *church talk*. Well, before we move on let us give Paul a moment to tell us just what he means in these very compressed statements. Because what is here is more than church talk, I promise you.

The four things Paul says in verse 25 contain both *less* and *much more* than I at least have been taught to find in them. What is Paul not saying here—and what *is* he saying? The four statements form a pattern: the first and third describe an act of God; the second and fourth give the reason for that act.

He was given up because of our wrongdoings and was raised because of our having been made righteous.

Let us take each of these things in turn.

Firstly, Paul says, Jesus was *given up* because of our wrongdoings. What does that mean? Not given up *to death*, despite the addition of this phrase in several translations. Of course the context of this giving up is indeed the death of Jesus, as the preceding verse indicates. But that is only the external manifestation of something much deeper. And immediately we remember the place where Paul has already used this word "given up," and used it with such deep seriousness: in his catalogue of human failure and wrongdoing in chapter 1.[24] "God *gave them up* to the lusts of their hearts," he told us there. "He *gave them up* to degrading passions . . . He *gave them up* to a debased mind, and to things that should not be done." (1:24, 26, 28)

As we saw back there, God's response to human wrongdoing is not, as we might humanly expect, thunderbolts and punishment. God's anger against all that spoils or mars his good creation is demonstrated by something far more serious: by his *withdrawal*, by his active *giving us up* to the consequences of the course we have chosen. Wrong deeds are only the fruit of the plant; the root is our active rejection of God (1:19–23). And in this terrifying phrase, three times Paul repeats the consequences of that rejection: "God gave them up." Now, here in chapter 4 he uses the very same word about Jesus. Because of our wrong deeds, he tells us, *Jesus* was given up. Because of our wrong deeds Jesus suffered that fall into the darkness. Can we grasp the force of that?

The next thing Paul says is that he was given up "because of our *wrong deeds*."[25] The church rightly or wrongly talks a great deal about wrong deeds (or, using the word in a quite different way to the way in which Paul uses it, about *sins*). And we all know the kinds of actions or attitudes that these terms describe. But what do all those different wrong things have in common? What is their fundamental nature? This will sound a little strange at first: the thing that is common to them all is *the lack of something*. The lack of what? The lack of love; the lack of truth; the lack of respect for others, the lack of honor or faithfulness. Wrongdoing means an emptiness where there should be something. It means turning our back on something essential to being human. Wrong deeds are a sign of something *missing*. They are a hole that we have torn in our integrity, in our wholeness as a person.

The central lack, as Paul made clear back there in chapter 1, is lack of godliness: the failure to allow God to be the center of our lives. That is the fundamental void from which all these other things derive. Whatever the effect of our wicked behavior on other people, wrongdoing is first of all slamming the door against God.[26] Trespasses, wrong deeds, sins, however we want to describe them, all are characterized by *the absence of something that ought to be there* in a fully human life.

Now, this isn't the normal way in which we religious people understand wrong deeds. We tend to think about them not as the absence but as the *presence* of something. They haunt us, they are powerful, and they come to have a life of their own. We feel that they are something which can accumulate, like a stack of rusted cars in a scrap yard, or a mound of garbage in the city dump. But this is incorrect in two ways. For a start, a wrong act is not a thing separate from the person who commits it. A wrong act isn't a kind of free-floating thing, it is *a person* who has done something false to themselves or to others. Wrong acts therefore cannot mount up. Their consequences can accumulate, but the deeds themselves cannot. They are not the kind of thing that can be counted. They are personal. And they are not a thing at all, they are the absence of something.

How then are wrong deeds to be dealt with? Instinctively, even with regard to our own wrongdoing, we feel that they deserve to be punished. People from every tradition across the millennia have sought to find ways to appease their gods and thereby to avoid punishment for their wrongdoing. But, Paul has told us, this is not how it is with the Living God. As he responded to God's call, Abraham discovered that he was not like the gods of paganism in any way. He did not keep count of good deeds, as they did. But nor did he keep count of bad ones. Relationship with him was of a different order altogether: it was personal, not commercial; it was based not on accounting but on faith, obedience, and unmerited grace. It was a free gift, as love must always be.

How are wrong deeds to be dealt with? The absence of something cannot be dealt with by punishment. It can only be dealt with by filling the absence with what ought to be there. Faithlessness can only be met by faithfulness. Hatred can only be defeated by love. Disobedience can be made right only by obedience. "Do not be overcome by evil," Paul will tell his Roman listeners later in the letter, "but *overcome evil with good*."[27] That is the only way in which it can happen. And this, Paul tells us, is precisely what God through Jesus the Messiah has done. He has been righteous where we were unrighteous. He has been faithful where we have been unfaithful. He has been obedient where we were disobedient. And he has done and been all this *on our behalf*. He has done it *in our place*.

This is not anything new. Paul has already reminded us how God passed over sinful deeds in the past;[28] and how in Messiah Jesus he made it possible for those who trust him to be made fully human in the way that Jesus was (3:25-26). But given the way human religion with its fears and pagan ideas about God tends to creep into the way we interpret these passages, we can't remind ourselves of that often enough.

ROMANS UNPLUGGED
THE SPACE BETWEEN THE STARS

Recognizing that wrong deeds are the absence of something rather than the presence of something is not to make light of their power. Everyone knows the damage that malice, or greed, or misuse of power, or lying, or broken faith can wreak in individual lives or in whole societies. We need to distinguish, though, between the *act* and its *effect*. The effect is destructive, but the *act* is a deficiency, the absence of something. Think about the idea of cold. What is "cold"? When you try to explain what it is, you discover that you cannot define it in terms of itself. Cold—even the cold of interstellar space—is not something in itself. It is *the absence of heat*. The fact that it is an absence does not make it less powerful or destructive, though. I am reminded of Robert Frost's poem "Fire and Ice":

> Some say the world will end in fire,
> Some say in ice.
> From what I've tasted of desire
> I hold with those who favour fire.
>
> But if it had to perish twice,
> I think I know enough of hate
> To say that for destruction ice
> Is also great
> And would suffice.

Frost knows about the power of evil. Our wrong deeds and selfish attitudes are tragically destructive. They undermine and cripple and warp and kill. But that they do so is not because of any power they have in themselves. Evil is not a thing in its own right. If it was, then either God would have created it or its source would lie somewhere other than God. Neither alternative is possible. Rather, evil is the rejection or the destruction of God's good creation. The power that evil wields comes ultimately from God. It must: there is no other source of power in the universe. But evil's power is stolen power. Any power that it has is merely the shadow cast by God's choice of something else. It is the power of God's choosing seen from a place that he has rejected. It is the power of creation seen from within the chaos that God denied when he gave shape and form to the world.[29] It is the power of the absence of good.

This explains why, in those three terrifying statements back there in chapter 1, Paul tells us that God *gives us up* to our disobedience and folly. He doesn't give us up out of carelessness or spite. He gives us up because what we are choosing is the nothingness, the state of disorder and chaos that he turned his back upon in the act of creation. God cannot follow us where he himself has chosen not to go. He cannot follow us into a place that he has rejected. The Creator cannot follow us into un-creation.

Or maybe—possibility beyond our imagination—he *can*. For what Paul is telling us in 4:23ff is that he *has*. Paul has not lost sight of the questions that arise out of the comprehensive failure of human beings to be faithful. He has articulated some of those questions in 3:1–8, and others lie close below the surface. If all have sinned and fall short of the glory of God, does that mean that the Creator God is helpless in the face of evil? Is God forced to watch sadly as we use the freedom he has given us to destroy rather than to create, to choose death rather than life, to unravel our wholeness and integrity as human beings made in his image? Not a chance, says Paul. For now in Jesus we see *God's* righteousness revealed. A great door swings open. The way we understand the world and our place in it changes forever. We see that God has taken responsibility for his world by entering it himself in the person of Jesus the Messiah. And for our wrong deeds, for the comprehensive failure of us human beings to be human, *he himself* was given up. That has to be one of the most astonishing sentences ever written.

I wonder how many readers of this book remember the classic movie *2001: A Space Odyssey* (dir. Stanley Kubrick, Stanley Kubrick Productions). At least, it is now a classic: I saw it as a new release back in 1969. Hmm. Dated as the film is in many ways, it contains one unforgettable image. One of the crew of an interplanetary spacecraft is working on a tether outside the vehicle. Inside, the computer controlling the ship has gone insane. As the engineer completes his repairs, the computer arranges an accident. The man's tie to the spacecraft is cut, and without that essential link he drifts away. At first you can continue to see him, as the sun reflects from the spacesuit. But then slowly he recedes further and further from the ship. The dot of light grows smaller and smaller. And then at last it winks out, lost against the background of the stars.

"Jesus our Lord was given up," Paul tells us. In Jesus' searing cry of desolation on the cross we hear the echo of a convulsion in the heart of God himself: "My God, my God! Why have you abandoned me?"[30]

WERE YOU THERE WHEN THEY CRUCIFIED MY LORD?

Why, in that moment, did God abandon Jesus? The second of our four statements gives the answer. He was given up, Paul tells us, *because of our wrongdoings.*

Not the wrong deeds of someone else: Paul does not say *them.* Nor would we expect him to. We have heard all that he has said so far, and realize how far we, like all humankind, fall short of the glory of God. We cannot step aside and pretend that in the death of Jesus we were somehow not involved. We were there. In the events of Good Friday we human beings not only failed him, we rejected him.

Think about the cascade of failures and betrayals during that crucial couple of days surrounding the death of Jesus. Firstly, although autocratic and brutal, the Romans were renowned for their system of justice. Trials were intended to be fair, and judicial verdicts were based on testimony and evidence. And yet Pilate, faced with the pressure of the crowds on the one hand and the blackmail of the religious authorities on the other, stepped back from justice, and knowingly condemned an innocent man to death.

It wasn't only Pilate. Above all nations Israel prided itself in the privilege of knowing and serving the one true God. And yet, for good religious reasons (to crush what they saw as false teaching that threatened the foundations of the faith) and for good political reasons (if things went on unchecked the Romans would destroy the nation and remove freedom of worship), the leaders of the Jewish church not only delivered Jesus over to the Romans, but insisted on the death penalty.

And it wasn't only the religious leaders. The disciples and other supporters of Jesus were of course not a party to these crimes. But knowing the consequences of criminal association as only those who live in a police state can, the disciples ran away. There was some support for Jesus in the corridors of power. Nicodemus and Joseph of Arimathea are two of the names we know; perhaps there were others. But that support was too little and came too late. Even the love of the women who followed Jesus to Calvary, and that of faithful John who stood at the foot of the cross beside them, was not sufficient to deliver him. Every human resource fell short.

Fearful Pilate, the jealous religious leaders, the ordinary people who had no power, the powerful people whose political reach or simple love was insufficient to avert catastrophe: these are our representatives. We were there. All of us were there. The human race was on trial, and we failed him. It has happened so often in the history of the world. But now, in this particular place at this particular time, the person involved is God himself, stepping into human existence, the Living God submitting himself to our judgment upon him. All of human history is summed up here. God comes into the world and we spit him out of it again. This is what we do to God, what we always do to God. The lies, the failures, and the betrayals that delivered Jesus to the cross were our wrong deeds. He was given up because of them.

Only one thing makes the burden of this less than insupportable. It is this: *there is yet another person in the story who is also our representative.* Where human beings fail, God does not fail. In majesty and utterly alone, on the cross Jesus takes his place as our representative. Having lived our life he now dies our death, obedient to the last to the way of his Father. In order to bring us back to himself, God in his Messiah goes into the heart of the negation of his own creation. He goes into death. He goes into the unmaking, into the lostness and desolation that we human beings choose for ourselves. He suffers our mortality. Human experience and the consequences of human failure and rebellion and weakness are taken up into the experience of God himself.

Don't rush too quickly over this. Of course we know how the story ends. And twice in these two verses the fact that God *raised* Jesus is mentioned. The actual death of Jesus is never presented in the New Testament except in the context of the resurrection. But die he truly did, physical death as the outward sign of something much deeper and more radical, something that runs right down into the foundations of reality. His death is our desperate shame—and our only hope.

ROMANS 4:23—5:11

THE SCANDAL

It is difficult for us in the twenty-first century to realize just what a challenge for belief the death of Jesus was for first-century Christians. The cross as a symbol of Christianity is so common in our culture it has become a cliché. Every church has got one. It is part of the familiar furniture of our belief. A symbol of torture and violent death has become a symbol of religion.

In the first century it was different. Crucifixions *still happened*. It was the standard punishment for terrorists, murderers, and rebels. Those who died in this way were violent men who had been explicitly rejected not only by their society but also by every decent person: the very way the execution was carried out was designed to demonstrate that to the world. And yet Christians proclaimed that a man who had been executed in this way was no less than the Messiah, God's chosen Deliverer, the bringer of judgment and grace to all the world. Twice in his letters Paul describes the proclamation of Jesus' death as a *scandal*: something offensive to every right-thinking person, whether religious or not.[31] And yet Christians speak only the truth when we say that, here at the center of this outrageous thing, the greatness and glory of God is being demonstrated. Jesus on the cross is God himself in his glory and in his majesty, acting to save. Human religion has nothing to say about this. We are talking about what God has done.

BECAUSE IT IS IMPOSSIBLE

Given up, then, *but also raised*. This is the engine that drives the message of the whole letter (1:4). And just as Abraham did not put his faith in the *promise* (because it was impossible) but in *the one who promised*, so we too do not put our faith in truths or in promises. We put our faith in the one who raised Jesus from the dead (v. 24). Christianity is not a collection of facts to believe. It is a relationship with a God who, just as once he brought life itself into being, still today brings life out of death. It is not some true *thing*, it is some true *one*, a person who can be trusted completely.

The one who raised Jesus from the dead! We need to be honest here. If the death of Jesus was shameful, then the story of the resurrection is absurd. We have already in an earlier section recounted the story of Paul's evangelistic encounter with the philosophers of Athens (Acts 17). As he addresses them, all goes well until he comes to the point where rule and authority are given to a man whom God has raised from the dead. "At that point many scoffed," Luke tells us, "though some were keen to hear more." How could one *not* scoff at such an outrageous flight of fantasy? Unless, breaking through every certainty, it actually happened.

As with the death of Jesus, the fact that he was also raised from death is so familiar to us that its meaning barely registers. We sing about it, we read about it, we celebrate it each Easter Sunday. But do we really understand what it is that we are talking about? We are talking about something that is *impossible*. The truth of this must force itself upon every thoughtful person. Arguing that what really happened on Easter day was not a resurrection but the disciples *coming to believe* in one, the fine New Testament scholar Rudolf Bultmann observed that "a resurrection from the dead is utterly inconceivable." Bultmann isn't wrong. Some of us may remember a publicity-seeking group of scholars and others a few years ago who called themselves The Jesus Seminar. At one media briefing reporting their conclusions about the resurrection they produced a couple of morgue attendants to tell the assembled reporters just how impossible it was for a dead person to come back to life. This seems slightly unnecessary, to say the least.

So let us be clear about this: when we talk of resurrection we are dealing with something that sits completely outside the range of possibility. If it happened, it constitutes a boundary-breaking event, something that utterly changes the way we think about everything. If a human being rose again from the dead then nothing in the way we understand the world can be the same.

One of my favorite Bible characters is the disciple Thomas. Returning to the disciples' safe house after a trip to secure supplies, Thomas finds the rest of the group bubbling with joy because—they say—Jesus has returned from the dead. Thomas will have none of it. Whatever happy pill his friends are on, he is not going to buy such manifest nonsense. And isn't he right? The church for years has called this man "Doubting Thomas." But to say this is to malign him. Thomas is sensible, practical, and has his feet firmly on the ground. He knows what every sane person knows: that dead men do not come back to life again. And when, at last, the risen Lord does appear to him personally, he among all the disciples knows precisely what it must mean: "My Lord *and my God*!" he cries. And with that startling identification John concludes his Gospel.[32]

So these are not bland truisms that Paul is invoking here. They are statements that shake the most fundamental beliefs we have about the world. The second-century Christian writer Tertullian puts it in a nutshell:

> The Son of God was crucified: I am not ashamed—because it is shameful.
> The Son of God died: it is instantly credible—because it is preposterous.
> He was buried, and rose again: it is certain—because it is impossible.[33]

The good news of Jesus has nothing about it that is either acceptable or explicable in terms of human religion, or indeed in terms of human thought at all. We are dealing with the outrageous, the impossible—and the true. These are the fingerprints of the creator God acting to remake the world.

ROMANS 4:23—5:11

THE STUBBORN AND SETTLED PURPOSE OF GOD

The climax of these concentrated couple of verses comes as Paul tells us *why* Jesus was raised. That he was raised was nothing that could have been anticipated. The resurrection wasn't inevitable; it was inconceivable. This isn't a fairy story, where after all the drama and the tragedy God with a wave of a wand makes everything all right again. Something much deeper was involved. What does the resurrection *mean*?

Verse 25 has the answer. Jesus, Paul tells us, "was raised *because of our being made righteous*." That is a bit of a mouthful in English, but the meaning is clear. The first half of the verse is about something we have done: our wrongdoings. The second half of the verse is about something *God* has done: making us righteous. The word Paul uses is rare: here and in 5:18 are the only two times it appears in the New Testament. The important thing to notice is that, like *righteousness*, it is a noun. It refers to a fact, to something real. An event has occurred; something has been settled and eternally decided.

What has been decided? For our part, we turn away. We reject God, and we reject God come among us; we nail him to a cross. *Our* decision about God is to reject him. But this rejection, Paul tells us, is not something that shakes the throne of heaven. Our rejection of him is not something God *reacts* to. How could anything we do or not do alter God's eternal purposes? Whatever we decide about him, God's decision about *us* is unshaken. In spite of the cross, Paul tells us, in spite of all our failure and folly, God's decision, his settled purpose, is that we be righteous. His decision about us is that we *will be* fully human, that we *will be* the people who can faithfully stand opposite him in a covenant relationship. Our decision about God is rejection. His decision about us is righteousness. And what God decides God does.

Throughout these chapters, Paul has been telling us about the way God has acted to put us right with himself, to make us whole and make us free. Here he declares to us the decision, the purpose, the settled intention, which lies behind those actions. Even though we reject him, nonetheless, God chooses us. He declares to the universe who we truly are, who we have been since the beginning of creation. Not rebels. Not failures. But people created, chosen and beloved. Failing and foolish though we are, in God's decision about us we are his counterparts, his covenant partners, created for relationship with him. God has decided that that is who we are. God has decided that this is who we will become. He will not settle for anything less.

This, Paul tells us, is why Jesus was raised from the dead. The resurrection of Jesus declares that God remains totally unwavering in his purpose for the good of humankind. Jesus was given over because of our wrong deeds: the resurrection says that God will not accept that as the final word. We reject and despise and fail the Son of God: the resurrection tells us that God's settled purpose for our joy and for our wholeness is not shaken. In the resurrection we understand that *there is nothing we human beings can do that can stop God loving us*. There is nothing that can shake his steady, certain, patient intention to have us for his own. He is the Creator. Sin cannot wreck his purposes. The Crucifixion is the most appalling event in all of history. But that, Paul triumphantly declares, is not the end of the story. Just as Jesus, standing in our place, was let go to fall into the nothing, to fall into the place God rejected when he made the world, so now in the resurrection God the Creator "gives life to the dead and calls into existence the things that do not exist" (4:17): Jesus is raised from the dead. This is not a happy ending, a magical resolution to a sad story. It is *a new creation.* And it is that because of a fact, because, Paul tells us, of our *being declared to be righteous.* The resurrection declares that it is God's stubborn and settled purpose that human beings shall be whole.

SEEING IN STEREO

And now nothing can be the same again. I stumbled across an intriguing news report the other day. Bruce Bridgeman, a 67-year-old brain scientist, had lived all his life able to see in only two dimensions. He had no depth perception. Everything that normal people see in three dimensions he saw as flat, like a photograph or a painting. This meant that he found it difficult to work out how far away things were. He did it by noticing that things that were close to you moved quickly, whereas things that were further away moved more slowly. Without being able to see the difference between objects that were close by and far away, he learned to work it out, by noticing the relative speed at which things moved across the flat panel of his vision.

But suddenly, all of that changed. Invited by friends to go to a screening of the 3-D version of a popular movie, he put on the glasses as a whim, just because everyone else was doing it. Watching the movie was unlike anything he had experienced before. And it didn't stop. As he left the theater, his jaw dropped. He was speechless. The world he saw was completely different to the one he'd left when he'd gone in. A switch had somehow turned on in his brain. For the first time in 67 years, he could see the life of the street outside in all its depth and richness and complexity. And the gift didn't go away. "Riding to work on my bike," he told a reporter, "I now look into a forest beside the road and see a riot of depth, every tree standing out from all the others."

An experience something like this lies behind Paul's excited exhortation in the opening verses of chapter 5. Having seen and understood what the death and resurrection of Jesus God's Messiah means, we look around the familiar territory of our everyday world and everything is different. What before we saw as a flat panel now suddenly leaps into three dimensions. What before we had to try to piece together with painful guesswork, now we understand with overwhelming certainty. And the picture that opens up to us is an *invitation.* We aren't called to gaze in wonder, but to move forward into the splendor of a life that opens out before us with every step we take. Where once there was only a flat panel, a wall, we now see a *world*, a three-dimensional world in which we are summoned to live.

ROMANS 4:23—5:11

PEACE WITH GOD

What does it mean to have peace with God? How can this be something that we are exhorted to do? A number of years ago when I was the sole staff member of a small Christian organization, a lady used to ring me up every now and then. We had never met, but somehow she had got hold of the organization's phone number, and found someone on the other end of the line who was happy to talk to her about God and about life. I have to confess that these calls were sometimes a trial, especially when I was pushing deadlines and knew I would have to work late into the night to meet them. However, remembering C. S. Lewis's observation that the people we most consider interruptions are in fact exactly those whom God has given us to care for today, I tried my best to be patient and caring of a lonely person who had no one else to talk to. Perhaps in the end I didn't get everything right, for there came a time when the calls stopped coming. But I do remember some of the things that we talked about, and in particular this lady's desperate anxiety in case she had not done enough or believed well enough in order to get into heaven. "I know that those who believe in Jesus get to go to heaven," she said, "but how can I be sure that that is me? How can I be *sure*?"

Somehow the Christian church that this lady attended was failing her. The God she knew about was a threatening and mysterious God, a God whom she knew she had to please in a way that wasn't quite clear to her, a God whose final attitude towards her she couldn't be sure of. But what Paul is saying here is that God's attitude towards us is something that we *can* be completely sure of. The death and resurrection of Jesus show us unmistakably that God's settled and certain attitude towards us is only for our good. No matter what we do—even to the extent of the rejection and unbelief and failure that led to the death of Jesus—*God believes in us*, and will have us as his own. We are *beloved*. It is this certainty that Paul is urging us to make our experienced reality. There is no place for fear or doubt any more. We can trust God. That he will never let us down is not just bland church talk. It is a fact that we know because of the death and resurrection of Jesus.

Peace with God is not, however, just the absence of fear. Conscious as we are of our inadequacy and sinfulness, we often struggle to bring positive content into our description of good things. We tend to think of holiness, for example, as the absence of sin instead of the presence in our lives of God's light and grace and joy. Much of our religious tradition understands righteousness as a matter of being squeaky clean, without blame before God, rather than being faith-*full*, reliable, a person who can be trusted to keep their promises. So it is with the word peace: in a world full of strife, distress, and fear we long for peace as being the absence of those things. But the biblical idea of peace goes much further than that. In biblical understanding, peace is the *presence* of prosperity and well-being.[34] It is a life lived in harmony with others. It describes a healthy and joyful community where everybody has their place.

Paul is exhorting us then not only to put our fear of God aside. He is calling us to step forward into the richness of life that is God's good intention for us. And this is something that daily we need to do. Peace is not something that falls upon us from heaven like fairy dust. It is something to be lived. It is something that we are called to step out into and make our own.

The seventeenth-century poet George Herbert understood this. He saw that because of what Jesus has done, having peace with God is, in fact, now a matter of obedience. In his poem "Love"[35] he imagines a dialogue between God and himself as the representative of all of us ashamed and fearful human beings:

> Love bade me welcome. Yet my soul drew back
> Guilty of dust and sin.
> But quick-eyed Love, observing me grow slack
> From my first entrance in,
> Drew nearer to me, sweetly questioning,
> If I lacked anything.
>
> 'A guest,' I answered, *'worthy to be here.'*
> Love said, *'You shall be he.'*
> *'I the unkind, ungrateful? Ah my dear,*
> *I cannot look on thee.'*
> Love took my hand, and smiling did reply,
> *'Who made the eyes but I?'*
>
> *'Truth, Lord, but I have marred them: let my shame*
> *Go where it doth deserve.'*
> *'And know you not,'* says Love, *'who bore the blame?'*
> *'My dear, then I will serve.'*
> *'You must sit down,'* says Love, *'and taste my meat':*[36]
> So I did sit and eat.

Here is someone who understands the first verse of Romans chapter 5.

A LIFE ANCHORED IN THE FUTURE

But what does it mean to have peace with God? What might a life lived at peace with God look like? It won't be a place of calm and untroubled passivity. Paul knows that human life is not like that. In the following verses he therefore calls us to shape our lives on the basis of two principles: one that anchors life in terms of its *goal*, and one that reconfigures life in terms of its *meaning*.

Remarkably, in both cases what he exhorts us to do is to *boast,* the very thing he has told us is impossible (3:27); the very thing that Abraham had no grounds for doing (4:2). But now, everything has changed. There he was talking about the spiritual pride that, by being religiously observant, thinks it has earned special treatment from God.

Here he is calling us to exult in a hope for the future grounded in the resurrection of Jesus from the dead. There couldn't be two more different grounds for confidence.

Firstly, the resurrection makes it clear that our life is not just an aimless stumbling from one thing to another, doing the best we can. It is a journey towards a destination. It has a purpose and a goal; it is open to the future. And that future is an eternal future.

Down the ages people in doubt, in danger, and in the agony of loss have asked the question: in the light of the marvel and the mystery that is a human being; in the light of the love we have for each other; in the light of tragedy and injustice and the uncompleted business in so many individual lives, is death truly the end? Can we believe that at death all the personality and creativity and passion and hope that is a human life simply winks out and ceases to exist? Ceases to exist *before God*? In Jesus' day, for many faithful readers of the Scriptures, the answer to that question was *no*. But back then that was nothing more than an intuition, a reasonable thing to believe. Now, says Paul, we know the truth of that belief in person.

Knowing the risen Jesus changes everything for us—and we need to allow it to. "Let us boast in our hope of sharing the glory of God!" Paul urges us. Allowing hope to seize our lives is something that we need to *do*. Paul is not offering us a pious idea that might console us in the tough times, as if to say "life may be filled with grief right now, but we're all going to get to heaven one day." He is talking about the way in which knowing that we have a goal and a destiny completely transforms our attitudes, our priorities, and our relationships now in the present. Life has a meaning. Nothing is unimportant. Nothing is wasted. Whatever happens on the journey of life, we have a future with God.

This is not to sentimentalize life or ignore the fact that we are mortal people. Even Jesus endured death, just as he shared every aspect of human life. Helmut Thielicke explains what that means for us:

> As a Christian I go down into this death with the complete confidence that I cannot remain therein, since I am one whom God has called by name and therefore I shall be called anew on God's day. I am under the protection of the Resurrected One. I am not immortal, but I await my own resurrection. I am one with whom God has begun to speak. God will not break faith with me and the fellowship he has established, nor will he let it be annulled by death. This is the certainty of my conquering death, founded not in me, but in God.[37]

Paul is calling us in the light of this hope to live with confidence now. Hope reaches out to us from the future, drawing us on. It transforms everything that we do; our life from now on will never be the same. And when we come to the end of the journey we will take the last steps in the company of the Lord who has walked the way before us. Death is a doorway: Jesus has proved it. And what that door opens onto is the glory of God. Not a glory that we will simply acknowledge. Not a glory that we will wonder at from afar. A glory that we will share.

ENDURANCE AND CHARACTER

The second thing that Paul calls us to boast in seems very strange. "And not only that," he urges us, "let us boast in our sufferings." At first sight—and perhaps at second sight as well—suffering seems the very last thing for us to become excited about. But what Paul is saying is that not only the *resurrection* of Jesus, but also *his crucifixion* transforms our understanding of life. In this new world, even suffering, even the painful presence of brokenness and disorder in our lives is no longer meaningless. The world God has made is not a fairy-tale world, but a living world, one to which God has given freedom, that freedom that makes possible all its richness and wonder. And in human life that freedom makes possible choice and thought and creativity and love. But with those things comes risk and danger. Freedom is an essential condition of life, but with it comes vulnerability. Tectonic plates can shift, and a city falls in an earthquake. A wildfire or a tornado sweeps through a community. Human bodies wear out or become damaged. People make wrong or evil choices, and those choices affect the lives of others in painful or tragic ways.

What Paul is saying is that Jesus' death and resurrection mean that we now can—mean that we now *must*—think about this quite differently. No longer is even tragedy merely a pointless bolt from the blue. The struggles and difficulties of this world, even the most painful, are in Messiah Jesus taken up into God's loving purpose (vv. 4–5). God has entered history and has made himself vulnerable to it just as we are. The perils, challenges, and chances of human life have been taken up into his life. We can therefore no longer see them as meaningless. In all of their strangeness and apparent disorder they have become part of God's own experience. They have become open to his creative and healing power, open to his redemption both of history and of all of our individual histories. Suffering therefore becomes something that under the hand of God can shape our lives to become more like the life of Jesus.

Let us not be all pious and triumphalist about this. We are talking about pain. We are talking about abandonment and loss. We are talking about desolation. Shame upon that cruel and superficial religion that preaches that we should be joyful in our sorrows, that what is needed is simply to trust the Lord, that subtly or unsubtly suggests that tears and heartache are a sign of lack of faith! Such blundering and wounding shallowness knows nothing of the spirit of the One who, even knowing what in that exceptional situation he was going to ask his Father to do, still broke down in tears and turmoil of heart at the grave of his friend (John 11:33–36).

What Paul is saying is something different. There is no magic wand that can make right the wrongs and chances of the world. There is no way out. But this verse tells us there is a way *through*. Because Jesus has entered our suffering, because he himself in his life and death has taken our chancy and tragic history into the being of God himself, now even suffering comes to us, not as a random calamity, but as something which can be redeemed, something which can be used in the infinite tenderness and grace of God to shape and even (let us say this with great care) enrich our life. What before was only destructive can now, in his grace, be redeemed. What before could only terrify can now be used under his loving hand to shape us for beauty rather than destruction. Because of what Jesus has done we now know that nothing is lost or wasted. "Suffering produces endurance, and endurance produces character, and character produces hope," Paul tells us (v. 4). Endurance: there is no magic wand. Character: the love of God poured into our hearts. Hope: the certain knowledge that our lives are held in his hand and that he will never let us go. Let us then, in the teeth of all the chaos and destruction in the world, *boast in our sufferings*.[38]

A FUTURE AND A HOPE

Notice that in both of these last two exhortations the key word is hope. Christian faith, Paul is telling us, is not something static. The righteousness that comes through it is not a status or a condition. Instead, what God has done for us in Jesus opens up for us a life to be lived; it leads us on into a future that is always unfolding. It shows us a destination which is certain, but towards which we have to journey.

You will remember the story I told earlier about the dramatic rescue of two Australian women from a raging river. Although I didn't mention it at the time, there was a sequel to that story. Because the newspaper photograph became famous, and because the appeal of the story was so universal, people started coming to the banks of the river just at that spot to hear the story told. It became a sort of tourist attraction. After a while there was a little group of skilled narrators who knew every detail. Some people came back to listen time after time. At first the organizers used a small marquee on rainy days, but as the gatherings became regular, a fundraising campaign was undertaken in order to build a more permanent structure. Of course the river itself was now quite a way away from the spot where the photograph had been taken, and under normal conditions it was just a quiet little stream. But screens were put up in the new auditorium upon which the picture of the actual flood and of the rescue could be projected. As numbers grew, the retellings became more elaborate. Sometimes actors reenacted the whole event, complete with sound and lighting effects. Songs were composed to capture the drama of the women's situation, and the excitement and wonder of the rescue, and the people sang them with gusto.

The strange thing about all this was that Tom, the rescuer, never came to these reenactments. Each week (for the reenactments had become weekly by now) the organizers sent him an email giving all the details, but he never showed. Sue and Cassandra, the two women who had been rescued, did come occasionally, when one of their old friends got married, when one of the regular attendees that they had known in the past was in trouble, or when there was a birth to celebrate. People noticed, though, that on these occasions they weren't as appreciative as one would have expected of the increasingly skillful efforts that were made to remember and to dramatize their rescue.

They seemed more interested in the concerns of the person they had come to visit than the powerful recreation that was going on up front of their delivery from drowning. One or two regulars wondered aloud whether they'd forgotten to be grateful.

Cassandra and Sue did, however, quite often get together with Tom. And others who knew about the rescue and were curious to meet him also found it quite easy to get in touch. He regularly answered his emails and was always very happy to meet. It was never at a café, though, or a drinks-after-work kind of meeting. He'd be visiting an older lady in hospital, and invite you to come with him. He mentored a couple of at-risk youths at the local high school, and you'd suddenly find yourself roped into an impromptu game of soccer, or hauled along on a weekend outing. On one occasion several went with him to a public meeting discussing ways to make housing more affordable for low-income families. Others shared his shift at the local food bank.

After a while the scattered group of Tom's friends discovered that they were becoming good friends with one another as well. Someone set up a Facebook page, and, as it turned out, little groups ended up getting together here and there to enjoy one another's company, to laugh, sometimes to weep, to learn, and to talk about the kinds of situations where they'd spent time with Tom recently. Tom would drop into these gatherings now and again. He never stayed long, but no one minded. He had a lot on his plate, and they knew they'd be doing something with him later in the week one way or another. Every time they got together there were always new things to learn, new friends to meet, and new stories to tell. There were some creative people among them and soon these little groups had their songs too.

But theirs were traveling songs.[39]

LOVE POURED IN

Hope, reaching out to us from the future, draws us on. "Hope does not let us down," Paul tells us, "because God's love has been poured into our hearts through the holy Spirit that has been given to us." What is this *holy* spirit? Those of us coming from the Christian tradition immediately know. Both words are normally capitalized: this is the Holy Spirit, the third member of what we call the Trinity. This is the third personal presence alongside the Father and the Son who together with them makes up the threefold being of God. This has been the formal doctrine of the church since the fourth century.[40]

But we can't start with that doctrine here. Whatever the strengths or limitations of this way of thinking about God, we need to gently unplug from that final formulation if we are to understand Paul's meaning as, just a few years after the resurrection, he writes his letter. Paul lived two or even three hundred years before the doctrinal debates that led to the establishment of our familiar doctrine of the Trinity. His writings, among others, provided the material out of which the doctrine was constructed.

But when he spoke of the Holy Spirit, he didn't mean the third member of a Trinity. He couldn't have, because the idea of the Trinity had not been formulated yet.

Does that sound surprising? But if he didn't mean that, what then *did* he mean? The best way to begin thinking about it is to consider how Paul uses the word "spirit" in other contexts. At the start of the letter, for example, he has told us "I serve God *with my spirit* in announcing the good news about his Son."[41] What he is saying is that he declares the good news with passion and with all of his being. In chapter 12 of the letter he exhorts the Roman Christians to "outdo one another in showing honor. Do not lag in zeal," he tells them, "*be ardent in spirit*, serve the Lord."[42] In other words, they are not to be half-hearted but to pour their whole selves into God's service. In his first letter to the church in Corinth, Paul says that visitors from Corinth had "*refreshed his spirit*"; in his second letter to the same church he tells them of the time when he had "*no rest in his spirit*."[43] In both cases of course he is speaking about nothing other than his inner self, the real Paul, the one who is in fact writing to them.

Now, in none of these passages is the "spirit" seen as a *part* of a person. On the contrary, it is the *essence* of the person: it is the person's self. When a person reaches out to us it is their spirit that we encounter; in thoughtfulness or in love or in laughter it is really and truly them.[44] This is the way the idea of spirit is used everywhere in the Scriptures. The handful of examples I have given here are all from Paul, but if you get a concordance and look up all the examples of the use of the word *spirit* as it relates to people in both Old and New Testaments you will not find a single example where a person's spirit is anything other than truly themselves, their innermost nature, the real them.[45]

This is how what Paul is saying in verse 5 must also be understood. When he speaks of "the holy Spirit"[46] he does not mean a part of God. He does not mean one aspect of a corporate personality. He means *God's own self*, the essence of who God is, God himself reaching out directly into our lives. This is why in the splendid wording of the Revised English Bible: "hope is no fantasy; through the holy Spirit he has given us, *God's love* has flooded our hearts." Paul is not talking about two things but about one thing. God has given us the holy Spirit, that is, his own self: this is what it means about our hearts flooded with his love. Love is not an idea or a quality. It is not a fact to be believed or a truth to be known. It is a person reaching out to us with their whole heart. That is what the holy Spirit is, then: it is God himself, the essence of who God is, reaching out to us; indeed, not only reaching out but living directly with us at the very heart of our life. And this is why hope is no illusion. It is no illusion because the promising God himself comes to us now. That is why we can journey on in hope, because the God in whom we hope travels with us.

GOD AND THE GODLESS

This is wonderful, but perhaps we have a doubt. How do we know God loves us? Well, says Paul, "while we were still weak, at the right time the Messiah died for the godless." It is a curious statement, isn't it? What does it mean? I guess it is probable that most of the readers of a book like this will be fairly decent people. People who read books tend to be people of a certain sort, and readers who are Christian select themselves out even more. Of course we are sinners too. We've got nothing to boast about before God. But the very fact that you've read this far suggests something about your seriousness: beyond the battle and the failings, you have a longing to live clear and true before God. That is what I want too. I've blundered and stumbled, and still do, but still I long to be a disciple of Jesus. To someone looking in from the outside we would probably seem to be basically good people. And what Paul is saying here is that Jesus didn't die for people like that. He died for the ungodly (v. 6).

If he had chosen to die for fairly respectable people like us, Paul says, that might not have been too surprising. People do really do that, in those times of need or crisis where one's fundamental impulses are laid bare: they let someone else go into the lifeboat before them, they step in front of the gunman's bullet, they go back into the burning building to find the missing child. Such situations are rare, and we rightly acknowledge such people as heroes, but we can understand the impulses that motivate them. We know about love, about its courage, its greatness, and its self-sacrifice. But Paul says, in the death of Jesus we are dealing with something stranger than that. Jesus didn't die for righteous people. He didn't die for good people. He died for the ungodly.

I have just found in my file the newspaper picture I was looking for: a young man in a dark red jumpsuit, sitting in a dock. His hair is dyed orange. His face is blank, except for his unnaturally wide eyes and his lined forehead. He looks very vulnerable. A few months ago this man walked into a crowded movie theater in Colorado just as the feature was beginning. Costumed as the villain and wearing black body armor he began to fire into the crowded audience. After his rampage 58 people lay injured and 12 were dead, including a six-year-old girl and an unborn child.

What was going through this young man's mind as he planned and prepared for this atrocity? What possessed him? What intoxicating narratives of power and revenge ran over and over in his mind during those days, as he intricately booby-trapped his apartment in the hope of maiming those who came to search it after the event? Whatever they were, it is all over now. There he sits in a prison dock, waiting. And he has lost his tether to the spacecraft. He has fallen into the space between the stars. He is just 22 years old.

What an amazing outpouring of grief and love swept over the country in the wake of that terrible event! How many hands were reached out in care and help to those who were affected! There were candlelight vigils across the country, and thousands came to the funerals. The president of the United States spoke for the nation in expressing his own heartache and pain. But all of this passed this young man by. Perhaps he heard some of the deep human outpouring as it came to him on the TV, if he had access to that. As a human being his heart could not but be stirred by it. But he has cut himself off from the fellowship of humanity, expressed in grief. He is utterly excluded. Not only that, but a great gulf now separates him from anyone he has ever known: his parents and family, consumed now in pain and shame; his friends, uncomprehending; his teachers and classmates in confusion; every girl he has ever dated; anyone who has ever smiled at him in the street. Even his name is not being mentioned by the news media. He is lost. Will he ever know human warmth again? How many years will he wait until someone for the very first time smiles at him? Do you sometimes wonder what reality might lie behind the grim warnings about hell and judgment that appear in some of Jesus' parables? Well, whatever other meanings there may be in those stories, without doubt this young man is in hell right now.

AND YET . . .

And yet? *Les, no, you can't be serious.* And yet? *I can see where you're going with that, and surely that can't be right. Can it?* But think about it for a moment. Can I ask you what Paul is saying here, if not that? It was not for good people that Jesus chose to die. He died not for the righteous, not for the good, but for *the godless* (v. 6). He died for us while we were still *in rebellion* against him (v. 8), while we were *enemies* (v. 10). He died for us human beings who rejected him, who scoffed at him, who despite our good intentions failed in the weakness of our love to deliver him; he died for us human beings who denied him justice, who tortured him and nailed him to a cross. And on that cross Jesus said, not to a victim, not to a good man treated unjustly, but to a self-confessed criminal, "Today you will be with me in Paradise."[47] How can we escape the conclusion? There is no doubt in my mind that, whether his life be long or short, that blank-faced and vulnerable-looking young man James Eagan Holmes (and we must give him his name, for before God everyone has a name) will before the end of it have serious dealings with Messiah Jesus. God will not impose his will on any person. But that Jesus died for him, died that he might be forgiven and be free, is beyond a doubt.[48]

Even as I write this I can feel the disappointment and even anger that such a statement might arouse in some of us. This is nonsense! What about the victims? And although at first it seems that Paul doesn't deal with the matter, don't we have to ask that question? Isn't it unjust, isn't it almost obscene to suggest that God might ultimately have mercy upon a calculating mass murderer, when so many people's lives have been ripped out of the world by him, when so much pain has spilled out into the lives of others because of it? This outrage cannot be brushed aside. After a day or two of shock and anger over an event like this, most of us move on to other things in our lives; we move on to other news stories, other atrocities. But for a whole community moving on is not possible, nor perhaps will it be possible for many years. And for those most closely involved, this tragedy will be part of their lives forever.

What can we say then on behalf of the victims of the godless? No clever or pious human explanation will do. The only thing we can point to is what Paul has been again and again pointing us to throughout the letter: the revelation in Jesus of *the righteousness of God*. What God's coming among us in Jesus the Messiah demonstrates is that he as Creator does not fail to take responsibility for his world. He has not set us loose in the world with all of its terrifying freedom, its absolute moral choices, its ever-present possibility of failure and mistake, without himself being personally committed to that. In all of the mixed and sometimes tragic history of the world, God is and has been with us every step of the way. The incarnation uniquely demonstrates this. In Jesus God submits himself to our history. He takes our sin and brokenness and pain. He takes the burden of our sinfulness upon himself. He does not step back: he takes personal responsibility for the world that he has made.

And that must mean that he takes responsibility for the consequences as well as for the choices. It must mean that he takes responsibility for the victims as well as for the perpetrators.[49] How will that work out? I do not have an answer. I am not sure that God has given us one. This is not something we can see in this age of the world. But that it will work out we must be certain. God holds the victims too, their lives, and the lives of those who love them in his hands. And we know that he can be trusted.

And then, even as we think about it, suddenly we realize that in fact Paul does deal with this issue. For Jesus is not only God himself being given up for us. We see him also as the incarnate God, suffering the violence of others. He too is the victim. Torn out of life in young manhood, abused, abandoned, denied justice, tortured, stripped naked, jeered at, and publicly scoffed at: Jesus takes the experience of the victim, the experience of all the victims, into the experience and the being of God himself. Yes, Jesus died because of our evil deeds. But he also took upon himself the evil deeds that others have done *to us*. It was because of them that he died. He took the shame and the pain and the outrage and the helplessness of the victim too into his own self. The purpose of his death was to heal us from the shame of those things that we have experienced. He rose to restore us to the fully human life that has been stolen from us. I ask with some understanding of what this might mean for some of my readers: can we dare to believe this?

HOPE FOR THE RESPECTABLE

Jesus died then, not for good people, not for the fairly respectable readers of Christian books. He died for the ungodly, for those in rebellion against him; he died for the enemy. Which means that, praise God, he did indeed die for us. Because if in any aspect of our lives we are good, we know that that is only so by grace. Goodness, love, faithfulness, truth: strictly speaking individual human beings own none of these. They aren't the kind of thing that can be owned. Sometimes we have the privilege of sharing in them, but they don't originate with us. They pass through us; they come to us from outside and flow on through us to others. They aren't a possession, they are a gift: a gift that we do not own, but that we participate in as they pass through our lives.

What does originate with us, what we do truly own, is of another kind: disobedience, failure, willfulness and rebellion. Sadly, these are the things that are truly ours. In our heart of hearts we know this. That knowledge is the source of our fear of God and our unwillingness to approach him. Whether our wrong deeds are in human terms great or small, the principle is the same. With all of our hopes and good intentions, still all of us are the ungodly, the sinners, the enemies. And therefore, Paul tells us, at the right time the Messiah died *for us*.

God will not let us go. In the death and resurrection of Jesus we know this with absolute certainty. His love doesn't depend upon us, or upon anything about us. It doesn't depend upon whether we are good or bad, whether we are lovable or unlovable. It is not shaken by our sinfulness. It is not deflected by our rebellion. It is the settled decision of the sovereign God himself about the truly human beings that he will have us become. Love is a choice, and God chooses; and his choice pre-dates any choices of ours.

Nothing is said about repentance, nothing is said about remorse. Repentance is not a condition for our restoration. Remorse and breast-beating are not the conditions for our restoration. There are *no* conditions for our restoration. Here is the gospel: "While we were still sinners Christ died for the ungodly. While we were enemies we were reconciled to God by the death of his Son." Remorse and breast-beating are not conditions. They are consequences. They are our response to this good news.[50]

While we were weak, while we were wicked, while we were rebels in arms, while we were enemies, God's Messiah died in order that we might be his. No matter what we've done in our life, no matter what blunders and follies, no matter what waste, no matter what wrong deeds so high-handed that we now feel they could not possibly be forgiven, still God's patient, certain, unshakeable love for us remains. God's love is not an idea. It is not a feeling. It is a settled, ongoing commitment: God's complete commitment of himself to rescue us and to make us whole. This is what the death and resurrection of Jesus show us so conclusively.

HOW MUCH MORE . . .

The words throb with intensity. Perhaps we can imagine Paul striding up and down the colonnade, with Tertius sitting by a pillar, his stylus racing over the wax as he struggles to keep up with the words that tumble out. Every time Paul preaches this it grips him afresh. These are not just facts among other facts in the world! He wants to speak it: he needs the living voice to catch the emphasis. He wants to see the congregation in front of him; he wants to catch the eye of this one and that one as he draws his listeners with him into the wonder of what he has seen. He wants his words to be like water and like light, like fire and like rain. He longs to see the word of God falling unerringly into the hearts of the living people, to the transformation of every aspect of their lives. For we are here right at the heart of the mystery of the universe, the secret of what it all means.

See how statement by statement the intensity mounts. Now that we have been made righteous people by participation in the Messiah's sacrificial death,[51] *much more certainly,* says Paul, will we be saved through him from wrath (v. 9). And if while we were enemies we were restored to friendship with God through the death of his Son, *much more certainly* will we be rescued by participation in his life (v. 10). But *not only that!*—and Paul drives on into the astonishing statements of v. 11. As we will see, the same sense of excitement runs all the way to the end of the chapter. We hear it in individual phrases: "for if indeed . . . *by how much more . . .* " (v. 13); "for if it is correct that . . . *how much more certainly . . .*" (v. 17). We hear it in words like *grace-gift* and *abundantly* and *overflowingly.* The things that so radically threaten our lives are not just neutralized but overwhelmed by the grace and the goodness of God.

Up to now Paul has been speaking about something that has happened in our past: an act of God in history that demonstrates his love for us and decisively restores the relationship that constitutes what it means to be human. Of course, anything done by the eternal God is effective and powerful over all of human time (3:25–26). In our individual experience, however, the act of deliverance is something that we look back to; it is in the past. But Jesus was not only crucified: in the power of God he was raised to life again. We don't have a dead Savior, however wonderful; we have a living Lord.

In verses 9 and 10, therefore, Paul first of all points out what that means for our future. All of us must one day stand before God to give an account of our lives. And as sinful people falling short of the glory of God, the most that we can expect outside of Jesus Messiah is wrath. Terrifying as it is, it's worth sticking with this word for a minute. We thought about it a little earlier when we came across it in chapter 1. God does not have attributes. He is not loving one day and angry another. He is always only ever himself. Of course we must speak about his love and also about his wrath,[52] but these are not descriptions of moods or attitudes of God, they describe *our experience* of the one reality of the living God as we encounter him. They are our view of him from one or another place in our lives. If we choose to turn away from God and live our lives against the grain of the universe, if we choose what he has not chosen and seek out that which he has rejected, then we can only experience him as wrath. But if we are in Messiah Jesus, that is, if our life has now been taken up into his risen life, then we have been rescued from the place in relation to God where all we could experience of him was wrath, and brought into a different place altogether. The relationship has now been restored. Our true humanity has been given back to us. Just as Jesus at his baptism once heard it, we now hear God say to us "you are my beloved son, my beloved daughter; I delight in you." This is the new place to which we have been brought.

And, as Jesus did that day, we step out of the waters of baptism and on into the life which he has won for us. "We *will be* rescued in his life," Paul says. It is a living thing. Our standing before God has utterly changed. But rescue is not a once-for-all but an ongoing experience, something that opens out for us day by day as we live our life in fellowship with the risen Jesus.

It is impossible to over-emphasize the extraordinary confidence and certainty that the good news brings in this regard. All good Jewish people believed in a future judgment. Most good Jewish people also believed in the resurrection—at the last day, the judgment day.[53] But the good news tells us that Jesus was raised from the dead at a particular moment *in history*. What before was only a belief about the future has become a fact in time. What does this mean for us? The resurrection of Jesus brings judgment day right into the middle of life, and the power of the resurrection right into our present experience. It means that these things are no longer somewhat mythical, located in a dreaded or hoped-for future. Instead in Messiah Jesus they have become a concrete practical reality, something that we enter into now. God's judgment is not an event that we wait for in a future time. It is a function of who he is. God passes judgment on us now, says Paul. And this is the judgment: when he looks at us, he sees Jesus.

"Jesus was raised because of our being made righteous," Paul said at the beginning of the section. We need to emphasize it again: neither being alive nor being righteous are abstract states. They are precisely living things that are only experienced by living a life. Jesus is living his risen life now, and through his spirit, he is living out that life through us. In him we will be rescued from wrath (v. 9), and the shape of that rescue will be the experience of a life lived in the spirit of Jesus (v. 10). Paul will have much more to say about this, as we will soon see.

BUT THAT ISN'T ALL!

"Let us boast in our hope of sharing the glory of God," Paul has urged us. "And not only that, let us also boast even in our sufferings!" But that isn't all, now he tells us. "We *boast in God* through our Lord Jesus the Messiah." What an extraordinary thing.

What does it mean, to boast? With regard to *religion* it means a kind of smug confidence that we've done all that God requires. And therefore he owes us: we have a claim upon him. Paul has shown us that this kind of boasting is not only presumptuous, it is sadly and terrifyingly misconceived. More than that, it treats God as if he were merely a god. Abraham had nothing to boast about before God (4:2–3); instead he put his faith in God's faithfulness. So too for us. Our boast is not in anything we have, but in God alone. But what a boast! What a claim!

Boasting here doesn't mean to brag, but to speak confidently of an assured possession. And that possession is not any *thing*, it is God himself, Creator of the galaxies, master of time and space and history, the source of everything that is. How could we ever imagine we would even be *noticed* by a God like that? Yet what this verse tells us, what everything that Paul has been telling us—indeed all that the long history of Israel from Abraham on through Jesus tells us—is that it is not a matter of being noticed. We are not just noticed, we are *intended.* We are not simply accepted in some casual kind of way. We are loved to the uttermost. We are at the heart of it all.

WHAT IT MEANS TO BE LORD

But none of these things are free-floating general principles. All of them, Paul tells us, are "*through our Lord Jesus* the Messiah." It is through him that we can have peace with God; through him that we have come to stand in this place of grace and privilege; it is he who has died for the godless; he who rescues us from the wrath; he whose risen life is our salvation. But what does the title mean? We have already looked at what it means for Jesus to be *Messiah*; what does it mean for him to be *Lord*?

Well, we all know what a lord is. Lords and ladies, lording it over somebody; we think either of something old-fashioned or of the exercise of power. We mostly use the word as a title. But the idea in biblical thought is much richer and fuller than that. And just like *Messiah,* the word isn't really a title. It too is a description.

It is so with regard to God. When we speak of God as the Lord, of course we are speaking of his authority and right to command.[54] But this is not the language of arbitrary power. Greek has another word for someone who wields that: *despotes,* which gives us our English term *despot*. But God is not a despot. Even in the Old Testament, where the one Hebrew word has to serve for both ideas, it is clear that speaking of God as "Lord" is the language of *relationship*; a certain kind of relationship for sure, but nonetheless a real interaction between persons bound together in mutual obligation.[55]

The case is the same when we come to talk about people. The Old Testament makes it clear. A lord is not just a specially privileged individual who has somehow made it to the top of the heap. Rather, he or she is the person *within* the community who has the particular responsibility of leading *on behalf of* the community. The lord (the king, for example) in a real sense *is* the community: he represents it; he in his own person embodies it.[56]

This is the essential background for Paul's description of Jesus as our Lord. His history is the history of God's saving act. Jesus is the representative before God of all humanity. In this real person who grew and learnt and laughed and cried, God takes up human being into himself. In his own person Jesus *embodies* humanity. He lives our life and he dies our death. In that death he takes upon himself our finiteness and mortality. He takes upon himself the shame and distress, the failure and the falsehood of the human condition. And out of death, because of his eternal purpose to bring human beings to himself, God raised him—and raised us with him. He is our Lord.

And so, says Paul, if we are restored to fellowship with God through the *death* of Jesus; how much more certain it is that we will be saved through his *life*. The resurrection is not merely a fact, it is a promise.

A building is ablaze: a small apartment building in a quiet suburb. There are people trapped inside. What does God do? There can be no magical rescue, no Star Trek transporter beam. Someone has to get to where the people are, and lead them to safety. God has to go himself. Messiah Jesus is the firefighter who enters the building, past the flames, and up the smoke-filled stairs. He comes to where we are and stands beside us. And he leads us out. He tells us what to and shows us how to do it. Crawling along the corridor to keep below the smoke. Edging past the glass from the broken window. Down the stairs, away from the crackling flames, along the hallway and out the rear entrance, into the light and the air. Two parents look at each other appalled: each thought the other had the baby with them. The Messiah is the one who goes back in to find it. God comes to where we are. He becomes our representative. Jesus is our Lord.

The metaphors could be multiplied, and they will be different for each of us. A word is simply a sign for something real; it is the reality that fills the word with content. It is therefore the living person of Jesus Messiah that defines the meaning of his lordship for each of us, as we experience his grace in our lives and walk the way of life in his company day by day. It is striking that nowhere in this crucial first half of the letter does Paul ever refer to Jesus as "the Lord." It is always "*our* Lord." He is not describing an abstract status but a living relationship. And so, he tells us, *we boast in God through our Lord Jesus the Messiah,* because *through him we have been given that restored relationship now.* The rescue that comes from him is not something wistfully or earnestly hoped for in the future. It is our possession now. And what we possess is not a thing, not an idea, not a standing before God. It is a person: Messiah Jesus our Lord.

11

Romans 5:12–21

¹²"*[In the Genesis story] it was through one person that sin came into the world, and through sin death; and so death spread to everybody, meaning that everyone sinned.*

¹³*This shows that sin was in the world before the Law was.*

Without a Law there is no means of defining sin, ¹⁴*but nonetheless death still reigned from Adam to Moses, even over those whose sinning wasn't, like Adam's, disobedience to a command. (In that regard Adam foreshadows the one who was to come.)*

¹⁵ *But the gift of grace is not like the wrong deed. If the one human being's wrong deed meant death for the many, by how much more has the grace of God, and in that grace the gift of the one human being Jesus the Messiah, overflowed for the many!*

¹⁶*Nor can the gift be compared to the effect of one person's sinning. It is indeed true that the just judgement upon one wrong act led to God's condemnation. But here a gracious gift following many wrong acts leads to an act of righteousness.*

¹⁷*If then because of the wrong deed of one human being death began its rule through that one, how much more certainly shall those receiving the abundance of grace and the gift of righteousness rule in life through the one human being Jesus the Messiah!*

¹⁸ *Therefore, just as a human being's wrong deed led to condemnation for all people, so now a human being's act of righteousness leads to the lives of all people being made righteous!*

¹⁹ *Just as through the one person's disobedience the many were made sinful people, so, through the obedience of the one, the many will be made righteous people.*

²⁰*Law came in order that the consciousness of wrong deeds might intensify. But where sin increased, grace increased far more,* ²¹*in order that, just as sin once ruled over us in death, so grace would rule through righteousness all the way to everlasting life through Jesus the Messiah, our Lord.*"[57]

Romans 5:12-21

THE PRESSURE OF JOY runs through every word that Paul has said so far. The second half of chapter 5 is equally joyful: the exclamation marks at the end of some of the sentences are absolutely demanded by their content. When we were discussing this passage recently in our Bible study group, one of the members broke in to say "And I think there is probably a "wow!" in there somewhere." Absolutely right. Do you hear what I'm saying here? Paul asks. Do you really see what God has done in Jesus? Wow! Paul has shown us how God in Messiah Jesus has taken our life upon himself, taking responsibility for it in all its brokenness and injustice and loss. We have seen Jesus following the path of obedience all the way to death. But what does that mean for us *now*? How does it make any difference to the life we now lead? What God is doing in us through Jesus: that is what the following section is all about.

This is another place in the letter where it is crucial to remember that Romans is in the first place an oral rather than a written text. If we try and read it in paragraphs, like a book, it will seem dense and complicated. But Paul is not a writer. He is an orator, and understanding that makes all the difference to how we read this or any of his letters.

We don't have a lot of experience of powerful oral communication in our print-oriented and video-clip world. In my country, New Zealand, though, there is among the Maori people a tradition of oratory that goes back a thousand years. It's instructive to see it in action. When delivering a speech of persuasion or of welcome, the speaker steps forward and with great energy delivers a carefully crafted couple of sentences. Then he walks back, or leans over his stick for a moment. Turning again, he delivers another couple of sentences. Once again there is silence and body language of some kind. Then another declamation and pause, and then another, as the speech slowly builds into a whole. The speaker's movement keeps his audience's eyes upon him. His silences enable his hearers to digest what he has just said, before he extends and explains it in his next statement. The effect is not so much linear like an argument moving from point to point, as architectural like a building going up, with floor then roof then walls.

The origin of this section in oral delivery is crucial to understanding it. This is why the text looks a bit unusual: I have laid it out in the periods of oral speech rather than in paragraphs of a written document. I have also italicized the second element of the repeated contrasts, which is really just the one contrast continually repeated and elaborated: the contrast between what human beings have done in Adam and what God has done in Messiah Jesus. Try reading the text out aloud yourself. Imagine you have your audience there. Make eye contact with them. Reach out to them with your words. Feel for yourself the power of the truth these words contain.

WHO WAS ADAM?

The second point to note is of a different kind. Paul has previously pointed us to the example of Abraham, a man who trusted in God's faithfulness long before the rituals and signs of belonging of Jewish religion existed. But now he needs to go back further than that. Why? Because he knows that what God has done in Jesus is more fundamental even than Abraham. What has happened is a change in the very fabric of human nature itself. And to talk about that Paul needs to go back all the way to creation.

The difficulty with that is that in our century we cannot read the creation story in quite the same way that Paul did. The force of his message is quite undiminished, as we will see. But Paul understood the Gen 3 story in a directly historical way that is not possible for us today. There are two issues. Firstly, like all believing people of his time, Paul thought that the first human being to walk the earth, Adam, had been created by God perhaps only three or four thousand years before the coming of Jesus.[58] He did not know—and could not have known—how vast the gap of time is between us and the first people on our planet. The second issue is that of death. Paul's understanding of the relationship between Adam's disobedience and death is subtle and complex, as we will see. For Paul, death is much more than merely the death of the body, and indeed this is something that is central to the Genesis story as well.[59] Both writers understand bodily death to be the *consequence* of a death of a much more far-reaching kind. Nonetheless it is a real consequence, and Paul shared the belief of his time that physical death was a consequence of Adam's sin. Neither of these beliefs, that the first human being lived only 5,000 years ago and that physical death entered the world through the disobedience of that one individual, is possible for us today.

Don't put the book down! For the leap I am asking you to make is exactly the kind of leap that Paul himself everywhere throughout his letter is asking his first audience to make. He is speaking to a community that, while Christian, has the instruction of the synagogue and the Old Testament faith in the marrow of its bones. And yet, step by step, Scripture by Scripture, Paul shows how all of that needs to be understood differently in the light of Messiah Jesus. Many things are fulfilled in him; other things—some of them central to what these good Christian people had always been taught—are superseded in him. If we feel a little nervous about rethinking something that for some of us has been part of our mental geography since childhood, then we find ourselves precisely in the place of those first readers of the letter.

It is important also to remember that Paul held a remarkably modern view of the origins of humanity, one that would have seemed offensive and threatening to many people in his day. In striking contrast to the lurid and confused mythologies of the surrounding cultures, he knew without a doubt that all human beings were the creation of the One God, made to be like him and to know him. The world was not founded upon chaos, nor was it the product of chance. It was a *creation*, ordered, purposed, and delighted in. As part of the creation human beings had an origin and a purpose in the mind of God. They were not an accident or a byproduct but the glory and crown of creation, granted God's own authority to name, to tend, and to rule. These things were a radical challenge to the paganism of Paul's world, just as they continue to be a challenge to our neo-pagan culture 2,000 years later; the whole of the good news is built upon them. What this chapter contains then is fundamental to the way in which we understand God and the world. We mustn't throw the baby out with the bathwater. The only things we happen to know more than Paul about are subsidiary matters: merely details of the *historical frame* in which God's creation and care is set.

What then do we know about the history of humankind upon the earth? That it is a very long history indeed. To find the first traces of walled towns in the lands of the Bible we have to go back to 9,400 BC, almost twice as far beyond Abraham as Abraham is distant from us.[60] But beyond that, to the first evidence of the existence of *homo sapiens*. As is clear from their shelters and campsites and the artifacts that they left behind, behaviorally modern humans first appeared in the upper Paleolithic era, that is, between 40,000 and 50,000 years ago.

That's an extraordinarily long history to look back on. Perhaps we might be able to accept that it could be possible. But were these people really human? Might there not have been a literal Adam and Eve in 4,000 BC from whom all *truly* human people have descended? To think so is, I believe, to both misread and misunderstand the Genesis story. There is much to say about genres within the biblical literature, and how to read particular passages as the kind of thing that they are, rather than the kind of thing they are not. To spend a lot of time on that right now, however, would, I think, distract us.

Already, though, the information we can glean from the archaeological remains has much to tell us. For example, consider the extraordinary paintings of animals, birds, and hunting scenes in sites like the Chauvet cave in what is now southern France.[61] A combination of dating methods shows that these imaginatively complex and technically skilled images were produced some time between 32,000 and 30,000 BC. And the paintings are not all: among other items discovered in this particular cave was a flute carved from the radius bone of a vulture; it is constructed to produce the pentatonic scale that is still commonly used in much modern music.[62] Art, music, sophisticated tool making, structured communities—and love and grief. Prehistoric graves are often stately, with ornaments, stone knives, and tools laid carefully beside the body. Pollen at burial sites from as far back as 16,000 BC show that flowers were regularly placed in or on graves. In a burial from around 4,800 BC a young woman, richly adorned with beads and necklaces, has her newborn baby beside her, laid on a swan's wing.[63] Undoubtedly these were human beings. Which means that God was there.

And that is precisely what Paul is saying. The knowledge of God was present, he tells us, *right from the very point that human beings became human*. The Jewish faith in which he and his hearers had grown up insisted that Israel was privileged above all other nations with regard to God: they alone had true knowledge of him. There is a sense in which that is true, and that God had chosen Israel to know him in a special way, in order that that knowledge might spill out into the life of the nations. But it is so easy to slip from the truth that Israel belonged to the living God, to the delusion that God in some way *belonged to Israel*, that outside Israel one could never know God, that only by submitting to Jewish culture and the Law of Moses (especially the distinguishing signs of circumcision, the Sabbath, and the food laws) could one find hope and salvation. This danger, ever-present for Israel, is an ever-present danger for the church as well.

It is to challenge precisely such a misunderstanding that Paul points to the Adam story and the first creation of human beings. God's business is not just with Israel, he tells us, but with all humanity. All are able to know him, all are responsible to him, all fall short of his glory—and all of this was the case long before the coming of religion. God was active in human life from the beginning, long before Moses and the Jewish Law—and from our point of view, certainly long before Christianity. To be human is to be Adam, to be named by God, to know his call to obedience, to have the freedom to either accept that call or to turn away to our own schemes for running a life. And that freedom is not a function of membership of a religious group. It is a creation right and responsibility.

The archaeology tells us about that aspect of things, too. Despite there being no written records it is clear that the knowledge of God has always been there. Among the remains of early human societies there are structures that were clearly designed for religious purposes. On the summit of a limestone hill in southeastern Turkey lie the remains of a complex and amazingly sophisticated communal temple which was constructed around 9,600 BC by people *who did not even yet live in permanent settlements*. They were hunter-gatherers, without townships or domesticated animals or plants. Yet the construction is massive, supported by eight-foot high, seven-ton pillars, each richly decorated with carvings depicting animals, birds, and human beings. With nothing more than chipped-flint stone tools, these pillars were carved out of the limestone bedrock and transported hundreds of yards by people who did not have the wheel or beasts of burden. The compulsion to worship, to reach out to God, is deeply ingrained in human nature.

But worship is not always innocent. In a settlement from about the same period in what is now modern Palestine there is evidence of a non-residential structure the walls of which once were hung with the skulls of wild bulls. Clearly it was some kind of shrine. The building has been deliberately burnt down. Gideon (Judges 6 and 7) was not the first to challenge false religion.

And of course, as the Genesis story itself is at pains to make clear, from the very beginning there was never a society without conflict and violence. Not that prehistoric societies were in continual violent upheaval, any more than ours are. There is lots of evidence of cooperation and peaceful coexistence, the huge Neolithic shrine in Turkey being one example of that. But intertribal and interpersonal violence was also common, just as it is today. A cave-burial in Germany from around 6,400 BC contains more than 30 skulls, buried with great honor and surrounded with precious objects. The majority of them are women and children. What tragedy happened here? Is this perhaps the bitter outcome of a raid upon a settlement by a neighboring tribe while the hunters were away? We have no way of knowing.

Human beings first came to North America around 11,500 BC, across the land bridge between Asia that is now broken by the Bering Strait. The owner of a skeleton found near the mouth of the Columbia River died somewhere around 7,400 BC—a date which fits exactly with the style of a stone spear point embedded in his thigh bone.[64] "Sin was in the world before the Law was," says Paul. "Long before Moses brought the Law death reigned over everyone who lived."

WE ARE ADAM

None of what Paul says here in chapter 5 is new to us. "Ever since the creation of the world the things about God that *can't* be seen—his eternal power and divine nature—have been evident in the things that *can* be seen, the things he has made," he has reminded us in chapter 1. And he went on: "When, despite not having it, people of other nations act instinctively in accordance with the Law, they are a Law to themselves. They show that the effect that the Law was designed to bring about is written in their hearts."[65] From the dawn of humanity the knowledge of good and evil, the awareness of God's command and his grace, have been part of what it means to be human. To know these things is in fact to *be* human. Being human is not a matter of biology. It is a matter of spirit.[66]

Nor is what Paul says here is different from anything that will come later in the letter. In chapter 7 he will draw us into his own struggle for obedience: knowing what is right to do and longing to do it with all of his heart, but nonetheless inexplicably doing the evil he doesn't want to do. What Paul describes here from the *outside* using the terms of the beginning story, he there describes from the *inside*, from within the experience of Adam himself. Adam is not, then, a figure from faraway in the past, someone whose one fatal disobedience helplessly doomed all his descendants to judgment.[67] Paul knows that he is Adam—and so do we. The tree of the knowledge of good and evil grows in my backyard, and in yours. The story of Adam and Eve's turning away from grace, their falling short of God's glory, describes what we experience every day of our lives. We don't need an historical Adam to account for our sinfulness. We know that from first principles. We know it from our own experience—and the Adam story itself is a reflection of that.[68]

If this was all, though, why would the beginning story itself be necessary—and why would Paul want to use it in this place in his letter? Because a broken relationship with the Creator lying right at the beginning of human history is central to the good news. It means that the potential for sinfulness—and for obedience—has been part of human existence from the beginning. The fact of sin that is made real in every human experience is not a *necessary* consequence but it is a *possible* consequence of the kind of beings that human beings are created to be. God did not make us sinful, but he made us human. And in making us human, he necessarily took responsibility for what he had made. He took responsibility for the potential for sin and for obedience that is built into who we are. This is what it means that Adam "foreshadows the one who was to come" (v. 14). Adam was completely responsible for his disobedience, just as we are completely responsible when, in ignorance or willfulness, we neglect God and go our own way. But behind these things lies a deeper responsibility, the responsibility of the Creator for his creation—and God does not step back from that responsibility. The coming of Jesus and his obedient life all the way to death on a cross is no emergency measure on God's part. It is no accident of a merely human history that begins with the sin of Adam. It is part of a divine history that begins at creation. God takes the responsibility for us, for our obedience *and for our disobedience*. The creation of human beings and the redemption that is in Jesus are not two things but one. They have been one from the start. Adam foreshadows the one who was to come. God takes responsibility for his creation: he enters into human life with all of its risk and hope and confusion and struggle. He lives our life, and dies our death—and rises again so that we, created human being that we are, can share his own life. This is Paul's good news.

GRACE OVERFLOWING THE CUP

This section of Paul's letter is not, therefore, about sin or human failure. The truth about that has already been made devastatingly clear in earlier chapters. Here his theme is *the triumph of God* in the gift of Messiah Jesus to human beings. Paul is not writing about sin: he takes that for granted. He is writing about the way in which, in our ordinary daily life, sin is overwhelmed by the undeserved goodness of God.

This explains the repeated series of rhetorical statements in the section we have just read. Paul sets up a contrast between Adam and Jesus, and then displays that contrast again and again from this aspect until gradually we begin to see it in its richness and completeness. Like a jewel held up and turned so that now one facet and now another reflects the light, so Paul takes this one thing and says it one way, and says it another. As he does so the light of the glory of God shines and gleams against the dark background of human sin and failure.

The things we do and what God has done are not similar in any way. They don't sit side by side on the same level. They are totally different in kind. Paul is not showing how, in response to one bad example God offers us a better example. He isn't describing how God *remedies* Adam's wrong deed with all its sad consequences. Rather, Adam is done away with altogether! What God gives us instead is *another human being, Jesus the Messiah* as source of the human race. God has stepped into human life himself and made it his own. This is God's gift. It is the gift of the new human nature in Jesus that now defines the life of every human being (v. 15).

As a result, our understanding of God has been transformed (v. 16). The Adam story tells us of a God who reacts to disobedience with a judge's verdict and with judgment. That is the only view we have of God from the place that disobedience leads us. But the Jesus story shows us a God who acts in grace, brushing aside our wrong deeds, giving freely, declaring his irrevocable commitment to us.[69] From the beginning human beings have found themselves oppressed by the fear and the power of death, the nothingness and emptiness into which our sin delivers us (v. 17). God's gracious gift is very different. He fills our life full, putting us back in control of it, as day by day we live it in the grace and the power of Jesus.

The strong statements follow one another in steady succession. Paul has preached this so many times, to so many audiences! Each phrase is honed and polished from many repetitions. What is the heart of the message? In words of one syllable, what are we talking about? We are talking about a change deep in the heart of human nature (v. 18). In Jesus, God has met us right there at the center of who we are. In Jesus he has wrenched human nature away from its destructiveness and futility. In Jesus he has given human nature back to us, so that we can be once again the people we should be.

And this has happened for *everybody* (v. 19). This is the crucial importance of the Adam story. This is why Paul has used it. Adam tells us of what we already know from our own experience: the universal sinfulness of the human race. *Jesus* tells us something beyond our experience or imagination: God's act of power to make all human beings whole.[70]

And that power, Paul tells us, is infinitely greater than even the best of human religion (v. 20). Religion is a funny thing. It is helpful in many ways, but it is not complete. Knowing what is right to do often just intensifies our realization that we don't do it. Paul is not running religion down. Being conscious of wrong is not a bad thing. That is why the Law came, Paul tells us, so we could know right from wrong. It is a knowledge fundamental to what it means to be human. The problem we have is that knowing it is not enough.[71] But, Paul says, "where sin increased, grace increased far more."

OIL IN THE GAS TANK

Stop, stop! What is this *sin*; what really is the *wrong deed* of the Adam in whom we all participate? We've talked about it, we've read about it, but what *is* it? Is it the breaking of a rule? No, it is not the breaking of a rule. It is the failure of all our own attempts to run a life. Adam (and Eve) didn't set out to be *disobedient*. They just felt they knew better than God did what choices they should make.

Is sin therefore the crippling weight of all our wrong deeds, weighing down our spirit and making us limp and stumble? No, because wrong deeds are not a thing. They are the absence of a thing. Sin is a child lost in a dark wood, blundering and afraid. Sin is our experience of the absence of a God from whom we have chosen to turn away.

Let me tell you a story. When I was a student at university, Dave, one of my best friends, turned up one day, not on his bike as usual but in a car. I knew he had sat for his license, but the car was a bit of a surprise. It was a Ford Anglia, eggshell blue, a little dented here and there, but it ran very sweetly and he was very proud of it. He drove me home, and on the way we stopped to buy some petrol. Now, Dave hadn't had a lot of mechanical experience: as far as I was aware the only thing he'd seriously driven before was a motor mower. And that became obvious when the attendant came to put the gas in the tank. "Half a liter of oil in it, please, and then fill her up," Dave instructed. "Not in the gas tank, surely," argued the attendant. But Dave is a pretty determined type, and is always sure he is right. After a lot of spluttering, the attendant did as he was asked, and we drove off—in a cloud of blue smoke.

The eggshell blue Anglia trailing its smoke-screen was a bit of a novelty around campus for a week or two, although it seemed to me that the engine wasn't running as nicely as it had at the beginning. Then one day we were driving home after class when there was a flop-flop-flop noise coming from the back of the car and the steering started to shudder. The Anglia drifted to a halt, with a perceptible lean to the right. The flat tire was obvious when we got out and had a look. I had never changed a tire before and didn't really know what to do, but I was pretty sure there'd be something to help us in the boot. But Dave would have none of it. He was thinking. Suddenly, I could see the light come on. He raised a finger and walked around to the lefthand side of the car. There was a long hiss, and all at once the car was level again. We climbed in, and Dave drove me home, both rear tires flopping and flapping noisily all the way.

Well, of course, this couldn't go on. Soon it was summer vacation, and I didn't see Dave for a couple of months. When I did rock around to his flat during orientation week there he was around the back, coming out of the passenger seat of the Anglia with two eggs in his hand. The car looked pretty sad: it was obviously immobile, one of the rear passenger doors sagged open, and the long grass had grown up around the wheels. But Dave seemed cheerful. "It's quite good really," he explained. "The fowls have started nesting in the back, and we are getting a couple of eggs a day."

Now, it is just possible that this might be a somewhat fictional story. The point I'm trying to make is, however, a serious one. *How do you run a life?* We think we know how to do it, and things go awry. Despite our hopes and best intentions things don't work out the way we thought. A stupid mistake brings really serious consequences. We live with a persistent feeling of failure. Something is wrong.

Of course the limits of the analogy are immediately apparent. It isn't that we need something like the *owner's manual*. A life is not a material, mechanical thing like a car, where the answer to each problem can be found in the instruction book. A life is a personal and gracious gift from the hand of God, and, in giving that gift, he does not take his hand away. Our life, every breath we breathe, every thought we think, depends upon that relationship. When we turn away from it, we die. We don't need the maker's manual. We need the Maker.

Sin therefore is a real power: it cuts us off from God. It cuts us off from the source of life. It raises a barrier that cannot be overcome from our side. It can be breached only from the other side, by God himself. And, Paul declares, *it has been*. In Messiah Jesus the Creator has stepped in to reclaim what is his own. God comes to us. Hence Paul's triumphant conclusion to verse 20: "But where sin increased, grace increased far more!" We fail, we stumble, we blunder and lose our way—and the tide of God's grace catches us up, heals us, restores us, and brings us home.

In verse 21 Paul brings all of this together in a last great contrast. Human beings are insufficient. For all our trying to do it ourselves, all we can create is the non-thing, the absence of God, the death-dealing power that we call sin. Death: coldness, sterility, and passivity. That is the air that once we breathed. That is *once* how it was, Paul says. But now the wave of God's grace sweeps inexorably over that barrier. God is the only one who can truly act. And he has. Now grace is the controlling force of our life. Think about that. The settled and determined good purpose of God for us is now what shapes who we are, and what we shall become.

DO YOU UNDERSTAND?

The way that happens, Paul tells us, is through *righteousness*. Several chapters ago I attempted to rescue this word from the narrow, sterile judicial meaning that has so often crippled our understanding of it. Righteousness: a living, creative, active thing. A righteous person: reaching out to others, dependable, true, committed, faithful. We are painfully aware how far we fall short of this. God knows about that—and ignores it. He is not interested in what we aren't, but what we *are*, and in what we will be. In an outrageous act of pure grace God declares us to be the righteous person, to be someone fit to stand opposite him in a covenant relationship. And through the risen Jesus he gives us the power *to be that person* in the actual day-to-day living of our lives.

It is important to notice that all of this is "through Jesus the Messiah, our Lord." The whole of this chapter is focused upon one person, and his crucial importance to God and for us.[72] These are not just beautiful religious ideas, but the practical result of something that has actually happened in the history of the world. God doesn't love us in theory, he loves us in a costly, committed, hands-on way. He doesn't just wish us well, he commits himself to us completely in an irrevocable act. Because of an act in history the nature of being human has been radically changed. These are facts in the world: not something to be gazed at through misty light from afar, but a possession to be stepped into, seized, and made our own.

Does what Paul is saying in verse 21 sound a bit familiar? If you look back, you'll see that in phrasing it is virtually a duplicate of verse 17. This is unusual: Paul very seldom repeats himself. But what Paul is saying is so important it needs this repetition. "Do you understand?" he asks. "Do you understand? Let me say it again!"

Do we understand? I'm not sure that we do. A long history of theological interpretation has taught us that we are rescued in the *death* of Jesus. A great cosmic transaction occurs there, by means of which all the terrifying punishment for sin that we would otherwise have to undergo after death is taken away. But Paul is not saying anything like that here. The rescue the good news tells us about is in the *life* of Jesus. Already this has been spelled out very explicitly earlier in the chapter, but we are so unfamiliar with the idea that it's easy to slip right by it. "If while we were enemies, we were restored to fellowship with God through the *death* of his Son," he tells us, "much more certainly, given that renewal of relationship, will we be rescued in his *life*" (5:10). Rescue is not an abstract thing. It is not a mysterious spiritual transaction that we can't touch or feel; a kind of electronic bank transfer where we can't check the balance, but have to trust that something has happened. God's rescue is tangible, real, challenging, and joyful. It is not an idea, not a theological concept, it is a life lived. It is the life of Jesus lived out through us.

And that life is a journey, a journey to a destination. It is this that makes a life a life rather than just an existence. This is one of the great revelations of the Christian message: that life has a purpose, a meaning, and a destination. Once we have grasped that life can never be the same again.

The expression Paul uses to describe that life, *everlasting*, has become a kind of religious property: long experience has taught us to identify it with the idea of "life in heaven with Jesus when we die." That is not what Paul is talking about. He is talking not about *duration* of life at all, but about its quality. He is talking about the grace and the power that enables us to live a truly human life *now*. Such a life does indeed lead on into the future! It leads all the way to the end of our life on earth, and it leads all the way past our death into whatever lies beyond. But eternal life is not something *for* the future. It is a gift, Paul says, that we are given now that leads on *into* the future.[73]

This is important for how we understand the idea of eternal life. God doesn't give us our whole life at once. He can't. A life is not a thing, it is something that must be lived. That is its nature. The gift Paul is speaking about here is given to us—can only be given to us—day by day. It unfolds. It is something that, as we choose and step out through joy and suffering, as we link our lives with others in love and service and friendship, we *create*. God gives us that privilege and responsibility: to create a life. This is the glory of being a human being. And of course we won't always get it right. Sometimes we will wonder or wander: that too is our privilege, to be free to make a mistake. But *grace is now the controlling force in our life*. Behind us, beneath us, before us is always the steady, unwavering, determined purpose of God for our good. This we know, because of the resurrection.

Such a life is eternal. The very character of God is at stake in that. When once God has had dealings with a person, that person's life is *already* eternal. We are seen and known by the living God. Time is touched by eternity. In Jesus our mortal existence has been caught up into God's own unending life. And from the deep places of the life of God himself is given to us the power and the joy to live our own. This is the good news.

12

Romans 6

¹What can we say then? If when sin increases grace increases even more, should we just continue living our sinful lives? ²Impossible! We have died to sin: how can we go on living in it? ³Have you forgotten that all of us who have been baptized into Messiah Jesus were baptized into his death? ⁴Through baptism we died and were buried with him, so that just as Messiah was raised from the dead by the splendor of the Father we too might live a new life.

⁵If we have become one with him in that symbol of his death, the same will certainly be so with regard to the resurrection. ⁶We know that our old self was crucified with him so that the sinful body might be rendered powerless, and we might no longer be enslaved to sin. ⁷For a dead person has had all sin's claims upon them cancelled. ⁸And if we have died with Messiah, we trust that we will also live with him. ⁹We know that Messiah, being raised from the dead, will never die again; death no longer rules over him. ¹⁰The death he died, he died to sin, once for all; but the life he lives, he lives to God. ¹¹In the same way you too must recognize that you are dead to sin and alive to God in Messiah Jesus.

¹²Don't therefore let sin rule in your mortal body, making you obey the body's desires. ¹³Don't any longer present any part of your body to sin as a weapon of wickedness. Instead, present your selves to God as those who have been brought from death to life, and the parts of your body to God as weapons of righteousness. ¹⁴Sin will not rule over you, for you are not under Law but under grace.

¹⁵What then? We are not under Law but under grace, is that a reason for us to go on sinning? Impossible! ¹⁶Don't you know that if you present yourselves to anyone as obedient slaves, slaves you are of the one whom you obey, whether it is sin, which leads to death, or obedience, which leads to righteousness? ¹⁷But thank God that, while you used to be slaves of sin, you have become obedient from the heart to the practical effect of the teaching to which you were entrusted. ¹⁸You have been set free from sin and have become slaves to righteousness.[19]*(I am using a metaphor from the everyday world to help you understand.) Therefore just as you once presented your bodies as slaves to impurity and to lawlessness, with deeper lawlessness as the result, so now present your bodies as slaves to righteousness, so that you may become holy.*

[20]*It is true that when you were slaves of sin, you were free of the claims of righteousness.* [21]*What fruit ripened for you there, though, in the heart of the things of which you now are ashamed? Where those things lead is death.* [22]*Now however, having been freed from sin and become slaves to God, you have a harvest of holiness, with eternal life as the goal.* [23]*For the wages of sin is death, but the unearned gift of God is eternal life in Messiah Jesus our Lord."*[74]

IN THE TOWN OF Bristol, Tennessee, police are called to a funeral home because a pair of vagrants have been found sleeping in the coffins. Not something that has ever crossed your mind to do? Why not? Those velvet linings must be pretty slinky to the touch, and the pillows look really comfortable. You could really make yourself at home.

Jesus calls across the barrier of death to bring his friend Lazarus back into the world of light and life. A fortnight later, after all the guests have left, are we likely to see Lazarus back at the tomb in the evening, sighing, looking around, maybe even taking a nap for a while on the shelf where the body had rested?

And here is a former slave, the price of freedom paid to his owner just a year ago by an acquaintance of the family to whom he had done a service. He has struggled to make the effort that freedom requires. In fact, he is nostalgic. Those leg-irons were cruel things at times, but you did get used to them. They were a kind of security, really, and at least you got fed when you were wearing them. The local polytechnic is offering night courses, and he is attending one of them. He is learning how to weld.[75]

These two images from his hearers' everyday world frame Paul's argument in this section. "You have been raised from the dead—why would you climb back into the coffin?" he asks (vv.1–14). "You have been freed from slavery—why would you weld the manacles back onto your wrists?" (vv. 15–23) Because, these are things that we can do. The freedom God gives us is real freedom. Life is not a game. Freedom means the genuine freedom to do what we like, to work out what we think is best, to follow our own way. And God will let us do that. That is how he honors us. He cannot give a gift with one hand and take it away with the other. We choose, and we get what we choose. But as we have seen from the Adam story and as we know well from our own experience, when we follow our own way the outcome is, somehow, not what we expected. Things go wrong. What promised so much turns out to be a cheat. We get what we want and find that it isn't what we wanted after all. And of course God knew all this long before we do. In the Genesis story, God's instruction about the tree was not a prohibition. It was a warning.

What Paul says here is intensely practical. At the end of the last section he described with joy the way that in Jesus the grace of God overwhelms our sinfulness, and gives us life and freedom—and all that he said there is true. If this was merely religion he would now move directly on to the challenging and inspiring end of chapter 8. What a wonderful ending to a sermon that would be! Our need, God's rescue; Jesus standing alongside us; a glorious destiny. After hearing all this, wouldn't any congregation leave the building feeling thrilled and exalted?

But Paul doesn't do that. He is not interested in religion and religious feelings. He is interested in life, real life, with its blessings and its joy, but also with its rough surfaces and sharp edges. He knows that it is in the real world that we have to live— and also that it is not in some vague religious world but precisely in the real world that God in Jesus meets us. As the Russians say, life is not as simple as crossing a field. Paul knows it well. His good news is about real help, hope that doesn't let us down, practical outcomes, real growth, and a joy that runs far deeper than mere happiness. But we have to choose. And the sign of that choice is baptism.

THE BAPTIZED LIFE

Notice that Paul is not calling his readers to be baptized. He assumes that this has happened. And it is a perfectly reasonable assumption, for the call to baptism has been an essential part of the good news from the beginning. "Every one of you, repent and be baptized in the name of Jesus the Messiah," Peter exhorts the crowd on the day of Pentecost—and 3,000 of his hearers respond. Riding home in his chariot with all his retinue, and overcome by the message of Jesus as Phillip unfolds it from the Scriptures, the treasurer of the kingdom of Ethiopia asks: "Look, there's water here. What's to stop me being baptized?" Desolate and blinded after a shattering encounter with the risen Jesus, Saul of Tarsus receives the laying on of hands from Ananias, and his sight is restored. "Thereupon he was baptized," Luke tells us, "and ate, and his strength was restored." What a matter of fact description! There was no fuss and no drama. Knowing what you now knew, it was just what had to be done next—and then you went on. Baptism was what happened when you became a Christian.[76]

Paul is not therefore talking in this chapter to anyone who hasn't been baptized. If we ourselves have not been baptized, we are listening in—and that is perfectly all right. But before we will be able to grasp the full meaning of what Paul is saying here, there is something we must do. Of course, the initiative is God's completely. The key is turned, the door opened—and we step into life.[77] We need to take the step. This is something important to keep in mind as we read on. Because Christianity is not something that one just drifts into. We have to choose.

Romans 6

Everybody's experience will be different, and I can only speak of my own. At Easter 1968 I rode my single-speed Raleigh bicycle from Invercargill, my hometown, 180 kilometers north to Queenstown, where a Bible camp was being held at a Christian campsite. I was 17 years old. It was a wild and stormy weekend. Stopping for the night with some friends of the family halfway up the road, we watched the grainy television pictures of one of the Cook Strait ferries grounded on a reef in Wellington Harbor, with the wind whipping spray off the tangled seas all around. More than 50 lives were lost. Pushing on the next day, I got drenched, buffeted by the wind, and lashed by horizontal rain. The camp, though, made it all worthwhile. I don't remember a lot about it now, except that the theme of the main talks was the Lordship of Jesus. It wasn't just that we had to believe something, the speaker said. Jesus wanted to be Lord of our lives.

And suddenly, there it was for me. It hasn't been very often that I've heard God speak directly. And there was no basso profundo voice, or any drama at all, really. I just knew that God was addressing me. And what he was saying was something like this: Well, Les, what are you going to do? Are you going to continue to be the golden-haired Bible class boy, the one who knows all the answers—or am I going to be Lord? I am so grateful that, in God's good grace, with all of my heart I said yes, he would be Lord. Though, I have to confess, it also ended up being a bit of a deal. He would be Lord, I said—but if it didn't work out, then I was off. If this wasn't a real thing, I had no desire to keep on being religious. Looking back, I think God did a smile.

And so, in the autumn sunshine I rode home out of the mountains. At the camp I had learned for the first time Charles Wesley's wonderful hymn "And Can It Be?" Its words followed me down all the long miles:

> And can it be that I should gain
> an interest in the Savior's blood!
> Died he for me, who caused his pain?
> For me, who him to death pursued?
> Amazing love! How can it be
> that thou, my God, should die for me?

> I remember actually singing it on the downhill bits, awkward and insecure teenager that I was, biking along all by myself. By myself, but not alone:

> Long my imprisoned spirit lay
> fast bound in sin and nature's night;
> thine eye diffused a quickening ray;
> I woke, the dungeon flamed with light.
> My chains fell off, my heart was free,
> I rose, went forth, and followed thee.

The day after I got home, I went to the elders of the church and asked for baptism.

As I've said, all I can speak of is my own experience. The circumstances will be different for each of us. But in every case what is involved is hearing the promise and the call of the living God, and stepping forward into that promise. I was talking to a friend about it the other day. "For me it was a decision," he said. "I was just sitting in church on an ordinary Sunday morning, and suddenly I realized I had to choose."

Many of us, of course, were baptized as infants. Way back, before we were aware of ourselves or of God, others took the vows on our behalf, including us in their own commitment to Jesus, promising to bring us up in faith in him. And God drew near. It is crucial to understand this. The way baptism happens is not important. Baptism is not something that we do, it is an acknowledgement of something that God does. God commits himself utterly and unreservedly to us in Jesus, and we enter into those promises with the obedience of our lives. So, whether we were baptized as a child or as an adult we don't look back to some ceremony in the past. That was just the beginning. We look forward, each day hearing the call, and each day answering yes, and yes, and yes. Baptism is not a status. It is the first step on the journey of a baptized *life*. That alone is what Paul is interested in here.

WALKING AWAY

What is the reality that baptism is a sign of? It is a sign of death. This is not just a metaphor. The death was real, and our participation in it is real.

We know what it is like to walk away after a graveside service. The prayers have been said, the coffin lowered into the grave, and the earth shoveled on top. It is very final. The person we knew has passed on. Where their living presence used to be there is a gap, a gap that will never be filled again in this age of the world. So it is here. Jesus died, and with him died the human nature that is subject to death. In all of its questionableness and weakness and failure and folly, that old nature was nailed to the cross. In his death it passed out of the world. Now, we walk away from the grave.

What does our being baptized *into* that reality mean? No sacrificial promise on our part! No emotional identification with Jesus! Baptism is not a promise that we make, it is a promise that God makes. Sin is a break in our relationship with God—but God pushes past that break, insisting on the validity of the relationship. He treats us as what we are not: new people, and he gives us the power and the grace to be that. For those who have been known by God, sin has therefore become a withered, defeated, and finished thing.[78] Sin is the absence of something; when that absence is filled with presence, sin dies.

Paul is talking not about a state or a thing but about a relationship. It is possible to misunderstand this, because elsewhere in the New Testament the word *sin* often refers to individual wrong deeds ("your sins are forgiven"). When Paul uses the word, however, he is never talking about individual wrong acts, but rather about *a fundamental orientation away from God and towards the self.*[79] He knows that what really matters is not what we do, but whose we are.

Paul understands sin not as a succession of wrong deeds but as a ruling power. It is not something that is at our disposal, as if we could choose to do or not to do an individual act. It is a power that dominates our life. We are at its disposal—until God in Messiah Jesus delivers us. This is what Paul is telling us.

Does what he is saying make any sense, though? Isn't the idea of sin as a power just a religious or even a mythological idea? Well, of course it is a metaphor. But it is a metaphor to help us grasp the nature of a real thing. We in the West have over the last two centuries become accustomed to the idea that matter, the patterns of energy and particles that make up every physical thing, is the fundamental reality of the universe. This is absurd. To suggest it is a bit like proposing that the fundamental reality of Dvorak's *New World Symphony* is the individual carbon atoms that make up the ink upon which the score is printed. As Christians we know that the fundamental reality of the universe is *personal*, for all that exists is the creation of the personal God.

This explains the seriousness with which Paul treats the problem of sin. If the fundamental reality of the universe is the Creator and we find ourselves oriented away from that reality, focused on ourselves rather than on him, then we do not have a minor problem. It is not something that can be mended. We are at war with our own existence. We are living our lives against the grain of the universe. We are separated from the principle of life. That is why we are so often at cross-purposes with ourselves. That is why it is so painful and so hard.

But, Paul tells us, because the essential nature of the world is personal, the absence of God doesn't leave just a hole. It leaves a *contradiction*: the willed absence of something that is fundamental to all reality. When we forget God, his very absence comes to have a power of its own. This power Paul calls sin. Sin is not a thing, it is the absence of a thing. It has no power of its own: it is merely the shadow or echo of something that isn't there. It has real power nonetheless. It is the power of the absence of God.

We are feeling our way through a huge cavern far from daylight. Suddenly against the wall beside us looms a figure vast and menacing and terrible. Moving relentlessly, it reaches out towards us in threat and in terror. We stop, paralyzed.

The shadow on the wall is not a person, but it looks like one. It is nothing in itself; it only mimics the acts of the person whose shadow it is—while at the same time grotesquely distorting them. A gesture of welcome becomes arms reached out to seize and take captive. A call to follow becomes a hand raised in threat. Sin is the power of the absence of God. We are facing the wrong way. The shadows terrify us: nothing in themselves, they exercise the power of God's absence.

God would continue to be absent if it was up to us. But God refuses to be absent. In Jesus he comes to where we are, and claims us as his own. He brings us, bodily, out of the darkness and into the light. And lo and behold, before us lies not a cavern with walls and a roof, but a sunlit landscape with a river running through it, and a path beckoning us onward. And in the presence of the light, the shadows melt away. They are not rendered powerless. They are not diminished. They are not defeated. They simply cease to be. This is the truth that Paul is telling us here. "You are dead to sin and alive to God in Messiah Jesus" (v. 11).

FROM AND FOR

"We have died to sin," Paul continues, "but that is only the beginning. If we have died with him, we trust that we will also *live* with him." God's deliverance is twofold: we are delivered *from* something, and we are delivered *for* something. The empty space in our life becomes full, as the tide of God's grace pours in to fill the gap. And how does that come about? It comes about because of the resurrection.

We need to ask God to lay upon us the in-your-face factualness of Jesus's rising again, to give us something of what the disciples experienced when they touched him or saw him eat an ordinary meal of fish and bread in front of them. For we are so familiar with the Christian story that it is easy to treat it as a child's tale. Tragically, the hero is betrayed and handed over to his enemies, who torture and kill him. Everything seems lost. But, lo and behold, God steps in to bring him back to life again! Everything turns out right in the end. What Paul is talking about is nothing even remotely like this. He is talking about an earthquake at the very foundations of reality. The power of death is shattered: a human being breaks through it, making a way for others to follow. An old world has died, a new world has been born. God has created a new humanity. Nothing will ever be the same.

Paul urges us therefore not to hope or wish for something but to *recognize* the fact of our new situation (v. 11). He is not suggesting that we sentimentally imagine that we are dead, or that we "kill ourselves" as an exercise in autosuggestion. What he is calling us to do is to recognize the reality of something that has objectively happened—and to live on the basis of it. Speaking of the reality of the cross, someone once said that if you ran your hands along it you would get splinters. Were you to go to the tomb, the stone shelf upon which Jesus' body had lain would be cool to the touch, and rough with the adze marks of its making. "Sin will not rule over you" (v. 14): Paul is not talking about a pious hope, but an actual, concrete reality. The statement is a *promise*: a promise that will not let us down because it is grounded in the actual events of the cross and resurrection.[80]

Generations of tradition have taught us that when Paul speaks about "also *living* with him" in verse 8 he is referring to life after death.[81] But Paul's interest is not in life after death. He is asking whether there is life *before* death. Are we alive, or do we merely exist? Jesus has been raised from the dead: with him we too are now alive to God. But the risen life is not something that we have, it is something that we *live*; it is a gift given day by day. That is what life is. We *have* died with Jesus; we *will* live with him; it is a promise of which we have to take possession, now, each day.

FREED TO FIGHT

Taking possession involves choice. It is our birthright. It is possible to allow sin to assert control. Don't therefore *passively* let sin rule, Paul urges us, and don't *actively* offer the parts of your body as weapons of wickedness either. Instead *do* actively offer your selves to God, and the parts of your body as weapons of righteousness.[82]

The military metaphor brings us up with a start. Important as they are to us, the choices we make, the lives that we live, are not just a personal matter. Everything that we do influences the lives of others, whether negatively or positively. Faithlessness, a lie, gossip, greed, neglect, failure to stand up for the needs and dignity of others: the destructive influence of things like these spreads out into the world like a stain. Faithfulness, truthfulness, speaking well of others, generosity, care, courage: these things actively build righteousness into the community. Paul depicts all this as a battle, a battle in which, whether we are aware of it or not, we are fighting either on one side or the other. It is a wakeup call. In the past we have unknowingly been offering our bodies as weapons of wickedness. Now with conscious intent we must offer them to God as weapons of righteousness. God will take what we offer and make it part of his work in the world.[83]

Notice that Paul is not treating the "don't" and the "do" as separable things, as if we could do the one without the other. The former is *only possible* in the power of the latter. Life is not about not doing things but about doing them. A life built upon not-doing creates an intolerable tension. The house is swept and cleaned—and the demons take up residence.[84] Righteousness, on the other hand, is a filling-full; it is the power and the joy of life. It is something that God alone can give. It is a sharing with him in the work of the new creation.

The best illustration of this that I know is in Luke's story of the calling of the first disciples in chapter 5 of his Gospel. Do you remember it? Jesus is teaching beside the Lake of Galilee. The crowds are so huge that people can't hear him, and indeed can hardly breathe for the press. Coincidentally some fishermen cleaning their nets just happen to be there on the beach, so Jesus asks them if he can borrow their boat to use as a floating pulpit. Later, when the crowd has gone, he suggests they go fishing.

Why? Does he have some deep spiritual purpose? I don't think so. Preaching and teaching is hard work, making yourself heard in this case, making yourself understood at any time. But now, the crowds are gone and the responsibility is over, at least until tomorrow. I think Jesus wants an adventure.

And of course, we know the story. The reluctance of the fishermen, who have been working all night and know there is nothing out there. The sudden massive school of fish that drives into the net. The hard, fast work, as the boats come together and the nets are secured and lightened as best they can be before they break. And then Peter (for he is the owner of one of the boats) understands. Suddenly he realizes what this means. He turns, and right there in the boat falls on his knees before Jesus.

Who does he turn to? An image search on the web for "miraculous catch of fish" will turn up some of the weird religious things that artists down the years have done with this story (the movies too). Does Peter turn in reverence to some white-robed, holy-looking blue-eyed Scandinavian? No, he turns to a big, burly Jewish man, stripped to the waist, hauling fish in as hard as he can go, and having the time of his life. How could we imagine it would be otherwise? "You're making a mistake, Lord," Peter bursts out. "I'm not the one you want. I'm a sinful man!"

Peter is telling nothing but the truth. He is not worrying about how he used to pinch half-crowns out of his brother's moneybox when he was a kid. He is a tough young fisherman in a hard-living, hard-playing harbor town. And we know what Jesus says, don't we? "Well, I'm glad you've realized that, Peter. You need to repent now, and turn your life around. And then maybe we can get to know each other better." Not a bit of it. Instead he completely ignores Peter's confession. "Come with me, Peter," he says, "and I'll teach you to catch *people* for God." When they had brought their boats to shore, Luke tells us, they left everything and followed him.

Don't—and do. The story takes us immediately to the heart of the good news. It shows how irrelevant to Jesus is our obsession with the things we have done wrong. It turns all of our religious ideas on their head. Knowing Jesus is not about a scorecard but about a relationship. Jesus isn't interested in what isn't there in our lives, but he is very interested in what will be. He isn't interested in the past, but he is deeply interested in the future; indeed he calls us to accompany him into it. And here is another shock. We are so used to the idea of having faith in Jesus that we can miss what is implied in that call. Not only do we have faith in Jesus, *he has faith in us.* He trusts us. He takes us on as learners. He enlists us as comrades alongside himself in the work of the good news.

What Paul says in verse 14 is not, then, an exhortation. It is simply a matter of fact. "Sin will not rule over you," he says. How can that be? "Because you are not under Law, where matters of right and wrong are measured by an impersonal standard. Rather, you are under grace, where the only thing that matters is God's outrageous and unmerited call into relationship with him."

Sin *will not* rule over you.

CHOOSE YOUR MASTER

Paul now switches to his second metaphor—and using it, says everything he has just said all over again. The parallels between the two halves of the chapter are obvious even when we are reading rather than listening. The arresting rhetorical question and point-blank answer in verse 15 is the same as that in verses 1 and 2. Paul has just called us to present the parts of our bodies to God as *weapons* of righteousness; now he calls us to present our bodies as *slaves to* righteousness (v. 19). And so on. Paul is not going further with this new illustration, he is going deeper.

Familiar as it was in Paul's every-day world, slavery is still a grim metaphor—but also a completely appropriate one as far as sin is concerned.[85] Notice that Paul does not contrast slavery and *freedom*. Freedom is surely what God intends for us, but it is not an absolute freedom. What a terrifying thing that would be! We can no more be absolutely free than we can exist without a body. Just as a human being is an embodied being, our freedom is freedom *for obedience*. We are born for this. It is the way we are made; it is a fundamental fact of who we are. We cannot be absolutely free.[86] We can passively or actively serve sin—or we can actively serve God, which is our freedom and our destiny.

Just as vv. 3–11 are not about baptism but about the death to sin of which it is a sign, so these verses are not about slavery or the status of the slave, but *the nature of the owner to whom we submit ourselves*. Paul's emphasis is not upon the owner's acts: he has already made clear that on God's part they are the acts of a sacrificial savior. His concern is the Christian's willing acceptance of God's ownership, and daily choice to live a life in dependence upon him. We are personal beings, made by the living God for relationship. In Jesus, God has acted decisively to restore that relationship. We cannot therefore any longer live in subjection to our impulses and desires and willfulness. It is a possibility that is closed to us. Paul is not offering us the choice between two types of life. He is talking about something that has already happened: "Having been set free from sin, you have become slaves of righteousness" (v. 18). This is the fact. This is the new reality. Presenting our bodies as slaves to impurity is something that we *once* did. It is now no longer a possibility for us. But what we *do* now need to do, Paul tells us, is to actively present our bodies as slaves to righteousness (v. 19).

Hmm . . . but is it really something that we want to do? The whole idea of slavery is repellent: how can Paul be expecting us to buy into that in the twenty-first century? And in fact, v. 19 shows that this isn't what he is asking. He is fully aware of the tension implicit in the comparison. He is using it to explain, not to define; it is "a metaphor to help you understand," he tells us.[87] The metaphor nonetheless describes something very real. Some of us out of bitter experience will be more aware than others of just what it means to be a slave to sin, but aware of it or not it is a reality for us all. "You've gotta serve somebody," sang Bob Dylan long ago. "It may be the devil or it may be the Lord, but you gotta serve somebody."[88] That is verses 15 to 19 in a nutshell.

COME WITH ME

But how do we *do* it? How do we "offer every part of our bodies as slaves to righteousness"? Isn't this just religious talk? Rather than anything practical the idea just sounds mystical and mysterious. We have, however, learned enough about Paul by now to know that nothing could be further from the truth. The secret lies in the word *obedience*, which Paul uses four times in two sentences (vv. 16–17).[89]

I wonder what you think about this word. For me, it conjures up memories of being told to do the dishes or mow the lawns when I was a boy, or, in my single-sex high school, having to keep my socks pulled up and my cap on. Obedience means doing something you don't particularly want to do because someone more powerful than you requires it. These are the connotations of the word in twenty-first century English. We have forgotten what it means to choose your lord; we have forgotten the joy of sworn allegiance to a trusted master. The word has come to have a negative connotation instead of the positive one that it has had throughout most of its history.

It is not a negative or mindless obedience that Paul is describing here. On the contrary, he rejoices in the way those who have been liberated from sin have become obedient *from the heart* to the outworking of the truths that they have been taught. The reversal is complete. In the one case we are *out of* control, slaves of sin; in the other we are *in* control, as obedient servants of God.[90] When we give up our freedom we become slaves. The body, or our impulses, or pressures from outside demand our obedience . . . and we give it. We give our freedom away. But when we become obedient from the heart the initiative is ours. We *use* our freedom; we choose. The obedience of the heart Paul speaks about is not then the teeth-gritting exercise of some human freedom. Rather, it is the stepping out into the free life that God alone can give. It is the lived experience of the freedom for which we were made. Now at last the goal of our lives is outside of ourselves. That was the slavery from which we need to be set free: the slavery of the self-enclosed self. But now we are free for God, and therefore free for ourselves.

Paul has already told us about this back in chapter 5. "Now that we have been restored to fellowship with God through the death of his Son," he told us back there, "how much more certainly will we be rescued in his life. *Through the obedience of Messiah Jesus,* all people will be made righteous" (5:9, 10, 19). Rescue, salvation, however we want to describe it, is salvation for obedience. Obedience is our participation in the life of Jesus. It is not an optional extra, but the very secret of life. Obedience is the state of being saved, both from and for.[91] "Come with me," says Jesus to Peter, "and I will teach you to catch people for God."

SHARING IN GOD'S WORK IN THE WORLD

That sounds fine, even inspiring, when you say it. But how do we *do* it? It was easy for the disciples: they could leave their boats behind and follow an actual human being down an actual road. But how do we today get to know Jesus? We can't see him, or hear an actual voice; we don't get any of the visual feedback that we get from a friend that shows they are really listening. How can we, in any meaningful way, come to know the invisible God? What practical sense does it make to talk about following Jesus today?

Paul will have much to say about these questions in the next couple of chapters. But in the meantime, he gives us one of the keys right here. Step back for a minute. How do we get to know anyone? We know about that perfectly well. We talk to them—and we also listen to them. Talking and listening are basic to getting to know someone. But that is not all that is involved in a relationship. The real way we get to know people is by doing things together. It is in shared activity that we really get to know another person. This is the way friendships are forged: in the sports team, in the workshop, on the committee, or in the drama group; in shared service, or in striving for a cause.

Why would getting to know God be any different? We already know something about it. Talking to God is what we call *prayer*. Listening comes in prayer as well, and perhaps especially through reading the Scriptures. God also speaks to us through others, through our own experience of joy and sorrow, and through our encounter with the natural world. But what about that third thing, the one I've suggested is the real key to building a relationship? How do we do things together with God? Paul tells us right here: by means of *obedience*. Obedience is our response to God's call to accompany him in his work in the world. It is not obedience to an impersonal instruction, it is response to a personal invitation. It is not morality, it is discipleship.

We can sometimes feel that we are the first generation to have these kinds of questions. Not so. During the Last Supper Jesus gave his disciples the startling news that his time on earth was coming to an end. He was going away, and they would not be able to follow (John 13:31–33). They were devastated, and their immediate question was exactly the same as ours. How are we going to get on? How is it possible to have a relationship with somebody who you can't hear, see, or touch? Jesus goes on to explain how it will be: the way in which their present life with him would not only continue, but become deeper and fuller (16:6–7). The way the Holy Spirit will come, that is, he will come back to them (14:15–20). How the Father will love them and Jesus reveal himself to them (14:21). How not only the incarnate Jesus but God the Father in all his fullness will come and make his home among them (14:23).

These are astonishing promises. But in every case there is what seems to be a condition. "If you love *me you will keep my commandments* . . . those *who have my commandments and keep them* are those who love me . . . those who love me *will keep my word* . . ."—and then in each case the promise follows. But the condition is not a condition. It is a statement of a truth about the world. This is how it works. What John describes as Jesus' commandments, his word, are exactly the same as his first call to the disciples to "come with me!" Obedience is *accompanying Jesus*. His personal presence and continuing revealing of himself to us through the Holy Spirit, and God himself coming to live with us: these are not *reward* for obedience, they are the *result* of it. They are what happen when we do things together with God. We step out on the way in company with Jesus—and so we come to know him.

A HARVEST OF HOLINESS

The result of all this, Paul tells us, is holiness. "Present your bodies as slaves to righteousness, *so that you may become holy,*" he exhorts us (v. 19). "Now, freed from sin and slaves of God you have *a harvest of holiness*" (v. 22). Good grief: what on earth is he talking about now?

In his splendid little book *The Fight,* John White lists the things that come to mind when he thinks about holiness: hollow-eyed gauntness, beards, sandals, long robes, no sex or jokes, hair shirts, frequent cold baths, fasting, wild rocky deserts, and getting up at 4 a.m. to pray.[92] Perhaps we all have a mental list a little like this. It is the fading echo in our culture of something important that has been lost. What is striking about this kind of description is that all the terms of it are negative in some way. They describe the absence of something: sin, I suppose, or at least the absence of things that we might see as *temptations* to sin.

But as soon as we unpack it like that, we realize how impossible an idea this is. For sin itself is not a thing. It is already in itself the absence of a thing, the absence indeed of the most fundamental thing in life. If *sin* is now absent that must mean the *presence* of something else—or of somebody else. The gap in our lives has been filled by the presence of God.

Holiness is therefore the presence of something, not the absence of a thing. But holiness is not just a human word. Think about it as it is applied to God. We speak of God as holy, and that is completely appropriate. But in what possible way could that mean the absence of something? On the contrary, as I once heard an old preacher say, the holiness of God is *the shining out of all that God is.*[93] And that is precisely what Paul means by "the harvest of holiness" as far as we are concerned: through obedience to the living Jesus, the shining out in our lives of all that God intends us to be, and which, through the resurrection, he gives us the power to be. Once there was nothing, now there is something; our lives have a goal and a purpose. The void in our lives has been filled.

Notice, however, that holiness doesn't fall upon us like fairy dust. It is something that we day by day present our bodies as slaves to righteousness *in order that we may become* (v. 19). It is a *harvest,* maturing slowly, with eternal life as its goal (v. 22). Paul is speaking about a life that is created day by day, decision by decision, choice by choice, a fully human life, the only kind of life there is. "Come with me *and I'll teach you,*" said Jesus. "Come, *with me.*"

THE TERROR . . .

In verse 23, Paul brings his two metaphors together: death and life, the wages sin pays and the unearned gift of God. It is a powerful statement that stands as both a promise and a warning. A warning? Paul undoubtedly means it as such. What, after all, is this death he is talking about? We know he doesn't mean merely physical death. But what does he mean?

We need a concrete example, and once again, I have to take it from my own experience. With shame and reluctance I have to tell you that, under particular circumstances of tiredness and isolation that I know very well, I have ended up involved with pornography on the Internet. On the computer I am using to write this, there is a program installed which is designed for parents to protect their primary school children from accessing inappropriate websites and images. My wife knows the password for this program, but I do not. It is necessary for me to have it there. I am not in peril every hour, but should the stars line up and that madness fall upon me, I need the protection. It is a matter of life and death.

This is difficult to write. In particular, I am aware of how disgusted and repelled one half of my audience will be by this. I may have lost you. But we have to be real. We can't talk in general terms about sin and death and grace and holiness, as if we were just shuffling religious tokens around. Too much of that has been done in the past, until what Paul is saying here has become completely divorced from real life. But the good news of Jesus doesn't live in some religious zone, in church perhaps, or in earnest religious experiences. It comes to us in the messiness of our compromised and tangled real lives, in the mud and the blood and the tears. That's where God in Jesus came to meet us. He didn't come to where we ought to be, but to where we are.

What Paul means by "death" I therefore know very well. Sin is not a thing, it is the nothing which God put behind his back in the act of creation. When we step into it, like the cold of outer space it sucks our life away. When I have surfaced from one of these incidents in the past, I have realized that something is gone. I'm aware that I'm diminished. I'm not the person I was. I'm available for *that*; indeed, sin lusts for us, it feeds upon the life that we have to offer it. But I'm not available for anything else, for God or for people. If there was some crisis to which I had to respond, I would be unable. If there was someone in need, I would have no resources. Indeed, I would probably not notice, for the essence of sin is to turn us in upon ourselves. We make ourselves comfortable all alone with the silk and the pillows, and the coffin lid slides across.

Outwardly, of course, nothing has changed. No one notices. It's like when your computer hard drive fails. There is the wonderful machine, sitting on the desk in front of you. It is as sleek and business-like as ever. You know its intricacy and complexity, and the wonderful things it can do. But that one tiny green light isn't showing, and that is the only thing that matters. Or it is like coming back to your parked car and finding that it won't start. You turn the key in the ignition, and nothing happens. No one around knows that anything is wrong. All they see is a person sitting in a car, waiting. Indeed, they may be pretty impressed: it is after all a BMW, and it's clear that you look after it well. But all they are looking at really is a small steel, leather-upholstered space, not much bigger than a cupboard. It's not going anywhere. It has no purpose.

We walk in life day by day, each of us, only by the grace of God. The boundary between life and death is different for us all. Sin comes in many shapes and guises. John Ruskin describes a nomadic Russian tribe that, when the head of house died, dressed him in his finest robes, and carried him in his chariot to his friends' houses. There he was placed at the head of the table, and all feasted in his honor. But, Ruskin asks, how it would be if it were possible for this to go on day by day *for a living man*, for such a person to be aware of what was happening to them, of the increasing riches and honor, of the pomp and palaces—and yet the spirit inside them be dead?[94] What profit is it to you if you gain the whole world and yet lose your own soul?

Do we fear the death that Paul is speaking about? O brothers and sisters we should fear it! It is the darkness of the night. It is the cold of deep space, and we have cut our tether to the spaceship. All alone we are falling into the space between the stars. It is from this death that God has committed his own self utterly and without reservation to rescue us. In Messiah Jesus we have died to sin. How can we go on living in it?

. . . AND THE GLORY

If not in that way, how then shall we live? We receive life, each day, as an unearned, gracious gift. The emptiness is filled. The presence of God replaces the void. We live "*in Messiah Jesus our Lord*," Paul tells us. The phrase is not just a nod in the direction of Jesus, but the whole of Paul's meaning. The life God gives us is no free-floating gift, no generalized benevolence. It is something specifically located in space and time, grounded in something that has been accomplished, embodied in a living person who now encounters and accompanies us. "In Messiah Jesus" is the *location* of life. And that life is not just living, it is eternal life. The life God gives us is the risen life of Jesus.[95]

Eternal life is life before death. Our culture likes to talk about "quality of life," but that is not what Paul is talking about here. Not a better quality of life, but a new human being! Not darkness, but light: the difference is absolute.

What does that life consist of? In John's Gospel, in the prayer that brings to an end the Last Supper discourse we were looking at a page or two back, Jesus himself tells us. He reminds God that he has given him "authority to give eternal life to all those you have given me. And this is what eternal life is: *to know you, the only true God and Jesus Messiah whom you sent.*"[96]

Eternal life is a relationship. The specific nature of that relationship Paul will describe in chapter 8. But before that, he has one more metaphor, one more comparison, one more unfolding of the meaning of the resurrection. Let us read on.

13

Endnotes
Chapters 4–6

1. **Notes to the translation:**
   v. 2 **"religious observances."** The common English translation "works" has led to many misunderstandings. Later in Christendom (the issue coming to dramatic focus at the time of the Reformation), church doctrine would come to conform to the perception still common to most human religious systems that a person's eternal destiny depended upon a credit balance of good deeds over evil ones over the course of their lives. The balance could be influenced in various ways, including doing acts of extraordinary merit value, the canceling of bad deeds through penance, and the purchase of merit from the church's treasury of surplus merit built up from the good deeds of Jesus and the saints (whose credit balance was far greater than that necessary to enter paradise). Exposing the essentially unchristian and even pagan nature of this doctrine was one of the great achievements of the Reformation; it was essentially the rediscovery by the church of its own good news. The intense importance of that reawakening has, however, meant that ever since it has been hard for Protestants to see that Paul in this place is talking about something completely different. (One is reminded of Carson's comment on Luther's Galatians commentary that the modern reader "has to make allowance for Luther's concern with the Pope in places where Paul is concerned with Moses." D. A. Carson in *New Testament Commentary Survey*, Grand Rapids: Baker, 2007, 106.) As is plain from the context, Paul is not talking about "good deeds" in general, but quite specifically about the distinctive practices (especially circumcision v. 9; the others were Sabbath-keeping and the food laws) that marked out Jewish people as, in the minds of those who practiced these things, exclusively God's chosen people. See further on v. 6.

   v. 3 **(also vv. 18–19) "Abraham put his faith in God"**: The word is *pisteuo*, to put one's faith in. I have tried to avoid the word "believe" where a personal relationship is involved: one can believe a fact, but one trusts or puts one's faith in a person (even with regard to facts, in biblical language acknowledgement of their truth is never passive, but implies a response). Hopefully the whole translation makes it clear that in every part we are talking about faith in God's faithfulness.

   v. 3 **"reckoned"**: The Greek word is *logizomai,* to evaluate, judge, consider something to be. To make clear English sentences I have translated the same word "considered to be" in v. 4 and "ascribes" in v. 6, considering that the meaning is clear without forcing the verbal parallel. Throughout the rest of the chapter I have continued to use counted/reckoned/ascribed/considered interchangeably, as the logic of the individual sentence demands (e.g., in the transition from v. 9 to v. 10). The crucial thing to note is that Paul is not speaking about "counting" or "reckoning" in any transactional sense. *Logizomai* always bears the sense of a personal or interpersonal *evaluation*: this is so even in v. 4, where Paul is not talking about counting out a particular amount of wages to be entered in a ledger, but about how the idea of wages is understood. This is doubly important when righteousness is involved. The issue is not a transaction, as in (as some theologies assert) we don't have righteousness, but God accepts faith as a substitute for it in the ledger. Rather, it is an interpersonal *judgment of character*; God considers us to be, treats us as, and trusts us to be *a certain quality of person*. This is his response to our trust in him: he trusts us in turn. "Counting" or "reckoning" therefore has nothing to do with a heavenly balance sheet; rather it is a door God in his grace opens to a personal future, to a life to be lived. The Greek text is very clear about this.

"as righteousness": The Greek word is *eis*, which has the general meaning "into" or "towards"; it carries the sense of goal or purpose. It is a preposition denoting not a status but a journey into or towards something.

v. 4 **"generosity/obligation"**: Not "gift/debt"; Paul is talking not about the wages but about the difference in the nature of the relationship.

v. 5 **"not someone working for a wage"**: The phrase is identical to that denoting "worker" in v. 4 with the addition of the negative. Paul is not talking about someone who *doesn't work*, but about *the nature of the relationship*. We are not God's hired worker. Rather, in his grace we are called into covenant, into a personal relationship with him.

v. 6 **"exactly this"**: *katheper kai*.

"works": i.e., observances, as in v. 2, considered as something done to gain credit or incur obligation, like the worker's wages in v. 4. Paul's point is that the forgiveness and free pardon that David speaks of was not the reward of the works of religious observance that the Law prescribed—and in particular, not the reward of circumcision, of which membership of the covenant community (and therefore the circle of his favor) was the sign. It was the result not of anything that humans do, but of the grace of God who acts in freedom. Grace is not dispensed to those within the community through the community's mechanisms. God's grace *creates* the community, and governs its composition at his good pleasure.

v. 7 **"pardoned"**: Lit. "covered."

v. 11 **"confirmation"**: Lit. "a seal of," i.e., the imprint of a signet ring confirming that an affidavit or document was genuine.

v. 13 **"the promise that he would inherit the world"**: Notice the way in which Paul's understanding of his text is not tied to a wooden literalism; rather the Old Testament text is renewed and reconceived for his own day in the light of the good news. The quotation in v. 17 comes from Gen 17:4 where the immediate "inheritance" in question is the land of Canaan (v. 8). But Paul realizes that to the ancestor of many nations, the promise of an inheritance has wider significance than just the narrow territory of the nation of Israel either politically *or* spiritually. Paul is not of course alone in this: cf. Matt 5:5.

"the righteousness of faith": We must be careful not to allow these two words to float away free into the superficial understandings of them that have historically plagued this letter. Their *relational context* must always be at the forefront of our minds. We are not dealing with abstract qualities or religious ideas, but about the relationship between people and God and (1) the integrity of character on God's side and (2) the gift of that same quality to human beings, that constitutes the ongoing experience of that relationship.

v. 17 **"makes the dead live again and calls things that don't exist into existence"**: although Paul is discussing an Old Testament text, his thought is nonetheless controlled by the fact of the resurrection; this will be made explicit in 4:25. What God declared himself to be in Abraham's day his act in Messiah Jesus has demonstrated: that he is the one who *in the present* gives life to the dead and who calls *the future generations* into existence, even though they do not as yet exist (v. 17b). Of that earlier promise the Christian community in Rome is part of the fulfillment; and the promise still stands, open to the future.

v. 19 **"no longer capable of begetting a child"**: Lit. "his body was as good as dead," a euphemism.

vv. 20–21 **"Acknowledging God to be God"** (1) The sentence is not commonly broken here. The first half of the verse is however complete in itself, with its verbal parallelism between wavering through doubt and being made strong through faith. The following two participial phrases then can be seen to be a description of faith *as it was lived in Abraham's experience*, leading directly into the *dio kai* of the concluding verse. (2) The idea of "giving glory" can often be a bit of religious vagueness. What Paul means, though, is very precise: it is the opposite of what is described in 1:21 (where the same Greek word is used). Paul doesn't therefore mean merely *praise*, except in the way that something consciously and deliberately lived is praise (and can be described as worship, Rom 12:1).

v. 21 **"he is able to do"**: Note the change from past to present tense: God's dealings with Abraham in history reflect his eternal character.

v. 22 **"this is what was . . . "**: Greek *dio kai,* introducing the repetition of the Gen 15:6 quotation that Paul started with. "This then is the conclusion to the preceding exposition as a whole; the second exact quotation from Gen 15:6 forming a frame with v. 3 in which the intervening exposition is set" (Dunn, *Romans 1–8,* 221). As we have seen once before, the traditional chapter division is in the wrong place. The next section of the letter begins not with 5:1, but with 4:23.

2. When Abraham's nephew Lot is captured with all his people and his possessions by the victors of a war between the local tribes, Abraham musters a force of 318 of his own retainers, follows the track of the raiders, surprises them by night, and sends them fleeing over the border. The stolen goods and stolen people are all recaptured (Gen 14). No pious dreamer here: this is a man of action, a resourceful commander and strategist. There's more: it's worth looking up these stories if you haven't read them for a while (Gen 12–25).

3. The word is *euriskō,* to discover (as in Archimedes's "Eureka!"); it has nothing to do with acquiring or gaining, as, e.g., NRSV renders it.

4. This last clause is often translated as if it were a kind of afterthought, a sort of polite nod in God's direction. In fact, given the question in v. 1, it is the climax and point of the verse. If Paul had had punctuation at his disposal (Greek text contains none) he would certainly have used an exclamation mark.

5. The Hebrew word is *hasab.* Examples of this word used in its primary meaning include Ps 144:3, "What are human beings that you *regard* them, or mortals that you think of them?"; Job 13:24, "Why do you hide your face and *count me as* your enemy?"; and Isa 53:3, "he was despised and we did not *esteem him.*" *Hasab* is translated in the Greek version of the Old Testament as *logizomai,* which is the word Paul uses here as well. On *logizomai,* see the notes to the translation on vv. 3–6 above.

6. Both of these quotations, slightly adapted for clarity, are from the *Mekhilta,* a first-century-BC commentary on the book of Exodus, as quoted by Cranfield, *Critical and Exegetical Commentary,* 229. He refers his readers to Strack and Billerbeck's *Commentary on the New Testament from the Talmud and Midrash* (Lexham, 2013), and notes that when expounding Gen 15:6 the rabbis regularly tended to replace "righteousness" in the verse by "merit." All of this would have been well-known to Paul and presumably also to those of his audience who had come under this kind of teaching.

7. We have noted earlier how in both Greek and Hebrew the word translated *faith* can mean (in English) *faith* or *faithfulness.* As *faithfulness in religious observance and in keeping the Law* (i.e., seeing faithfulness as a set of obligations to fulfill, rather than as one side of a mutual relationship) is how Abraham's faith is being interpreted in these passages. According to this understanding of the Genesis verse, Abraham's faith in God meant his faithfulness *earned God's favor.*

8. 1 Macc 2:51–52. Abraham's actions, not God, make him righteous!

9. Matt 9:13, repeated in all three Synoptic Gospels.

10. If your translation says "justifies" here, that is what to justify means. See translational note "Justification or being declared righteous?"

Endnotes: Chapters 4–6

11. There isn't space here to discuss this theory in detail; besides, it seems more important to concentrate on what Paul is saying rather than what he is not. Sufficient here to note the long history of this kind of thought. We have already seen some examples from rabbinical Judaism. But it occurs also in Christian theology from earliest times. It is at least partly a translation issue. Because the early theologians of the church used the Latin translation of the New Testament, in which the word righteousness was translated as "justice," the idea that *making righteous* or *justification* (this is where the word comes from) is about a legal declaration appeared to be both natural and, at a verbal level at least, also biblical. That same Latin translation was the standard text (indeed, the only text) in use right across Europe until the fifteenth century.

    But to understand declaring to be righteous as a legal declaration is totally misleading, and totally at odds with what Paul is actually saying here. Again and again in the commentaries one finds the assertion that vv. 7–8 demonstrate that "reckoning as righteous" is equivalent to "not reckoning sin," i.e., to *forgiveness*. This is (1) an extraordinary confusion between a positive act and a negative one; (2) it perpetuates the idea of a legal fiction on God's part; (3) it incorrectly sees the focus of the verses as being on the nature of righteousness instead of the meaning of "reckoning"; and (4) it limply assumes that Paul is simply repeating himself in vv. 6–8, rather than advancing the argument.

    It may come as a surprise to those of us who have been brought up on the forensic doctrine, but verse 7a contains the only mention of forgiveness in Romans, and one of the very few in the whole Pauline corpus. The word only appears here because it is a part of a quotation from David, which Paul is invoking not because of this word but because of the word *reckon* in v. 8. Dunn notes the perplexity caused by the fact that "Paul elsewhere, and when expressing his own theology, seems to avoid so completely the thought of God's forgiveness (*aphesis* only in Col 1:14 and Eph 1:7), as also the conjoint idea of repentance" (*Romans 1–8*, 1:206). The reason Paul doesn't use this terminology is given in precisely this passage. God, as Paul understands him, is not a God who operates with a system of merits or demerits. There are no accumulated demerits to forgive. Instead, God calls us to follow, to trust, to enter into a living relationship—and provides the transforming power to enable us to do that. Paul virtually never uses the word "sin" in the singular. Rather than repentance and forgiveness his words are *righteousness*, *grace*, and *faith*, all of which speak of relationship rather than accounting.

    For a striking illustration of this truth in action, see the story of the call of the disciples in Luke 5:1–11. Faced with a display of joyful power that is quite beyond his experience Peter says to Jesus (my paraphrase): "You've made a mistake, Lord! I'm not the man you want. I'm *a sinful man*!" And he was a hard-working, hard-playing young fisherman in a lakeside town: he knew exactly what he was saying. Jesus completely ignores it. "Don't be afraid," he says. "Come with me and I'll teach you how to catch people for God!" And Luke concludes: "When they had brought their boats to shore *they left everything and followed him*."

12. The older NIV translation is therefore right in understanding that there is indeed a righteousness *that God gives*. Its mistake is in reading that into Paul's discussion of the righteousness *that is proper to God himself* (in 1:17 and 3:21).

13. Paul uses the Scripture with authority and freedom. Like Jesus in the synagogue at Nazareth (Luke 4:18–19) he stops his quotation half way through a sentence, where the second half of that sentence would have blurred the point.

14. If that is the case, does that mean that it doesn't matter what we do: good or bad, it is all the same to God? Hmm . . . where have we heard that question before (3:8)? How foolish! Of course what we do matters to God. Have we forgotten what Paul said back in 2:6–11 about God's attitude to lives that are shaped by deeds that are good or by deeds that are selfish and wicked? Paul hasn't forgotten—and his and our passionate longing for the power to live a righteous life is the engine that will drive all the rest of the letter. But his concern in these verses in chapter 4 is quite specifically with the meaning of the word "reckon" in Gen 15:6, and what that indicates about the character of God.

15. Gen 32:23–33. According to the tradition Abraham had other children, including Ishmael (Gen

Endnotes: Chapters 4–6

16) and those born from his marriage to Keturah, after the death of Sarah (Gen 25:1–6). Those of Jewish descent do not acknowledge these lines as part of the community of Israel.

16. Given the nature of the Roman community, Abraham is no random choice of example. He is precisely the model for the Christians in Rome, the majority of whom have themselves left the security of the paganism in which they had been nurtured, to follow the One True God of Judaism. That God has now revealed himself to them and to Israel in startling new clarity in the person of Jesus the Messiah; they are literally in the place of Abraham, discovering something totally new about the kind of God this God is.

17. Matt 21:31, 20:1–16, Luke 23:43.

18. Because we have no verb "to faith" in English, many translations have "believe" here. But more is involved than bare belief. The word implies trust and commitment in a relationship, which implies trust and commitment on the part of the other party. It is not a state; it is what a relationship looks like from inside it. It is the first step in an ongoing journey.

19. The relational context is not unique to the Greek word *pisitis*. The same is true for the Hebrew word *āman*, which *pistis* translates in the LXX of Gen 15:6.

20. 2 Chr 20:7.

21. In Gen 15:6 the particular point at which Abraham put his faith in God was the promise of a son, and of physical descendants as innumerable as the stars. The expression 'father of many nations' comes in a later elaboration of that promise (Gen 17:4–5); there too it refers to actual descendants. In Romans, however, Paul recognizes that the important thing in the promise is not the initial pressure point in Abraham's life from which it arose (the perpetuation of a family line) but its grounding in the character of God, who is God of the nations and whose purpose with Abraham is to bless the whole earth (Gen 12:3). In the Genesis story the single individual Abraham appears immediately after the primeval history, full of the chaos and challenge of human history, which ends with the story of the tower of Babel. This is not a narrowing of the focus of the story: the point remains the way God deals with the *world*. Abraham's faithful encounter with the faithful God and his physical descendants are not individual benefits but the bearers of God's promise and means of his deliverance for the nations. Paul wrenches the theology away from Abraham and back to the God in whose promise Abraham trusted. The *descendants of Abraham* are therefore not those who physically descend from him, but those (whether of his physical line or not) *who share his faith in the faithful God*. Compare Gal 3:25–29, where, in a different context, the same point is made.
Note that the word "nations" is the one that is usually translated "gentiles" in our English versions (e.g., in 3:27–31); Paul's emphasis upon it here is part of his continuing argument that the good news is not only for those inside the community, but also for those from "among the nations." Verses 9–11 of the present chapter have already made the point, of course, that Abraham, at the time of his call, was one of the latter.

22. Again we note the way Paul uses the Scripture with prophetic freedom. He takes from his passage the message he hears there from God for his Roman congregation, not allowing himself to get bogged down in all the other details of the story: the Ishmael episode, for example, or Abraham's later children by his second wife, Keturah, after the death of Sarah (Gen 16, and 25:1–6).

23. **Notes to the translation:**
v. 23 **"not only about him"**: Although the common translation "for him" (i.e., for his benefit) is linguistically possible, the context rules it out. Gen 15:6, with which Paul concludes the previous verse, is not (as is Gen 17:4) a *promise* to Abraham, it is a *report of his experience* in encounter with God. Paul is not here exhorting us to live by faith as Abraham did—exhortation begins with verse 1 of chapter 5. Rather, he is declaring the *fact* that what Abraham experienced we will also experience, as we too live by faith.

v. 25 **"because of"**: *Dia* with the accusative: Matt 10:22, Acts 21:34, John 7:13, Phil 1:15, etc.
"Wrongdoings": Not "sins" (NIV); see endnote 25 below.

5:1 **"let us"**: see Appendix 2.

vv. 2–3 **"let us"**: Reading *kauchōmetha* as the subjunctive, following the exhortation *exōmen* in v. 1.

v. 5 **"the holy Spirit"**: I have chosen not to capitalize the word "holy," in order to distinguish what Paul is saying from the later concept of a Holy Spirit, where the *description* becomes a *name* for a distinguishable person or persona within the being of God. Paul is not thinking in those terms. He means nothing more (and nothing less!) than *the essential being of the One God himself*, who enters history in Jesus to deliver and to claim us. Cf. Dunn: " . . . the power of Christ's risen life, or, alternatively expressed, the Spirit of God" (*Romans 1-8*, 1:269). We will hear more of this in chapter 8.

v. 9 **"made righteous"**: Righteousness always qualifies a personal subject. It is not an idea; it is not something that can exist independently. There are only ever righteous *persons*— and this is what we have been made in the offering of Jesus.

"in his sacrificial death": Paul's prepositions are different in each of the clauses of this verse (*en* his blood and *dia* him), whereas in v. 10 the order is reversed: " . . . we were reconciled *dia* the death of the Son. . .we shall be saved *en* his life." This cannot be accidental. Most English versions translate the *en* in both verses as "by," in other words, *by means of*. But Paul is not speaking of instrumentality, he is speaking about participation: the Messiah's full participation in humanity, living our life and dying our death. And our participation now, as part of all humanity, in that death (v. 9) and in his resurrection life (v. 10). That Paul's *en* means *participation in* should not need to be argued: in the next section he will use baptism as another visualization of something that he assumes his hearers understand to be fundamental (6:1–4). Note that the issue here is not the use or otherwise of particular words. The issue is the way in which the substitution of "by" for "in" not only flattens the text, but changes the underlying linguistic metaphor from one of *participation* to one of *instrumentality*: Jesus' death becomes a mechanism.

"in his sacrificial death" (literally *"in his blood"*): At its most basic level (as is common throughout the New Testament, Luke 11:49–51, Matt 27:24–25, Acts 20:26, etc.) the term "blood" is a synonym for the death spoken of in vv. 6–10. But it is not simply that. Paul's use of blood language in this verse indicates that the underlying image is that of the Old Testament sacrifice (compare 3:25, the only other place in the letter that image occurs). He is surely also referencing Jesus' own use of such imagery to make the same points about the uniqueness of his death and the way his followers will participate in it: "Take, eat; this is my body . . . drink from this cup, all of you; for this is my blood of the covenant, which is poured out for all for the forgiveness of sins" (Matt 26:26–28; well-known of course to Paul himself: see 1 Cor 11:23–26). Again: "Very truly, I tell you, unless you eat the flesh of the Son of Man and drink his blood, you have no life in you. Those who eat my flesh and drink my blood have eternal life, and I will raise them up on the last day" (John 6:53–54). In using such imagery today we run the risk of slipping into a kind of blood mysticism, where blood ceases to be a vivid *metaphor* for (violent) death, and instead becomes a magical mystical *substance* in its own right. But the blood of Jesus refers to nothing more—and nothing less—than the obedient death of Jesus, his life laid down in faithfulness to his Father. Nor does it refer in a religious way back to the Old Testament sacrifices; rather, they point *forward* as an acted metaphor within their own cultural context to this very specific act of God in history. As to what "participation in his blood" might practically mean, Jesus spells that out too: "If any want to become my followers, let them deny themselves and take up the cross and follow me" (Mark 8:34). We are made righteous not in some instrumental way, but precisely through participation in Jesus' righteousness, that is, his faithful obedience to the Father all the way to the cross. Note the way in which all of these passages are concerned with something that God has decisively done—but which we nonetheless are called to intimately participate in.

v. 10 **"restored to friendship"**: The word is traditionally translated "reconciled," which in modern English tends to carry connotations of unemotional or even resigned acceptance. In contrast the connotations of the Greek word are warmly personal; it can, for example, be used of the coming back together of a husband and wife who have been separated. Notice the phrasing:

it is not *God* who is restored to relationship with us, but *we* who are restored to relationship with God. What Paul is describing is not a mechanism to somehow turn God's heart towards us. It has always been turned towards us! The incarnation, the cross, and the resurrection demonstrate that conclusively. A way needs to be found to restore *our side* of the relationship; it is this that the death of Jesus accomplishes.

v. 11 **"that restored relationship now"**: Paul's point is that this hasn't happened in the end of time, it has happened *now*. Without that time signal the clause would simply be a repetition of the previous verses. This is the crucial extra information that Paul is adding at this point: all those things that in Jewish thinking had been considered to belong to the final judgment at the end of time are because of Jesus, part of our personal experience in the present.

24. The verb is *paradidōmi*; the correspondence between our wrong deeds and this expression make the link back to chapter 1 unmistakable. Notice the theological care in the statement; the verb is active in chapter 1 (God gave them up), passive in 4:25 (Jesus was given up). Paul allows no paradox: he doesn't say *God* gave Jesus up, because Jesus is the Son, that is, God himself entering history to redeem us. For Paul, God is always One. On being given up *to death,* Buchsel notes that "It is striking that we never find [this expression] in relation to Jesus" (Kittel, *TDNT* II, 170).

25. Not (for those using the NIV) given up because of our *sins*. Apart from two occasions when he is quoting from the Old Testament (4:8, 11:27) Paul doesn't in this letter use the word "sin" in the plural: compare this with 49 occurrences of sin in the singular. As already noted the word often translated "sins" in 3:25 is another word better translated "sinful acts." While the NIV chooses on other occasions as well to translate other words for wrongdoing as "sins," it is possible that in this case there is an assimilation of Paul's text to the LXX translation of Isaiah 53:12, to which some commentators see an allusion. If that is so, although Paul doesn't signal that he is quoting from Isaiah here, the NIV makes him do so! The very fact that Paul does *not* use the word "sins" in this verse (as the Greek Old Testament does in the Isaiah passage) seems to count against such an allusion. Moreover, Paul is constantly quoting the Old Testament in support of his arguments throughout the letter, dozens and dozens of them. In the light of that it seems strange that he would not formally indicate a reference to this extremely significant Isaiah passage if that was indeed his intention.

26. As, in the midst of the personal and social consequences of his grievous wrongdoing, King David recognizes: "I have sinned *against the Lord*" (2 Sam 12:13; this perhaps is echoed in Ps 51:4).

27. Rom 12:21.

28. The NIV translation ("left unpunished") in 3:25 is not merely inadequate here, it is wrong. It introduces a concept alien to Paul's discussion, a concept that both in chapter 3 and later in chapter 4 he is at pains to exclude.

29. When the airliners smashed into the Twin Towers or the New York World Trade Center on 9/11, *nothing* was contributed by the fanatics who flew the planes *to* the power of the explosion and the fall of the buildings. It was the energy, the resources, and the creative power that went into the making of those great structures being explosively released that caused their fall, with all the terrible consequences of that. This image also demonstrates the way in which the power of evil is *limited*. What is built can be brought to destruction. But once a building is reduced to ground level there is no further that it can fall. Evil has no creative power—and ultimately no destructive power either. For God alone is the Creator and his purpose is never shaken. Evil has nothing of its own, only God's power misused for a time.

30. Mark 15:34.

31. 1 Cor 1:23, Gal 5:11.

32. John 20:28–31. Chapter 20 is an additional recollection that was added by John at a time near his death (cf. 21:20–24).

33. Tertullian, *De Carne Christi* V, 4.

34. In secular Greek, the word *eirene* commonly means simply the absence of war. The New Testament writers, however, understood the word as a theological term through the Septuagint, the Greek translation of the Old Testament, where *eirene* is consistently used to translate the Hebrew *shalom*. The influence of the richer, more positive content of *shalom* is evident wherever *eirene* is used in the New Testament. The relationship between righteousness and *shalom* was a natural one in Jewish thought. Compare, for example, the famous verses in Ps 85:10–13, surely well-known to Paul (the clarifications in square brackets are mine):

    Steadfast love [on God's part] and faithfulness [on humanity's part] will meet;
    [God's] righteousness and peace [in human experience] will kiss.
    Faithfulness will spring up from the earth,
    and righteousness will look down from the sky.
    The Covenant God will give what is good;
    our land will give its crops.
    Righteousness will go before him,
    and will make his steps a path [for those who long for salvation to follow, vv. 4–7].

    Faith, righteousness, faithfulness, peace: the psalm could well stand as a powerful summary of what God has done in Messiah Jesus, as Paul has described it. Or, rather, what God has done in Jesus shows how the hope of this ancient prayer has been fulfilled.

35. Sometimes titled "Love III," the poem is available on the web, and published in many collections. Readers who have not come across this great poet of the Christian church might like to look online for the following poems as a further sample of his work: "Redemption," "Prayer," "Vanitie," "The Collar," and "The Agonie." As poems written in the seventeenth century they require a little work to understand, work that is richly rewarded for those prepared to do it.

36. Readers who are principled vegetarians may be relieved to know that the word "meat" was in Herbert's time a generic term for food of any kind.

37. Thielicke, *Death and Life*, 198.

38. This insight into what the death and resurrection of Jesus means is not unique to Paul: see for example Jas 1:2–4.

39. Needless to say, while the original event was real, this sequel is purely imaginary. In essence, what I am exploring here is the meaning of the command of Jesus at the Last Supper to "do this *in memory* of me" (Luke's account, 22:19; also the form of the words received by Paul, 1 Cor 11:24). Does Jesus mean "in the future you will do this to remember a key saving event in the past"? In one sense, yes: Christianity is not about a general principle but is news of an act of God in human history. But the remembering is not something that looks back nostalgically. The bringing to mind is "a positive force which affects one's behavior in the present" (Bartels in Brown, *NIDNTT*, 3:241). The Communion is just that, a present participation in the death of Jesus and in the risen life of Jesus. Paul himself makes this clear in another letter: "The cup of blessing for which we thank God, isn't sharing in that sharing in the blood of the Messiah? The bread we break, isn't sharing that sharing in the body of the Messiah?" (1 Cor 10:16; compare 2 Cor 4:10–11, where he describes what this means in his own present experience).

40. After many years of discussion and debate, the Council of Constantinople in AD 381 is commonly recognized to have produced the final synthesis (Kelly, *Early Christian Doctrines*, 87–88).

41. Rom 1:9.

42. Rom 12:10–11.

43. 1 Cor 16:18, 2 Cor 2:13 (where both NIV and NRSV translate *pneuma* as "mind"—for which, if Paul had intended this, there is another Greek word).

44. Hence the familiar threefold description of a human being as body, the physical substance; life, that which animates the body; and spirit, the thinking, laughing, creating, communicating *person*.

Endnotes: Chapters 4–6

45. The word *spirit* in both Hebrew and Greek is the same word for *wind* or *breath*. Hence the differing translations of Gen 1:2; hence the wording of Luke 23:46; hence the point of Jesus' discussion with Nicodemus in John 3:5–10. We are dealing with metaphor from deep in the past that is nonetheless part of the consciousness of both of the biblical religions and of the cultures from which they come. The use of the word suggests both the impossibility of separating the idea of spirit from the living person and also the way a living person reaches out into the world. Both of these aspects are unforgettably illustrated in John 20:21-22.

46. There are of course no capital letters in Paul's text. We add them for clarity—and sometimes as a reflection of the way we understand the text. But Paul's words here are not *a title*, they are *a description*.

47. Luke 23:43.

48. If this is a problem for us we need to consider: if Jesus did not die for the mass-murderer, where would we draw the line? At someone who commits a *single* murder? At a violent person? At a person who wishes someone else were dead? At someone who is angry with his or her neighbor (Matt 5:21-26)? Our own security is at stake here. The other relevant passage is the last chapter of the book of Jonah, where the prophet—sent to the equivalent in his day of the Nazi hierarchy, perpetrators of the Holocaust—refuses to accept that when they repent, God could have mercy upon them. Jonah is Israel, of course; and we are Jonah. It is a question of idolatry: are we prepared to allow God to be the God who he shows himself to be, or do we want a different kind of God: a grimmer, more retributive, more god-like God, perhaps?

49. That God *is* concerned for the victim as well as for the perpetrator should not be in doubt. Gen 4:10, Luke 16:19–31, and Rev 6:9–11 among many other passages make that completely clear.

50. Rutledge, *Not Ashamed*, 146.

51. In an earlier note we pointed out that Paul says not that we have been made righteous *by* his blood (i.e., his sacrificial death), but *in* his blood; he is not talking about instrumentality, but participation. What does that participation mean in practice? Paul is not talking about some weird ritual of blood mysticism. Blood is a symbol here, but what the symbol is doesn't matter as much as what it means. The key word is the one Jesus used at that last supper with his disciples: *covenant*. A covenant is a binding agreement. In ancient Middle Eastern culture when a solemn treaty or formal agreement between two parties was concluded, the seriousness of the matter for each party was shown by sealing it in the blood of a sacrifice. Strange? But although our culture uses different symbols, we do similar things today. When a man and a woman commit themselves together in a lifelong partnership, for example, they exchange rings, which each of them will wear as a sign for the rest of their lives. The gold of the marriage rings (and the diamonds in the engagement ring that has been given earlier as a sign of the seriousness of the promise), symbolize costly value, beauty, and indestructibility. It is not the gold or the gems themselves that matter. It is what they mean. In the symbolic world of ancient peoples, blood meant *life*.

It is a striking fact that even today we have no idea what life is. We can describe what it does, we can explore its chemistry and its physics and the wonderful mechanisms of its natural history. But what life itself actually *is*, what it is that breathes fire into the molecules and the cunning structures to bring about the difference between inanimate matter and a living organism: of these things we have no more idea than Paul had. What ancient peoples *believed*, though, was that that energizing principle was the blood: that the actual red stuff that ran through the veins of living creatures was life itself. Hence the power of blood as a symbol. And it isn't only an ancient symbol. Many cultures have even up to quite recent times maintained traditions based upon the symbolism of blood. The idea of "blood brothers," for example, is known from many cultures. Sometimes that was solemnized by two warriors each cutting their arm and pressing the two wounds together. The mingling of their blood was a powerful sign of commitment.

These then were the kinds of idea that underlay the Old Testament understanding of sacrifice. The blood of an animal was understood to be something given by God, and as God's gift, offered by a human being both in place of their own life and as sign of commitment of that life to

Endnotes: Chapters 4–6

God. The taking of the animal's life symbolized and solemnized the restoration of the covenant by God, after human failure to keep it. The symbolism appears strange to us, but it was powerful picture language to describe the very deepest things in the relationship between God and people. So it is natural that, as we have seen in chapter 3 (the only other time where this expression occurs), this became one of the central metaphors that Paul uses to explain what Jesus did on the cross. But with this one massively significant difference: the relationship is restored through the faithfulness of *his own* death (3:25).

52. Notice that, despite most English translations, Paul does not say *God's* wrath here. How could he, when he has just declared that all of God's grace is directed towards the ungodly—among whom we are included? Although Paul regularly makes clear that wrath is *God's* wrath (1:18, 2:8) he never characterizes God as wrathful. He uses the word and some occasions as a synonym for *judgment* (2:5); in others he treats it as a simple reality, an objective fact, as he does here. This is indicated by the use of the article ("*the* Wrath"); cf. 12:19, 13:4–5 (but not 4:15). English translations characteristically ignore the article, either gratuitously adding the word God (NRSV, NIV on 12:19) or translating *orge* as *punishment* (13:5, NIV). These liberties are in my opinion indefensible; they reflect a view of God that is different from Paul's. The comments above are not an attempt to soften or argue away the wrath of God: we have seen how important it is, because it affirms God's good creation against all that would destroy it. But it does reflect Paul's recognition that God is centrally the God of deliverance and good news: wrath is something from which God has gone to extreme lengths to deliver us.

53. The Sadducee party in Jesus' day represented the alternative view. For the orthodox understanding see, for example, Martha's declaration in John 11:24—and note the light that Jesus' reply in the following verses sheds on our present passage.

54. Sorting out how the word is used for God in the Old Testament is confused by the fact that virtually all English versions substitute "Lord" (often in small capitals) for the covenant name, Yahweh. See footnote 9 on Rom 1–3.

55. Noting of course that the word LORD (usually printed with small capitals) in our English translations of the Old Testament translate not the word "Lord" but the covenant name *Yahweh*. This convention is the source of endless confusion. What we are talking about here is not the covenant name, but the word Lord.

56. This explains all those psalms that rejoice in the king and pray for his welfare. There are many, but Ps 72 is particularly clear in spelling out how the relationship is understood. In these psalms people aren't praying that some individual will live long and prosper. They know that the king is *their king*: in his person he embodies the whole community, and his welfare is the welfare of the whole society. The people obey the king, the king rules in such a way that justice is done, and hence the country is kept safe from enemies and the whole society prospers. It is not a case of arbitrary rule and servile compliance but a relationship of mutuality in which each person plays their part.

57. **Notes to the translation:**
v. 12 **"it was through one person"**: The emphasis is upon the person, not the sin. The passage is about persons, their acts, and, in the case of Jesus, the act of God in him and the grace of God through him.

"meaning that": Lit. "on the basis of which." Theological debates about original sin have so influenced the environment of thought about this verse that commentators find it extremely difficult to see what the Greek text actually says. The theological interest in sin so dominates the view that we fail to see Paul's equal interest and emphasis upon death, in the widest sense of that term. (Notice how in v. 21 *sin* and *death* are considered together, not just as cause and consequence; see the note on that verse.) In the current verse *eph' ho* is a true relative clause: the *ho* (masculine dative relative pronoun) refers to the immediately preceding *thanatos* (death). As Dunn points out (*Romans 1–8*, 273) the statement is a chiasm:

sin came into the world and through sin *death,* meaning

death spread to all with the result that all *sinned.*

Paul is not speaking about the passing on of sin, leading to death, but the passing on of death, leading to sin. Adam's turning from God's command led to death. That is, the essential connection with God was broken; as a consequence he became mortal. His descendants are therefore also mortal. Their integral connection with God has been lost, and they are therefore subject to sin. For a full discussion of the interpretation of the Greek text, see Fitzmyer *in loc*, and Longenecker, who praises Fitzmeyer's treatment while himself preferring a different solution on contextual (i.e., theological) grounds. See endnote 16 on chapter 7 for further discussion of the idea of original sin.

v. 13: The first part of v. 13 is not, as the use of a variously placed dash in many translations suggests, merely indirectly related to v. 12, it is precisely the conclusion towards which Paul is leading in that verse. The translation I offer holds back the *hōsper* with which v. 12 begins until this point in order to make that connection clear. Paul's point is not (what has become an historical fascination in Western theology) Adam as the source of human sin, but the fact that *sin pre-dates the Law.* The role of the Law is therefore supplementary rather than definitive of what sin is. Paul cites the example of Adam as the ancestor of all people both Jew and pagan, as more fundamental than that of Moses as the giver of the Law, which Judaism claimed as its sole authority. The example of Adam pushes Paul's message—and God's claim upon human life—back beyond the distinctives of Jewish religion, to its basis in creation itself.

v. 14 **"disobedience to a command"**: see Kittel, *TDNT* 5:740 and compare Rom 4:15.

"Adam foreshadows": Lit. "is a *typos* of." A "type" is not a prophecy, a kind of secret code buried in past events. It is something that an expositor discovers, "a way of using Scripture for the illumination and confirmation of faith." "These important relationships [that is, between the fulfillment and the type which sheds light on it] have not been developed from general speculation about man as originally created or about redemption. They are revealed in the presence of the glory of Jesus the Messiah to the man who studies Scripture and in whom a divine miracle has caused the light of the new creation to shine" (Both quotations from Goppelt, *Typos*, 135). In Rom 5:14, therefore, Paul understands that "the destructive power of Adam . . . is *the distress that cries out for the Messiah's saving power* and it is the promise that points to that power within the framework of God's eternal plan of redemption" (Goppelt, *Typos*, 130, italics mine). Because we are unfamiliar with the language of typology today, we must translate the *idea*, not transliterate the *word*. While the way the New Testament uses the Greek word is distinctive, there is nothing mysterious or especially religious about its meaning. "Foreshadowing" seems to me to be as close as we can come in English, as long as we understand by that an *illustrative example* that an expositor discovers in Scripture which sheds light on gospel truth, and the sense he or she has that in some way that illustration was waiting there to be discovered. Notice that Paul doesn't say that Adam *was* a type, but that he *is* one: he is one now, for the purposes of this illustrative argument.

v. 15 **"wrong deed"**: Often translated using the archaic and specialist word *trespass,* the word Paul uses here is a general description, presumably in order to incorporate the wider context (those whose fault was not the breaking of a specific command) indicated in the first half of the preceding verse. While still carrying culpability, and sometimes used in parallel with the word *sin,* the word can also include not only explicit disobedience but ideas such as mistake, blunder, wrongdoing. As in 4:25 we here translate it "wrong deed."

"one human being": Here and in v. 17 where Jesus is, in contrast to Adam, explicitly identified as "the one *anthropos* Jesus the Messiah," the translation "human being" in both clauses seems more appropriate than the usual "person."

"the one . . . the many": Not "many" without the article, as if there were some outside the category. Zerwick notes that the sense is: "not *many* but *all* (who are many), the fact of a great number being more prominent to the Semitic mind than the fact of totality (cf. Matt 20:28)" (Zerwick, *Grammatical Analysis, in loc*). This is the case with the two similar constructions in v. 19.

"how much more": We should note here that the way Paul phrases the whole passage in such a way as to make the Adam material serve and illustrate the Jesus material—not the other way around. The two do not have equal weight. Adam is a *foreshadowing* of the glory that we see in the Messiah; he is the question, so to speak, that looks forward to this decisive answer of God. This is so throughout the passage: Adam's function here—and his *only* function—is to shine a light on Jesus.

v. 16 **"just judgement . . . led to God's condemnation"**: the words are *krima* and *katakrima*, a progression from decision to the result of that decision in practice. The logical progression from the one to the other is not easy to convey in English. *God's* condemnation is added to make clear what is implicit in *katakrima,* and later in *dikaiōma:* Paul is not speaking about ideas but about most personal acts. The focus of our attention must not be allowed to slip from God as the central actor in the drama to a general anthropology and absorption in consequences, as has so often been the case.

"An act of righteousness": The English translations almost all read "justification" (being made righteous) at this point, and the commentaries explain by suggesting that Paul, meaning *dikaiosis,* instead chose a related *-ma* word to match the others in the sentence. This is to mistake the nature of the contrast in the second half of each clause. What is at issue is not the effect upon people (hence judgment/being made righteous), but *the action of God* in each case (effecting judgment/acting righteously.) Reading *dikaiosis* for *dikaiōma* gives a meaning to the latter word that would be unique in the New Testament, and which is also at odds with the way Paul uses the word elsewhere in the letter—especially just a few sentences later in v. 18, where it is translated (correctly) as "an act of righteousness." It is also to blur the meaning of 4:25 and that same v. 18 of this chapter, the two places where Paul actually uses *dikaiōsis* (to be made righteous). *Krima* (judgment) leads indeed to *katakrima* (condemnation)—but, in contrast, Paul says, *charisma* (God's gift of his Son, v. 15) leads to *dikaiōma* (that is, an act different in kind to Adam's act; an act fulfilling rather than despising God's purpose). That God's act is in view is confirmed by the context. As we have already noted *dikaiōma* appears again in v. 18, just two verses later where it is clearly the righteous act of Jesus (notice how God's act and Jesus' act are indistinguishable in Paul's mind); in v.19, its synonym is *obedience.* Paul takes up the word again in 8:4, where he speaks of the *fulfillment* of the law in those whose lives are not controlled by the body but by the spirit. That is, God's own fulfillment of the law's requirements in his incarnate Son becomes our possession too. A general definition for *dikaiōma* might be "something that formally expresses right action within a covenant or relationship." This brings together the two different ways that the word is used in the New Testament. When God is the subject, *dikaiōma* is a command or judgment considered as an act (e.g., Luke 1:6, Heb 9:1); when human beings are the subject, it is a corresponding righteous act, an act of obedience (e.g., of Jesus in Rom 5:16, 18, 8:4; of Christians in Rev 19:8). Translating the word as "justification" in 5:16 potentially reflects a diminished understanding of *dikaiōsis* itself, taking that word to mean merely *acquittal,* escape from condemnation. Such an understanding comes from too cramped and limited a vision of God. The problem of human sin isn't dealt with by wiping some imagined judicial slate clean. God's deliverance is not so limited a thing. Sin, falling short, failure can only be dealt with on God's side by *making the person whole.* It can only be dealt with on our side with by *being re-made.* And that is what God has done.

v. 17 **"one wrong deed . . . one human being."** The expression is *tou enos* in both cases; the noun must be supplied. Most English translations read "one man" in both cases, thus rendering the verse clunky and opaque. It is as if there were no context. But the verse is identical in sense to v. 15, and the idea of one human/one wrong deed is repeated and applied in every statement of the section. Paul's audience, who are not painstakingly translating verse by verse but listening to a living voice, could not have failed to understand this contrast here as well.

v. 18 **"being made righteous"**: This is the same word that Paul uses in 4:25; these are the only occurrences of it in the New Testament. Notice once again that being made righteous is not an abstract standing, it is a *life* that is made righteous.

v. 19 **"all"**: See the note on v. 15 above on "the one . . . the many" and compare the explicit use of "one" and "all" in the two parallel phrases in the preceding verse. Taken as a whole, the Greek text of these verses declares in the most explicit way the universal scope of grace.

Endnotes: Chapters 4–6

v. 20 **"that the consciousness of wrong deeds might intensify"**: i.e., there was now an actual command of God to be obeyed or disobeyed. The verse reads literally "But Law entered in order that the wrong deed (singular) might increase." Paul has been arguing strongly against a Law-dependent religion (cf. vv. 13–14), so it is tempting to think that he might be overstating here for polemical reasons—suggesting that the Law came (and of course the old religion didn't see it as "coming" but as being given) in order to *increase the number* of wrong deeds (plural); i.e., it had a negative effect. But that can't be correct: despite its weaknesses in chapter 7, we will soon see the high respect Paul shows for the Law. In the second half of the verse, *epleonasen he hamartia* is in the singular. Wrong deeds are a *symptom* of sin, that is, of a broken relationship with God. It is Law that objectifies wrong deeds as things in themselves, diverting our attention to them and away from the broken relationship of which they are a sign. But *grace* is the living God brushing past these insubstantial things to call us to himself, to replace a broken relationship with a faithful one, to confront death with life through Messiah Jesus, our Lord.

v. 21 **"ruled over us in death"**: Gk *en*: not *through* or *by means of* death (although *en* can sometimes express this): Paul is not describing the way sin rules, but a condition of sin *and* death. In contrast, in the second half of the comparison he *is* talking about the way in which something comes to be: grace, the active power of God, rules through (*dia*) righteousness.

58. Whether this calculation was even performed is, however, doubtful. The more traditional measure was counting the generations: at the start of his Gospel, Matthew provides us with an ordered scheme of three sets of 14 generations from Abraham to Jesus; Luke gives a longer list for that period, and provides a further genealogy for Abraham that brings the number of generations from Adam to Jesus to 77. It is important to realize that these lists have a function quite different from that of modern family trees and were in any case concerned with pedigree and not duration. The intuition that human history reached back much further in time is perhaps reflected in the great ages of the patriarchs given in Genesis 5.

59. "You won't die if you eat of it," said the snake in the garden. And Adam and Eve *didn't* die, not then, anyway. Was the snake right after all? But, the story compels us to answer, Adam and Eve did die that day—and physical mortality is only the consequence of that broken relationship.

60. See for example https://en.wikipedia.org/wiki/Jericho#Natufian_Hunter-Gatherers_c._10.2C000_BC.

61. The best collection of high-definition images (among much else) is at the official Chauvet site at http://archeologie.culture.fr/chauvet/fr. The site descriptions are in French but the paintings are not! A good alternative in English is here: http://www.bradshawfoundation.com/chauvet/. Some readers might also consider looking for the superb feature-length documentary film by Werner Herzog on Chauvet called *Cave of Forgotten Dreams.*

62. Flute: see video at https://www.youtube.com/watch?v=yUCBBDV2Tzk; also this clip about a purportedly Neanderthal but more probably Aurignacian flute made from the femur of a young cave bear, discovered in Slovenia in 1995: https://www.youtube.com/watch?v=sHy9FOblt7Y.

63. Prehistoric gravesites: see the summary article, mentioning this burial among many others, at http://www.spoilheap.co.uk/burial.htm. Use of flowers in burial: see http://www.sciencedaily.com/releases/2015/05/150508091527.htm and http://www.livescience.com/37881-ancient-grave-flowers-unearthed.html

64. The examples in these paragraphs come mostly from Stephen Mithen, *After the Ice: A Global Human History 20,000–5,000 BC* (Harvard University Press, 2006): the tomb in Turkey (Göbekli Tepe) p. 66–67, (but see also the much more detailed article at http://ngm.nationalgeographic.com/2011/06/gobekli-tepe/mann-text/1); the shrine at Jerf el Ahmar and its deliberate burning, p. 64; the massacre at Ofnet cave, p. 176; the Colombia River skeleton, p. 227.

65. 1:19–20; 2:14–16.

66. Which is surely what the Genesis writer means to indicate when he describes God shaping the earth-creature (the *adam*), and breathing into its nostrils the breath/spirit (the word means both

things) of life. "And the man became a living being" (Gen 2:7).

67. The apocryphal book of 2 Ezra expresses the idea most poignantly: "This is my first and last word, that it would have been better if the earth had not produced Adam, or else, when it had produced him, had restrained him from sinning. For what good is it to all that they live in sorrow now and expect punishment after death? *O Adam, what have you done?* For though it was you who sinned, the fall was not yours alone, but ours also who are your descendants" (7:116–118). While the same sentiment has also sometimes been expressed in popular Christian theology, it is only by ignoring everything else in Paul's letter that we could argue for such a conclusion from our current passage. On the idea of original sin see endnote 16 for chapter 7, "the snake in the garden."

68. For which way does the story run? Is it only in the light of the Genesis story that we are able to comprehend our situation as sinful people? Or rather, when the writers of the book of Genesis came to tell the Beginning Story at the start of their history, was it not the history itself that determined the manner of its telling? The biblical Beginning Story is quite different from the origin stories that were told by other cultures. Here God creates from nothing. His creation is rich and beautiful and good. He himself calls human beings into existence and actively seeks their company. These insights about God's nature do not come from the Genesis story itself. The Genesis story is written in the light of the insights. The God in the Genesis story is not one of the random, capricious gods of paganism. He is Yahweh, the God that Israel had come to know through long years of relationship. The knowledge of sin that the story so powerfully embodies comes out of Israel's long experience of human weakness and failure and deliberate wrongdoing—and God's pursuing grace and faithfulness through it all. Where else could it come from, but through God's self-revelation through that history?

Whether we are male or female, then, the roles of both Adam and Eve in the Genesis story should be recognizable to us all. It is interesting to note the absence of Eve from Paul's argument in this chapter. It is a crucial clue for understanding the way in which he is handling the Genesis story. In the temptation story, as we know, Eve is a major player: the one who was first deceived, and the first to eat of the fruit of the tree. Paul will use those details in another place to buttress a very different argument (1 Tim 2:11–15). But just as the point he wants to make *there* controls the way in which he uses the story, so the way he uses the story *here* is controlled by his central purpose, and that is to shine light upon what God has done in Jesus the Messiah. All the other details in the story are therefore stripped away leaving only Adam's representative significance. All of humanity is drawn back to a point in him, all human experience to a single individual; he becomes both the source of physical life and the inaugurator of spiritual death for all humanity. Paul is indeed reaching back beyond Moses, and beyond Abraham to the primal Adam story, but he uses it not merely as an argument against Jewish religious privilege (vv. 13–14). He is going much deeper into the problem of sin than that. Sin is not just a matter of individual transgressions, he is telling us, but a condition, an environment, that involves the whole human race. A condition, Paul tells us, that *already implies within it the incarnation and the work of Messiah Jesus* ("Adam, who is a type of the one to come"). This is what the early church meant when it spoke of the death of Jesus being something "destined before the foundation of the world" (1 Pet 1:20), and of Jesus himself as being "the Lamb slaughtered from the foundation of the world" (Rev 13:8). That is, it understood the atonement not as a secondary reaction to the problem of human disobedience, an emergency measure put in place by God to rectify a primal disaster, but as something *implicit in creation itself*. Paul presents the Adam story in this passage in precisely the way required to cast the necessary light upon the fact of Jesus the Messiah, and the transformation that he has brought about within the human nature that Adam represents. Paul has no interest in Adam himself. His sole focus in the passage is the person and work of Jesus. Adam functions merely as a foil in order to make that central message clear.

69. This is what Paul means by an act of righteousness: not a good deed, but an act of faithfulness and commitment towards us that declares and demonstrates God's character.

70. This is a point that Paul will make again at the end of chapter 11, and one he makes in other

letters as well: Phil 2:10–11, 1 Cor 15:20–28, Col 1:15–19, for instance. When I was a young man I remember preachers on the first of these passages teaching us that all would indeed confess his name, the redeemed willingly, and the damned only through gritted teeth from the depths of hell. Which is not, I think, what Paul is saying in that passage.

71. As we will see later in the letter, Paul is adamant that the Law serves an important function. In another letter he will describe it as being "our tutor, leading us to Messiah" (Gal 3:19–26).

72. This phrase comprising one name, *Jesus,* and two descriptions, *our Lord* and *God's sent and chosen one* sums up the chapter, and indeed, the good news itself. For the phrasing look back especially at 4:24, 5:1, and 5:11, but note that the individual terms appear in virtually every verse of the chapter; and indeed the whole line of thought continues seamlessly all the way through to the great conclusion in 8:39.

73. Compare Jesus' prayer in John 17:3: "Father, the hour has come; glorify your Son now so that he may glorify you, for you have given him authority over all people, to give eternal life to all whom you have given him. And this is eternal life, *that they may know you, the only true God, and Jesus Messiah whom you have sent.*"

74. **Notes to the translation:**
v. 1: The Greek text reads "shall we continue in sin in order that that grace might overflow the more?" This is another case where the chapter division causes problems, obscuring the fact that Paul is drawing an implication directly from what he has just said in 5:20. It is essential to translate in such a way that that link is made clear; otherwise this chapter appears to begin out of the blue as a new topic.

"Continue our sinful lives": not "go on sinning" (NIV), "sin to our heart's content" (Phillips). These kinds of translation come from a moralistic understanding of sin, seeing it in terms of individual wrong acts. This use of the word is alien to Paul, who, here and everywhere in his letters, instead describes sin as an enslaving power, a defining orientation of the life away from God and towards the self.

v. 5: *The gar* indicates that v. 5 is extending the thought of v. 4; the "likeness of his death" therefore refers to the symbolism of baptism, as therefore does also the mention of resurrection in the second part of the verse. In a similar way v. 5 is the heading verse for what follows: vv. 6–7 expand v. 5a; vv. 8–11 v. 5b.

v. 6: "rendered powerless" (NIV), not "destroyed" (NRSV, NEB, etc.), which would imply an actual death and resurrection. That is something we could only conceive in some kind of mystical fashion. But Paul is not dealing in mysticism. The body is an essential part of being human. In the next chapter Paul will speak of his own wrestling as a Christian with this "body of death." And it is precisely in our human bodily nature that Jesus Messiah has won the battle for freedom and for holiness on our behalf.

v. 7 **"all sin's claims upon them cancelled":** an unusual expression, literally "has been righteoused from sin." Paul is picturing sin not as individual wrong actions (for which he uses other words) but as a personal power able to enslave, a power which, as we submit to it, gains rights over us. There is something that we owe to sin, our death. The image is the opposite of the one Paul will use in v. 23: "the wages of sin is death." In that verse death is something that sin pays to us; here it is something that we owe to sin. A person who has died, however, has paid that debt; they have therefore been "righteoused" with regard to that relationship. "Sin demands the death of the culprit; it cannot demand more than that, or less" (Schlatter, *New Testament Theology*).

v. 8: The adversative particle *de* indicates that this is the explication of the second part of v. 5.

"trust": Lit. *have faith;* an awkward construction in modern English. The word *trust* is better than *believe,* where the focus is upon the thing believed, rather than the person who promises.

v. 11: **"recognize that you are":** an idiomatic phrase, literally "count/regard yourselves to be." *Logizesthe* is the word used of God's "reckoning" Abraham (and those who share the faith of Abraham) to be righteous: it is not a way God thinks about Abraham, but a declaration of fact regarding him. In this case, translating the Greek idiom literally gives the impression that an effort of thought on our part is required to make the death and life of Jesus effective in our lives! On the contrary, Paul is saying that the death and life of Jesus have changed human reality: because of what he did, the way human beings are human is now different. The death and resurrection are therefore not pious remembrances; they are the actual foundation of our real lives. This is the new reality; now we must live in the light of it. The time for dreaming even pious dreams is over.

v. 13 **"weapons"**: Another metaphor, characteristic of Paul's vivid, popular style. Wickedness and righteousness are pictured as opposing powers in the world, using the resources we put at their disposal to extend their respective territories.

v. 14 **"sin** will not": The italics expressing the force of the *gar,* "truly, indeed, the fact is."

v. 17 **"thank God"**: Lit. *"charis* to God": the same word means both grace and gratitude. Just as is the case with the ideas of faith/faithfulness and righteousness, grace and gratitude are not qualities or attributes in their own right, but express one side of a mutual relationship. Just as faithfulness elicits faith, and faith faithfulness, so grace elicits gratitude—and, if we understand grace not as the gift itself but as the joy and good will of God from which any gift springs, also vice versa.

"the practical effect of the teaching": The word is *typos,* not referring to the "form of" teaching, as in its kind or content, but to the effect of it upon their lives, as a wax seal has an effect upon the wax.

v. 19 **"present your bodies"** (twice): Lit. "present your members," idiomatic: we do not today speak about the "members" or "parts" of a body, but use the noun simply, as inclusive of all of its parts.

"deeper lawlessness": To capture the force of the *eis,* "into." Paul is not talking about a simple state but about a progression, as step by step we find ourselves drawn further in.

v. 20 **"free of the claims of righteousness"**: In other words, one was not obliged to be faithful to one's undertakings. Sin is not trespasses or individual wrongdoings here, it is unrighteousness, lack of integrity regarding others, the failure to keep one's promises.

v. 21 **"What fruit ripened?"**: The Greek word in this and the following verse is *karpos,* lit. *fruit.* It can be translated blandly as *result, advantage, benefit,* but retaining the metaphor helps to capture Paul's tone of voice here (and he has already told us that he is using metaphors to help us understand). V. 21 in particular cannot be translated blandly: it is directly adversative to the second clause of v. 20, and carries strong emotional content. Paul is saying, "Sure, when you were slaves of sin you were free of the responsibility of being righteous. But what was the actual outcome of that 'freedom'? What did that really feel like? What was your actual experience?"

v. 23 **"unearned gift"**: *Charisma,* "grace-gift," is not simply *dorea,* a gift, but specifically *an expression of grace.* I have used "unearned" to capture something of that, and also to emphasize the contrast with "wages" in the preceding clause. This terminology runs through these first chapters of the letter: see 3:24; 5:15–16, for example. Cf also 4:3–4 where the concept of working for wages (but in this case "the works of the law") is contrasted with God's gift (also *charisma*).

75. The circumstances are dramatized for the sake of the metaphor. Except for criminals and prisoners of war, slaves in the ancient world were not shackled. For general information about slavery in Paul's world, and in contrast to the more recent history of slavery in the eighteenth and nineteenth centuries, see endnote 122, chapters 1–3.

76. These stories are from Acts 2:14–42, 8:26–40, and 9:1–20.

77. Barth, *Epistle to the Romans,* 188.

78. Barth, *Epistle to the Romans,* 191.

79. The contrast in v. 10 makes this clear: "The death he died, he died to *sin,* once for all; but the life he lives, he lives *to God."* A life lived without God, and the negative power of that: this is Paul's definition of sin.

80. Notice the boldness of Paul's answer to the question in v. 1. Because our lives are now shaped by grace, should we just continue living sinfully? No, Paul says, and that precisely *because* our lives are shaped by grace. Grace (the out-reaching good will of God towards us) and sin are fundamentally incompatible. When the room is filled with light, the darkness isn't simply muted, or isolated in

Endnotes: Chapters 4–6

only half of the space. Where the light is, the darkness is not. They are fundamentally incompatible.

81. The same goes for v. 23, despite v.11 and 13, and for 8:11 despite v. 10.

82. The first "present" is present imperative, the second, aorist imperative (i.e., a describing a particular action). In Greek the difference is contained in the shape of the word itself: the play upon the different forms of it would have been obvious in speech. The aorist indicates that presenting ourselves to God is a decisive action. In this verse notice two further things (1) the difference between "your members" in the first clause and "your *selves*" in the second. (2) Our dealings with *God* are always only active: God will not overmaster us as sin does. Being able to offer ourselves to God is our freedom, and our high dignity as human beings.

83. Do we experience the struggle with sin as a battle? That we do so is not surprising. It should encourage us. "How could man fight against sin, as long as he is the slave of sin and bound in its service? Only after he is freed by Christ from his captivity can he belong to the army whose mission it is to fight sin . . . Precisely because we are free from sin, we have to fight against it . . . He who is not free from sin cannot fight against it, for he is the slave of sin. That which he does serves sin. Only he who, through Christ, has been freed from sin can enter the battle against it" (Nygren, *Commentary on Romans*, 246, 263).

84. Luke 11:24–26.

85. Compare John 8:31–36—and note that this discourse also invokes the example of Abraham. Was Paul aware of that encounter between Jesus and his opponents?

86. The technical term for the search for absolute freedom is *sin,* and God in his grace has made it impossible for us ever to achieve it. Only God is absolutely free. For a commentary, see Gen 3:4–5.

87. And it is one among others: the "slave" terminology will, for example, become "son" terminology in chapter 8.

88. Dylan uses a different metaphor here. Both are metaphors; what is important is the reality they describe.

89. It is an important word elsewhere in the letter also: see 1:5, 10:16, 16:19.

90. The word *doulos* means both servant and slave; most servants in the ancient world were in fact slaves. My use of "obedient servant" here is intended to suggest the difference between the service required by power and the service freely given by someone who chooses their lord.

91. This provides a helpful perspective upon the nature of baptism. As we saw earlier, baptism is a sign of what God has done. On our part, it is not merely a sign, but also a reality. In its nature as a choice, baptism is the actual beginning of the life that we are saved for. It is not merely a symbol, but the real thing. It is not a mysterious religious ceremony but a genuinely human act. It is obedience. It is our first exercise of the freedom Jesus has won for us. It is the beginning of the new life.

92. White, *Fight,* 179.

93. Compare John 1:5–7. Light is not the absence of darkness; rather, darkness is the absence of light. Darkness is a void. It has no existence. When the light comes it is not just forgotten or swallowed up: in an absolute sense it ceases to exist; all the space which it might have occupied is filled full.

94. John Ruskin, *Sesame and Lilies* (1895), lecture 1.

95. V. 23 is almost identical to 5:21; it is the one truth that is being explored and explained in both chapters. Notice the progression of thought, as Paul goes deeper: the "through" in 5:21, referring to what Jesus has done *for* us, and, here, what the risen Jesus is doing *in* us, as we in our turn live "in him."

96. John 17:13.

14

Romans 7:1–25a

"Or aren't you aware, brothers and sisters (for I am speaking to people who know the Law) that the Law rules over a person only during that person's lifetime? ²Thus a married woman is bound by law to her husband for as long as he lives. Should her husband die, however, the law regarding the husband no longer applies to her. ³If she lives with another man while her husband is alive she will be called an adulterer. But if her husband dies she is free from the law, and, if she marries another man, is not an adulterer.

⁴So then, brothers and sisters, when the Messiah died you too were put to death as far as the Law is concerned, in order that you might belong to someone else, to the one who has been raised from the dead in order that we may produce a harvest for God. ⁵While we were living only on the physical level the consequences of the sins identified by the Law were at work in our bodies to produce a harvest for death. ⁶But now, having died to that to which we were bound, we have been taken right out of the sphere of the Law, in order that we might serve, not in the old way of the written code, but in newness of spirit.

⁷What then should we say? That the Law is sin? Never! Still, I wouldn't have known what sin is if it wasn't for Law. I wouldn't have been aware of illegitimate longings if the Law had not said, 'You shall not set your heart upon what you cannot have.' ⁸But, seizing an opportunity in the commandment, sin produced in me all kinds of longing for things that I cannot have! The fact is, apart from Law sin is dead. ⁹I was alive once, apart from Law. But when the commandment came, sin sprang to life ¹⁰and I died: the very commandment that was supposed to give me life led to death. ¹¹Seizing an opportunity in the commandment, sin deceived me—and through it killed me.

¹²If the Law is holy, and the commandment is holy and righteous and good, ¹³has a good thing then become death for me? Not at all! But, that its true nature might be clearly seen, sin produces death even through that which is for my good. That it does this through the commandment demonstrates that sin has no boundaries.

¹⁴For we know that the Law is spiritual; but I am merely physical, sold into slavery to sin. ¹⁵My own behavior perplexes me: I don't do what I want to; instead I do the very thing I hate. ¹⁶I acknowledge the authority of the Law in this, for if I do what I don't want to do it is only the Law that could have taught me not to want it. ¹⁷The fact is, it is no longer my true self that does it, but sin that lives within me. ¹⁸I know that nothing good lives in me—in my bodily nature I mean. I can will what is right but I'm powerless to do it. ¹⁹The good I want to do I don't do; instead the evil I don't want is what I end up doing! ²⁰Now if I do what I don't want to do, it is not my true self that does it; it is sin living in me.

²¹This is how it is, then: when I want to do what is good, that is exactly the time when evil lies close at hand. ²²In my inmost self I delight in the Law of God, ²³but I see in the various parts of my body another law at war with the Law I so value, making me captive to the law of sin that lives in them.²⁴Wretched person that I am! Who will rescue me from the body that in this way leads to death? ²⁵Thank God—through Jesus Messiah our Lord!"!

I WONDER WHAT YOU made of that. I can't remember ever hearing anyone preach on this section of Paul's letter. Chapter 7 is often seen as puzzling and obscure: we skip quickly on to chapter 8 where the real action happens. But that is like starting a movie in the middle. Chapters 7 and 8 are part of one continuous line of thought.

Having said that, though, mightn't we feel this first section to be obscure because it *is* obscure? How can what Paul is saying here mean anything for us today? What is all this business about marriage and husbands who die? Later on Paul seems to go on and on about the Jewish law: how does that have anything to do with our ordinary lives in the twenty-first century? Well, in fact it has a great deal to do with them. For what Paul is speaking of is not something strange and obscure from long ago. He is speaking about the value and the limitations of *religion*.

THE PARADOX OF RELIGION

Does that sound strange? How can religion be a problem? Isn't religion supposed to be a good thing? When he speaks about the Law Paul isn't talking about some strange pagan thing, but precisely about the Scriptures and the moral code and the worship and the prayers: all the well-intentioned human practices that gather around the truth of God. How can these things be something to which we must die? And even that is not the right way to put it. Dying to religion is not something that we *must* do, Paul tells us, but something that *has happened.* "When the Messiah died," he writes, "you too were put to death as far as the Law was concerned."

As we have seen already, all this is of intense importance for Paul and his listeners. The faith in which they had been brought up had taught them that salvation was a matter of community membership, defined especially by the markers of circumcision, Sabbath-keeping, and the food laws. If you did those things, you were accepted; you were assured of God's blessing both in this world and the next. I grew up in much the same kind of environment. A Christian was someone who celebrated the Lord's Supper every Sunday, who attended the prayer meeting and gave to mission work, who tithed their income and sought to be honest and responsible in everything they did. Those who didn't do this, friendly and goodhearted though they might be, were outsiders, unbelievers. At present, anyway.

But God's act of deliverance in Messiah Jesus has blown all that away. What God has done is not simply to tinker with the externals of religion, but to change the nature of what it means to be *human*. On that basis there can be no privileged community, no "in" or "out." What God has done affects every human being. And if we define religion as the way in which human beings out of their own resources seek God, ask for his forgiveness, pray for his help, and try to please him, then all of that is done away with as well. Not because it is bad, but because it is redundant. For God has sought *us, he* has reconciled us to himself. He has stopped at nothing—even the death of his Son— to make us his own. Jesus was raised from the dead so that we might live a totally new life, a life given by God day by day through his Spirit. There is nothing we can do in response to this except hold out our empty hands to receive the gift, and give thanks. Religion as a way to please God has become simply irrelevant.

Notice though that Paul is not dismissing religion or what we learn through it. "The Law is holy, and the commandment is holy and righteous and good," he tells us. The problem is not that religion is a bad thing, but that it *has no power*; indeed, in some ways it makes the situation worse. Religion operates on the level of precept and behavior: it teaches us the truth, and how we should live in response to that truth. To know these things is an extraordinary privilege. But it is not enough. The power of sin runs deeper than that. We know what is right to do—because religion has taught us it—and yet we find ourselves powerless to do it (vv. 15–16). Religion's concern is with what we know and what we do; God's concern is with who we *are*. It is right down at that deep place in our lives that God's power reaches, not to help us understand more clearly, but to make us new. Jesus didn't come to teach us a better and truer religion, he came to deliver us. In him God himself has accomplished a transformation within human nature in places deeper than religion could ever reach.

This is what Paul means when he speaks about us being "put to death as far as the Law is concerned" (v. 4). Once again he uses an image from everyday life to make his point. One of the things that godly religion teaches us is the importance of the marriage covenant. But when a marriage partner dies, the requirements of the marriage covenant are not modified, or relaxed or revoked. They just cease to exist: one of the partners to the marriage is dead. So it is in this case. When the Messiah died, we died with him. All people did. So it is not a case of a modified or even a new kind of religion. On the contrary: we have passed right out of the zone where religion has any claim upon us (v. 6). We don't, however, go into some kind of free fall. We died as far as religion is concerned *in order that we might belong to someone else*: to the risen Jesus. This is the very reason why he was raised, Paul tells us: so that we might serve in spirit rather than merely in letter. So that we might produce a harvest for God.

This is an extremely powerful metaphor. The resurrection is not just a happy ending to the story of the death of Jesus; it is an event of power, the creation of a new human being. The cross and the resurrection are not a sideshow. They are not an emergency measure on God's part. The outcome is not unexpected. It is what God intended from the very beginning. Paul is talking about the harvest of creation.

"YOU TOO, PAUL!"

My first encounter with the section beginning at verse 14 for the first time was electric. I was 17 or 18, earnest, adventurous, open to God as a result of good teaching by word and example—and yet continually wracked with sexual desire and a battle for holiness that I seemed never to win. Reading through Romans for myself for the first time, I came to this section of the letter, and it fell into my heart as a gift from the Lord himself. I remember the reaction so vividly: "You too, Paul!"

Suddenly I understood that what I was experiencing was not some aberrant thing, but part of the battle of the normal Christian life. God knew about it—and if he knew about it there was hope. Knowing that didn't make the battle go away (would we want it to go away?) but it did rob it of its domineering power. It put in its right place what had seemed to be an untamable larger-than-life monster. My identity lay not in this thing, not in what I did or didn't do even when there was failure, but in being named and called by God; in a power given by him that, despite all my mistakes, was making me more and more like Jesus. Paul's struggle gave me hope. And it gave me courage, because I realized I wasn't alone. Paul had walked this way before me; indeed Jesus had walked this way before me (8:17). It was therefore a *way*: a path, not a swamp.

Of course, Paul is not speaking exclusively about sexual issues here. There are many temptations that well up into our life from our bodily nature: appetite and envy and anger, the desire to dominate and the fear of the stranger: you know what these things are in your life as I do in mine. But the struggle for sexual holiness is certainly one of the things he is talking about. What other "parts of our body" (v. 23) seem at times to have a mind of their own? (Oh yes, the tongue: that too.) Christians are sometimes accused of being obsessed with sexuality. But that is nonsense. Every human being, one way or another, experiences sexual desire as a compelling power. Sexual desire is created by and therefore is the gift of God: why would we imagine that he would not still have an interest in how it fits into our lives, for blessing or for harm?

Of course, *moralism*—do this or don't do that—whether with regard to sexuality or any other of our bodily impulses, is a problematic thing. Paul makes that very clear here, too. "I wouldn't have been aware of illegitimate longings if the Law had not defined them as that. But, seizing an opportunity in the commandment, sin produced in me all kinds of longing for things that I cannot have!" (vv. 7–8) Knowing what is life-giving behavior and what is destructive is hugely important. Such knowledge, if heeded, will protect us from damaging our own lives and those of others as well. But, as Paul confesses so agonizingly from his own experience, knowledge alone is not enough. What we need is not only to know what is right, but the power to *do* it. Such power is God's alone. It is the power that he gives us in the resurrection of Jesus the Messiah.

THE BATTLE FOR HOLINESS

Paul's honesty and willingness to talk about his weaknesses as well as his strengths is both startling and encouraging. Even being an apostle of God doesn't mean that you have it all together, or live a life free from struggle and questions. This gives what Paul says a unique authority. He doesn't speak down to us from some holy height, but stands alongside us in a battle that we all share (7:25). And battle it is: "I don't do what I want to do; instead I do the very thing I hate . . . In my inmost self I delight in the Law of God, but I see in the various parts of my body another law at war with the Law I so value, making me captive to the law of *sin* that lives in them." Are you daunted by the note of conflict here? I suggest that, far from being daunted, we should be encouraged. For this is the battle into which redemption plunges us, and in 6:13–14 Paul has already urged us to take our part in it. The struggle with sin is a sign of hope: it is a sign that our lives are grasped by God.

"When the commandment came, sin sprang to life," Paul tells us in verse 9. How can we visualize this? It is like coming in from the dark into a room full of light. Suddenly we realize, because now we can see, the dirt, the stains, the raggedness of our clothing, and we are ashamed. One winter's day in 1916 on the remote sub-Antarctic island of South Georgia, three men walked into the Stromness whaling station. Part of the crew of a ship trapped and crushed in the ice of the Weddell Sea, they had sailed 1,500 kilometers across the Southern Ocean in a small boat to reach help. Forced to land on the wrong side of the island, the three had trekked for 36 hours across the un-mapped, mountainous, and glaciated interior to reach the whaling station. They were tired, ragged, filthy, and evil-smelling, their hair and beards long and matted with salt and blubber. One of the three, Frank Worsley, recounts that as they approached the whaling station, he tried to adjust his torn and ragged clothing. "What are you doing that for?" asked the leader. "Boss, there might be women here!" To the amusement of the others Worsley produced three large safety pins and proceeded to pin himself together, succeeding only, however (in the words of one of the others), "in drawing attention to his own deficiencies." It's a humorous story, but the point is a serious one. There were no women at the Stromness whaling station. But what if, out of the dark and cold, we are brought by a Rescuer into the light of the presence of the living God himself? Paul knows: "sin sprang to life." Only Christians know about sin. Those who are not yet Christians may have a sense of guilt, of having done things wrong. But only Christians understand sin, because sin is not about breaking a commandment but about being far away from a *person*. Later on Paul will say "you can be sure you have the spirit of Messiah Jesus, because that is what it means to be a Christian." Here we could equally truly say that we can be sure that we are really a Christian because we struggle with sin.

I have tried to be careful in my terminology. We experience sin as a power; it is a reality that we struggle with. But the good news is not about a battle with sin. Paul never describes it in that way. He speaks about sin being at war with *us* (v. 23) but never about us being at war with sin. To do so would be a nonsense: how can you fight against nothing? Sin is not a thing; it is the absence of a thing. What Paul is describing is not a battle *against* something, but a battle *for* something. Despite the rawness of the experience he describes, Paul's topic is not the dangers of sin, but the longing for holiness.

That we do long to be clean and straight and true, to live a life filled with grace and the power of God, Paul takes for granted. But that kind of life isn't delivered to us on a silver platter. A life can only be lived, moment by moment, day by day. In Messiah Jesus God has given us eternal life, but that is not a static thing. It is something that unfolds as we live it, and at certain times we experience that unfolding as a battle. Holiness is something that we reach out for, something that we fight in order to gain. That we are quite unable to gain it using our own resources is Paul's personal testimony. That it is nonetheless a battle in which we must joyfully engage he is equally certain.

Jesus makes the same point in the Sermon on the Mount. He doesn't say "Blessed are the righteous." Righteousness is not something we can attain on our own. Those whom he says are blessed are those who *hunger and thirst after it*. The Christian life is not one of passive self-congratulation. "Forgetting what lies behind and straining forward to what lies ahead," Paul tells us in another of his letters, "I press on towards the goal of the high calling of God in Messiah Jesus." This is the joy of the runner reaching out for the finishing line. It is the joy of a human being fully alive. "Christ did not come to give us peace," said William Barclay, "but to give us glory. He did not come to make life easy. He came to make it great."

It is winter in New Zealand at the time I'm writing this. A couple of weekends ago my wife and I drove into the mountains, left the car, and trekked up a side valley. The sounds of the highway dropped away. At last we came into a long clearing, the river flats stretching across to the forested slopes on the other side of the valley, the snowfields sunlit on the peaks, the silence profound. I went to the river to get water and plunged my hands in. It wasn't cold. Words like that fail. It was simply itself, elemental, intensely real, masterly. It wasn't "pure." It was itself wholly and completely, neither containing nor needing any other thing. The words we use are about the suitability of something for our use. But the water wasn't unsuitable for me; it was I who was inadequate for the water. Out in the channel a salmon was beating her long way into the headwaters to lay the eggs from which the next generation of salmon would come. Life! She was at home where we were not. And she was swimming upstream.

THE VIEW FROM THE DEEP WATER

"Who will rescue me from the body that carries this death within it?" (v. 24) Paul's cry is raw and genuine. The Christian life is not a matter of niceness and pious phrases and ready answers for everything. Paul has no time for that. These things may be the stock in trade of religion, but religion is not enough. There are places in life where clichés and platitudes fail, and only God will do.

A few chapters ago the story of a real-life rescue from a flooded river helped us understand the commitment that, in Jesus, God makes to deliver us. But the newspaper photograph that depicted the scene was taken by a spectator *standing on the bank*. What does rescue look and feel like from the maelstrom of the current? What does it feel like to stand there, clinging to the power pole, with the weight of the roiling water plucking and tearing at your foothold? What is the taste of fear? And what does it feel like as you see, through the noise and turmoil, your rescuer steadily approaching, bringing the line with him?

It is only those who know this kind of experience who can tell what rescue truly means. Paul takes us inside salvation not as an onlooker, but as a participant in the battle and in the rescue. This is not a cool, dispassionate description, but a letter from the front.

Paul's agonized cry is at the heart of what we mean when we talk about deliverance. Salvation is not just a pious religious word referring to going to heaven when we die. It is rescue in the deep water, the struggle, the clinging on moment by moment at peril of our lives. The pious and the comfortable have no idea of what rescue means. They can only read this chapter and the next from outside as a kind of theological exercise. To those who like Paul struggle with sin, who pray "forgive us our trespasses" and "deliver us from evil" because they need to, what he says here comes like bread for life, like water in the desert, like the dawn that follows the night.

POWERFUL AND PERSONAL

Before we move on to the first verses of chapter 8, there is one puzzle we still have to unravel. Paul experiences sin as an enslaving power (v. 14): he can will to do what is right, but then comes up against what he experiences as a power (v. 17). Sin is not only therefore something that we willfully do; there is a sense in which we feel ourselves at its mercy. How are we to understand this? First of all, for example, what is this "sin" that lives within us? Where does its power come from? Is Paul just using mythical language, or is he talking about something real?

There is a quick and certain answer to the question of power. The power of sin is God's power—out of place. There is no other source of power anywhere in the universe. It is noteworthy that Paul doesn't use the idea of the Satan in this passage. That too is a personification of a power, and Paul elsewhere does occasionally speak in those terms. But not in this place. What is happening here is something that is wholly between us and God. We cannot wriggle out of it, or make excuses. There is no third party.

Paul describes sin as an almost personal power. It can seize an opportunity, deceive, and kill; it enslaves us and lives within us. How can that be? We know that sin is nothing real. It is a turning away from the living God: it is a nothing, a vacancy; it is the absence of something. How can the absence of something exercise the power that Paul ascribes to sin? It can do so precisely because it is the absence of something *personal*. The power that we experience sin as having is reflexive; it is the shadow that is cast by the absence of God.

And this is the key to our deliverance. The power of God's *absence* can only be overcome by his *presence*. And it is. In Messiah Jesus God comes to us, fills our lives with his spirit, and frees us for obedience—to him. The reflexive power disappears. It must, because the real power is present. The power of sin, twisted out of shape though it may be, is ultimately God's power. Our experience of sin as a malignant almost-personal power testifies directly to the power of the God. Knowing this is a powerful weapon in the battle for holiness.

THE SNAKE IN THE GARDEN

Paul experiences sin as something arising out of his *bodily nature* (v. 18). At war with his will, sin's power is expressed physically, through the parts of his *body* (v. 23). What is this "bodily nature"? It is our animal nature, our nature as physical, created beings.

That a human being was an animal (but not merely an animal) was as obvious in Paul's world as it is in ours. In the twenty-first century we know from paleontology and from genetics that our distant ancestors, before being touched by God, were primates of hunting and foraging. Not that we need these rather recent sciences to tell us this: every time we eat, or sleep, or perform any other of our bodily functions, it is obvious that we are not angels but physical, mortal creatures. And that physicality, says Paul, *still has power*. We are called by God to be human, to be fine, to live, in fellowship with him, a fully human life. The Law testifies to that. But we are torn. We hear God's call, but alongside it also experience the animal nature with its violence, its selfishness, its irrational subjection to bodily appetites. While it is not at all the most important fact about who we are, nonetheless the animal nature is part of the experienced human reality.

Now we begin to see what Paul's point is in this chapter. In the first part of the letter he has confronted us with sin as disobedience, and shown how Jesus has dealt with that: his faithfulness instead of our faithlessness, his obedience instead of our disobedience. The second part (from 4:23) has been a sustained call to live the new life that Jesus has won for us: to live at peace with God, to rejoice in our hope of glory, to face our sufferings with courage, confident in God's love (5:1–5). Risen with Jesus, how could we contemplate returning to death? The chains of slavery have been broken: how could we go back to what is so utterly and completely gone (ch. 6)?

Now Paul takes us *inside* what up to now he has described only from the *outside*. Now we are in the lived experience of the struggle for holiness. Sin is more than merely disobedience, for it was in the world before the Law was given (5:13). Now Paul points out that it produces death even *through* God's commandment (7:13). Sin has no boundaries: it runs deeper than even the commandment can reach. It is not therefore just a matter of failing to do what is right. A force that lures us away from God lives within our bodily nature, our animal nature. Created and called to be truly human, open to God, free to choose and to shape our lives before him, nonetheless, our animal nature still talks to us, and at times it speaks with compelling power.

The writer of Genesis 3 knows this. He describes the snake in the garden as the shrewdest of the *animals*; it represents the subtlety and the compulsion of the animal nature. And it calls to us. It asks "Did God say?" It points out how wonderfully the thing that lies on the other side of God's protective prohibition would satisfy the bodily appetite, fulfill our desire for beauty, and satisfy our longing for wisdom (Gen 3:6). What more could be desired? And, like Eve, from within our own resources alone we can find no answer.

It is not that our responsibility for wrongdoing is taken away. None of us are under any illusions about that—nor is the writer of the Genesis story. Recognizing the source of the sinful impulse in our bodily nature is an insight, not an excuse. Nonetheless, this temptation to live on the purely animal level, to live a life turned away from God, is always there. Paul testifies to it, aware that it is our experience too. "Who will rescue me from the body that carries this death within it?" he cries. And the answer comes immediately: "Thank God! Through Jesus Messiah our Lord." The prison door swings open, and we step through, into the light.

This shout of triumph is the point to which everything has been leading. For chapter 7 is not about the inadequacy of human religion. It is not about the power of sin, or some desperate battle for holiness. It is about a saving act of God. Paul is a realist. He describes our actual experience as we seek to live as Christians in the real world. Sin and failure, he makes clear, are part of that experience. Nonetheless *even in sin and failure* we find ourselves encountered by the good news of what God has done in Jesus. Messiah Jesus has come and found us. The barrier has been overcome—by God himself.

Paul will go on now to unpack what God's deliverance in Messiah Jesus means. As we move on into chapter 8 we must not allow the reality of what he describes here to drift away. Only the person who has faced the challenges that chapter 7 describes can understand what the "no condemnation" in 8:1 means. There is no magic wand in the Christian good news that immediately resolves all our struggles and takes away all our temptations. The life God gives us is a *life*: not a static, inert gift, but something that must be lived. The battle for holiness, the daily choice between life and death; this cry "who will deliver me?"—these are a part of it. How terrible if it was not so! These things are precisely the context of the power and the glory—through suffering—that Paul will speak about in the next section of the letter.

15

Romans 7:25b—8:13

"To sum up, then: I myself am with my mind a slave to God's Law, but in my bodily nature a slave to sin's law. But at the same time [8:1] *there is now absolutely no condemnation for those who are in Messiah Jesus,* [2]*for the law of the spirit of life in Messiah Jesus has set you free from the law of sin and of death.*

[3]*God has done what the Law, weakened by the bodily nature, was never able to do. By, in order to deal with sin, sending his own Son with a bodily nature just like ours, he brought the sin within the bodily nature to judgement.* [4]*This was so that the righteous outcome that the Law was intended to bring about might be accomplished in us, who live our lives not according to the bodily nature but according to the spiritual nature.*

[5]*Those who live according to the bodily nature focus their attention on the things of the body, but those who live according to the spiritual nature focus their attention on the things of the spirit.* [6]*To focus the attention on the body is death; to focus the attention on the spirit is life and peace.* [7]*This is why the mind that is dominated by the bodily nature is hostile to God. It does not submit to God's Law, indeed it cannot;* [8]*and those who are absorbed by the bodily life cannot please God.*

[9]*But that is not you. Because God's spirit lives in you it is not the bodily nature but the spiritual nature that is the driving principle of your life. Someone without the spirit of Messiah isn't his in that way.* [10]*Since Messiah is in you, although the body is dead because of sin, the spirit is life because of righteousness.* [11]*More than that: if the spirit of the One who raised the man Jesus from the dead lives in you, then he—the One who raised Messiah from the dead—will, through his spirit living in you, bring your subject-to-death bodies to life as well.*

[12]*So then, brothers and sisters, we have no debt to the bodily nature that obliges us to live a merely bodily life.* [13]*If you live a merely bodily life you are doomed to die. But if by spirit you put to death the impulses of the body, you will live."*

THERE IS NO PAUSE. We are breaking the text into sections to make things more manageable, but the line of thought flows on unbroken. The first couple of sentences here are both Paul's summary of what he has been talking about in chapter 7, and his introduction to what he is going to say next.

His report from the front line of the battle for holiness doesn't end with struggle, but with triumph and praise. In a decisive act of God the battle has been won on our behalf! There is therefore (the expression is emphatic) absolutely no condemnation for those who are in Messiah Jesus.

Two things need to be said about this declaration. In the first place, we must learn to hear it. It is striking that Paul never quotes the words of Jesus or refers to any of the events in his life beyond the cross and resurrection. The carefully preserved memories and sayings that would later become our gospels were, in his day, still circulating orally among the young Christian communities, and we have no idea how much Paul knew of them. One story from Jesus' life, however, strikingly demonstrates what he is saying. Jesus is invited to dinner in a rich man's house. In that time there could be no privacy for such an event: members of the public came and went, and people looked in from every window. As the meal progresses a woman comes up to Jesus with a flask of extremely costly ointment, breaks it, and, weeping, pours it over his feet, wiping them with her hair. "And," says John, "the house was filled with the aroma of the ointment."

What led the woman to do this? What had Jesus done in her life? We have no idea. She knew, and Jesus knew. In spite of the host, who recognized her as a woman of the streets, and in defiance of the pious economics of those who were simply bystanders, Jesus rises to her defense. He says of her something he said about no one else: "Wherever the good news is preached in the whole world what this woman has done will be told in memory of her." And here we are, telling her story now. This is the good news. For this woman, Paul's "thank God!" was no meaningless exclamation. It was an *act*, love from the heart, the pouring out of the most precious thing that she had. "No condemnation" was for her not just a familiar phrase from a famous Bible passage. It touched the depths of her life.

As with all of the Gospel narratives, we all find ourselves somewhere in the story. Perhaps we are the host, the pious Pharisee, innocent of the gritty realities of life, secure in our own righteousness, deciding the *kind* of woman this is instead of seeing the *person* that she is. Perhaps we are the earnest do-gooders, calculating the cost instead of seeing the meaning. For these sins, too, forgiveness is possible. Or perhaps we are the woman. You know who you are. Whether male or female, if you are the woman, what Paul is saying here is said for you.

The second point can also best be made by way of an illustration. One holiday Angela and I trekked up a remote valley, heading for a hut in a clearing at the foot of a spectacular mountain range. It was a challenging trip: the trail was badly overgrown, and interrupted by windfalls and washouts. Where at one point we had to cross the stream, I took a couple of photographs that, thinking about it afterwards, seemed to me to summarize what Paul is speaking about here. Looking downstream, the creek quickly disappeared in a chaotic tangle of rocks and fallen trees. No calendar photo, this: just a jumble of obstacles, and no sign of a path anywhere. Looking upstream, the view was dramatically different. Down level after level of its rocky bed the stream came on, the air rich with the sounds of water and life. Annie Dillard said once that there must be something amiss with a person who, when crossing a bridge, looks downstream rather than up. There was no bridge in our little piece of wilderness, but nonetheless, here it was, rising from a source unknown, tumbling and streaming down inexhaustibly, the grace of God coming on towards us. *No condemnation.*

How hopeful and liberating it is that this declaration occurs here! If Paul had said it earlier in the letter it could have come to us as an idea about judgment averted, something to be believed in an abstract and theological way. But here it is now, right at this point, in the context of Paul's agonized cry, in the context of battle and indeed of failure, in the context of real Christian living in the real world. God doesn't give us a certificate to hang on the wall, but, with open hands, a life to be lived; and, along with that life, the grace and the power to live it.

SPARROWS AND BUTTERFLIES

Chapter 8 is one of the most astonishing and wonderful passages in the whole of the New Testament. But once again, in order to understand it, we need to unpack some familiar words and phrases. Right here, for example, Paul doesn't merely say that there is no condemnation, he says that there is no condemnation to *those who are in Messiah Jesus*. What does that mean? A few verses later, we find him talking about Messiah being *in us*. Us in him, him in us: are you confused by this language?

Although it only occurs occasionally in Romans, in his other letters Paul uses the expression "in Messiah" all the time. Preachers use it as well, speaking in solemn tones, making us feel that what they're talking about must be very wonderful—if we knew what it was. What does it mean to be "in Messiah"? Well, let me ask you something different: how does a sparrow know how to be a sparrow?

It is not an idle question. A sparrow's nest is very distinctive. The first time a female sparrow builds a nest, how does she know how to build one? She hasn't seen a nest since she was fledged. She hasn't ever learned how to build one. She just does it. And a sparrow's nest is different from a robin's, or a grey warbler's, or a fantail's. All the birds have the same *needs*, but they all build different *nests*. Not different by individual, but different by species. We call this "instinct," but that is a description, not an explanation. We don't know what it is that the description describes. We don't know where instinct is located, or what it consists of, or how it is passed on. It is just something that happens.

How does a monarch butterfly know where home is? In North America, monarch butterflies complete an epic 2,500-kilometer migration each year, flying steadily from the upper limit of swan plant growth in the northern states of the US all the way down to Mexico, where, in their tens of millions, they spend the winter hibernating in the fir trees. And then they fly back. But *it is not the same generation who make the return journey*. The lifespan of a monarch after hibernation is only a month or so. It is not the original butterfly, but the second, third, or even the fourth generation which eventually arrives back in their home territory. How does the second generation know where to go? Where is the memory of the journey their parents or grandparents or great-grandparents took the previous year located? How could such a memory be passed on from one generation to the next? A biologist called Rupert Sheldrake has an interesting theory about these questions. He suggests that each type of creature might have something like *a species-wide memory*, stored in a temporal field. The sparrow's or the butterfly's brain then would be less like an individual library of instruction manuals, and more like a radio receiver. Each sparrow learns how to be a sparrow by tuning into the species-wide memory. And as each individual learns and adapts, it contributes this learning back into the species memory, where it becomes available for another generation of sparrows to access. In other words there are lots of individual sparrows or butterflies, but they are all also bound together as a whole by a corporate memory which every sparrow or butterfly shares.

It's a very interesting suggestion, and explains a number of otherwise puzzling facts about living things. But I don't want to talk about biology here.

Whether or not Sheldrake's idea is true of creatures, it gives us a way of thinking about something that is certainly true of human beings.

Are we human beings just a collection of individuals, like the individual grains in a handful of sand? Or are we more than that? Think back, for example, to the prehistoric burial site in Denmark that we mentioned above. It contained the body of a young woman, adorned with beads and necklaces, and beside her a tiny newborn baby, laid on a swan's wing. These few details tell a whole story. Immediately we are back there, so long ago. A cherished young woman, perhaps the daughter of a chieftain, has died in childbirth. And the little one has been placed beside her, cupped tenderly in the wing of the regal bird. Love and care are apparent in every detail of the burial. And as the earth is piled on the grave we can see the tears on the weather-beaten faces of the people who loved her. We know what is going on in their hearts. We see them, supporting each other, walking away down the valley into the rest of their lives.

Is what we feel just sentimentality? Or is it not that we feel the emotion because you and I are bound inextricably to this young woman and her child, bound inextricably to the mourners who wept and prayed that day all those millennia ago? Because, although we are individuals, we are also *one thing*. We are part of something called humanity.

There are many terrible things in the world, and the newspaper and the television news collect them all together in neat little packages for us to agonize over every morning. The other day I was reading a story I would normally avoid, about the plight of women and children under ISIS rule, about rape and sexual slavery: things to stop the heart. But in the same report there were other stories. A girl named Mysa, now 18, told how a Kurdish family bought her from an ISIS fighter for $1,500, an astonishing sum in that environment, and then helped her to escape from ISIS-held territory. Another described how a man to whom she had appealed for help in the street risked his life to hide her and smuggle her to Turkey.[1] And the heart leaps with joy and pride.

Why? It is not *our* courage, *our* deeply sacrificial generosity that we are proud of (oh that we might act that way in such a situation). But our pride is not misplaced. These are deeply human acts, and in that humanity we, across the world and even across the ages of the world, *participate*. We are bound together, we human beings, in the good and in the bad. In the wrong that we do, and in the right that, in God's grace, we also do, we are part of this thing called humanity. Each of us is individually called into being, individually loved and prized by God, individually responsible to him for our lives. This is our glory. But God does not see us as merely a collection of individuals, rattling around like marbles in a box. He sees us *together*.[2]

None of this should be strange. The Bible uses several metaphors to describe the way in which human beings are interconnected. Jesus speaks about a *vine*, with every individual branch growing and thriving and bringing forth fruit, yet still one thing, drawing its life and sustenance from him. Paul speaks about a *body*, with each of the parts having its own individual function, and yet part of one whole. Another picture, one which goes back to the Old Testament, is that of a *building* where every individual stone contributes its function and beauty and yet is part of one thing—a place for God himself to live.

We are familiar with all of these images as pictures of the church. And of course they are that. But as Paul has made clear from the beginning, the church is not an exclusive company. It is simply the firstfruits of the harvest of all human kind. "God has imprisoned all in disobedience," Paul will declare in chapter 11, "*in order that he may be merciful to all.*" "Through his Son," Paul will tell the Colossian church, "God was pleased to reconcile to himself *all things*, whether on earth or in heaven, by making peace through the blood of his cross." And to the church at Philippi, he describes how, because of Jesus' obedience all the way to the cross, "God highly exalted him, and gave him the name that is above every name, so that the name of Jesus *every* knee should bow, in heaven and on earth and under the earth, and every mouth should confess that Jesus Messiah is Lord, to the glory of God the Father."[3]

All human beings are intimately bound together by God's call and God's design. We are *individually* part of *one thing*. This is not a wish, it is a truth. When in church we say as part of our worship "we who are many are one body," or hear the call to "keep the unity of the Spirit in the bond of peace," these are not just pious exhortations for us to get along with each other. They proclaim a fundamental reality of the universe. They spill out far beyond the confines of the congregation to include all people everywhere.

We are one. We can act that way or we can fail to act that way, but the truth remains: it is so. And the question is not will we choose to be nice to other people or some such superficial thing, but will we live our lives with the flow of the universe? Or will we in defiance rub our hand back against the grain of the world—"kicking against the goads," to use the risen Jesus' words to Paul on the Damascus road—and damage ourselves and others in the process?[4]

BODY

To be *in Messiah Jesus,* then, means to be fully human. In Jesus, God himself stepped into human existence, subjecting himself to the perils and chances of our life. He took upon himself the same bodily nature that we have, with its insistent needs and its vulnerability to the call of the animal world: "He was tested in precisely the same way that we are," the writer to the Hebrews tells us—yet without sin."[5] Remember how in chapter 5 Paul contrasted with the *disobedience* of Adam the *obedience* of Jesus? In his patient and steady obedience all the way to the cross, Jesus brought the sin within the bodily nature to judgement (v. 3). Sin is a turning away from God, but this was a turning *to* God, a wrenching of human nature back to its true home in the freedom of obedience. This is the judgment upon sin in the bodily nature. There is no longer any place for it. God himself has come.

This is not just an idea. We are not talking about some kind of fairy-tale, where a god comes in disguise into a human situation, does god-like things, and ends up rescuing everybody. This is a real man, with real challenges and temptations, who faces the perils we face, who fights the battles we fight, a man who, in the last desperate hours of his life, felt that even God had abandoned him. It is about God taking responsibility for his creation, subjecting himself to the conditions of human life as it is really lived.[6] Because this is *God* living a life, it changes everything. Human being has been taken into the life of God. Jesus is *the* human being: in his resurrected life he is the way a human being becomes truly human. He is not just an example to follow, but the source of power to be.

BONE

Obedience all the way to the cross: that is the point upon which everything converges. Alone among the four Gospels Matthew's account of the crucifixion describes not only an eclipse but also an earthquake. It is an apt symbol. In the death of Jesus the powers of the whole physical world were shaken. Because of our sin, and on our behalf, the Messiah *died.*

We could talk lots of theological talk about this, but let me give you an illustration. When I was two years into the writing of this book, a blood test showed that a condition for which I had been being monitored for several years had turned into full-blown leukemia. And suddenly our world changed.

I am not sure how much you know about leukemia, but the problem is this: the bone marrow, where our blood is produced, stops working properly. Blood is a complex substance: among other things it contains the hemoglobin which carries oxygen to the cells, the platelets that seal a cut or wound so that we don't bleed to death, and the white cells which protect us from infection. When bone marrow goes bad it starts producing small, imperfect forms of these cells. Little by little the imperfect cells start to outnumber the normal ones. Little by little the basic functions of life start to fail. Something is wrong at the very core of a person's being, something deep in the marrow of their bones.

The treatment is radical: all of the old bone marrow has to die. Powerful chemicals infused into the bloodstream attack the bone marrow until no single cell of it is left. This means that the patient becomes intensely vulnerable to the most ordinary infections: they are kept in strict isolation, and depend upon regular blood transfusions from others. And then comes the most remarkable part. A matching donor is found who submits to a procedure that, while making them feel sick for a week, releases some of their bone marrow cells into their bloodstream. These cells are harvested, transported with the utmost care (sometimes from halfway around the world), and then infused into the leukemia patient's bloodstream. And little by little, those cells find their way deep into the bone marrow. They make themselves at home there. They become part of the body. The old has gone, the new has come.

There couldn't be a more powerful image of what Paul is describing in these chapters. We human beings have a deadly problem. Deep down in our bones something is wrong. We have heard Paul describe it: "I know that nothing good lives in my bodily nature. The good I want to do I don't do; instead the evil I don't want is what I end up doing." Nothing external can help: the problem lies deeper than even God-given religion can reach. But into that place *God himself* can reach. In Messiah Jesus he does so. He doesn't send somebody, he comes himself. Something has to die. Bundled out of the world by us sinful human beings, Jesus dies our death. He dies—and the sin that sent him there, the sin that inheres in the bodily nature dies with him. That is what has to happen. The cross is the bitter chemotherapy that utterly destroys the old bone marrow. There is no other solution.

But the cross is only half of the story. God raises Jesus from the dead. Again the word *Messiah* is crucial. If Jesus was just a single person, the resurrection would be merely a fairy-tale wonder. But because he is *Messiah,* because he is our *Lord,* because he is (as he described himself) *the* human being, his life, death, and resurrection are not just events that happen to him, but things that happen right at the heart of the human nature that he shares.[7] The cross means the death of the old life. The door is shut upon it. We cannot go back. Resurrection is the infusion into our veins of the new bone marrow: the life of God himself transfused into our life, settling deep into our bones, steadily and surely making itself at home. "This was so that the righteous outcome that the Law was intended to bring about might be accomplished in us, who live our lives not according to the bodily nature but according to the spiritual nature" (v. 4).[8]

SPIRIT

The spiritual nature? What does that mean? We feel like we ought to know. The word "spirit" is such a basic Christian word. Like faith and righteousness it is part of the stock-in-trade of religious talk, and in one form or another it appears in virtually every verse of this chapter. I have to confess, though, that for me it has always been rather loosely defined. I've tended to think about it in one of three ways. Firstly, as something to do with being religiously serious: a spiritual person is one who speaks about God a lot, who prays and reads their Bible, and is regularly at church on a Sunday. Secondly, the spirit is the part of us that goes to heaven when we die. And thirdly, with regard to God, the Spirit is one of three persons within the unity of God, the third member of a Trinity. But wherever these ideas might have arisen in the Bible or in Christian tradition, none of them, not even the third, has anything to do with what Paul means as he uses the word in this chapter of Romans.

What does Paul mean then? As in all the ancient languages, the word in Greek that means *spirit* is also the word for *wind* and for *breath*.[9] The writer of the creation story in Genesis makes the correspondence between breath and spirit explicit: he pictures the Creator God calling the first human creature into existence by breathing into it his very own breath (Gen 2:7). This is what a human being is. God's in-breathed spirit makes us, not an animal in an environment, but a person in a world. This means that life is not something we possess; it is something we are given—for a time—by God. In his last moments on the cross Jesus prays "Father, into your hands I give back my spirit." "Having said this," Luke tells us, "he breathed his last." That is it precisely. The spirit, the breath: it is the same word.[10] To be spiritual, then, for Paul, doesn't mean to be religious. It means to be human.

And immediately we can see that the second of my three ideas about the meaning of spirit is simply wrong, for Jesus rose again. He had a body you could touch. On at least two occasions after the resurrection he shared a meal with the disciples. He died as a human person, and he rose as a human person. We are not an assembly of parts. The idea of a pure spirit that leaves the gross and physical body behind at death is a pagan idea; a human being, in biblical thought, is always an *embodied* being. Christians believe not in the immortality of the spirit, but in the resurrection of the body.

The third idea, that there is a Holy Spirit, who is in some degree distinct from a Father and a Son within the unity of the one God, we need to treat more carefully. There is much to be said about the doctrine of the Trinity, but saying it here would only distract us. Suffice to say that, as we've already noted, Paul in the first century did not know about a Trinity, the doctrine of which was developed long after his time—though of course he knew the truths which that doctrine is designed to protect. If we are to be fair to him, then, if we are to understand him, we cannot introduce these later categories into what he writes here. Many of the English translations do just that, though, capitalizing the word "spirit" virtually everywhere it appears. Paul doesn't need the capitals. He is always careful to indicate when he is speaking about the spirit of God (vv. 9, 11, and, later on, 14ff.) as distinct from our spirit. In every other place where he uses the word, he is referring to *our spiritual nature as persons*. There is a bodily nature, which we share with the animals. But there is also a spiritual nature, which we share with God. And, "if God's spirit lives in you, it is not the bodily nature but the spiritual nature that is the driving principle of your life" (v. 9).

FOCUS

There are two things I've wondered about here. Firstly, what does it mean for God's spirit to live in us? Is it like having two personalities inside our head? Mightn't that be a bit crowded? Wouldn't God's spirit tend to overwhelm our spirit? (On the other hand, if we don't feel overwhelmed, might it be that we don't really have the Spirit after all?[11])

But "in" has nothing to do with spaces. God's spirit in us is not like the air in a tire. It is not like a diamond ring put into a box: before there were just buttons in there; now there's a ring as well. "In" means not location but participation. It's the difference between being in the clubhouse and being on the team.

How does participation work? Paul assumes what we know: that we already have a spiritual nature breathed into us by God. Although it is Creator and creature, there isn't a difference *in kind* between our spirit and God's spirit. If there was then it would have been impossible for God to enter human nature in Jesus.

When God did enter human nature, he changed it forever. By his death he won it for obedience; by his resurrection he won it for joy. God's spirit in us doesn't therefore mean that there are two spirits controlling things, sitting side-by-side like the pilot and co-pilot of a plane. Rather, it means the fulfillment of what God intended for human beings from the moment he breathed us into life. What was foreshadowed there is now filled-full by God himself. Not only do we participate in the risen life of Jesus, he participates in ours. We are in the team. I once heard someone describing Louis Armstrong's experiments with instruments other than his signature trumpet. "But learning wasn't what Louis did, really," said the commentator. "He took an instrument and taught it to sound like Louis Armstrong." And that is what the spirit of God does in our lives. He takes human beings and teaches us—and enables us—to sound like Jesus.

My second question about v. 9 has been what it means for the spiritual nature to be the *driving principle* of our lives. Do we perhaps have a glum foreboding as to what it might mean: longer prayer times, more Christian activities, making sure we are mixing only with Christians, making the local Christian music station the default setting on the car radio? God forbid! Paul means nothing like that. To focus our attention on the spiritual nature means to choose to be, rather than merely animal, truly human.

What has become transparently clear in chapter 7, though, is that becoming truly human is not something we can do by ourselves. The list of supposedly "spiritual" things above assumes that the spiritual is a human quality of religiousness, something that we simply need to put more effort into. This couldn't be more wrong. The spiritual is a divine quality. What makes us human is the spirit of Yahweh God breathed into us, making us a person as he is a person. It is an ongoing process: like our physical breathing, even if we don't notice it, the Spirit's work goes on all the time. Spiritual life is therefore not *religious*, it is *relational*, directed towards God in the first instance, and because of that, towards others.

BODY AND SPIRIT

The bodily nature focuses on material things—and that is not *completely* wrong. God has made a world which he himself declared to be very good, and he has given us the curiosity and the passion to explore it. We have seen how the Genesis writer describes the fruit of the tree in the garden: good for food, beautiful, able to satisfy the longing for wisdom. These are all good things. The problem is not in the qualities in themselves, but in the fact that the qualities are sought in a *thing*; in the Genesis story, the fruit of a tree. A thing is chosen instead of the personal context which alone makes those qualities mean anything. No mere object, the story tells us, can confer those good things upon us. Only God can do so—and God is the one factor that has been excluded.

This then is where focus on the bodily life brings us: to, like a teenager's bedroom, a world littered with objects. Even when other people are involved, the impulse of the bodily life is to treat them as things. When he describes himself as harried by all kinds of longing for things that he cannot have, sexual desire is, as we have seen, at least one element of what Paul is talking about. And the change in terminology for sexual intercourse in my lifetime has been striking. Once (whether or not the promises that protect such a powerful thing were in place) we used to talk about *making love*. Now we talk about *having sex*. There is the difference in a nutshell.

Or think about the different ways we deal with money. What is money? It is human work and effort. It is the time, sweat, skill, wisdom, or creative passion of human beings, converted into a form that can be exchanged. People who need our gifts and skills pay us for our time, and we in our turn use that money to pay others for *their* time in providing the goods that we need. The dollar in our pay packet or bank account is not just a commodity. It is charged with personal significance. How we use it will tell us a great deal about whether the bodily nature or the spiritual nature is the driving principle of our life. Do we, for example, look to pay a fair price, or to drive the hardest bargain? Do we take pride in paying people a living wage, or offer them the lowest amount that they will put up with in order to stay employed? Are we intent on building an investment portfolio, "adding house to house and field to field until there is room for no one but us, and we are left to live alone in the midst of the land" (Isa 5:8)? Or do we follow the principle of "enough," releasing our resources in ways that empower people and relieve hardship and build community?

The bodily life is a life of things, all revolving about us. The spiritual life has a different center. It is about *persons*: a life in which we are empowered by the spirit of God, and surrounded by the glory of other people made, like us, in his image. When Paul speaks about the spirit of Messiah being in us this is what he means: not an infusion of extra religiousness, but a life learning to see with the eyes of Jesus, daring to speak and act the love and the holiness of God into people's lives, being free to laugh and to rejoice and to walk free in the sun and the air of his good earth, being open to reach out with the hands and heart of Jesus towards others and to experience their reaching out of heart and hand towards us. The Spirit is not an additional quality added to our life. It is the experience of being led by Jesus into freedom.

POWER

Paul doesn't describe what this experience feels like. How do you describe how it feels to live a life, with all of its light and shadow, its joy, its struggle, and its steady growth? Instead, he makes clear the sure and certain foundation upon which such a life is founded. Firstly, the power source: God's spirit lives in us (v. 9).[12] Not the bodily nature, then, but the spiritual nature is the driving force in our lives. Secondly, because the Messiah, *the* human being, lives in us (v. 10), our spirit is life because of the righteous life he enables.[13] Finally, because it is the spirit of *the One who raised Jesus from the dead* who lives in us (v. 11), *our* subject-to-death bodies will be brought to life as well.

I was always taught that this bringing to life meant the resurrection at the last day. But why would Paul suddenly leap from the intense practical realities of living a life to the promise of some remote and ideal future? Of course we will rise to new life on the last day! But this is the response to Paul's agonized cry in 7:24. Paul is talking about something that is happening *now*, a process that we might not be aware of in the moment, but looking back can recognize: little by little the Spirit is shaping us to become more like Jesus. Part of the process is bringing even that unruly, subject-to-death body to life.[14] I have to confess that sometimes for me that prospect seems very remote. Paul, though, is talking not about what we see, but what God sees. Whatever we feel or don't feel, this is the fact. This is what God has done.

This then is the answer to Paul's agonized cry in 7:24. This is how we overcome the impulses of the body (v. 13). Paul is not summoning us to battle against them. Such a battle is already foredoomed: we have in chapter 7 seen what happens when we attempt it. Battling against the impulses of the body is simply another way of focusing upon them. In contrast, the spirit of Jesus wrenches our attention away from the body, and focuses it upon something else. As we live in the spirit, open to God, open to others, we are actively putting those other impulses to death. The body is still there, but now it has its right place. We have no obligation to it. Open to God and other people, graced by his love and theirs, God's own life lives within us. Is this not extraordinary?[15]

16

Romans 8:14–30

¹⁴All who are led by God's spirit are God's sons and daughters. ¹⁵You haven't received a spirit of slavery to fear all over again. Rather, you have received a spirit of adoption into the family—in which we cry out, 'Abba! Father!' ¹⁶The Spirit itself answers that cry, confirming to us that we are sons and daughters of God. ¹⁷And if children, then also heirs, heirs of God and joint heirs with Messiah. Only we must suffer with him, if we are to share his glory.

¹⁸I am convinced that the sufferings of the present are slight compared to the glory that is about to be revealed in us. ¹⁹The creation awaits with eager anticipation the revelation of God's sons and daughters. ²⁰For it was subjected to futility, not because of anything inherent in itself, but because it was made that way by the one who created it, in the confident expectation ²¹that it, the very creation itself, will be released from its bondage to decay into the freedom of the glory of the children of God.

²²Up to now, as we know, all creation groans together in the pains of childbirth; ²³not only that but we too, who have the Spirit as the first fruits of the harvest to come, groan inwardly while we wait for adoption, for our bodies to be set free. ²⁴For we were saved in expectation of something. Expectation that is fulfilled is no longer expectation: who waits for what is already here? ²⁵But if we wait confidently for what we know is still to come, we wait for it with patience.

²⁶ In the meantime the Spirit helps us in our weakness. We don't know how to pray about things properly, but the Spirit itself prays with groans that words cannot express. ²⁷ The One who searches hearts knows what the Spirit means, because the Spirit prays for God's people in God's way. ²⁸More than that, we have come to see how God works alongside those who love him, shaping every circumstance for good—alongside those who are being called, just as he intended. ²⁹For those whom he knew beforehand he destined beforehand to be formed in the image of his Son, so that he might be the firstborn among many brothers and sisters. ³⁰*And those whom he destined beforehand he also called, and those whom he called he also declared and empowered to be righteous, and those whom he gave the power to be righteous he also made glorious.*¹⁶

"God's sons and daughters": this is something startling and new. In fact it is utterly astounding. But do we realize that anymore? Centuries of Christian piety have made our family relationship to God almost a cliché. "Of course God will forgive me, it's his job": so said the cynical Heinrich Heine on his deathbed in 1856. We wince at the shallowness. But do we share it? Of course God is our Father: why wouldn't he be?

The problem is that we Christians start at the wrong end of things. The Old Testament saints knew who God was. He was Creator of everything in the universe, the God of fire and earthquake. He could be described using the imagery of a thunderstorm: the rain lashing down, the lightning with unbearable light tearing the heavens apart, the earth trembling at its stroke. This was the One so much more real than any created thing that encounter with him would instantly burn out a human being's fuses. "Alas for me!" cried the prophet Isaiah, "I am lost, for my eyes have seen the King, Yahweh!"¹⁷ Marching across the desert guided only by a pillar of cloud by day and a pillar of fire by night, the newly liberated Israelites find themselves at the foot of a volcano. There Yahweh God meets them and binds himself to them in an everlasting covenant. It is a terrifying experience. The mountain is in eruption: through the vast column of smoke and debris lightning flashes continually, gas pours out of vents with an ear-splitting shriek, the earth trembles underfoot. This is the setting for a unique encounter: "Moses would speak, and God would answer him in thunder." That was how it had to be, for the people were so terrified they had implored of Moses, "You speak to us, and we will listen; but do not let God speak to us, or we will die."¹⁸

The God who revealed himself to Israel is the lordly Creator. That he could also be encountered and trusted did not qualify his fundamental reality as a God of fear and danger. It was *that God* who encountered people in those other ways. When Paul says that "You haven't received a spirit of slavery to fear all over again," then, he is being realistic about our instinctive response to God. And, until we learn more, it is completely appropriate to feel that way. If we aren't afraid of God, we should be. *But if we are, we don't have to be.* "For," Paul goes on, "you have received a spirit of adoption into the family."

How are we to understand this? Is Paul saying that the God of terror and of glory has a softer side? That is ridiculous. God is God. God has no attributes: he is always only himself. What has changed is *where we stand with regard to him*. Once we were enemies (5:10), inhabiting the shadow zone of sin and disobedience that God rejected in his making of the world. The only God we can see from there is, looming threateningly over our lives, a God of wrath and judgment. But in Messiah Jesus, God has seized us and torn us from that place. He has brought us into the zone of obedience, of a life lived with rather than against the grain of the universe. Now we see God from the same place that *Jesus* saw him. He is Father. We can be at peace with him. He has given us the confidence of those welcomed into the family. We recognize, and God himself stands alongside us in testifying, that we are his *sons and daughters*. This is no casual religious truism. It is a truth of the universe.

GETHSEMANE

What is remarkable is the circumstances in which this realization breaks in on us. We noted above that, beyond the facts of cross and resurrection, Paul seldom alludes to anything in the Gospels. But here we have an exception. The cry "Abba," translated immediately as "Father," is *Aramaic*, not Greek. Now, why would an Aramaic term appear in a letter to a congregation with no native Aramaic speakers? Aramaic was the language of Palestine. Jesus spoke it, but unlike Greek and Latin its use was strictly local. There can be only one reason. Paul is referring to something that is *already well-known and precious to the Roman church.* But not only the Roman church. Clearly it was well-known and precious among the churches in Galatia also, because Paul uses it in his letter to the Christians there as well (Gal 4:6).

This is a puzzle. Why would this so simple expression have become part of the worship vocabulary of the little Christian communities as they spread across the world? The answer is startling. The only other place in the New Testament where the expression occurs is in Mark 14:36. And that is the account of Jesus' agony in Gethsemane.[19]

To address God as Father, not with the crassness of a Heine but at God's own invitation, is an astonishing privilege. "Father" is the first word of the Christian life. How striking therefore that in the churches the primary remembered location of *Jesus'* address to God as Father should be not the other places we might expect: the parable of the prodigal son, perhaps, or John 17, or the Lord's Prayer, but the description of his agony in the garden! Gone is all sentimentality regarding the word Father! This is not about smiling and indulgent parenting. It is love in the heart of the fire. It is the total dependence that remains when all the chips are down.

The word "Abba" is a diminutive, indicating the intimacy of the relationship, but its repetitiveness of form also conveys a sense of urgency. And, says Paul, it is something that we *cry out*. On one occasion our small daughter and her cousin spent a night at their grandparent's house. It was the first time she had slept away from home. Due to a series of misunderstandings it was a really bad experience. When I came to pick her up the next day, as soon as she saw me she was running across the room. "Daddy, I fell over!" she sobbed. And of course she hadn't fallen over. But those were the words that meant distress. They meant being picked up and comforted. They meant the security of her father's arms.

Abba is a word like this. Do we dare to think it through? "Daddy, I fell over!" cried the strong man Jesus, in Gethsemane as he faced the abandonment, the hate, and the agony that was to come. *"Abba! Father!"* Was his cry not heard? Indeed it was. God *went with him* into the hate, the fear, the lostness, and the pain. Jesus suffered what we suffer, but his suffering was also God's suffering: God's suffering on behalf of his world; God's own journey into the dark to find us, to catch us up in his arms, and to bring us home. So it was that as the churches of Jesus Messiah spread out across the world this cry was part of their heritage. No platitude: "Abba! Father!"

Recognizing that Paul is speaking not about a general idea of fatherhood but about Jesus' cry in Gethsemane is crucial for understanding the rest of the chapter. The chapter itself is famous. Individual verses from it have been a source of consolation for Christians down the ages. *But consolation is not its primary purpose.* In every part its purpose is to give God's people hope and courage for the adventure of living a life like that of Jesus. Paul is not writing for those who merely exist, even as Christians. He is writing for fighters; for those who hunger and thirst after righteousness; for those who, despite their hands being full of thorns, still reach out for the rose.[20] Paul knew that those to whom he was writing so long ago were such people. God knew that we who would read these words so many years later would be such people. And that means you. He knows who you are.

And here is the next surprise. Those who live like this are not insignificant in the scheme of things. Despite their stumbling and foolishness, *God has chosen them to inherit the world* (v. 17). But the path to that inheritance is, as it was for Jesus, the way of suffering. As we will see.

HEIRS

If we are sons and daughters, Paul tells us, that means we are also *heirs,* heirs of God and joint-heirs with Messiah. The two parts of this statement are equally jaw-dropping. What does he mean?

We tend to think about an heir as *the person who will inherit the property*. Actually *being* the heir is nothing very much, really. It is just a kind of slightly uncertain waiting, with, as Charles Dickens put it, "great expectations." The worthiness of the heir is irrelevant; the important thing is the inheritance. Thinking about inheritance in this way makes Paul's statement either fantastically fairy-tale (we get to own a palace and a kingdom!) or somewhat embarrassing (is this about some sort of reward?). But of course Paul means something quite different. He is talking not about *what we inherit*, but *who we are*. In Jesus Messiah we have been brought into the same relationship with God which he has. God's own spirit leads us just as it led him. Just as he in his time walked the world in lordly freedom, so in God's grace do we. We are heirs as he is heir, sharing his God-given freedom and authority, sharing his standing in the world. And what is our inheritance? We are the inheritors of all that God had in mind when he created the world.[21]

Torn out of context, that could go to one's head, couldn't it? And so immediately Paul reminds us what it meant for Jesus, of what is implicit in the cry of "Abba!" and therefore what it will mean for us. It means *suffering with him*. Now this too is a remarkable statement. Sharing Messiah's sufferings? Haven't we all along been talking about God sharing *our* sufferings, of his taking responsibility for his world by entering human life himself, opening himself to the pain and the struggle that we experience? But here we hear about our sharing *Messiah's* sufferings. As we think about that, we find ourselves standing on the threshold of a door into another world.

THE FIRST TO CRY

In the movie Selma (dir. Ava DuVernay, 2014), a group of three black friends in 1960s Alabama flee the violent breakup by armed police of a peaceful march. Seeking cover in a nearby restaurant, they pretend to be studying the menu. A policeman high on anger and excitement bursts in, sees them, and fires several shots. He runs back into the street, leaving one of the three dead, a young man in his early thirties. It is a traumatic moment. Sometime later, Martin Luther King Jr. comes to visit the young man's father. "There are no words that could comfort you," he says. "But I know one thing for certain: *God was the first to cry*." A hand reached out across an abyss of pain, King's response carries within it a profound insight. Our suffering means suffering for God. Even before it was ours, it is his.

This truth lies at the heart of the Christian message. The early theologians of the church, influenced as they were by Greek philosophy, could never accept it. For them suffering meant being passive.[22] It meant being powerless in the face of someone or something stronger than oneself. Neither of these things could ever be so for God.[23] And of course—if that is what suffering means—they were right. That certainly is what human suffering means. But what about suffering, not as something *passively endured*, but as something *actively chosen*? What about suffering understood as God's taking responsibility for a world in the process of being born?

The answers to these questions are crucial. What kind of God do we have? It is not as if we are in a position to decide what God could be like. We are totally dependent upon God to tell us who he is. And, as it turns out, we just don't have a Greek-style God, majestic, supreme, living in some heavenly place far above the earth, looking down on what happens there with concern and even with sorrow. The cross blows that fantasy to shreds. What instead it tells us is that we have a God who is now and who has constantly been involved with his creation, rejoicing with it, agonizing with it, steadily and patiently working to bring it to the completion he had in mind from the beginning.

When, in the Genesis story, Adam and Eve were expelled from the garden, did God stay there in paradise, wandering the empty groves, sadly wishing it had never happened? What nonsense. When they left the garden, *God went with them*. Every story and history in the rest of the book declares that to be true.

It's so important that we understand this. How otherwise could we comprehend all the individual and communal suffering throughout history? How could we understand for example the Black Death which swept across Europe in the fourteenth century, killing between 30 percent and 60 percent of the population, men, women, and children? Where was God while that was happening? In the light of Jesus Messiah we can answer with utter confidence: not in some high and heavenly place, looking down with horror and dismay. He was *there*, right there among us, sharing the agony of the dying, strengthening those who helped, standing alongside the grieving, just as Jesus too had wept beside the grave of his friend.

How otherwise could we understand the world we live in today? As I write, war is raging across the Middle East. Saudi warplanes are dropping bombs on Yemeni cities. Syrian forces are using barrel bombs and sometimes nerve gas to terrorize rebel-held towns and villages. In northern Iraq, in the great city of Mosul, suburb by suburb the occupying Daesh forces are being driven out. It is the violence that makes the headlines. But in all of these places families are trying to make a living: parents are doing their best to provide food and shelter; children are cowering in fear when the aeroplanes come, or, on a good day, finding games to play in the rubble. It is impossible to comprehend what it is like to live this way. The real question, though, is not what is it like, but *where is God* in these situations? And the answer must be: not looking on, appalled, as we do, only from a slightly higher vantage point. The cross tells us that he is *there*.

I have a vivid memory of dropping my five- or six-year-old son off at school one day, and thinking how small and vulnerable he looked as, with his little backpack, he headed out into a world where I could not follow. I ached to protect him from whatever perils might be out there. Is that how it is for God? Does he give us free will and creativity and authority and skill and then send us toddling off to see what we will do with them, responding with anger and frustration when we make a mistake, giving us perhaps a pat on the back when we do all right? Impossible. The cross of Jesus Messiah tells us that we have a different God to this. The God we have is one who comes. As individuals and as communities *God accompanies us* in our life in the world. He takes responsibility for what he has made. He shares the risks and the joys; he shares the struggle. Whether we are believer or unbeliever he is close to us as a breath. When I was younger I saw the cross as a kind of one-off emergency measure. Now I understand it to be a kingly declaration of the kind of God that God is. It tells us about the kind of God that he has always been, through all the struggles and tragedies of human history. It tells us that this is the kind of God he is now, and that therefore we can trust him.

Romans 8:14–30

TAKE IT UP

But, says Paul, we must suffer with him (v. 17). I remember how grim passages like this used to sound when I was younger. Worryingly, they were there in the Gospels as well. "If anyone wants to be my disciple, he must take up his cross and follow me."[24] Gulp. I wasn't sure that this was quite what I'd signed up for. But neither Jesus nor Paul is describing a fate to be endured. Rather, the one is issuing and the other passing on a joyful and lordly invitation. It is an invitation to join our Master in his work in the world.

What is the suffering that Paul is referring to here? In the early centuries there was a tradition among the super-spiritual that suffering was something to be actively sought, and that the highest grace for a Christian was to be thrown to the lions or martyred in some other dramatic fashion.[25] What sad nonsense—and how unnecessary! Like death itself, suffering comes knocking without any invitation. It is one of the conditions of life in this age of the world. Sometimes its forms may surprise us. The immediate context here, for example, is the struggle for integrity of life that Paul describes in chapter 7. As we have seen, among other things that means sexual self-discipline: choosing not to be drawn back to a merely animal existence, but in God's grace to live a fully human life. Recognizing that the tension of sexual self-control was a form of suffering was enormously helpful to me. Instead of a battle with wicked and lustful thoughts that came from some rotten spot within me, I was dealing with a call from God to be whole and true and free. It wasn't a matter of a pitfall to be avoided, but of a prize to be gained. It was something worth fighting for.

But this is just one aspect of something that has deeper roots in the letter. It's worth looking back to 5:1–8 to see what Paul said about the matter there.[26] He urges us to step out into the three great gifts of the good news: peace with God; a life of hope because our future is secure; and suffering understood now not just as a random bolt from the blue, but as something which under God's hands can help us grow into real people. And it can do that because of *God's* own suffering: while we were weak the Messiah died for the godless (v. 6). God shows his love for us in that while we were still rebels the Messiah died for us (v. 8). These statements are not just random bits of history but reach deep into the heart of God. What kind of God do we have? This kind of God.

Knowing the kind of God that God is cannot but spill out into the lives that we live. Let me mention just two ways that happens. Firstly, as we have seen, God's suffering is not something *passively endured*, something to which God is subjected, but is something *actively chosen* as part of his covenant faithfulness to his world. Understanding this makes all the difference. Rather than something to be avoided, suffering tells us about Jesus himself. We are not passive in the face of it. It is part of our journey with him. As we actively embrace it as part of the journey, it produces endurance and character and hope; it creates a point of weakness through which God's love is poured into our hearts (5:3–5).

Secondly, as we step out into the new life, the spirit of God will inevitably open our eyes and hearts to the suffering of the world. The call to take up our cross and follow Jesus is not a command to go; it is an invitation to come. It is not as if we Christians, like knights of love and virtue, are sent out to bring God's presence into situations of need. How presumptuous that would be. Long before we even knew about any particular need, God was already there. But the God who has opened our eyes and ears and hearts invites us *to join him where he already is*, in the nakedness of need, in the heart of the struggle. He gives us a share in what he is already doing in the world.

In its understanding of suffering, Christianity is unique among the religions. Buddhism seeks above all things to avoid it. Judaism and Islam see it as a thread of judgment or perhaps tragedy, which ultimately comes from God. Hinduism sees it as a consequence of sins committed in a previous life, but also as a power within the world, to be placated or even celebrated. Perhaps there are other ways of thinking about it too. But we don't have the liberty to speculate. All we have is what God himself has revealed about the truth of his world, and of his own intimate and costly involvement in it. The only truth we have to proclaim is, as Paul said in another of his letters: "Messiah Jesus—and him crucified."[27] It is no mistake that the symbol of Christianity is a Cross. Just as suffering is at the heart of the mystery of the world, so the way God takes personal responsibility for it is at the heart of the good news.

LABOR PAINS

What Paul says now is not something I've ever heard preached,[28] though it seems to me to be one of the most profound and hope-filled passages in the letter. Paul lives in the same kind of world that we do. He looks around and sees it as it is: clearly a creation, yet just as clearly an incomplete and disordered one. He knows about the brutality of Archelaus and Pilate, about the crucifixions and the persecutions. He knows the terror of the elements, having suffered shipwreck; he knows, he must know, about the diseases and disorders that plague human life (things which the Gospels often characterize as demonic.) He knows the world isn't perfect[29]; it is disordered. But because God is God, that apparent disorder *can only be part of the Creator's plan*. And what is that plan? It is that you and I might come to be. Here is how Paul puts it:

> The creation awaits with eager anticipation the revelation of God's sons and daughters. For it was subjected to futility, not because of anything inherent in itself, but because it was made that way by the Creator, in the confident expectation that it, the very creation itself, will be released from its bondage to decay into the freedom of the glory of the children of God.

There could not be a more direct challenge to the unexamined presuppositions of twenty-first-century secularism. That "religion" says that the randomness and disorder that we see in the world is precisely what we would expect. In that view, the Big Bang, which brought the universe into being, was a totally chance and random event, and its astronomically precise fine-tuning to be the kind of universe that could sustain life was merely a fluke.[30] The universe is driven by random, impersonal, and irrational forces, and if order and beauty and truth have happened to have arisen out of that fundamentally meaningless environment, they are an aberration of no more significance to the life of the universe than the colors on a soap bubble.

We have already seen how the knowledge of the Creator challenges this dreary nonsense at every point. But if truth and beauty are the challenge for a materialist world-view, the challenge for those who believe in the Creator is *suffering*. All that Paul has been saying about the covenant faithfulness of God to his creation, and a suffering and rising Messiah, has already taken us deep into that question. But here he focuses upon the apparent randomness and futility of the physical world and what happens within it. And what he says is this: that God himself has made it that way, *because this is the only kind of world in which God's sons and daughters could come to be*.

For us to be free the universe has to be free and open to possibility.[31] In order to be the kind of world in which things can go right, it must be possible for them to go wrong. For love to exist, there must be the possibility of hate. For obedience to be real, there must be the possibility of disobedience. Such a world must be open to opportunity and vulnerability, pregnant with the possibility of both joy and sorrow. And this, Paul tells us, is the kind of world that God has made, subjected for a time to futility, in order that, breaking through the debris of chance and change and sin and suffering might come the children of God, fully human people, people like Jesus. That such a people can emerge is, Paul says, the purpose of creation. Creation longs towards its own fulfillment. The struggles and pains that it now endures are not meaningless. They are *labor* pains: something is coming to birth.

And *we are a part of that*. Paul is realistic about the struggles and challenges of life. We have heard him describe his own battle for holiness, heard his despairing cry for deliverance from the body whose impulses betray him into death. We have listened as he has described how, like Jesus in Gethsemane, out of the very heart of the fire we cry "Abba!"—and how that cry is answered by the spirit of God himself. We have heard him make clear that the lives of those who follow Jesus will be marked by suffering; as in the life of Jesus, the way is not out, but always through. But none of these things, he tells us, bear comparison with the glory that is about to be revealed in us. We, like all of creation, are straining towards something that is in the process of being born. We are part of a story that is not yet complete. This is the nature of our life in the world.[32]

FIRSTFRUITS

The striking thing that Paul is saying here is that human beings are at the very center of this process. We are not, as the religion of our world would teach us, merely an accidental afterthought, an intelligent mammal stumbling into history by chance, the life of our whole race just an infinitesimal blink of the eye in the vast reaches of time. That might be the case in a universe where matter and forces were the fundamental realities. But in a universe which is a *creation*, a universe in which intelligence and purpose are the fundamental realities, things are very different. In a universe where truth and faithfulness and joy are part of the structure of reality, those who share these things are at the center of the universe's meaning. So far from being an accidental afterthought, the coming to be of the sons and daughters of God is what creation is *for*, the crown and completion of its long struggle.

Paul isn't telling us this as part of some abstract theology. He is speaking from the middle of a battle that he and his audience share. Just as all creation groans in the pains of childbirth, "so we too, who have the Spirit as the first fruits of the harvest to come, groan inwardly while we wait for adoption, for our bodies to be set free." There is no calm and carefree place from which we can contemplate timeless truths about God. Faith is forged in the fire.

Paul is dealing with something extraordinary and struggling to find metaphors to describe it. Here is a second one, "*we who have the Spirit as first fruits of the harvest to come.*" What does that mean for those of us who get our food from the supermarket? Unfamiliar as it sounds to those of us who live in cities, Paul couldn't have found a better metaphor. For this is one of the deep mysteries of life: the way in which, without any input from us, the plant produces the bud, the bud becomes the blossom, and the blossom becomes the fruit: in Paul's day, grain, olives, figs, and all the other crops that sustain life. Something is coming to birth, Paul has told us; that is, a *harvest* is coming, and already we see the fruit starting to appear.

The harvest is the coming to be of God's sons and daughters (v. 19). All creation longs for it; it is why the world was made. But, Paul tells us, this harvest is not merely a hopeful idea about the future. *Already* God's spirit lives in us (v. 9); all who are led by God's spirit *are* God's sons and daughters (v. 14); the Spirit *answers our cry* to the Father, confirming that we are sons and daughters of God (v. 16). That is, *the future has already begun*. Here, in the midst of our struggles and sufferings the Spirit lives within us. We are the firstfruits of the harvest of the earth.[33]

The metaphor, then, contains a key insight into how we live in this age of the world. It helps us realize that *we are still in the middle of the story*. That being so, we can wait confidently for what we know is still to come. And in the meantime God's spirit helps us in our weakness (v. 26). How does he do that? In two ways: firstly, by shaping our *prayer*; and secondly, by shaping our *lives*.

Romans 8:14–30

GROANING

Paul isn't writing deep theology in these verses. He is reporting on experience. This is how the Spirit helps us. This is what we have come to see about the way God works in our lives. The pronouns are all "we." Paul is not writing *to* the Romans, he is standing alongside them, reflecting on an experience of God's presence that both he and they share.

"We don't know how to pray about things properly," Paul says. Hmm . . . I'm not so sure. When I was a young man I did know how to pray; in fact I was a hero of prayer. Confident, articulate, whether in my own private devotions (I had an extensive and well-organized prayer list) or in a prayer meeting I could pray compellingly for just about anything. It was all very earnest and genuine. I wasn't pretending. But my prayer life was pretty much under control; I didn't feel I needed any help.

Under control? It makes me smile now. The God of space and time and history; the still, small voice; the wind that blows where it pleases: when we come into the presence of God we *give up* control. We enter a zone of power where God is God. We call upon him to be that God in our lives and in his world. It is a risky thing to do. God is not at our disposal that we might influence him by even the most earnest prayer. *God* is in control: that is what prayer is an acknowledgement of, and we are fooling ourselves if we expect to come away from the encounter unchanged.

I remember the first time that I began dimly to be conscious of this. Two good friends were about to get married, and only months before the wedding one of them was beset by a severe bout of depression. On a sunny day I was walking around the park going through my prayer list, and when I came to their names my heart was full of concern and anxiety. And then suddenly I was aware that God was speaking to me. No voice from heaven or anything, just something that I knew with utter conviction. And the message was this: "This is not the time for anxiety. It is the time for rejoicing." And the whole nature of my prayer changed.

Slowly and painfully since then I have learned some other things about prayer that I never knew. That, for example, instead of blundering into God's presence with advice as to how he could help out in people's lives it is much more important to wait and to listen. It has to be, not "Here's what I suggest you do" (to God!), but "How do you want me to pray about this?" Prayer is still necessary,[34] but it is God, not us, who directs it. Often enough, these days all I can do is name a name, bringing that person with me into God's presence, and as it were leaving them there, confident that God knows how to deal with their need much better than I do. I join my small prayer for their good with his great one. What more can one do? In public, my prayers have become more and more inarticulate. Even saying the blessing over a meal I can find myself tongue-tied. We are talking to God! Where to start?

But the Spirit helps us in our weakness (v. 26). How does he help? What are these "groans that words cannot express"? Precisely because words fail, those who have had such experiences find them hard to describe. Unbidden a cry suddenly wells up from the depths of one's being, that carries the whole of one's need and longing directly into the heart of God. That's what happens, but saying it leaves out just about everything. Those who practice glossolalia, "tongues-speaking," may find that the gift has to do less with praise than with prayer in situations where human effort and ingenuity fail.[35] Whatever the ways in which we experience what Paul describes, the context is always intense need and the inadequacy of every human resource. "Groans that words cannot express": we are talking about suffering, tragedy, desolation; some of us may need to translate that into what at this moment may be relatively safe and protected lives.[36]

IMAGE

On a sunny day, Copenhagen is a charming town, but today it is bleak and grey, with a bitter wind blowing in from the North Sea. The rest of my party have yet to fly in, so I'm heading downtown, to find a bookshop perhaps, and later on someplace to get lunch. The main shopping streets, pedestrian only, are crowded with Danes pursuing their own agendas for the morning: hundreds and hundreds of black-coated figures, all heading purposefully off on their own particular errand. And suddenly it strikes me like a blow that I am an alien here, a stranger. This is not my country, not my world. All of these people have homes, and friends, and lives to live. But I have none of this. I am a stranger looking in on something to which I don't belong. If I was to suddenly vanish, nothing here would change. All these lives would just go on. No one would even notice.

What gives a life meaning? What is it that anchors it in reality, what makes it a *life*, rather than just an existence? We know the answer of twenty-first-century secularism: there *is* no meaning or value except that which we create. Life itself is alien to the universe: the astronomically improbable result of chance processes, among other things it constitutes a violation of one of the basic principles of physics.[37] Human life is only sophisticated animal life: we posture and preen and compete and pass on our genes and we die. That is it: anything else is window-dressing. The question is meaningless.

To this sterile foolishness Paul has the most complete answer. "We have come to see," he tells us, "how God works alongside those who love him, shaping every circumstance for good—*alongside those who are being called, just as he intended.*" Just as he intended! Your life is not a chance happening. The universe was created vulnerable to futility because only out of the freedom and risk of such a world could people like us come to be. But "coming to be" is not strictly correct. For God *intended* us. We are not an accident. We are not just one of the billions of people alive on the planet. God knows us personally. It is he who has called us into existence. He knew we were coming. And knowing we were coming, Paul tells us, God created a place for us to come to. We don't just stumble into life. God has destined us to be like Jesus, to be "formed in the image of his Son" (v. 29).

It is an extraordinary statement. There was not a person in Paul's audience who did not know the conclusion of the creation account in Genesis 1:

> So God created humankind *in his image*,
> *in the image of God* he created them;
> male and female he created them.

And Paul now identifies Jesus as that image, that pattern. He identifies him as the shape of the place in the world that, long before we were born, God destined us to occupy.[38]

CALLED

When our children were small, one of the pre-Christmas rituals was to make stained-glass-window biscuits. The biscuits were shaped using a cookie-cutter. When they were laid out on the baking tray, holes were cut in the center of each biscuit, and into the hole was sprinkled some crushed-up boiled sweet. When the biscuits were baked, the boiled sweet crystals had melted and spread to make a beautiful stained-glass window in the middle of the biscuit. We hung them on the Christmas tree—and at least some of them managed to survive until Christmas!

Is that the kind of thing that Paul means when he speaks about us being destined beforehand to be shaped in the image of his Son? A kind of cookie-cutter uniformity? God forbid! God does not destine us to a *state*, he destines us to a *life*. Three strong verbs in v. 30 make this clear: God has *called* us, he has *declared and empowered us to be righteous*, and he has made us *glorious*. Each of them describes something that God has done—and each implies a response from us, a stepping-out into the life to which we have been destined. We have learned much earlier in the letter about how God puts his own credibility on the line in declaring us to be righteous, and how along with that declaration comes the power to live righteously. The other two words, though, *called* and *made glorious*, are less familiar. What do they mean?

To be *called* means that God gives us a name.[39] He calls us into being as a specific person, in all our individuality. With your strengths and your weaknesses, your talents and your flaws, in all of space and time there will only ever be one person like you. God doesn't make generic human beings. There is no standard model. He isn't interested in mass-production. God makes individuals, and he is passionately interested in our individuality, in the unique person that we are. He has *called* us, Paul tells us; that is he has called us to become the person that we are, to become the person that we alone can be. He has given us a name.[40]

And he has *made us glorious*. I suspect that for most of us this is the most puzzling of these three acts of God. And yet Paul has talked about glory several times already in the chapter. "Only we must suffer with him, *if we are to share his glory*," he told us in v. 17. And he has described the way all of creation longs for release from its bondage to decay into *"the freedom of the glory of the children of God"* (v. 21). How are we to understand this glory business?

It is interesting to do a Google search and see the kinds of images that appear when you type in "glory." There are people with raised hands standing on a beach at sunrise; there are rays of light bursting out of clouds; and, even, heaven forbid, there are pictures of Jesus, a pale and sentimental figure in the sky, wearing 2,000-year-old clothes that shine with light. If that kind of picture makes you uneasy, you are not alone! For glory is a very different thing to this.

Let me give you just two examples. The first is from John 2, where Jesus turns water into wine at a peasant wedding in Cana. As a result, John tells us, "the disciples *saw his glory.*" What does that mean? Did they see his robes suddenly flash with light? Did they wonderingly notice a halo? Not at all. There was none of that, no spectacle at all; indeed, no one knew about the miracle except a few. All there was for them to see was a big cheerful man laughing with friends, joining in the dancing, shaking the hand of the bridegroom. But in what had happened the disciples had seen something shine out. Something was revealed to them about who he was. They saw his glory, and they put their trust in him.

The second example is from Romans 8 itself. God's spirit testifies that we are sons and daughters of God, Paul declares in v. 16. "And if children then heirs, heirs of God and joint heirs with Messiah. Only we must suffer with him, *if we are to share his glory.*" What is this "glory"? Some kind of numinous brightness that will surround everybody when we get to heaven? No. That would be to introduce an extraneous idea that has nothing to do with the rest of the passage. Paul has already told us what the glory is that he is referring to. Jesus' glory is to be God's son, God's heir (v. 17). And we also are sons and daughters of God, co-heirs with Messiah Jesus! That is, in his glory as the Son *we share*. But we don't share his glory passively. Sons and daughters of God don't sit around congratulating themselves on their status. Sons and daughters are only sons and daughters *as they live a life.* And if we are truly to live that life, to share his glory, we must also share his sufferings.

Glory is not therefore an external thing, a rapturous experience, or something that we passively receive. It is the *inner identity and quality of character* which a person has, invisible to others until it suddenly shines out in something that they say or do. This is the glory that the disciples saw in Jesus. This is the glory that, as sons and daughters of God, we share with him. And this, Paul tells us, is something that God has *accomplished*. He has called us, he has declared us to be righteous—and finally he has glorified us. His work in us is complete. He has made us the people he intended.

Hold it right there! That can't be right. Paul, this is a wonderful ideal, but our experience makes nonsense of it. We aren't like Jesus. We aren't complete. We stumble and struggle and fall short. We see God's dream for our lives as if through the wrong end of a telescope: beautiful and precise but very far away. What you are saying sounds like church-talk: all very fine on a Sunday morning, but something that brings guilt and discouragement on Monday.

And of course Paul isn't saying that we have already arrived. We have heard his anguished cry in 7:24—and from God's side the answer to it. The answer is not a pinch of fairy dust that magically makes us holy. It is a life, and the grace and the power to live it. And even as we live that life, we are still in the middle of the story. "Even we who have the Spirit as the first fruits of the harvest to come, groan inwardly *while we wait for adoption, for our bodies to be set free*" (8:23). So when Paul speaks of God having glorified us, he is not speaking of a perfect and saintly life. He is talking about who is in control. We have a life to live but that doesn't mean us trying to be as holy as we can. The life of Jesus is not an ideal for us to imitate, it is the image in which we have been created. God has already established the destination. He has already secured the landing-place. We are already the people that we shall become. *Those whom he gave the power to be righteous he also made glorious.* And so we step out into life unafraid.

17

Romans 8:31–39

³¹*What can we say about all this? If God is for us, who could be against us?* ³²*He didn't spare his own Son, but gave him up for us all: will he not with him give us everything else also?* ³³*Who will bring a case against those whom God has chosen? God declares us to be righteous:* ³⁴*who will condemn? Messiah Jesus, who having died has been raised, who is at God's right hand, prays for us!* ³⁵*Who will cut us off from the Messiah's love? Calamity, or distress, or persecution? Hunger or lack of clothes? Or danger and violence:* ³⁶*as the psalm says,*

'for your sake we face death every moment; we are regarded merely as sheep to be slaughtered'?

³⁷*No: in all these things we more than conquer through him who has loved us.* ³⁸*I am convinced that neither death nor life, supernatural beings or human oppressors, nothing now and nothing to come, nothing* ³⁹*that would overwhelm us from above, nothing that could undermine us from below—neither these nor any other created thing will be able to cut us off from the love of God in Messiah Jesus, our Lord.*⁴¹

PAUL PAUSES HERE FOR a moment, and so must we. He does so in order to bring all that he has said together, and show how it practically applies in our lives. What can we say? We can say *this*. We need to pause for a different reason. There are two ideas that come from later theology from which we need to unplug if we are to understand this extraordinary passage. The first is about the *Messiah*, and the second, what we mean by God's *love*.

The Messiah, then. Once, during a discussion I was involved in, the topic moved to how we might share the good news with Muslim friends. Someone pointed out how accurately Rom 10:1–4 describes the situation of faithful Muslims, and noted

Paul's call to mission to such people in verses 14 and 15 of the same chapter. "Yes," said someone else excitedly. "After all, they probably don't even *know* that God has a Son." And then there was a little silence. For the truth is this: *God does not have a Son.*

Does that startle you? Indeed, isn't it immediately refuted right here in the passage we are dealing with: "God didn't spare *his own Son* but gave him up for us all" (v. 32)? What does that mean if God has no Son? And that is precisely the point. We cannot understand what Paul is saying in v. 32 if we hear not what Paul says in that verse, but what later theology tells us that he meant.

When we were discussing what Paul says about the Spirit of God earlier in the chapter, we noted how impossible it would be to understand if we were to interpret it in the light of the later doctrine of the Trinity. The same is true of what Paul says here about Messiah Jesus the Son. Trinitarian doctrine teaches us that there are three personal centers within the unity of God: the Father to whom Jesus prayed, a Son who became incarnate in Jesus, and a Spirit who, now that the mission of the Son is completed, is the primary way in which God is active in our lives. Much could be said about this that would only distract us now. Our only responsibility here is Paul's message: to be true to what he wrote. But that means that we cannot use Trinitarian categories to interpret it, for they were unknown to him. That is particularly so of the "Son" language in v. 32, where Paul is not speaking about a *part* of God but precisely about *God himself*. A person has no parts.

As Paul reminded us right at the beginning of the letter,[42] the title Son of God is not a divine title but a human one. In Israel it was the title of the king, the one who bore God's authority, and in his justice and righteousness represented God to the people. Jesus was no earthly king, but his rising from the dead in power declared him unmistakably to be the One who bore God's image and exercised his authority. But no mere human representative this time: in Jesus Paul recognizes God himself entering human existence, changing it forever. And this is what Paul means by God's *own* Son in v. 34: not a part of God, not an aspect of his character, but God himself, taking responsibility for his world by taking human nature into himself. And, Paul says, he did not *spare* his own Son; that is, in Jesus he did not spare *himself,* but suffered the betrayal, the rejection, and the hate; in Jesus allowed himself to be pushed out of his world onto a cross, shamed and naked for all the world to see.

Does this sound sacrilegious? Of course it is sacrilegious! It is outrageous and impossible, an offence to all religious people. Isn't it beneath the dignity of God? Surely there must be some part of God that stands aloof from this! But this is precisely the good news, that there is no part of God that stands aloof, that he is completely and totally involved in our salvation. He does not spare his own Son,[43] that is, he spares himself not all; there is nothing that he will not spend including his dignity, his honor, his own safety in order that he might win us for himself. If only a part of God is involved in the drama of rescue then we do not have rescue at all. But if we have such a rescue then nothing on earth and heaven can shake it—and Paul knows this! The words tumble out: not this, not that, not this other thing either; subjected as it is to futility and as rejecting of the Messiah's people as it was of Messiah, nothing in all of the creation can cut us off from the love of God in Jesus our Lord. God did not spare his own Son: this is how much he loves us. This is what his love means. This is the unshakeable truth that lies at the heart of the universe.

And now we can come back to v. 31. What can we say about all this? Paul asks. That is, not just the last few verses but the whole of the good news as Paul has unfolded it step-by-step throughout the letter. And now he asks: what does this all mean for us? There is one single answer. It means that without the slightest reservation *God is on our side*. In his Son he has given us all that he is: what remains that he would possibly withhold from us?

Don't rush on from this. Read those sentences again.

NO ONE AND SOMEONE

When I was a young man I was taught that the initial chapters of Romans were structured like a great courtroom scene. First the pagans were brought before the divine Judge—and condemned. Then the Jews with their self-righteous religiousness were called to judgment. Next came the astonishing sight of Jesus the Messiah being convicted in our place, with the result that those who put their trust in him were forgiven and free. On that model, what Paul says here is the final scene of that drama.

Paul's concerns in chapters 1–3 of the letter are, however, very different, as we have seen. These verses then are not the last but the *first* mention of the idea of a court case in the letter. And it is something like a parody of a court case. Who could be the prosecutor in such a situation? Nobody! On the contrary, we have an advocate so powerful that so far from being *accused* we are permanently *affirmed* as those upon whom God's favor lies.

Why does the idea of a court case arise just at this point? As always, Paul's concern is the character of God. To understand we need to think back into the pre-Christian understanding of God in which Paul and his Roman listeners grew up. The Old Testament is full of the knowledge of the good news of God's grace, as Psalms 51, 23, and 130 and great passages such as Isaiah 40 and Jeremiah 31 testify. But in the life of ordinary people, then as now, there was always a doubt. How could one be sure that one was forgiven and accepted? Were the sacrifices enough? Wasn't the God of covenant grace also "a jealous God, punishing children for the iniquity of parents to the third and fourth generation" (Exodus 20:5)? How could one be sure one was among the faithful? This was not a matter of unbelief, but the earnest concern of good people who knew how often in their daily life they fell short of God's glory. One reflection of this theological uncertainty was the idea of the Satan, a member of God's court whose responsibility it was to test whether people demonstrated in their lives the reality of what they said they believed.[44] God was indeed the gracious God, but there was also a part of him which kept account and searched out sinfulness. And there would always be something.

And in these verses it is as if Paul looks at the place where such a figure might stand—and finds it empty. The idea of an accusing God vanishes forever.[45] God's character is whole; his commitment to us is complete. Then Paul looks again and sees that that space is not empty! For Messiah Jesus stands there.[46] Instead of an accuser, God himself declares that we are righteous, and that we are his.

Messiah Jesus stands there! The Jesus who, because of our failure and faithlessness, *died*. The Jesus whom God, declaring void our judgment upon him and disregarding our failure in that judgment, *raised* to new life, bringing us with him. The old has gone, the new has come. Messiah prays for us. What does that mean? Not I think intercession as a kind of separate benevolent activity. The whole being of Messiah Jesus presents us to God as new people. He is himself the prayer.[47]

This is not abstract theology, pious platitudes, and a memory verse or two. This is truth in the heart of the fire. These are the weapons we need when our hearts misgive us. This is what gives us courage to step out into life. If God is for us, who can be against us? And courage is needed. Verses 35 and 36 take us into the life-experience of the Roman church, and of all the little Christian congregations in those dark and dangerous days. If you are reading this, as I am writing it, in a Western country with a stable government and an intact social fabric, then we need to make an effort to understand. If we imagine Paul's audience as like a well-to-do middle-class congregation gathering enthusiastically to listen to the famous teacher Paul's latest YouTube video, or perhaps coming as it were to something like a friendly and interesting neighborhood Bible study, then we imagine wrong. Calamity. Distress. Persecution. Hunger. Poverty. Danger and violence. These were the realities of the Roman congregation's world, just as they are the realities for our brothers and sisters in Messiah in a dozen countries around the globe right now—and indeed in one way or another of many hidden people in our apparently safe and well-off and tolerant societies in the West as well. (God sees you!) What Paul was writing is not encouragement for the contented, but unshakable certainty and hope for those who are living daily only a step away from the edge.

Verse 36 is a quotation from Psalm 44, and it is worth turning the psalm up and reading it all. Psalms 22, 44, and 88—I have no idea why the coincidence of numbers—the psalms of desolation. No answer is given to the agonized questions they pose. Still, they are there in the Bible, preserved as a testimony to a genuine part of Christian experience. And Paul takes one of the most bitter lines of the most anguished of these poems and asks, will even this experience of dehumanizing violence separate us from the love of Messiah? Think about the question before rushing on to the answer!

And what is the answer? The answer is *no*. "In all these things we *more than conquer* through him who has loved us." No one can simply say this. These are the words of someone who has lived through these kinds of experiences.[48] But more than that, they are the words of someone who knows that, whatever his own experience, God has been there before him. "We more than conquer *through him who has loved us.*" Love: not a feeling, but an act that costs God everything. This will stand though the galaxies fade and die. This is something to build a life upon now.

LOVE

At the start of this section I noted that there were two things that we need to think about if we were to understand it correctly. The first was the meaning of Messiah; the second what Paul means by God's love. And what *does* he mean by that? There are two questions to ask, *who* and *what*. Already we have looked at the first of these. When we were talking about God acknowledging us as sons and daughters, we noted how a long and sentimental Christian tradition has made this almost a truism. Of course God is our Father: why wouldn't he be? But the God Paul is speaking about is not some warm-hearted grandfather in the sky. He is the Creator of the universe, the God of terror and of glory; the untamed God, sovereign and free. *This* is the God who names us sons and daughters. To be loved by him is an awesome thing.

The second question is *what*, and we need to think carefully about this, for the culture we live in has many ideas about love, and virtually all of them are wrong. The river, which should be alive and free, deep in the pools and foaming over the rocks, has become a shallow meandering creek, something you can splash across without getting your feet wet. Much is sung and said about love, but barely anything is known.

In the first place we need to say this: *love is not a feeling*. Does that sound strange? We will talk about emotion in a minute, but in the meantime I'd like to suggest that love that is real includes three things: *choice*, *commitment*, and *action*. We will draw our examples from human love. I realize these may not be part of the experience of every reader. Yet we have to use the tools we have. May God himself show us how much or how little these things are a help in understanding his ways with us.

When we say that love involves choice we are talking about freedom. This is another thing our culture knows little about. Freedom is not about having a range of possibilities from which to choose. That is the *potential* for life, but not life itself. A teenage desire to keep all the options open is a sign of immaturity. You only know freedom when you choose. You only know freedom when you give it away. I remember coming home after the date on which (surprising myself perhaps more than her) I had asked Angela to marry me. And I thought "You fool! Now you've said it. You can't take it back. You've burnt your bridges now." And another part of me said "But perhaps, for the first time in your life, you've been a man." It felt pretty terrific. Freedom is about choosing. It's about taking all of your life and putting it in one particular place, and standing by that choice, for good or bad, as long as you live.

Love is about commitment. When a young woman or a young man says "I love you" they are not reporting on the state of their hormones or their feelings. Whether we are aware of it or not, "I love you" is always a promise. It means I *will* love you: I commit myself to your good and your welfare from this time forward. I joyfully take upon myself that responsibility. It is reciprocal: met by an answering declaration of love it signals the binding together of two lives. It is this element of promise in the declaration of love that makes the breakup of even the most casual of relationships so painful. Love means commitment.[49]

And love means action. Love is not something that we fall into. It is not a state or a condition. It is a life that we live. When in the musical *My Fair Lady* Elisa Doolittle finds herself subject to her young man's high-flown protestations of love, she bursts out in frustration:

> Don't talk of stars
> Burning above;
> If you're in love,
> Show me!
>
> Tell me no dreams
> Filled with desire.
> If you're on fire,
> Show me!

The demonstration Eliza is looking for is a lover's embrace, but the principle is absolute. Words are fine, but love is demonstrated not by what we say but by what we do. And it is a powerful thing, this turning away from one's own self-preoccupation to the prizing of the life of another person. Love enables us to see the one we love not in their relation to us but in our relation to them—and to act accordingly. It involves not merely feelings or general goodwill but a life lived towards the other. This too is reciprocal, and that reciprocity worked out through the years is one of the deep joys of life.

Do we already begin to see what all this means for the way we understand God's love? It is not as if we were using human examples to imagine how it might be for God. The correspondence runs the other way: whatever we know of love in our human experience is only real because, whether weaker or stronger, it is a reflection of what is already there in God himself.

Love, Paul tells us, involves God's *choice* (v. 33). God intended us from the beginning. He knew we were coming. He created a place, the image of his Son, to receive us (vv. 29–30). Love is God's pure freedom in committing himself, not in general, but to you, you who are reading these words, now and forever.[50]

Love means God's *commitment*. With the creation of free beings comes responsibility. We would not have known that unless we had seen God's taking up that responsibility in Messiah Jesus (3:21–26). God enters our experience and makes it his own. He does not ask us to live a life that he would not live himself. He *has* lived it (8:3–4). You and I are responsible for our lives—and God also takes responsibility for them. That is the good news.

And God *acts*. What Paul describes here is the love of God *in Messiah Jesus* (v. 39). God doesn't love us in a general way, but quite specifically in a costly act, an act in which, without qualification or reserve, he gives us all that he is (v. 32). The risen Jesus is our *Lord* (v. 39).[51] We are in him, and he stands at God's right hand. You and I have a place in God's own heart, a place that has been won for us through conflict and sacrifice. God looks on us and is glad.[52]

EMOTION

Is this, though, all that we can say? I was talking with a friend once about how love is not just about feelings, which involve us on the surface, but is something that reaches much deeper into our lives. And at one point he burst out "But it's all so bloodless, Les! Choice, commitment, action: sure. But what about *being in love*? What *about* the feelings? What about *passion*?" They are good questions. Dare we ask them here as well, about God?[53] Is God benign towards us in a bloodless and abstract way? Is his love dispassionate, all about choices and strategies? It cannot be so, and everything Paul says in chapter 8 confirms that. We haven't been delivered in some general way; we've been adopted into the family (v. 15). Creation itself is an act of love; joy is the engine that drives it. And all of creation waits with eager longing for God's sons and daughters to be revealed (v. 19). Before time began God knew us, each one, called us into being, and prepared a place for us to come to (v. 29). And those to whom he gave the power to be righteous he also made glorious (v. 30). These are not the actions of an abstract strategist. They are the acts of a *lover*.

I remember our wedding day. The previous weeks had been filled with preparation, and even that morning there had been last-minute things to do. Now I was standing with my best man at the front of a church full of excited and expectant people. And here on her father's arm came Angela down the aisle. She was wearing a dress that she had made herself. There were flowers in her hair. And she had made herself beautiful for me.

Was I unmoved by this? I was not.

In our own case, of course, it is God who in the grace of his Spirit is making our lives beautiful for himself. But as he, as it were, sees us coming down the aisle towards him, is he unmoved by what he sees? He is not. In his choice, his commitment, his costly acts toward us we are used to the idea of being loved by God. But what does God's love for us feel like *for God*? Think about that.

Romans 8:31–39

When a woman makes an altar cloth, so far as she is able, she makes every flower as lovely as the graceful flowers of the field; as far as she is able, every star as sparkling as the glistening stars of the night. She withholds nothing, but uses the most precious things she possesses. She sells off every other claim upon her life that she may purchase the most uninterrupted and favorable time of the day and night for her one and only, for her beloved work. But when the cloth is finished and put to its sacred use, then she is deeply distressed if someone should make the mistake of looking at her art, instead of at the meaning of the cloth; or make the mistake of looking at a defect, instead of at the meaning of the cloth. For she could not work the sacred meaning into the cloth itself, nor could she sew it onto the cloth as though it were one more ornament. This meaning really lies in the beholder and in the beholder's understanding, if he, in the endless distance of the separation, above himself and above his own self, has completely forgotten the needlewoman and what was hers to do.

Soren Kierkegaard, preface to *Purity of Heart is to Will One Thing*

18

Endnotes
Romans 7–8

1. *Christchurch Press*, Jan 2, 2016.

2. Paul has made this point strongly in Rom 5:12–21. We are Adam. Each of us turns away from God as individuals and are individually responsible for that. But we are not *merely* individuals. We are also bound together as part of a wider humanity. Hence Paul's talk there of "one man . . . one man": not in each case one *individual* person, but one *representative* person. "Just as a human being's wrong deed led to condemnation for all people, so now a human being's act of righteousness leads to the lives of all people being made righteous" (5:18)—this would be impossible if we were merely individuals.

3. Rom 11:32, Col 1:20, Phil 2:9–11 (citing Isa 45:22–25). These things are merely a reminder of what Paul has made so clear in the earlier chapters: Christians don't own the good news. Paul is not talking about a matter of *religion*. If it was a matter of religion, Jesus would have called himself the Son of Israel, or a Son of the Temple, or a Son of the Scriptures. But instead he called himself the Son of *Man*: the Human Being. Where is the church in all this, then? Our high calling is the same as that of historic Israel: we are "a chosen race, a royal priesthood, a holy nation, God's own people, in order that [we] may proclaim the mighty acts of him who called [us] out of darkness into his marvelous light" (1 Pet 2:9, referencing Exod 9:6). That is, we are *a missionary community*. Through no merit of our own we are given the responsibility of standing between God and people in proclamation and prayer, our only reason for being the gospel service of those who are not yet members. Paul will have more to say about this in chapter 10 of his letter.

4. Acts 26:14.

5. Heb 4:15. The whole passage in Hebrews and especially 2:10–18 and 4:14—5:10 provides an excellent commentary on these verses in Romans. We should note in passing that God could enter human existence in this way is our glory: we are the kind of being within which this is possible.

6. "Taking responsibility" is my phrase, but it represents what seems to me to be a crucial aspect of what Paul is speaking about in vv. 3–4. The Law, that is, the instruction manual for living a whole and free human life *that God himself gave* to people was never able to bring that life about, because it was weakened by the bodily nature (v. 3). While God's intention for human beings goes beyond it, the bodily nature is nonetheless God's creation: it is how we were made. In taking that nature upon himself, God takes responsibility not by, for example, accepting the punishment for other people's wrongdoings, or in somehow reversing the consequences of a universal Fall. Paul speaks of neither of these things. What God takes responsibility for is *human nature*

itself: he takes that nature upon himself and brings to judgment the vulnerability to sin that is within it. The Genesis story helps us once again. It does not only tell of the sin of humankind (by sin meaning not the disobedience of chapter 3, but the breaking of the relationship which that disobedience represented). It also tells of the creation of humanity as the kind of being that *could* sin—because it could also love. The story is not only about the taking of the fruit of the tree, but about the creation of the tree itself in the first place (Gen 2:15–17): a part of God's good creation, before the temptation to sin ever arises. Of course we are not talking about a literal tree, but within the story a symbol of a capacity to choose one's own way *that is inherent in the ability also to choose God's way*. Created for love and obedience yet the very existence of those things necessarily allowing the possibility of their opposite, this is the human nature to which the animal world calls, and to which, sadly, we so often respond. It is this created human nature that God takes upon himself. Through the faithful obedience of Jesus all the way to death he has judged the sin within it, robbing it of its power. In this way he completes the purpose he had in creating human beings at all, opening a door for all people (as the resurrection declares) into eternal life. For the resurrection as implicit in creation, see Rom 4:17b.

7. Of course none of this is new. Paul is simply showing us in a different context and in a fresh light something that has been there from the beginning. "Don't you remember that all of us who have been baptized into Messiah Jesus were baptized into his death?" he asked back in chapter 6. "Through baptism we died and were buried with him—so that just as Messiah was raised from the dead by the splendour of the Father we too might live a new life." *So that we too might live a new life*: this is the good news.

8. "So that the righteous outcome that the law was designed to produce might come to be in us." We would expect at this point for Paul to spell out what this means, what the characteristics of the righteous life might look like; that he would begin to instruct us. But he doesn't do that. What such a life will look like in its both individual and corporate aspects will be the topic of the last three chapters of the letter. But here Paul merely *mentions* the outcome; his whole concern is bent upon something else. The rest of the chapter is not about a *result* (that is a secondary outcome) but about a *relationship*, about a *person*. The second guarantees the first; there is no first without the second.

9. Hence the play on words, invisible to us, in what Jesus says to Nicodemus in John 3: "The wind blows where it chooses . . . So it is with everyone who is born of the Spirit."

10. Luke 23:46, *pneuma, exe-pneusen*. Compare John 20:21–23, "he *breathed* on them [*enephouēsen*, the same word used in Gen 2:7 LXX] and said, "receive the *Spirit*." The idea of the inbreathed Spirit as the principle of truly human life is found in numerous Old Testament passages. It is common in the Psalms, but perhaps the most striking example is the mighty vision described in Ezek 37:1–14.

11. In contrast to tribal religions, and some forms of Eastern religion, e.g., Hinduism, Christianity has no concept of being possessed by the god. On the contrary, being filled with God's spirit means being more truly one's self, being more fully alive. It is true that, under the influence of powerful emotion, phenomena such as ecstatic speech and, in group settings, other more bodily manifestations may occur, and the emotions that *generate* these may certainly be a response to God. That was surely the case on the day of Pentecost, in Cornelius and his company's response to Peter's sermon in Acts 10, and on other occasions recounted in that book. The unusual nature of such phenomena does not, however, guarantee that they are spiritual in nature: similar phenomena are widely attested in religious contexts very different from Christian ones. The body has a limited range of responses to overpowering experience, and the experiences that trigger those responses can be of many kinds. Are the tears we weep tears of joy or of grief? Is that lurch of the diaphragm the beginning of fear or of love? Is this the laughter of joy, or of despair? The apostle John instructs us to test the spirits to see whether they are of God (1 John 4:1), and it is important that we do. Physical manifestations alone are not a sign of the spiritual. Something is going on, but what is it?

How do we test the spirits? Firstly, the Spirit is the spirit of Jesus: anything that is truly his will demonstrate his character. How do we match what we see with the Gospels? Secondly, we must remember what Paul states here as a truth: *every* Christian has the indwelling Spirit. It is our birthright. There is no other spirit than the one we have received. Confident in that, we should take our own reactions seriously. Do the exhibited phenomena honor the God we have come to know through Jesus? Do they lead us into praise and joy, or do they make us anxious and uncomfortable? Do they generate obedience, or merely excitement? I once spoke to a group of younger people who were hugely keyed up about dramatic manifestations, and indeed were specifically seeking them. Out of my (I recognize even now very limited) experience I said that biblically it seemed to me that there were three unmistakable signs of the Spirit's presence: joy, suffering, and people becoming Christians. This was not the comment that was expected.

The other biblical control is Paul's discussion of spiritual gifts in 1 Cor 12–14. Among other things he includes ecstatic speech and indeed acknowledges it as part of his own experience. He clearly sees it as a private matter, however, and lays down strict conditions for its practice in the congregation. While spiritual gifts (that is, gifts of God given through an individual for the good of others) are to be earnestly sought, Paul singles out prophecy as of especial importance. We tend to limit the range of this gift to predictions, pictures, and individual messages, which, while in the mouths of godly people to be taken very seriously, are only the fringes of prophetic activity. The prophet is the one who has the ability and the responsibility to stand up and speak the truth of God into the life of the community—something always crucial, but especially so in those early times when there was no written New Testament.

We should also note that in this passage chapters 12 and 14 bracket chapter 13, the latter often taken out of context for use at weddings and so on, but in fact dealing with something more important than even the greatest spiritual gifts (1 Cor 12:31). This is, of course, the true test of the presence of the spirit of Jesus Messiah; cf. also Gal 5:22–26. Readers interested in setting particular phenomena in a richer and deeper context might consider (among others) these two articles by (1) Helmut Thielicke "Speaking in Tongues," available here: http://www.ccel.us/between.toc.html#5 and (2) C. S. Lewis, "Transposition," available here: https://www.gutenberg.ca/ebooks/lewiscs-transposition/lewiscs-transposition-00-h.html .

12. It is crucial not to allow later theological ideas to trip us up here. A person's spirit is not anything separable from *the person themselves*. A person is an indivisible substance. The spirit is *precisely* the person: that is what a spirit is. Paul is not, then, talking about a part of God, or something given to us *by* God. God has no parts: the Spirit is God himself.

    I noted a little earlier, that, while Paul did not know about the idea of the Trinity, he knew the truths that that doctrine was developed to protect. This is one of them: that when we speak about the spirit of God we do not speak about something commissioned by God, something like God, or a merely God-associated power: when we speak about the Spirit we speak about God himself. The other truth that the doctrine of the Trinity was developed to protect is what technically we call the divinity of Christ: that in the man Jesus we likewise encounter not merely a godly man, not a prophet, not a semi-divine being, we encounter none other than God himself. Paul is not affirming this truth here, he is taking it for granted. *"God's spirit* lives in you . . . those without *the spirit of Messiah* . . . but if *Messiah* is in you . . . *the spirit of the One who raised the man Jesus from the dead* lives in you": these different expressions unmistakably refer to the same reality, the personal presence of God himself in the heart of our lives.

    The extraordinary ideas in this chapter are not unique to Paul. John's Gospel records Jesus as saying "I and the Father are one" (10:30) and "Don't you know that I am in the Father and the Father is in me?" (14:10) Later in the same chapter he uses a different set of metaphors to express the truth that Paul too is reaching for in this passage: "If you love me, you will keep my commandments, and the Father will give you another Friend, *the Spirit of truth* . . . I will not leave you orphaned; *I am coming to you* . . . Those who love me will keep my word, and my Father will love them, *and we will come to them and make our home with them*" (14:15–18, 23–4). God doesn't give us something, God himself comes. God has taken our life into his; now we, simply receiving, take his own life into ours.

13. Notice the change from adjective, *dead,* to noun, *life.* The spirit is not a concrete thing like the body, something that can be described. God's gift is not, like death's wages, a state. It is life itself.

14. Notice that the tense of the verbs has changed from present to future. Paul knows that the deliverance of which he speaks is not an instant transformation, but the steady outcome of a life lived daily in the company of the risen Jesus. The image of a bone marrow transplant continues to help us here. Once the new bone marrow is in place there is a period of adjustment. The body recognizes that something alien to itself has been inserted. It fights against it, trying to reject it, causing various symptoms that are known as "graft versus host disease." But slowly, over the weeks and the months, all of that goes away. The bone marrow steadily goes about its business of producing the blood which provides oxygen, heals wounds, and protects from infection: all of these things are counterparts of what the Spirit does in the life of the Christian. Finally the resistance ceases; the body is whole and complete.

15. We tend to think of the spiritual as something ideal and ethereal. For Paul, however, the spiritual is more real, not less real, than anything else we know. Recognizing the spirit to be the driving force is not wishful thinking, then, but a matter of the more real, the more powerful bringing under control something that is weak and impermanent. This daily decision to live as a human person is what Paul means in v. 10 when he speaks about "the spirit being life *because of righteousness.*" Righteousness is not a negative thing, the absence of sin. It is a positive thing, a joyful quality of character given us by God himself.

16. **Notes to the translation:**
    v. 14 **"All who are led . . .":** Understanding the *gar* that introduces both vv. 14–15 as a connective the force of which can best be expressed in modern English by the bare statement..
    "sons and daughters": Lit. "sons," but this is a generic term, including both men and women, cf. vv. 16, 17, 19, "children." Where the extended phrase is used, we need to make sure the link between Jesus as Son and our standing as sons (and daughters), v. 19, doesn't get lost. Compare the parallel passage Gal 4:4–6, where the NRSV does lose it by translating "sons" as "children."
    v. 15 **"rather, a spirit of . . . ":** Omitting the repeated "have received."
    "adoption into the family": while the word includes *"huios"* (son) Paul is not comparing a slave and a son, but the quality of the relationship.
    "spirit . . . spirit . . . in which": The Greek text has the article in neither occurrence of the word: Paul is contrasting two types of spirit. It is "the fear of the servant contrasted with the love of the son" (Luther, *Lectures on Romans*, 231). The distinction is not between fear and love, but between two kinds of person, two different places within a household. The second term of the current verse cannot be the spirit of God; grammar apart if that were so then the "spirit" in the first term would be also some external spirit (cf. Augustine, who thinks it is Satan). Rather this is our (God-given) spirit crying out; this is the spirit alongside which the spirit of God testifies that the cry we have made is heard and its truth witnessed to (v. 16). It is important by the way to read the text here on its own terms, rather than forcing the sense into that of Gal 4:4–7. There the sequence of thought is the reverse of what it is here, v. 15a corresponding to Gal 4:7, and vv. 15b–16 to Gal 4:6.
    "Abba!": Paul retains the Aramaic word and its translation as one expression, and so must we.
    v. 16 **"the Spirit itself":** We are required to retain what Paul wrote (a neuter pronoun reflexively referencing a neuter noun). Translating "himself" here and elsewhere is to allow a later theological idea to retrospectively alter what the text actually says. If that later idea is correct then it will be defensible on the basis of what Paul actually wrote, rather than it being necessary for us to supply what we feel he might have written if he had known the later doctrine. The only occasions in the New Testament when a spirit is considered as a personal subject is when it is demonic. Otherwise a spirit is always the spirit of a personal subject—just as the body or the life are not themselves personal, but rather individual aspects of a person's existence in the world. The comparison is not frivolous. We have already seen that the spirit is not the "ghost in the machine" of the body, as the Greeks believed. In biblical thought the person is precisely an

embodied spirit. Speaking of the Spirit as "he," therefore, would have been as incoherent to Paul as our speaking of someone's body as "she." When Paul speaks of the Spirit testifying, therefore, he is speaking about God testifying (v. 14.) He places the pronoun up front for emphasis; "the Spirit itself!"

"**answers that cry**": Here is a place where a literal translation ("the Spirit itself testifies with our spirit") cannot possibly convey what Paul is describing. *Symmartyrei* is not a bland and formal agreement: it is the deep cry of our heart in v. 15 being heard and answered from the side of God himself. Cf. Heb 5:7 "... and he was heard!"

v. 18 "in us": *Eis*, something that we experience, compare v. 20 where *eis* is translated "will obtain" (NRSV), "will be ... brought into" (NIV).

v. 20 "because it was made that way by the one who created it": Lit. "because of the one having subjected it." This can only be God. Who else has the power to determine the nature of the creation? Hence "it was made so by God" (JB), "God subjected it" (NEB mg.), "because in God's purpose it has been so limited" (Phillips).

v. 21 "the very creation itself": *Autē*, brought to the front of the sentence for emphasis.

"**will be**": I have retained Paul's change of tenses, implying as it does a Creation which is not a past and finished event, but a process in which we now participate.

v. 22 Lit. "groaning together and in labor together."

v. 23 "of the harvest to come": Not in the Greek text; added to make clear the meaning of the term "first fruits." To take the term in a merely cultic sense, as many commentators do, seems perverse. (1) There is nothing in the context to suggest this. On the contrary, Paul is speaking about creation yearning for a completion that is about to come, of something coming to birth that all creation waits for with expectation. Where in the grandeur of this vision could we find any suggestion of the narrow cultic idea of "first fruits"? (2) The cultic idea (ubiquitous across the Middle East) involves something offered to the gods or to God; but here we have a promise or a foretaste given by God to people. (3) The suggestion ignores the purely metaphorical ways in which the New Testament writers use the word: of the first converts in Asia and in Achaia respectively (Rom 16:5, 1 Cor 16:15), and of the Messiah as "the first fruits of those who have died" (1 Cor 15:20, 23). Closest to Paul's idea in Rom 8 is Jas 1:18—"In fulfilment of [the Father's] own purpose he gave us birth by the word of truth, so that we would become a kind of first fruits of his creatures."

v. 26 "in the meantime": The idiom we would use in English; in Greek "moreover in the same way" (looking back to a time-related sentence).

"**pray about ... prays for**": The first of these phrases translates the generic word for prayer, speaking to God; the second that for praying on behalf of someone (also, with the *hyper* broken out, in v. 26b and v. 34). This second of these verbs (*hyperentynchanei/entynchanei hyper*) is normally translated "intercedes." This has not only become a Christian jargon word ("intercessory prayer"), but also restricts the range of meaning. *Hyper* suggests either something done (a) for our good, as in "pray for me," (b) in our place, i.e., pray for me, or (c) as an advocate representing us or testifying for us: pray for me. Which of these does Paul intend? The English "intercede" implies (c), but the context of v. 26 requires (b)—without necessarily excluding the other senses. In v. 34 the same construction is used in sense (c), but, given that Paul is clearly referencing vv. 26–27, the other senses are not far away there either. Hence the "prays for" in the translation, as an attempt to keep that breadth of meaning available.

"**itself**": We must translate the text before us in which the pronoun is neuter (cf. Dunn, *Romans 1–8, in loc*). Paul does not treat the spirit as itself a person, he understands it to be the Spirit of God. God is the personal subject. There is therefore no question of a mere power or influence. The Spirit helps us, the Spirit prays on our behalf: these are personal actions of God, is always understood.

v. 27 "the Spirit prays": To avoid the awkwardness in English of "it prays," which is what the neuter noun would otherwise require. The Spirit Paul refers to is not that of later theology, a separate person within a collective Godhead. A person is indivisible: the spirit of a person is precisely the person themselves, reaching out in encounter with others. Throughout the whole chapter the Spirit Paul speaks of is therefore no more and no less than God himself; here assisting us in our prayer. But how can God pray to God? We can only respond that it is a mystery: that is, something that from our place in space and time we don't yet have the perspective to understand. It is not the only mystery! We have already encountered that of the incarnation of Jesus. How can God become his own creation, dependent upon himself; how can he pray to himself? We have no way of explaining this, all we can do is experience it and testify to it. And then we see that the two mysteries are one: what we are dealing with in this verse is the mystery of the incarnation of the spirit of God in us. The questions then present themselves somewhat differently. How can God's spirit be in us without overwhelming our humanity? How can prayer truly be ours if it is also the spirit of God that is praying? Recognizing that there is more here than we can understand, we can only point to the way in which the incarnation has, from God's side, blurred the line between God and people. In the incarnation God has taken up humanity into himself. As a result we are "in Messiah," part of a new humanity that lives in the power of the resurrection. Our prayer must be ours alone, for prayer is the very essence of being human. But, Paul tells us, while ours it is also the prayer of the spirit of God within us, the prayer of Messiah Jesus, who stands at God's right hand (v. 34).

Somehow, in Jesus Messiah, we have been taken up into the life of God. Paul has already made this clear, of course: we have been welcomed into the family; we are sons and daughters of God; we are heirs of Messiah and fellow-heirs with him. These are not just comforting sayings: he means us to take them seriously. The Spirit of God within us, so far from diminishing our personal initiative and responsibility, is what precisely makes us truly human, just as God's breathing his breath into the *adām* so long ago created us, not an animal in an environment, but a person in a world. We, now, experience the beginning of the fulfillment of the purpose that was implicit in that act so long ago: the completion of humanity; the reason God created the world.

"God's people in God's way": Lit. "according to God for the holy ones." The superb English rendering is gratefully borrowed from NEB.

v. 28: "we have come to see": Perfect tense; Paul is not speaking about abstract trust, but about something that has been proven in experience.

"God works alongside . . . shaping every circumstance for good": Despite its fame (I learned it as a memory verse as a child) the traditional translation "all things work together for good" (still in NRSV) cannot be correct; Paul's strong statement has been replaced by the sentimental truism that (for those who love God) everything will work out for the best. A literal rendition of the Greek might be: "we have come to know moreover that regarding those loving God in absolutely everything he works in partnership for good." *Panta* cannot be the subject: its inflection excludes it as a possible subject of the singular verb. Its placement before the verb is for emphasis (cf. 7:25b for another example of this common practice, the equivalent of, in English, placing something in italics), i.e., "in absolutely everything" (accusative of specification, cf. Acts 20:35, 1 Cor 9:25). As the whole passage is about God's intimate involvement in our lives, it is hard to see why we would be seeking a different subject—and difficult to understand how we could imagine things working alongside us to do anything at all. Is the subject of the verb then the Spirit spoken of in the preceding verse, or the God who is loved (in the participial phrase)? The question is meaningless. For Paul these choices are not mutually exclusive: when he uses the words God and Spirit he is not referring to two things, but to one: the spirit of God, the spirit of Messiah, the spirit of the One who raised Jesus from the dead, that is, precisely God himself. And so he can immediately go on to speak about "those whom he called," and, two verses later, about "God" being for us.

The traditional translation dies hard. The verb must have a personal co-referent, in this case "those who love him"; it cannot be used in the sense of the Spirit working things together, i.e., weaving circumstances towards an outcome (Longenecker, *Epistle to the Romans,* 527–30). Paul is certainly talking about an outcome rather than merely a general goodness, but the word that indicates that is not *synergei* but *eis*; hence, in the translation offered here, "shaping every circumstance for good." The latter phrase has been chosen instead of the bland English "everything" to make clear the link Paul makes between the Spirit's expression of our cries and his practical assistance in the circumstances that give rise to them. For, despite the fact that most translations start a new paragraph here, and some even insert a heading, v. 28 is not the start of something new, as the *de* surely indicates. Rather it is the final statement of a unified block of teaching about the work of the indwelling Spirit of God who in v. 6 is also declared to *stand alongside (synantilambanetai)* believers in their weakness, and whose work in the believer is also described as *hyperentynchanei* and *entynchanei* (26b, 27). This is precisely the "God" who is loved in v. 28: the theme reaches back to vv. 9–13, and Paul's terminology flows unhesitatingly from one to the other alternative term for describing the same reality.

While this is not the only place where a famous saying does not express what Paul actually wrote (12:1 is another, as we will see), hearing what he really says here is important. The traditional translation expresses an abstract and pious principle that is hard to square with the experience of real-life tragedy or disaster. But Paul is not dealing with abstractions or pious principles. He is describing a deeply personal joint venture of the Spirit of God with our spirit, standing alongside us and shaping every aspect of our lives—even our sufferings, 5:3–4—for good.

"Being called": A present participle. God's action is described in the next verse; however, from within our experience God's call is not a once-for-all thing, but a continuing invitation to step forward into life.

v. 30: The verbs here, in contrast, denoting God's action, are all in the aorist tense, denoting a completed action. God knew us long before we knew him—and destined us to become like Jesus. In our personal experience he then called us, declared and empowered us to be righteous, and glorified us. From our point of view some of these things are in the past, some in the present and some in the future. But from God's point of view, this has all been settled from before the dawn of time: we experience in our own lives the outworking of his settled purpose for human beings from the moment of creation.

"Knew beforehand," "destined beforehand," etc. These are non-defining relative clauses, that is, they describe the individuals, not individuals in contrast to others. Paul's whole focus is upon his Christian audience, in assuring them of God's eternal knowledge of them, purpose for them, and high destiny for them. In that context asking how God might deal with others ("does God's calling of some mean he doesn't call others?") merely demonstrates how badly we have missed the point of the passage. (The *hous . . . toutous* in each of the clauses cannot be read as "these, *and only these,*" for the second element in that phrase is alien to the whole discussion. The *toutous* is, rather, an intensifier: "these, precisely these." Compare Jesus' use of a similar idiom in Luke 11:9–10.) This is not to say that concern about the destiny of unbelievers is unnatural or out of place—after all, each of us knows and loves so many of them. Having already hinted at some answers earlier in chapter 2, Paul will turn his whole attention to this matter in the next three chapters—though even there, as we will see, his primary concern is pastoral, and the overriding question is not the destiny of people but whether in the light of unbelief God can be trusted.

"made glorious": Or, startlingly but in line with the usual use of the term, "gave glory," i.e., praised and honored. Cf. vv. 17–18: this is the conclusion of the line of thought begun back there.

17. Isa 6:5. The full title given there is "the King, Yahweh of Armies," the latter being "any group, human or divine, called upon by God to mediate a divine objective, which may or may not be military in nature" (Fretheim in VanGemeren, *NIDOTT* 4:1298).

18. Exod 19, 20. The New Testament, for all its message of grace and of hope, never loses this understanding of God's glory. When the risen Messiah appears to John of Patmos the experience is so overwhelming that "I fell at his feet like a dead man" (Rev 1:17). Calling a suffering community to faith and courage the Hebrews writer reminds his readers of the encounter at Sinai, and assures them that they are faced now by something far more awesome and compelling: "Once more I will shake not only the earth but also the heaven." "Since we are receiving a kingdom that cannot be shaken," he urges them, "let us give thanks, thus offering God true worship, with reverence and awe. For truly our God is a consuming fire" (Heb 12:26–29).

19. The use of the expression in Mark 14 makes it clear that Paul is not using "Abba" in a general

way, as an echo of Jesus' language on all the other times he spoke of God as Father. The Gospels use the Aramaic word nowhere else, as they surely would if it was the word rather than the location of the saying that was important. It is not, either, as if Paul picks up the expression from the oral tradition behind Mark. Rather both Mark's and Paul's accounts reflect something that was already of wider currency within the life of the churches. Mark places the source of the cry in Gethsemane; Paul's quotation of it is therefore as specific a reference to that incident as his use of Jesus' words on that other occasion is to the Last Supper (1 Cor 11:23–25). It shifts the balance. Western theology places all the emphasis upon the cross, which is seen as something transactional. Gethsemane becomes merely a kind of preface. The early church (Heb 5:7, for example) and Eastern Orthodoxy put the crisis in the garden much more in the center, recognizing that the heart of the matter is relational. So then, across the churches, bread and wine, a cry, and a cross: the three summing up the early church's experience of the atonement.

20. This metaphor borrowed from the song "Southland of the Heart" (a contemporary rendition of Matthew 11:28) by Bruce Cockburn, lyrics available from many sources online.

21. The Genesis writer understands this. "Then God said: 'Let us make humankind in our image, beings patterned after our being, so that they may rule over the fish in the sea and the bird in the sky, over the livestock and all the wild animal, and over all the creatures that move along the ground'" (Gen 1:26). Human beings are different from the animals: they are created to be persons, aware of themselves and of God. They are the heirs of creation, sharing God's freedom regarding, authority over, and responsibility for the created world. Note too that this is not the first time in the letter that Paul speaks like this: remember the promise to Abraham that he would "inherit the world" (4:13), and the promise that those who receive God's grace will "rule in life through Jesus the Messiah" (5:17).

22. Passion is the Greek word for suffering.

23. Although at that time he only dimly understood who Jesus was, Peter's remonstrance in Matt 16:21–23 illustrates our instinctive reaction to the idea. Jesus' response is very crisp. We human beings are not in a position to decide what kind of God we have. The thought is preposterous. We are totally dependent upon God to show us the kind of God that he is. "No one has ever seen God; God's only son, the one nearest to the Father's heart, has shown us who he is" (John 1:18). "He is the shining-out of God's glory, the exact imprint of God's very being" (Heb 1:3). There is, these texts declare, no hidden God standing mysteriously somewhere behind Jesus. On the contrary, Jesus is precisely the revelation of God as all that he is.

24. Mark 8:34-37 and parallels.

25. Of course there was active persecution in the early years, and many Christians did indeed meet their deaths in these kinds of ways. What was pathological was the active seeking of martyrdom by some on the crazed fringes of the church.

26. Chapter 5 seems a long way back, but in fact it is only a few minutes reading or listening time in Paul's letter. And as we look back, those first few verses should sound very familiar. Remember that we are dealing with an oral not a written document. The final verses of chapter 4 and the first verses of chapter 5 are the initial heading statement that Paul has been unpacking since then, a movement of thought that comes to completion at 8:39. (With 5:1 compare 8:1–11, 31–39; with 5:2–5 compare 8:18–25, 30. But such an exercise soon spills out to encompass the whole chapter.)

27. 1 Cor 2:2.

28. One of the reasons for this may be the extraordinary way a number of commentators (Dunn, Cranfield, Käsemann, Fitzmeyer) accept without question that the "futility" is imposed upon the world by God as a result of the sin of Adam. Hence it is something only secondarily *permitted* by God rather than, as the text insists, something that was part of his creative *purpose* from the beginning. The whole of Paul's point is thereby sabotaged: the "futility" is seen as a consequence of something far in the past, rather than as a factor built into creation in confident expectation of

a glorious outcome in what is still our future.

Where does this God-diminishing idea come from, so alien to the text as it stands? Chapter 5 shows that Paul is perfectly able to talk in clear language about Adam when he wishes to. If Adam was in view here, why would he use this shrouded and opaque language? But Paul does not invoke Adam at this point. In chapter 5 Paul used the Adam story to shine a light upon Messiah Jesus, and particularly to show that, just as the sinfulness of which Adam is the symbol is universal, so Jesus' faithful obedience has universal power to transform every person. But that point has now been made. Here we have a doctrine of creation, and of futility within it, in which Adam has no explanatory place.

What we have in these commentaries is *eisegesis*: that is, an interpretation of the text not in terms of what it actually says, but in terms of an extraneous doctrine to which we have to make the text conform. But if we are going to understand what Paul is saying we need to read the text on its own terms, not through a distorting lens that comes from some other place. I need to be blunt here. Despite its foundational significance for the church's doctrine from the earliest times, it does not seem to me that the idea of a primal Fall which changes the nature of the created order is a biblical doctrine—not even Rom 5, which we have already looked at in its own place, suggests that. On the other hand, what Paul is saying here *is* a biblical doctrine: here it stands at the center of the most systematic and strategic of all his letters. And it is not just Paul. Consider the symbolic portrayal of the forces of disorder in the book of Revelation. In the great throne room scene in chapter 4, as the great hymn of praise ripples out from the center until all of creation is ringing with it, close to the throne John sees four "living creatures." These represent precisely the living creatures: the wild animals, the domestic animals, human beings, and birds. *But no sea-creatures!* Why not? Because in Old Testament symbology (remember the Hebrews were people of the hills, not the coast), the sea represented the forces of chaos and disorder. Revelation takes up that idea in several places: it is out of the sea that the beast comes, full of blasphemies and evil, making war upon God's people and conquering them (chapter 13). And yet, in that extraordinary depiction of God and his creation in chapter 4, although there is no representative of the sea-creatures to sing praise, still John saw in front of the throne "something like a sea of glass, like crystal." The sea from which later we will see the forces of chaos and disorder spilling out upon the earth is *God's* sea. It is part of his creation, under his gaze and under his authority. Until, that is, in Rev 21 we come to the new heaven and new earth, when John sees that *the sea is no more*.

29. Perfect is a Greek, not a biblical concept; yet Christian thought has often been influenced by it. In Gen 1 God doesn't say that the universe is perfect, he says that it is very good, that is not static but open to growth and development, as is everywhere implied in the creation story. Our hackles should rise every time the word "perfect" crops up in theological discussion. A particularly important place where the Greek concept has insinuated itself, with baneful effect upon generations of earnest Christians, is Matt 5:48, which is often translated "You must be perfect, as your heavenly Father is perfect" and described as "the impossible demand." But the word is *teleios*, having arrived at the goal, complete, full-grown, mature. This is the sense in which it is translated almost everywhere else in the New Testament (e.g., Jas 1:4, Eph 4:13, 1 Cor 2:6, 14:20, Phil 3:15, etc.) Despite this we still persist in translating it as "perfect" when Jesus uses it. It is a holy habit—and a barrier to understanding.

30. The number of possible ways in which the four fundamental constants could be configured is 10^{500}. Considering that the total number of fundamental particles (not atoms and molecules, but the zoo of tiny particles which comprise them) in the visible universe is around 10^{80}, this is a number so vast as to be impossible to conceive. Despite the screen of other arguments surrounding it, multi-universe theory (multiple universes) has been devised exclusively to provide some kind of rationalization of this extraordinary fact within the model of an accidental and random cosmos.

31. The Genesis writer already understood this: "Let the earth bring forth vegetation . . . let the waters bring forth living creatures in all their multitudes . . . let the earth bring forth living

creatures of every kind." We aren't presented with something like a series of engravings from an old-fashioned book, but a tumbling, teeming creation joyfully spreading out to fill the environment. So it is with human beings, too. Within the created world, made to be like him, God commands humans to multiply and fill the earth and subdue it (Gen 1:11, 20, 24, 28). It is the gift of freedom.

32. This should give us great confidence in our individual lives. I remember back in the eighties seeing a T-shirt which read "Have patience, God hasn't finished with me yet." It is a cheerful and somewhat lightweight version of what with intense seriousness Paul is saying here: that a great work of God is in progress, that we are a part of that work, and that its completion is sure because it is grounded in the character of God. It should also give us peace of heart as we live our lives in a tangled and chaotic world. I remember the ebullient Bishop Desmond Tutu saying on one occasion "It's all right! I've read the end of the book! Jesus wins!" It is in the light of that certain outcome that we live our lives in such a world. We live in a world subjected by God to futility in order that something wonderful may come to be. We don't yet see that consummation, but we know it is coming. Jesus is going to win (Col 1:15–20).

33. The key interpretative question is what the harvest is of which the Spirit is the firstfruits. It is true, as Paul says, that as part of creation we too struggle as we "wait for adoption, for our bodies to be set free." But we do so as part of creation. The thought that in his understanding of what the harvest might be Paul would narrow that creation-wide vision down to merely something that will come to completion in our own lives is to slip back into a religious attitude that he has long ago set aside. Such a mindset sees the grace and power of God as something that is for our benefit—rather than something that brings all of creation to completion, and in which we are privileged to share. It is also to give firstfruits a purely internal meaning that is narrower than the ways in which the phrase is used elsewhere in the New Testament (see the references in the notes to the translation, and particularly 1 Cor 15:20–23 and Jas 1:18.)

34. How is that? When God made a world like the one he made, he did an unprecedented thing. He made beings with freedom. We take that for granted. But implicit in that making of free beings is a voluntary limitation upon God's own power. He gave us a part of the moral world where we are able to choose, and free to act. The whole biblical record is testimony to this freedom. This means that God cannot step directly into that human world to enforce his will. To do so would be to destroy it. But when we pray we line up our will with his will. In our full freedom as human beings we invite God to act. Prayer opens a channel for God's grace to work in the world.

35. For a particularly striking testimony to this, see Jackie Pullinger, *Chasing the Dragon*, London: Hodder and Stoughton, 1980, chapters 5 and 15.

36. If the Spirit is the spirit of God himself, how are we to understand the Spirit's *prayer*? How does it make sense for God to pray to God? We can only think of this in the light of a larger mystery: to whom did Jesus pray? How could God become his own creation, become a human being, totally dependent upon God as all human beings are? This is the mystery of incarnation, and what we see in these verses is a reflection of this in our own lives (not too bold a statement, given vv. 14–17). Without diminishing our humanity—in fact completing it—the Spirit of God becomes incarnate within us. When we don't know how to pray he prays through us, taking the finite concerns of human life and bringing them into the light of the infinite life of God. It is a mystery: we can experience it but not explain it.

37. The second law of thermodynamics states that everything in the universe moves from a state of relative order to one of increasing disorder. Life, in contrast, is a different kind of thing from any physical process: it progresses from a state of relative simplicity to increasing complexity. No face-saving fudge about open and closed systems can obscure the fact that in this regard the laws of physics alone are unable to fully describe the real world.

38. *Theologically*, the extraordinary thing in this statement is the direct identification of the Son, Messiah Jesus, with God himself. The God in whose image we were created (Gen 1) is the God whom we see revealed in Jesus. God, Paul is saying, is Jesus-shaped. In Jesus we see the nature

and character of God most perfectly revealed. There is no other, hidden God beyond what we see in him. *Practically*, Paul is talking about something that, despite all our awareness of falling short, is actually happening in our lives. It was a wonder to him: "And all of us . . . seeing the glory of the Lord as though reflected in a mirror, are being transformed into the same image from one degree of glory to another; for this comes from the Lord, the Spirit" (2 Cor 3:8).

39. The verb *kaleo* is very common in the New Testament, and has a range of meanings that is similar to those of "call" in English, namely to *call to particular service* (Rom 1:1, Matt 4:21); to *summon or invite* (Acts 24:2, Matt 22:8–9); and to *name* (Matt 1:21, Rev 19:13). Note (1) that the essential thing in all of these uses is that it is a particular designated individual who is called or invited or named. The call acknowledges or actually bestows a personal name, and (2) that the call in every case implies an answering response, whether to perform an action, or to live a life worthy of the name given.

40. In one of the letters to the seven churches in the first chapters of Revelation the risen Lord says to those who conquer that he will give them "a white stone, and on the white stone written a new name that no one knows except the one who receives it" (Rev 2:17). Although there may have been a contemporary meaning that we have lost, in its purity and permanence the white stone is probably a symbol. But what is important is what is written on the stone: a wonderful thing; a name that only God and the recipient knows. My wife's name is Angela, but I always call her "Angel." Once a friend came around and began to call her Angel too—and it was wrong. Her name is *Angela*. "Angel" is our private name, the name of intimacy and of our long journey together. What the risen Jesus says in this verse is that for each Christian he has a name like that, a name known only to him and to us, a name of intimacy and shared experience. Think about that!

41. **Notes to the translation:**
v. 34 **"was raised"**: Emphasized to capture the sense of Paul's *mellon de*.
v. 35 **"Who will"**: The third of the sequence of *tis* clauses; that Paul retains the "who" (rather than "what") makes clear that the series of abstract nouns that follow are not impersonal: these are sufferings brought about by the ill-will of others.
v. 36 **"we face death every moment"**: See commentary in Knox, *Holy Bible*.
v. 38 **"neither . . . nor"**: What follows here and in v. 39 is a sequence of ten nouns each prefaced by *oute*, a rhythmical sequence that cumulatively is very powerful. This rhetorical intensification is at least as important as the meaning of each individual noun. At the same time the nouns need to be translated into terms that mean something for a twenty-first-century reader; a literal word for word translation is inadequate for this.
"spiritual beings": The word is *angeloi*, angels, but Paul is not referring to an angel as a messenger of God (to think that such a one would separate us from God's love is absurd); rather, he is referencing the popular veneration of semi-divine angelic beings in first century culture (Heb 1:1—2:9, Col 2:18, John 12:29, Acts 23:9), understood to be either threatening or beneficent powers.
"or human oppressors": *arche* can be used of both earthly and supernatural powers. Paul's series of antitheses (life and death, height and depth) suggest that encompassing the extremes is his intention here as well, i.e., "no heavenly power, no earthly one" rather than "no heavenly power whether good or bad" (cf. NIV "angels or demons").
I have omitted Paul's word "powers" which, if it means "supernatural beings" is hard to distinguish from *angeloi* earlier in the verse. Instead I have read the term in relation to the following "height and depth," understanding those terms not as purely spatial references but as the location of potentially threatening powers.
v. 39 **"overwhelm us from above . . . undermine us from below"**: Lit. "neither height nor depth." No one is sure what Paul meant by these terms. Either his first hearers recognized them instantly, or Paul meant simply that nothing "above" or "below" us in either spatial terms (in the terminology of the Gospels, heaven or hell) or metaphorical terms (overwhelming or undermining powers) can do us harm. I have chosen to translate in the second of these senses; it

is, however, important to recognize that in the whole list the exact meaning of individual words is of much less importance than the cumulative effect and overall point: the powerlessness of anything we could name to separate us from God's love.

"in Messiah Jesus": not "that is in" (NIV), which suggests weird ideas about locality. The pronoun is demonstrative: "that love."

42. Rom 1:4.

43. Trinitarian doctrine shifts the focus away from God's act of deliverance in Messiah Jesus to a postulated drama within God's self: a costly choice on God's part (the word "God" now being understood to mean the Father figure) to send the Son figure to act on the Godhead's behalf. Whatever one thinks about the theological validity of this, with regard to our current passage such a scheme renders what Paul is saying forever unintelligible. One symptom of the incoherence to which a Trinitarian interpretation plunges this verse is the suggestion common in the commentaries that Paul is referencing Abraham's sacrifice of Isaac. Three things should be said about this: (1) Paul never elsewhere mentions this story: why he would suddenly without explanation merely *allude* to it here? (2) In Romans Paul has used Abraham as an example of one who lived by faith, especially with regard to the promise of the birth of a son. But then, in order to widen the scope to all humanity, he moves on to the example of Adam, and then on to other things. As examples these figures have served their purpose: to imagine that Paul intends a continuing reference to them as the letter progresses is to sow confusion. (3) But most importantly, if Paul is referencing Abraham here, then he really is teaching that God has a Son. As we have seen, nothing could be further from his mind. God does not have a Son. Rather Jesus Messiah is the Son, God himself entering his world to bring about its liberation and achieve its completion.

44. On the Satan as an externalizing of an aspect of God's sovereignty over both good and evil, compare 2 Sam 24 with the much later retelling of the same story in 1 Chr 21. The classic depiction of the Satan as a member of God's court is in the first two chapters of the book of Job, where the Satan acts as a mechanism to bring Job to the point of utter prostration at which the dramatized exploration of the meaning of suffering can begin. We should note that throughout the rest of the book Job's argument is with God alone; even in the ironically fairytale ending the Satan figure does not reappear. The Satan's role in Zech 3:1–2 is similar. Elsewhere in the Old Testament the word is used in its general sense of an adversary (e.g., 1 Sam 29:4 of David; Num 22:22 of the angel who stood in Balaam's way). New Testament usage reflects the variety of ways in which the concept was understood in the thought of the day, including that of an evil *opponent* of God (something which would be developed in the dualism of later Christian doctrine). The original concept of the Satan as hostile to people yet nonetheless a servant of God is still strong, however, as seen, for example in Matt 4:1, where Jesus is led by the Spirit into the wilderness *in order to* be tested by the devil (aka the Satan, v. 10, Mark 1:13); and Luke 22:31 where Jesus says that "the Satan has begged earnestly to sift you all [i.e., the disciples] like wheat."

In the Old Testament the designation of the Satan as a function was indicated by the article; in Greek of the New Testament, because the article also commonly accompanies proper names, it is less easy grammatically to distinguish between *the* Satan as a function and "Satan" considered as a proper name (as the translational tradition has uniformly interpreted it to be). The difference should not be pressed however, for, just as "Messiah" is not in the first instance a personal name, but a description of the office of the one whom God would send, the name *satan/satanas* is also in the first instance descriptive of a *function,* i.e., it is the nominal form of the Hebrew verb to accuse or oppose. (The Greek synonym *diabolos,* the devil, which occurs the same number of times, has the same etymology.) It could be argued that where it occurs *satan* was retained because it was the (transliterated) word that was actually used in the religious talk of first-century Palestine, while *diabolos* was chosen in at least some of its occurrences, e.g., as we have seen, Matt 4, specifically to avoid the confusion with a proper name. Be that as it may, it is worth considering how our understanding of passages like the following would be increased by recognizing that we are not dealing with a personal name but with a function: "He was in the wilderness for 40 days, tempted by the Satan" (Mark 1:13); "We wanted to come to you but the Satan blocked our way" (1 Thess 2:9); "After he (Judas) received the piece of bread the Satan entered into him" (John 13:27); "We do this so that we may not be outwitted by the Satan" (2 Cor 2:11). And so on.

45. Cf. Jesus, "I saw the Satan fall like lightning from heaven," Luke 10:18. *"The accusing God vanishes"*: how do we reconcile this with the wrath of God that Paul speaks about in chapter 1? We need to remember (1) the rhetorical context of that passage, designed as it is to bring every human being to the terrifying confrontation with the righteous God described in 2:1–5; (2) the way the good news unfolds from that point for every person; (3) the way in which the wrath of God is exhibited there, not in fiery judgment but in God's *giving us up* to what we choose—meaning that we find ourselves in the place that God rejected in his act of creation; (4) the way in which, seen from that place, God can appear only as the judging and rejecting God. God in his grace and power has not changed, only the way we inevitably must encounter him when we choose a path that from the beginning of the world he rejected.

46. We mustn't let the extraordinary nature of this pass us by. The person Paul is speaking about is not some remote spiritual figure but *his own slightly older contemporary*, someone who almost certainly he heard speak on more than one occasion. And without hesitation he proclaims that that same person, incorporating all of humanity in himself, now stands at the right hand of God. Is this not an astonishing thing? McLeod Campbell puts it unforgettably:

> Now, my dear hearers, consider Christ's present place. The man Christ Jesus, our brother, bone of our bone, and flesh of our flesh, is at this moment upon the throne of Almighty God. And observe he is there, not because he is God, for that was his eternal glory. But he is there in his human nature. He is, in his humanity, exalted to that high place. . ..
>
> When you think only of his divinity—when you only think of him as God, it appears no strange thing that God should sit upon his own throne; it appears no great thing to tell us that he who is God sits upon the throne of God. But, when you see that he is there in humanity—when you see human nature there—when you see one in whom you are taught to see your own flesh and blood. . . when you see the particular person who was known upon this earth as Jesus of Nazareth, who was seen going about on the face of it, just like other men, and mingling with them as their brother—when you see him now on the throne of God, this surely is a matter to be searched into with *deep, deep interest*.
>
> It is, on the one hand, a deep and glorious mystery, to see God upon the earth as a man. And, on the other hand it is a deep and glorious mystery to see a man upon the throne of God. Both these things are seen in Jesus Christ. . .
>
> My dear hearers, if you but understood fully. . . what is contained in these doctrines concerning yourselves, then would you see your own salvation in them. For this is our connection with them, that what Christ did he did for us, and that the glory which he now has he has for our benefit: and that in all his humiliation, and in his present exaltation, we are to see him not as one who needed either the one or the other for himself, but as one who has become concerned both with the one and the other for our sakes.

> *Love is of the Essence: an Introduction to the Theology of John McLeod Campbell*, edited by Michael Jinkins, Edinburgh: Saint Andrew Press, 1993, 10–68.

47. "At God's right hand": it is worth reminding ourselves that expressions such as these are purely metaphorical. The same is true (as is the case with all of the symbolism in that book) of the great throne room scene in Revelation 4 and 5. God does not have a right hand, or a throne; the reference is to authority and sovereignty and (especially in the case of the Revelation passage) identity, rather than to anything physical or spatial. The purpose of such imagery, wherever it

occurs, is to tell us something about God, nothing else. The pagans imagined a physical location for their gods within the world, but for Christians questions about physical space and place are meaningless. The classical statement of this is in Solomon's prayer in 1 Kgs 8:27. The metaphor in our current chapter of all of creation groaning in the pains of childbirth is also suggestive. The unborn child knows something of the world outside: it can recognize its mother's voice, and snatches of music or laughter filter through. It can move a little. But how could you describe to it the experience of running down a grassy hillside, towing a kite in the wind? It doesn't have the concepts to even begin to imagine what that might mean. That is our situation too, with regard to our own selves, let alone with regard to God. "We know only in part, and we speak God's word only in part; but when the fulfilment comes, the partial will come to an end" (1 Cor 13:9,10). "Beloved, we are God's children now; what we will be has not yet been revealed. What we do know is this: when he is revealed, we will be like him, for we will see him as he is" (1 John 3:2).

48. For a (on Paul's part reluctant) summary, see 2 Cor 11:23–29, 12:6–10.

49. It is worth mentioning what several people have reported to me, the way in which commitment to the other calls out from us the desire, in order to be faithful to that commitment, to be a better person than we are. Perhaps there is a theological lesson here too: the way in which the love of God experienced no matter how distantly or imperfectly calls out from us the "hunger and thirst after righteousness" that Jesus speaks about in Matt 5:6.

50. *And forever* is not merely a pious phrase. A particularly powerful statement of what it means is in Helmut Thielicke's book *Death and Life* (198–99):

> As a Christian I go down into this death with complete confidence that I cannot remain therein, since I am one whom God has called by name and therefore I shall be called anew on God's day. I am under the protection of the Resurrected One. I am not immortal, but I await my own resurrection. I am one with whom God has begun to speak. God will not break with me in the fellowship he has established nor will he let it be annulled by death. This is the certainty of my conquering death, founded not in me, but in God. . . .
>
> Just as [in justification] I stand with empty hands before God and remain standing, just as I can only beseech God nevertheless to accept me, in just this fashion do I move into my death with empty hands and without any death-proof substance in my soul, but only with my gaze focused on God's hand and with the petition on my lips, "Hand that will last, hold thou me fast!"
>
> In dying I come before God, who holds not only judgement but also life in his hands, and I come with the confidence that I have no need to trust in my good works nor my immortal soul. . . .. I remain in fellowship with him who is Alpha and Omega, and with this knowledge I walk into the night of death, truly the darkest night; yet I know who awaits me in the morning.

51. It is worth reminding ourselves about these titles. *Son of God*: the one (historically the king) in whom God is embodied. *Lord*: the one in whom the community is embodied; of Jesus, the one who sums up and represents humanity in himself. See the more detailed discussion on chapters 1–3 (Son of God) and chapters 4–6, (Lord).

52. It is worth underlining again how astonishing this is. That God could love individuals, in the sense that Paul describes it here, is alien and incomprehensible to every religious tradition. Human religion characteristically seeks to please or to placate the god, while recognizing that the god is too exalted to pay *particular* attention to individuals. Even if it were conceivable, such attention may well be something to be avoided. A god may perhaps show dispassionate interest, even a general benevolence. But *love* in the sense that Paul understands it involves mutual commitment, and such a thing is inconceivable: it is alien to the nature of a god. And the nature of that commitment: that the Creator would step into his world, taking responsibility for it,

living our life and dying our death! (It is interesting to see how, in response to the challenge of Christianity, the love of God is portrayed in Islam, for example here: www.en.islamway.net/article/45779/god-is-love. Islam is in this regard the Israel of chapters 9–11, standing, as we all do, under the indictment of 9:30—10:5, the call to mission in 10:14–17, and the proclamation of grace in 11:30–32.) The truth that Paul declares here is the death of all religion—and the birth of grace.

53. Scholastic theology was very reluctant to ascribe feelings to God. God was, by their definition, impassible, unable to suffer. Feelings make you vulnerable; they open you up to suffering. The Bible writers were far less reticent, freely using human examples as ways of expressing the love of God. "Can a woman forget the baby at her breast, or show no compassion for her own child? Even these may forget, yet I will not forget you" (Isa 49:14). "'When Israel was a child, I loved him, and out of Egypt I called my son" (Hos 11:1). "As the bridegroom rejoices over the bride, so shall your God rejoice over you" (Isa 62:1–5). "And I will take you for my wife forever; I will take you for my wife in righteousness and in justice, in steadfast love, and in mercy. I will take you for my wife in faithfulness; and you shall know the Lord" (Hos 2:19). For similar imagery in the New Testament, see John 3:29, Eph 5:31–32, Rev 19:6–9, 21:1–14.

Appendix 1

The Nature of the Roman Christian Community

We know nothing about the Roman Christian community beyond the information we can deduce from Paul's letter itself. Yet what we can learn from the letter is by no means inconsiderable. Because Paul had never visited Rome in person we don't get the kinds of questions coming from the church itself, or glimpses of its inner life, personalities, and controversies that we do in some of his other letters. But the way Paul frames his letter and shapes his arguments gives us a very clear picture of the kind of community that he understood the Roman church to be. It was a largely gentile community that was deeply rooted in the Old Testament faith of Judaism.[1]

Not more than a handful of its members were *racially* Jews or were circumcised. Beginning at 1:5–6, Paul makes it clear throughout the letter that he understands most of his hearers to be from among the other nations (i.e., not from ethnic Israel). But he also assumes without question the deep understanding of and commitment to the Old Testament faith of those to whom he speaks. He speaks about Jesus as the Messiah, the one promised in the Old Testament Scriptures. He assumes the authority of those Scriptures for his hearers: the letter is stacked with supporting quotations from them. He assumes their familiarity with the promise to King David and the title Son of God; with the Law, the Torah, as a way of life; and with circumcision and the other marks of covenant belonging. How can that be?

It is probable that to a thoughtful observer the Roman Christian community would have appeared indistinguishable from the local synagogue. Converts were baptized, but this was a common rite for gentile converts to Judaism.[2] The shared meal

---

1. I am using "gentile" here in the commonly accepted English meaning of "non-Jewish." In Paul's day of course the word translated as gentile was a collective noun meaning *nation*. It was only rarely used of individuals, or as an adjective, and then in the sense of "someone from another nation." "Judaism" too is a word more appropriate for the period post–AD 70 than for Paul's day; I use it here as a convenient shorthand for "the religion of the Jews."

2. It was of course also familiar within Judaism, as John the Baptist's use of it shows; the Qumran community also had it as a central feature of their ritual.

and the reverence paid to Jesus were unique, but these would not to an observer have appeared markedly different in kind to the revered teachers and special practices of other Jewish denominations. The doctrine of the coming Messiah was well-known to be central to Judaism: the only difference apparent to someone from outside would be that this particular group believed that the promised Messiah had in fact come. Any *Christian* distinctives would have been completely invisible compared to the contrast between the worshipers of the One True God, whether Jewish or Christian, and the paganisms and proliferating mystery religions of the day.

THE OVERLAPPING CIRCLES

Today we are of course used to seeing Christianity and Judaism (alongside Islam, Buddhism, etc.) as *separate religions*, and that reality of our world is all too easily read back into the New Testament. Discussion of Romans 1–3 in the commentaries usually assumes this without question. But this is an anachronism. In Paul's day the two circles of Jew and Christian were not exclusive, but *always overlapped*, and *sometimes overlapped completely*. Jesus himself, of course, and all of the leaders of the early church, including Paul, were Jews. And they never ceased to be so.

But Judaism was also a missionary religion.[3] In Matt 23:15, for example, Jesus speaks of the Pharisees as those who would "cross sea and land to make a single convert." He assumes that the existence of an organized missionary program is familiar to his audience.[4] In John 7:35, upon hearing Jesus speak about the limited time he has with them and that soon they would search for him without success, his audience asks, "Does he intend to go to the Dispersion among the Greeks (that is the non-Jews) and teach the Greeks?" The fact that this possibility comes to mind for some at least among Jesus' listeners indicates that the idea of such a mission is not strange to them. Other religious leaders have left Judea in order to undertake such a ministry. Is that what Jesus is going to do also?

With these passages in mind, it should come as no surprise to hear that the vast crowd assembled in Jerusalem for the first Pentecost after the resurrection included *both Jews and converts* from regions and people groups across the Mediterranean and

---

3. It was only after the formal split between Christian congregation and synagogue—which, in the case of Rome would occur within less than a decade from the date of Paul's letter—that Judaism turned its back upon foreign mission, retreating inwards once again to its identity as an exclusive "chosen people."

4. It is worth noting that Jesus is not denying the validity of the enterprise itself—only the Pharisees' blindness, which produced converts who were "twice as much a child of hell" as they were themselves. We do not know whether what Jesus was referring to was an organized movement. However, it is not hard to see how such activity would have appeared to be the fulfillment of the Old Testament promises such as Ps 87:4–5, Gen 12:3, Mic 4:1–2, and many others. The quietly growing interest from outsiders in the Jewish faith must have suggested to many Jews that the age-old role of Israel as witness of the truth of God to the world was being rediscovered.

APPENDIX 1: THE NATURE OF THE ROMAN CHRISTIAN COMMUNITY

beyond.[5] Contemporary secular sources confirm that all over the Roman world there were significant numbers of people outside the ethnic Jewish community who nonetheless attended synagogue, because they were strongly attracted to the doctrine of the one true God.[6] As with the ethnic Jews who formed the inner circle of the faithful, such people were deeply taught in the Old Testament and instructed in the Jewish religion. While only a small number chose to be formally incorporated into Israel through circumcision, the significance of circumcision and the Sabbath, the food laws and the other marks of covenant belonging must have been well understood, and for many were part of their own religious practice. That variegated crowd present in Jerusalem for Pentecost demonstrates that.[7]

As at Pentecost, across the Mediterranean world it was to this *mixed* community that the word of the gospel first came. The book of Acts describes Paul's missionary strategy. In whatever city he visited he went first of all to the synagogue. There he preached to the assembled company, including "Jews" (i.e., ethnic Jews) and "Greeks" (or "God-worshiping Greeks" as Acts 17:4 has it), i.e., *non-Jewish* converts and fellow travelers.[8] Around every synagogue, as well as members of the ethnic people of Israel, a company of those from outside the formal Jewish community also gathered, coming week by week with equal interest in hearing the teaching of the One True God.[9]

The initial Christian mission was not therefore among what we might call "pure" pagans. It was among those who had already been prepared for the gospel by the Old Testament witness through long association with the synagogue, and it was this group

5. Acts 2:5–13. The word "Jews" in v. 5 is missing from key texts: it seems most probably that "devout men" here included "both Jews and converts" (v. 10, cf. Peter's double address in v. 14).

6. Dunn cites a number of Greek and Roman sources bewailing the growing fashionableness of the Jewish religion, and warning of the dangers that it posed for the established religion of the Empire (Dunn, *Romans 1–8,* xlvi, l). The phenomenon was not limited to the Mediterranean world, as the story of the (presumably racially African) financial controller for the Queen of Ethiopia in Acts 8:26–40 shows.

7. The existence within the religious community of those not ethnically Israel is of course as old as the nation itself. For an example late in its history, see Ps 118:1–4, where the cantor calls first of all to the Israelites (v. 2), and then to the priestly class (v. 3), and then to the wider circle of the "God-fearers," i.e., non-Jewish fellow-travelers within the community (v. 4), in order to evoke from each the response "His steadfast love endures forever!"

8. E.g. Acts 13:5, 16, 26, 43, 48 (note that this is in the congregation, not outside it). See also 14:1, 17:4, 18:4 among many examples. It could almost be said that Paul, the apostle to the gentiles, preached almost exclusively to gentiles who were already part of the penumbra of the synagogue; with Acts 17:16ff one of the few exceptions. Note also, among those appointed alongside Stephen and Philip as the first deacons, "Nicolas of Antioch, a former convert to Judaism" (Acts 6:5).

9. Behind this lies a different organizational conception to the one we are used to, where, for example, a congregation can gather together in a building with no one from outside the group present. With the mystery religions as an exception (and having one of their advertising points in that very circumstance) both individuals and organizations in the ancient world operated in a relentlessly public space. Consider, for example, that even at a dinner attended by Jesus in a private house, a street girl was able to enter and anoint his feet while he was at table (Luke 7:36–50). Organizational meetings of all kinds would regularly attract a penumbra of interested observers, coming for reasons ranging from polite entertainment to keen interest.

which formed the backbone of many of the early churches.[10] Because of successive imperial edicts which forbade Jews from living in the city, it is possible that the Roman community may have been less mixed than those in some of the other Mediterranean cities.[11] But educated in the synagogue many if not most of its members had certainly been: everything in the letter points to this being the case.

In Romans then Paul is writing (1) to a largely non-*racially*-Jewish community, which is however (2) deeply enculturated in the Jewish Scriptures, worship, and religious practice, and for whom therefore (3) the term "Jew" is synonymous with "worshiper of the One True God," i.e., something which they own and strongly identify with. The two circles are distinct *ethnically*, but map onto each other exactly in terms of teaching and of emotional and religious commitment. They are precisely *one* community.

No other model does justice to the evidence of the text. Chapters 9–11 are especially clear. Note in 9:1–5 Paul's pronouns: "*my* people, *my* kindred humanly speaking;" and then "*they* are Israelites . . . to *them* . . . from *them* . . ." Paul identifies himself with ethnic Israel, but assumes that his audience does not. On the other hand he as a Jew identifies with his gentile audience *as a Christian*. "What shall *we* say?" he asks. "*You* will say to me, then . . ." "*Brothers and sisters*, my heart's desire and prayer to God for *them* is that they might be saved."[12] Paul's identification with his gentile audience is maintained in 11:1, *alongside* an affirmation of his own racial heritage in Israel. We see exactly the same pattern in 11:13–14, where Paul specifically addresses the Roman Christians as gentiles—and in the same breath acknowledges Israel as "my

---

10. When, after regular debate in the Corinthian synagogue with "both Jews *and Greeks*," Paul's message is eventually rejected by the Jews (Acts 18:6), he declares his intention to take his message to those traditionally outside the Jewish community. But those to whom he goes are by no means pure pagans: he goes to the house of a non-Jewish God-fearer whose house is right next door to the synagogue (v. 7). From the synagogue itself the presiding official also joins the Christian congregation; and so the mixed-ethnicity, *Old Testament-grounded* church in Corinth is born.

11. There seem to have been two separate expulsions, probably in AD 41 and 49 (see Acts 18:2, and the contemporary sources cited in the commentaries). There has been much discussion about the possible effect of these expulsions upon the Christian community, including the suggestion that Paul's letter was written not for the reasons he himself gives, but to attempt to unify a church divided between its gentile members and returning Jewish Christians who felt disempowered by what had happened within the group during their absence. The resolution of tensions between gentile and ethnic Jewish Christians is thus elevated into a major interpretative paradigm for the whole letter. There is however no hint of such a problem in the text itself—unless we read it in, that is by, for example, seeing chapter 2 as a debate between parties rather than the prophetic confrontation of the whole Roman church that it is in fact. Knowing Paul as we do from other letters, can we believe that he would not address an issue like that directly, even to a church unknown to him? The theory confuses rather than clarifies our understanding of the letter.

12. From 9:1–5 and 11:17ff it is clear that ethnic Israel has rejected the gospel. The Roman church is not the synagogue. However, this clearly does not for Paul alter the close identification of the church with the Old Testament faith. The implication of 11:17–24 is that this gentile congregation is now an integral part of historic Israel, in a way that (in Paul's view, temporarily) unbelieving Israel is not. One is reminded of Paul's closing benediction at the end of his letter to the Galatian church: "peace and mercy be upon them, upon the Israel of God." (Gal 6:16).

APPENDIX 1: THE NATURE OF THE ROMAN CHRISTIAN COMMUNITY

own people." These passages occur in three chapters that contain at least 30 direct quotations from the Old Testament, the Scriptures of the synagogue. It is clear that the Roman church is a gentile Christian community. It is however so deeply steeped in the Old Testament faith that it can be described in 11:17 as being "*grafted into* the rich root of the olive tree" that is Israel. The force of this metaphor should not be lightly dismissed. It provides as clear a description of the nature of the Roman community as could be provided. Ethnically gentile, these are people who have been grafted into the faith of the One True God as declared in the Law and taught in the synagogue. They have a new identity, a new belonging. And now that identity is both confirmed and fulfilled in the coming of Messiah Jesus.

DISTINCTION OR IDENTIFICATION?

With these insights in hand, we can now return to chapter 2, and Paul's sudden challenge, to *this* audience, in *this* letter: "But if you call yourself a Jew, and rely on God, and boast of your relation to God, and know his will . . ." (v.17) How does this kind of address make sense in a letter to an audience most of whom are gentiles? To answer we need to go back to the start of the rhetorical movement that begins at 1:18 and which climaxes in the confrontation of 2:1. Ignoring the crazy placing of the chapter division, it is clear that Paul's prophetic "sting" is addressed directly to the Roman congregation itself. No other audience is possible. To suppose that the "you" in 2:1 is different from the "you" in 1:6–15 is to engage in an extraordinary semantic contortion. Of course it is not the Roman Christians exclusively: "you who judge others, *whoever you are*." But to imagine that Paul suddenly without any signal moves to address a notional "you" which does not include those to whom he is writing is just nonsense.

With his *gentile Christian* audience firmly in his sights, then, Paul goes on immediately to talk about God's impartiality as between "Jew" and "Greek" (2:9). It is important to recognize that the "Jew" in this phrase does not at this point have a primarily ethnic reference. "Jew and Greek" is a global expression for "everybody."[13] In that phrase Paul is using "Jew" as shorthand for the good God-fearing person who knows the Law, in contrast to the "Greek" (also not a racial reference) for those outside the religious community who nonetheless show that the knowledge of God is written on their hearts. The issue is not ethnicity in either case. If it was, then there would be no category within which the Roman Christians could find themselves.

Eye to eye with his audience of racially gentile Christian believers, Paul in 2:14 describes the situation of gentiles who, while not possessing the Law, nonetheless do what it requires. But this is not of course the group with which the Roman church

---

13. A classic misunderstanding of this is to read the summary statement in 3:9 as meaning that what precedes deals with the Greeks (understood as *pagans*) in 1:16–32, and with the Jews (understood as *unbelieving* Jews) in 2:1–3:8, leaving Christians (those who have faith in Christ, whether Paul's audience or ourselves) as a third category somehow excluded from the "all."

Appendix 1: The Nature of the Roman Christian Community

identifies itself, nor does Paul make that identification.[14] They, while racially gentile, *do* in fact possess the Law. If this were not so the prophetic confrontation of 2:1ff would be meaningless. So the Roman Christians are not the *Greeks*, outside the pale of the Law, who nonetheless may possibly do what it requires. Where they must identify themselves in that phrase, and where Paul undoubtedly expects them to identify themselves, is with the term *Jew*. The majority of them are not ethnic Jews. Rather, they are what we might call *theological Israel*: outside the racial boundaries, but nonetheless deeply rooted in and committed to Jewish religion. They have been grafted into the rootstock of Israel and are inheritors of the promises. *It is this same theological rather than ethnic shorthand that continues in 2:17*. Paul's confrontational gaze does not waver. The pronouns are still "you" all the way. Those he addresses in 2:17 are the same as the "you, whoever you are" in 2:1.

This is where our literary (rather than oral/aural) culture and our distance from the historical situation become a problem for us. We come to 2:17 and the word "Jew," and say "aha, this is what he is talking about! He is talking about the Jews, who are different from Christians. Therefore he can't really have been talking to us after all! In all of this he is actually talking to those sad failures, the Jews." And so from then on we ignore the pronouns and the whole thrust of the rhetoric. Flicking back and starting again, we construe the passage from 2:1 as if it was descriptive not of us good Christian religious people, but of somebody else.

The problem with this strategy is that it doesn't work. Within an oral culture such a move was not possible. You couldn't turn back. You couldn't move back and forth within a document. At 2:17 the original audience was still gripped by the relentless flow of Paul's prophetic confrontation. Just as they have recognized that all of chapter 2 up to this point applies directly to them, here too they hear themselves being addressed, this time in the guise of the central owners of the God-fearing religion to which they have been converted. Paul has no other language, no other category with which to address them that would have as much impact or seriousness.

If in any part of this chapter Paul was talking to Jews *in distinction from* Christians he would have needed to clarify that up front. Otherwise what he was saying would have been incoherent to an audience receiving this not as a written but as a spoken message. But in fact, he never makes that distinction at all: on the contrary, he is at pains to emphasize that the spiritual poverty he speaks of is the situation of every individual, including those in the church to which he is writing. It is always "you, whoever you are." In 2:17ff, then, Paul is not addressing *Israelites* in contrast to his *gentile Christian* audience. Rather he is using the term Jew and mentioning circumcision as the key sign of covenant belonging as the *epitome of the good religious person set apart for God, which the Roman Christians know themselves to be*. This is not the language of distinction, it is the language of identification. It is not the language of

---

14. The pronouns alone make this impossible.

ethnicity but of allegiance. This is the aspiration, this is the model, this is the source of the Roman Christians' knowledge of God up to this point.

Deeply rooted in and committed to the truth of the One True God as they had heard it taught as part of the penumbra of the synagogue, the gentile Roman Christians could not have understood the term "Jew" in Paul's phrase as anything other than a term of identification. Not direct *ethnic* identification, of course: Paul makes that clear in chapters 9–11. (But even there, "not all Israel is truly Israel": ethnicity is specifically *not* the central issue.) But it is an identification close enough for Paul to cite the Jewish Scriptures in virtually every line of the letter, an identification so close that Paul can without hesitation in 4:1 refer to Abraham as "our forefather, humanly speaking." No less completely than any modern Christian claims the Old Testament, the Roman Christians understood the Scriptures to be their own: that is, with precisely as little *ethnic* warrant for that, and with as completely real and genuine *spiritual* warrant. When Paul talks about Abraham as "our forefather, humanly speaking" (4:1) the gentile Roman Christians didn't have to think twice about what he meant. The thought of ethnic literalness didn't cross their mind any more than it does ours. Abraham belongs to us all.

And so it is with perfect consistency that Paul can ask in 3:1, "What advantage then does the Jew have?" and then in the very next breath (to a primarily gentile congregation, remember) rephrase the same question: "What then? *Are* we any better off?" (v.9) No more than at 2:17 has he here suddenly started talking to ethnic Jews. "Not at all!" he answers in response to that second question. "For we have already charged that both Jews and Greeks are under the power of sin." Now, some of the Roman congregation may have been literally ethnic Greeks. But not a one of them would have seen themselves in the second of Paul's categories here. For these are not ethnic but religious categories.[15] What Paul is saying is that both *religious* and *non-religious* people, both those inside the faithful community and those outside it, are under the power of sin and therefore under God's judgment—and, astonishingly, also under his mercy and his grace.

GO THE ALL BLACKS!

Where might we look for an example to illustrate this? In my country people sometimes joke that the national religion is rugby football, a very fluid and exciting running and passing game. Top players are royalty: people hang on their words, and take their advice in buying products of every description. Small boys grow up with dreams

---

15. This usage is not exclusively Pauline. "Greek" is used in the New Testament by more than one other writer as shorthand for "pagan": Mark 7:26, John 7:35, Acts 11:20, 19:10,17, 21:28, etc. Within the native American communities of the Pacific Northwest in the mid-nineteenth century, the white settlers were known as "Bostons," no matter what city or district—or indeed other country—they came from. The term "Greek" functioned in a similar way among the Jewish communities of Paul's world.

of someday becoming an All Black, a member of the national team. So maybe we can imagine the coach of a high school rugby team talking to the boys about the need to submit to the discipline of training, and eating properly and getting enough rest between key games. In that situation he might say, "You have to think rugby all the time. An All Black doesn't stoke up on hamburgers, he eats properly. An All Black keeps up his training throughout the week. An All Black doesn't get drunk the night before the big game and arrive on the field with a hangover!" The coach is not giving his team the negative example of despised *soccer* or *basketball* players and how poor they are at discipline and keeping fit. No, he is speaking to them directly: not literally, but in the language of their aspiration. This is what Paul is doing in these chapters.[16]

We see this confirmed as we move on through chapter 3. For Paul (as for God himself, 2:9–10!) there is no distinction: he includes himself alongside his gentile audience everywhere. Notice the inclusive pronouns in in 3:5, 7, and 9—and consistently all the way through to 4:23–25. Or do those latter verses not apply to us? There is no indication anywhere that Paul shifts his focus from the one set of addressees, among whom he includes himself, to someone else. The one exception is 3:3, where he speaks about "some" others who have been unfaithful. It is at *that single point* that he is speaking about others: he will not include his Roman audience in the category of the unfaithful. But then immediately he returns in v. 5 to the second person plural pronoun. Paul never allows us to drift off into contemplation of the situation of some theoretical "others." It is always we who are face to face with the challenge of the living God. And is this not what we would expect from a prophet and from the word of God?

LEARNING TO LISTEN

Where does the idea come from then, repeated in virtually every commentary, that somewhere in these chapters (at 2:17, or even at 2:1!) Paul steps away from addressing his audience, and starts an imaginary dialogue with a postulated unbelieving Jew?

---

16. Another modern illustration might be the way in which a new immigrant to a country, while still having only the status of a permanent resident, is addressed in the terminology appropriate to a citizen. But the prime example is the way in which we Christians everywhere appropriate the Old Testament and read it as our own. We don't come to it to learn about the religion of someone else. In the God of Israel we recognize the one whom Jesus taught us to call Father, and in Israel's journeying with that God we recognize our own mistakes and disbelief and obedience and glory. When we read "Hear, O Israel, the Lord our God, the Lord is one; you shall love the Lord your God with all your heart and with all your soul and with all your mind, and with all your strength," we as Christians take that to ourselves, despite the fact that Jesus is quoting something addressed quite specifically to Israel as the people of God. When we read in Isaiah 40 "Comfort, O comfort my people, says your God!" we read on through those wonderful chapters, hearing the promises as spoken to us, taking heed of the warnings as addressed to us, knowing the grace and faithfulness of God spoken into our own lives—all of this despite the fact that the prophecy is addressed to Jerusalem, and to God's historical people in exile. Nothing in the way in which Paul addresses the Roman Christians in these three chapters is different from this common fact of our experience in reading the Bible.

Appendix 1: The Nature of the Roman Christian Community

To some extent the problem is one of genre recognition, of understanding different modes of speech. We need to remember that Paul is using the language not of academic precision but of rhetorical impact. There is a potential trap here for those of us who read academic articles and have shelves full of commentaries. Paul is an intellectual but he is not an academic. He is a preacher and an effective rhetorician; he knows how to capture an audience and draw them with him; he knows how to lure us, and involve us, and confront and challenge and excite. The mechanisms and categories of such discourse are very different from that of the biblical commentaries that are so often the sources to which we as preachers go to for information about the meaning of these powerful texts. While the commentaries are essential for detailed information, their very nature tends towards the consideration of individual trees rather than the forest. Those of us who are teachers in the church need to wrestle with the large structures, to listen with the ears of a preacher, and to foster our sensitivity to the originally oral nature of the material. We need to get out more.

I suggest that four factors contribute to the common misunderstanding of these chapters:

1. Failure to identify 1:18–2:5 as a prophetic confrontation of the Roman Christians themselves. The chapter division could not be more strategically placed to destroy Paul's argument in that section, and to throw our understanding of the whole first three chapters into confusion. Compounding this is the culture of specialization within biblical studies. New Testament scholars tend to be classically trained and steeped in the culture of the Graeco-Roman world of the first century. As a consequence precedents for Paul's rhetorical techniques are sought from first-century sources (the Stoics, Epictetus, etc.) rather than from the Old Testament prophetic tradition in which Paul had actually been trained. We have forgotten how to identify prophetic speech.

2. As suggested earlier in the paper, an anachronistic reading of the relationship between church and synagogue at the time Paul was writing, that sees contrast and opposition where there was in fact identification and ownership.

3. A literary rather than an oral/aural reading of the passage, which allows those of us brought up in a literary culture to pause and turn back and reformat our thinking about an earlier section in the light of something in the text that, when the specific cultural situation of the Roman church has been forgotten, appears inexplicable. This was not possible in Paul's oral/aural world. The necessary signals that he is moving into a new style of discussion (an imaginary dialogue!) are simply missing.

4. A diminished capacity to "hear" the text as Scripture. How could we ever suppose that a man like Paul would allow us to sit back while he in some oblique way (through the device of an "interlocutor" or "dialogue partner") exposed the hypocrisy and failures of Judaism, for our edification and self-congratulation?

Appendix 1: The Nature of the Roman Christian Community

When were the addressees of any Old Testament prophetic book, Gospel, or New Testament letter ever allowed to simply observe as disinterested onlookers? How could we imagine that this would be the case here?

This is not a minor issue. Our misreading of these chapters has fundamental significance for our understanding of Paul's letter as a whole. Reading them as we tend to do puts us on the wrong foot immediately, and results in a completely different kind of Romans. Much is at stake.

Appendix 2

Romans 5:1
"We Have or "Let Us Have" Peace with God

A CALL TO LIVE is what these first verses of chapter 5 certainly are—not that you would realize that from any of our standard English versions.[1] This is another of those curious translational oddities that we've noticed before. Every commentary agrees that in the best text of these verses Paul is urging us *to have* peace with God, *to rejoice* in our hope of sharing the glory of God, and *to rejoice* in our sufferings. And then in the very next breath virtually all of the very same commentaries insist that he cannot be doing so. "Although *let us have* is supported by the greater weight of manuscript evidence . . . on grounds of intrinsic probability *we have* is what Paul must have intended," runs one typical comment. What he must have *intended*? Hello?

I suggest that, having journeyed as far as we have with Paul in his letter, ordinary thoughtful readers are as well-equipped as anybody to gauge from the context what, on the grounds of intrinsic probability, Paul must have intended. What do we find in the immediate context? We find that in the previous three verses (the last three verses of our chapter 4) Paul is at pains to point out to us that the story of Abraham is not merely for our abstract interest but is *an example for us to follow*. We look on to the coming three chapters where we are called to *forsake sin*, to *seize obedience*, to *suffer and pray and rejoice*. All of this is passionate and full-hearted exhortation. How then could we imagine that Paul might pause here in these first verses of chapter 5 merely to offer us a list of theological facts, however wonderful those facts might be? We've been given back our sight: the world suddenly springs into rich three-dimensional life. Is it likely that Paul would keep us standing on the edge of the pavement while he tells us about the brain science that explains what has happened to us? Isn't it rather that he is calling us to step out with him into this new world, as wonderful new perspectives

---

1. Exceptions are the 1881 Revised Version and the New English Bible.

open around us on every side? Don't we know Paul well enough now to be absolutely certain that he is calling us to do the latter?

Very few translations are brave enough to go with what Sanday and Headlam describe as "overwhelming textual authority" for *let us*.[2] The English Revised Version of 1881 did so. As did the New English Bible—though its later revision, the Revised English Bible, reverted to tradition. Of the older commentators, both Luther and Calvin read *let us*; as among the moderns do R. C. H. Lenski, William Barclay (in his Daily Study Bible), and C. H. Dodd. Two notable contemporary voices are Robert Jewett (Hermenia, 2007) and Richard Longenecker (NIGTC, 2016).

How do those who prefer *we have* explain their preference for the much less authoritative textual reading? Bruce Metzger explains why the majority of the United Bible Societies' translation committee came to their decision:

Although the subjunctive *exōmen* ['let us have'] . . . has far better external support than the indicative *exomen* ['we have'] . . . a majority of the Committee judged that internal evidence must here take precedence. Since in this passage it appears that Paul is not exhorting but stating facts ("peace" is the possession of those who have been justified), only the indicative is consonant with the apostle's argument. Since the difference in pronunciation between them in the Hellenistic age was almost nonexistent, when Paul dictated *exomen*, Tertius, his amanuensis (16:22), may have written down *exōmen*.[3]

One can't but smile at the suggestion that the "error" might have been there *in the original manuscript*, because Tertius somehow misheard Paul say the word *exōmen* (with a long vowel) when really what he had said—as we 2,000 years later are very sure he must have done—was *exomen* (with a short vowel). Perhaps he had been up too late the night before, and wasn't concentrating?

I suggest that this is a classic example of the reason why we need to "unplug": because here, as so often with Romans, pre-judgments are driving the way the text is read. The Committee *already knows* the kind of thing that Paul's letter is. They *already know* what Paul is intending to say, and therefore are confident about the actual, specific words that he must have used to say it, even when all the principles of textual criticism suggest otherwise. I am sure such a judgment is well meant. Nonetheless, it is a failure of the translator's specific responsibility. For how can we ordinary Christians ever hope to know what Paul is really saying, if our the translators of our basic English texts abandon the best textual tradition for a less reliable one?[4]

---

2. Sanday and Headlam, *Epistle to the Romans*, 120.

3. Metzger, *Textual Commentary*, 511.

4. I do not want to suggest that textual criticism is a simple matter, nor that theological judgments may not from time to time be both appropriate and necessary as an aid to establishing the best text. I do want to strongly assert that such judgments should, within the discipline of textual studies, be used with the utmost caution, perhaps even as a last resort for the resolution of an otherwise insoluble difficulty. Such is certainly not the case with the text before us.

Appendix 2: Romans 5:1

That other reading ("we have") is, however, there in many texts, including one or two quite early ones. How could that have come about? I think there is an answer to this. In the introduction to this book we considered the difference between Paul's world, where communication was primarily *oral* with writing down as a secondary thing, and our world, where even oral presentations (lectures, news bulletins, sermons) are first of all *written* and only later orally delivered. In this confusion between two forms of a word I believe that what we see is a misreading of a *primarily oral* textual tradition by a *primarily literary* culture.

You are reading the paragraphs on this page as *a written thing*. But if you could beam yourself back into Paul's world that would not be the case. Instead (provided of course you were one of the minority that could read) you would instead be reading *a spoken thing written down*—in fact even if you were alone you would actually be speaking it out aloud, for no one for many centuries after Paul ever read anything silently. The distinction is important. Writing in Paul's world was always *transcription of speech*. In those days no one wrote a letter; no one wrote a book. They *spoke* a letter, they *dictated* a book, and an amanuensis, a scribe, wrote it down for them. And what the scribe wrote down was quite specifically *what was heard*. The words inked onto the page had to capture not just the words, but all the cues that signal meaning in a spoken utterance.

In our sophisticated literary culture we have many written cues that weren't available to Tertius: punctuation marks like full stops and commas to indicate pauses, and question and exclamation marks to indicate tone of voice, and whether something was a question or a statement. What Tertius did have, though, was something that is much less common in our language: *the shape of the word itself.* And this could be very economical. An English translation will always contain more words than a Greek text because we need many more individual words to convey information that in Greek is coded into the shape of the words themselves.

Which brings us to the question of whether Tertius perhaps misheard what Paul said, and put down one word rather than another one. And immediately we see how impossible that is—unless Tertius was a very poor scribe indeed. For what is at issue is not which of two words Tertius used, but the *form* of *one* word. The long vowel form ("let us have") is precisely *a written representation of the way in which the word is sounded orally*, i.e., with the intonation that signals that this is an exhortation rather than a statement.[5] The long or short vowels operate in precisely the same way that a question or an exclamation mark in English does, in signaling the tone of voice which would be necessary for someone reading aloud to convey to a reader that a particular phrase was a statement or a question or an exclamation.

Now Metzger's suggestion that "the difference in pronunciation (between *o* and ō) in the Hellenistic age was almost non-existent" may be true, although in the

---

5. I think this can be argued for all senses of the subjunctive, within their context in a longer grammatical unit, not just the hortatory.

absence of a tape recording or a native speaker this must necessarily be a deduction made purely on the basis of written texts. But it is beside the point in this situation. Is Metzger suggesting that people of the period had regular difficulty distinguishing between a statement and an exhortation? For what is at issue is not the precise tonal value of an individual vowel, but the ability of a scribe, by choosing one written form of a word over another, to represent the whole complex of signals that enables us to distinguish the mood and intention of a spoken statement.

If we imagine from our own heavily literary perspective that it was Paul's intention to include a particular *written word* in his letter, then we may be able to entertain the possibility of an amanuensis mis-hearing Paul's vocalization of that word. But if on the other hand we understand the *spoken* form to be primary (Paul is in the first instance speaking to people, not "writing" to them), we will recognize in precisely such cues as the use of the subjunctive a transcription not only of the bare words, but also of the tonal context which governs them. On this understanding the idea that Tertius somehow "got it wrong" is just nonsensical. Would a twenty-first-century secretary taking dictation, even one suffering from a hangover, fail to put a question mark at the end of a question?

The shift from a primarily oral to a primarily written culture is the explanation, I believe, of the minority textual tradition of the indicative ("we have"). When, as the years went by (and even our best texts are not originals, but copies of copies of copies) the letter became understood primarily as a *written* text by people whose business was dealing with written texts, it is easy to see how reading the word as an indicative (i.e., as a statement) might seem in the context more appropriate to a copyist than reading as a subjunctive (i.e., as an exhortation). It is understandable too—if rather sad given the principles of textual criticism—that commentators coming from our heavily literary culture might also tend to confirm the misunderstanding that appears in the minority texts. We have forgotten how to listen to a text rather than just to read it. It is noteworthy that the testimony of the majority of the Greek fathers is to the subjunctive.

This is not the only example of this kind of thing. A similar confusion arises in 1 Cor 15:49, where most translations choose to translate a clear subjunctive as a future ("we *shall also* bear the image of . . . " instead of "let us also bear the image of . . . ").[6] In cases like this the footnotes that appear in biblical translations suggesting that "*some* ancient texts read *let us*" are less than honest when in fact the overwhelming textual evidence is for the subjunctive. The result of decisions like this is to flatten and intellectualize the text: we find ourselves contemplating systems of ideas rather than stepping out into a life to be lived. The common argument that Paul can't in these verses be exhorting us to enter into the possession of something that is already ours is unimaginative in the extreme. A passage such as 2 Cor 5:20 gives the immediate lie to it. "We beg you on behalf of Christ," Paul exhorts the believers at Corinth, "be

---

6. On this passage see Fee, *First Epistle to the Corinthians*, 794–95.

APPENDIX 2: ROMANS 5:1

reconciled to God" (verb in the subjunctive). All translations render the text correctly here. But are the Corinthians not already reconciled to God? Of course they are (v. 18, 19)! But Paul is exhorting them to *take possession* of that reconciliation; to walk on through the door that has been opened for them, to *live as reconciled people*. This is precisely what he is urging upon the Roman church in 5:1–6.

A final example from elsewhere in the New Testament is Hebrews 10:22–24, where we get almost precisely the same structure as in Romans 5:1–6: "*Having therefore . . . confidence to enter the holy place in the blood of Jesus*" the Hebrews writer begins, " . . . *let us* approach with a true heart . . . *let us hold* fast the confession of our faith . . . and *let us* stir up each other to love and good works . . . " The Hebrews writer's identity is unknown, but the sequence of a participle followed by three verbs in the subjunctive matches both the structure and the tone of Romans 5 exactly.

Returning then to Romans 5, the subjunctive form of the verb ("let us have") as it stands in the best texts, is in fact *the closest we will get to a tape recording of the tone in which Paul spoke*. It makes it clear that in this passage Paul is not merely stating wonderful truths, but urging us to practically seize hold of a life the possibilities of which have been totally transformed by what Christ has done.

Appendix 3

Adam and the Creation Story (Romans 5)

THERE IS AN IMPORTANT truth to consider here about the nature of the Bible. The whole of Genesis, for example, is not about the individual people it describes. It is about God. None of the characters are heroes—far from it. The hero of the story, the central character upon whom all interest is focused, is God. The Adam story therefore (the story of *the adam*) is not about Adam, it is about God, and how he relates to us, and how we relate to him. The historicity or otherwise of an "Adam" is an irrelevance, it is the wrong question. The real question is, who is God?

Paul knew all this through his reading of the creation account in Genesis, the title of that book itself proclaiming that it was the story of the Beginning. And within his world he could not but take seriously the genealogies which linked the beginning stories of chapters 1–11 with the account of the call of Abraham, and then linked that to the record of Abraham's descendants, right down to his present day. Those genealogies, although they differed in details (compare, for example, the two lists of the ancestors of Jesus given in Matthew's and Luke's Gospels) suggested that Abraham, of whom Paul has been writing in chapter 4, appeared in the history somewhere around 20 generations from the first creation of human beings upon the earth. From Abraham (according to Matthew's carefully symmetrical reckoning) there were then fourteen generations to Israel's great King David, a further fourteen generations to the disaster of the exile, and from the exile fourteen generations to the Messiah. This was the chronology of Paul's biblical world.

We now know, without a shadow of a doubt, that while the *theology* is correct, the *historical details* are not. The way that sentence is phrased should not obscure which of these two factors is the most important! But let's consider the one that is of lesser importance for a moment.

Dates were not a central concern of the biblical scholars of Paul's day. But if they were, and if they had ever thought to count up the generations, the best estimate for the original creation of human beings that Genesis could provide would have been around 6,000 years before Jesus. That the actual appearance of human beings on the earth was so much further in the past—and that the earth itself had existed for three billions of years before human beings walked upon it at all, was something that would have been totally inconceivable to anyone in Paul's generation. There was not the conceptual framework to even begin to understand something like that. (Come to think of it, do we understand it, really? It is easy to feel smug about knowing facts that earlier generations did not. But does our imagination really grasp that huge span of years, to think and to wonder?)

Recognising the authority of the Bible does not require us to mentally squeeze ourselves into the necessarily limited view of the physical world that its writers had. To insist on doing so would be to dishonor the Creator who is the subject of Genesis itself. He made us in his image as curious and thinking beings, and, as Psalm 19 tells us so vividly, alongside his written word spreads out the Word of his physical creation for us to explore and delight in. Jesus reminds us that we are called to worship God with all of our heart and all of our soul and all of our *mind* and all of our strength.[1] This means that with regard to knowledge about the physical stuff of the world, its history and its place in the universe we must live in our own time, not that of Paul, or even that of the Genesis writer long before him. It was God himself who gave human beings authority over the world to understand and control it, and the knowledge we have of these things comes to us because of our obedience to that commission.

About this matter of detail, then, we know more than Paul did. What difference does this make to the way we read this text in the twenty-first century? Well, in one sense, it makes no difference at all. We know that the Bible is not intended to be a magic book, some kind of encyclopedia of everything, a supernatural document in which all the secrets of the universe are locked away somewhere. Its real function is different and of much greater importance. We find little in it to satisfy our ordinary curiosity. Instead we find ourselves personally gripped and confronted. The Bible's record of the encounter that the people of the past had with the living God plunges us into that very same encounter. We find *ourselves* named and known, *we* are judged and liberated, *we* are addressed as people who are responsible before God, *we* are called to follow. The Bible's prose and poetry, history and song, saga and proverb and prophecy, written by many writers over hundreds of years is Scripture because through it the church still hears the voice of the living God, the creator, the lord of history and of our individual lives. The Bible is not meant to teach us science or history or cosmology. It is meant to open our ear to his voice, and our hearts to obedience.

We are therefore no more bound to think of Adam as a literal historical figure[2] than we are to see the earth as the first chapter of Genesis depicts it. There, once again

---

1. Mark 12:30.

2. It is worth noting that some thinkers who accept the facts I have noted about the emergence of human beings on the earth still propose that two among those first *homo sapiens* must have been specially touched by God and made responsive and responsible beings in a way that they had not been

Appendix 3: Adam and the Creation Story (Romans 5)

in what for its time was absolutely cutting-edge thinking, the earth is seen as a vast flat disk lidded over by the huge bowl of the sky (the "firmament"). This bowl holds in place the sun, moon, and stars, and also separates the earthly seas and rivers from the reservoirs of the sky (the "waters above the earth") from which the rain falls. It is a magnificent vision—and, we now know, wrong in virtually every detail. How could it have been otherwise in that age of the world? But the account was never intended to teach us geography or astronomy. Its real purpose is to teach us about God and his relationship to the world.

The cultures among whom this account was written, the peoples who surrounded Israel on every side, saw the earth as a mysterious place, charged with dangerous spiritual forces, and subject to the whims of inscrutable and terrifying gods. The message of the creation story blows away such an understanding. It dethrones the pagan gods, and disempowers the spirits that were thought to inhere in sacred places or particular animals or birds. It removes the possibility of worship from the sun and the moon (thought to be sacred by many nations, but in Genesis 1 not even named!) The power of the fertility of the earth is not to be worshiped either: the gift of growth and reproduction belongs to the Creator God.

Thus the world is stripped of its spiritual power; it becomes a *creation*. The living things lose their totemic influence and become merely *creatures*. The world is demythologized. But once that understanding is in place it is immediately lit up with power of a different kind and with joy. For this is not a *mere* thing, it is a world called into being by the One True God. The Spirit of the Lord of time and of space himself breathes upon the primordial chaos to bring earth into being, and calls forth from it creatures in all their forms to flourish there. Neither the world nor any part of it is to be worshiped: it is a creation. But, Genesis tells us, the creation has a Creator, and to know him is the secret of life.

And human beings are also a part of this creation. Human beings are not divine, but at the same time we are quite different from the rest of creation. While the earth and the water and the sky are called to *bring forth* the birds and animals and the fish in their multitudes, human beings are *created in God's image,* capable of response and of responsibility. They are themselves addressed, and blessed, and commissioned, and given authority as regents to rule over and to care for the wider creation.

---

before—and that they thus became the ancestors of all modern human beings. This goes way beyond what we can ever know. As a theory it seems biologically improbable (what happened to the descendants of all the other early humans?); however a more fundamental point is that it is based upon a confusion of genres both *within the Bible* (the Beginning-story being treated as in some way historical), and also upon inconsistency of interpretation *within the story itself* (some aspects of the Genesis 3 account being correctly understood as story, while others are treated as historical or semi-historical.) That Paul also treats this story as history is no excuse for us to be blind to the strong internal evidence that it is something else. Paul does not have the knowledge of humanity's long pre-history with which to operate, but we do, and we must be consistent. We don't need to rescue Paul. And trying to "save the appearances" of biblical authority in the Genesis accounts only reveals our own uncertainty about that very thing. God is perfectly able to authenticate his own Scriptures, and he does.

Bibliography

GENERAL NOTE

THE MOST SENSIBLE DISCUSSION of **the challenges English readers have in understanding Paul's letters** that I know is found in "An Essay for the Understanding of St. Paul's Epistles, by Consulting Paul Himself," the preface to John Locke's *A Paraphrase and Notes on the Epistles of St. Paul to the Galatians, Corinthians, Romans, Ephesians*. Originally published London, 1707, and available online here: *https://books.google.com/books?id=1wRaAAAAIAAJ*.

On the challenge of **hearing Paul's message as a living word in the contemporary world**, see the successive prefaces to Karl Barth's *The Epistle to the Romans*, translated by Edwyn Hoskyns, Oxford, 1933. **Individual journal articles** are too numerous to mention: those interested in exploring scholarly discussion of individual passages and issues should consult the bibliographies in Dunn, Fitzmeyer, and Longenecker.

Augustine. *Propositions from the Epistle to the Romans & Unfinished Commentary on the Epistle to the Romans.* Translated by Paula Fredriksen Landes. Riga, Latvia: Scholars, 1982.
Barrett, C. K. *The Epistle to the Romans, Revised.* Black's New Testament Commentary. Peabody, MA: Hendrickson, 1991.
Bartchy, S. S. "Slavery." In *The International Standard Bible Encyclopedia*, edited by Geoffrey W. Bromiley et al., 539–46. Grand Rapids: Eerdmans, 1986.
Barth, Karl. *Dogmatics in Outline.* London: SCM, 1949.
———. *The Epistle to the Romans,* 6th edition. Translated by Edwyn C. Hoskyns. Oxford: Oxford University Press, 1968.
———. *A Shorter Commentary on Romans.* Translated by D. H. van Daalen. London: SCM, 1959.
Brown, Colin, ed. *New International Dictionary of the New Testament.* Grand Rapids: Zondervan, 1975.
Bruner, Frederick Dale. *The Christbook: Matthew 1–12.* Grand Rapids: Eerdmans, 2004.
Calvin, John. *The Epistles of Paul the Apostle to the Romans and to the Thessalonians.* Translated by Ross Mackenzie. Edinburgh: Oliver & Boyd, 1960.
Bultmann, R. *Theology of the New Testament.* 2 vols. New York: Scribner's, 1955.

BIBLIOGRAPHY

Campbell, Douglas A. "The Crisis of Faith in Modern New Testament Scholarship." In *Religious Studies in Dialogue: Essays in Honour of A.C. Moore*, 163–74. Otago: University of Otago Press, 1991.

———. "False Presuppositions in the ΠΙΣΤΙΣ ΧΡΙΣΤΟΥ Debate: A Response to Brian Dodd." *Journal of Biblical Literature* 116 (1997) 713–19.

———. "Romans 1:17—A *Crux Interpretum* for the ΠΙΣΤΙΣ ΧΡΙΣΤΟΥ Debate." *Journal of Biblical Literature* 113 (1994) 265–85.

Cranfield, C. E. B. *A Critical and Exegetical Commentary on the Epistle to the Romans*. 2 vols. Edinburgh: T. & T. Clark, 1975 and 1979.

Dawkins, Richard. *The Selfish Gene*. Oxford: Oxford University Press, 1976.

Dillard, Annie. *Teaching a Stone to Talk*. London: Picador, 1984.

Dodd, C. H. *The Epistle of Paul to the Romans*. New York: Harper Collins, 1963.

Donfried, Karl P., ed. *The Romans Debate, Revised and Expanded Edition*. Peabody, MA: Hendrickson, 1991.

Dunn, J. D. G. *Romans 1–8*. Word Biblical Commentary 38A. Dallas: Word, 1998.

———. *Romans 9–16*. Word Biblical Commentary 38B. Dallas: Word, 1998.

Fee, Gordon D. *The First Epistle to the Corinthians*. New International Commentary on the New Testament. Grand Rapids: Eerdmans, 1987.

Fitzmeyer, Joseph A. *Romans: A New Translation with Introduction and Commentary*. The Anchor Bible. New York: Doubleday, 1993.

Gaventa, Beverley Roberts, ed. *Apocalyptic Paul: Cosmos and Anthropos in Romans 5–8*. Waco, TX: Baylor, 2013.

Godet, F. *Commentary on St Paul's Epistle to the Romans*. 2 vols. Translated by A. Cusin. Edinburgh: T. & T. Clark, 1986.

Goppelt, Leonard. *Typos, the Typological Interpretation of the Old Testament in the New*. Grand Rapids: Eerdmans, 1982.

Hay, David M., and E. Elizabeth Johnson, eds. *Pauline Theology, Volume III: Romans*. Minneapolis: Fortress, 1995.

Hays, Richard B. *The Faith of Jesus Christ: An Investigation of the Narrative Substructure of Galatians 3:1–4:11*. Grand Rapids: Eerdmans, 2002.

Hebert, Gabriel. "'Faithfulness' and 'Faith.'" *Theology* 57 (1955) 373–79.

Howard, George. "The Faith of Christ." *Expository Times* 85 (1974) 212–15.

Jowett, Robert. *Romans: A Commentary*. Hermeneia. Minneapolis: Fortress, 2007.

Käsemann, Ernst. *Commentary on Romans*. Translated and edited by G. W. Bromiley. Grand Rapids: Eerdmans, 1980.

Kelly, J. N. D. *Early Christian Doctrines*. 5th ed. London: A. & C. Black, 1977.

Kierkegaard, Soren. *The Last Years: Journals 1853–55*. London: Fontana, 1965.

Kittel, Gerhard, ed. *Theological Dictionary of the New Testament*. Grand Rapids: Eerdmans, 1964.

Knox, Ronald. *The Holy Bible: A Translation from the Latin Vulgate*. London: Burns and Oates, 1950.

Leenhardt, Franz J. *The Epistle to the Romans*. Translated by H. Knight. London: Lutterworth, 1961.

Lenski, R. C. H. *The Interpretation of St Paul's Epistle to the Romans*. Minneapolis: Augsburg, 1961.

Longenecker, Bruce. "ΠΙΣΤΙΣ in Romans 3:25: Neglected Evidence for the Faithfulness of Christ?" *New Testament Studies* 39 (1993) 478–80.

Bibliography

Longenecker, Richard N. *The Epistle to the Romans.* New International Greek Testament Commentary. Grand Rapids: Eerdmans, 2016.

Luther, Martin. *Lectures on Romans.* Louisville: Westminster John Knox, 1961.

Metzger, Bruce. *Textual Commentary on the Greek New Testament.* London: United Bible Societies, 1971.

Moo, Douglas. *The Epistle to the Romans.* New International Greek Testament Commentary. Grand Rapids: Eerdmans, 1996.

Nygren, Anders. *Commentary on Romans.* Translated by Carl C. Rasmussen. London: SCM, 1952.

Robinson, John A. T. *Wrestling with Romans.* London: SCM, 1979.

Ruse, Michael, and Edward O. Wilson. "Moral Philosophy as Applied Science." *Philosophy* 61 (1986) 173–92.

Rutledge, Fleming. *Not Ashamed of the Gospel: Sermons from Paul's Letter to the Romans.* Grand Rapids: Eerdmans, 2007.

Sanday, William, and A. C. Headlam. *Critical and Exegetical Commentary on the Epistle to the Romans.* Edinburgh: T. & T. Clark, 1986.

Schlatter, Adolf. *New Testament Theology.* 2 vols. Translated by Andreas J. Kostenberger. Grand Rapids: Baker, 1999.

Schrenk, G. *Righteousness.* London: A & C Black, 1935.

Stanovich, Keith E. *The Robot's Rebellion: Finding Meaning in the Age of Darwin.* Chicago: Chicago University Press, 2004.

Stendahl, Krister. *Final Account: Paul's Letter to the Romans.* Minneapolis: Fortress, 1995.

Thielicke, Helmut. *Death and Life.* Philadelphia: Fortress, 1970.

———. *Evangelical Theology, Volume 1.* Grand Rapids: Eerdmans, 1974.

Thornton, Agathe. "Two Features of Oral Style in Maori Narrative." *Journal of Polynesian Studies* 94 (1985) 149–76.

Torrance, Thomas F. "One Aspect of the Biblical Conception of Faith." *Expository Times* 68 (1956/7) 111–14.

VanGemeren, Willem A., ed. *New International Dictionary of Old Testament Theology.* Grand Rapids: Zondervan, 1997.

Von Rad, Gerard. *Old Testament Theology.* 2 vols. Edinburgh: Oliver & Boyd, 1962.

White, John. *The Fight: a Practical Handbook of Christian Living.* Downers Grove, IL: InterVarsity, 1977.

Zerwick, Max. *Biblical Greek.* Rome: Gregorian Biblical Bookshop, 1962.

———. *A Grammatical Analysis of the Greek New Testament.* Rome: Pontifical Biblical Institute, 1974.

www.ingramcontent.com/pod-product-compliance
Lightning Source LLC
Chambersburg PA
CBHW081145230426
43664CB00018B/2809